FROM CARE
TO
ACTION

MARTIN HOLDGATE

FROM CARE
TO
ACTION

MAKING A SUSTAINABLE WORLD

IUCN
The World Conservation Union

EARTHSCAN
Earthscan Publications Ltd, London

First published in the UK in 1996 by
Earthscan Publications Limited

A catalogue record for this book is available from the British Library

ISBN 1 85383 306 1 Paperback/1 85383 317 7 Hardback

Printed and bound in England by Clays Ltd, St Ives plc

For a full list of publications please contact:

Earthscan Publications Limited
120 Pentonville Road
London N1 9JN
Tel: 0171 278 0433
Fax: 0171 278 1142

Earthscan is an editorially independent subsidiary of Kogan Page Limited
and publishes in association with WWF-UK and the International Institute
for Environment and Development.

C O N T E N T S

ABOUT IUCN – THE WORLD CONSERVATION UNION

Many environmental organizations have become household names: The World Wide Fund for Nature (better known simply as WWF), Greenpeace, Friends of the Earth, Conservation International, The Nature Conservancy, The National Wildlife Federation, and so on. All are members of IUCN, yet IUCN itself has been described as the conservation world's best kept secret.

IUCN is the oldest, broadest and in some respects most unusual world conservation body. It was created in 1948 through the joint initiative of the government of France, UNESCO and the Ligue Suisse pour la Conservation de la Nature. It was designed as a United Nations for Nature. Like the UN its central policy-making body is a general assembly in which all its members meet on equal terms to exchange information and experience, discuss major issues that affect conservation and the sustainable use of living resources, and decide the policies the Union as a whole should follow. Like the UN it has a series of standing committees, or commissions, and these now bring together over 6000 volunteers with an immense range of expertise. The Union has a worldwide secretariat, now about 400 strong and based in over 30 countries. But unlike the UN, it has government agencies and non-governmental organizations as full members alongside governments. The members are grouped in governmental and non-governmental 'chambers' when it comes to voting, so that neither group can impose an unwelcome policy on the other.

IUCN has led many of the major world environmental initiatives of the past 45 years. In partnership with the UN Environment Programme and WWF, it produced the original *World Conservation Strategy* (IUCN/UNEP/WWF, 1980) and its successor and complement, *Caring for the Earth: A Strategy for Sustainable Living* (IUCN/UNEP/WWF, 1991). It prepared the text of the World Charter for Nature, adopted by the UN General Assembly in 1982. It began the processes that led to the Ramsar Convention on Wetlands of International Importance, the Convention on International Trade in Endangered Species and the Convention on Biological Diversity. It has assisted over 50 governments to prepare national conservation strategies. It has published red data books on threatened species, and action plans for their conservation. It produces, under direct mandate from the United Nations General Assembly, the World List of National Parks and Protected Areas, and has developed a wide range of regional and national strategies for protected areas. And so on – the full list would fill a volume as big as this one.

Martin Holdgate, the author of this book, was Director General of IUCN from February 1988 until April 1994. The book is yet another contribution from IUCN to the most important debate in the world – how nearly 6 billion people alive today can shape the courses of development so that the 8 to 10 billion people that we expect will inhabit the Earth a century from now may live peaceful lives of high quality, in harmony with the world of nature on which we all depend.

IUCN – The World Conservation Union – has its headquarters at Rue Mauverney 28, CH1196 Gland, Switzerland. John Burke, the Director of Communications and Corporate Affairs, will be glad to tell readers more about this unique organization.

I N T R O D U C T I O N

'Of the making of many books there is no end, and much study is a weariness to the flesh.' So wrote the author of the Old Testament book *Ecclesiastes* over two thousand years ago. Anyone who scans the bookshelves, groaning under the weight of environmental volumes, reports and prescriptions today, has cause to echo those words.

How is the wearied flesh to be stirred to action? For the fact is that people have never been so aware, at all levels from the global leadership to the rural peasant and the urban poor, of the need to live in harmony with the world of nature of which we are part. There have never been so many widely publicised disasters involving the breakdown of human societies, the disruption of the environment and the extinction of species. There have never been so many gloomy forebodings. And there have never been so many attempted prescriptions of cure.

In his poem *The Hollow Men*, the British poet TS Eliot wrote:

> Between the idea
> And the reality;
> Between the motion
> And the act
> Falls the shadow.

Why is this so? What is the nature of the blockage – and why should such obstructions be tolerated when the world community is so aware of the need for action, and of the fact that every year of delay increases the cost, the loss, the suffering and the risk of tragedy? The problem has been summed up well by Lester Milbraith (1989) in his book *Envisioning a Sustainable Society*: 'Many millions of people now recognize that we must transform society, but they have difficulty imagining what a new society, designed to be sustainable, might be like.'

As conference follows conference, and report follows report, that is emerging as the central issue. For while any one of us can *design* a new society – and most of the books and reports do just that – it can only come into being if people want to move in that direction. And for that to happen, they must see the new vision as more attractive than the present reality, not just for everyone else, but for themselves. Moreover, they must see that the way ahead offers benefits (or escape from danger) at each step. It is rather like the evolutionary challenge of changing *Eohippus*, the ancestor the size of a fox terrier, into a horse over 50 million years – every stage of enlargement and specialization has to offer survival advantages over the preceding stage so that all the intermediaries succeed as well as the final model.

In addressing this challenge with yet another book, I may be accused of jerking in the usual reflex and once again offering words because deeds are more difficult and more costly. But that is to misunderstand the nature of the process on which we are embarked. Books are not action, it is true. They are no substitute for blood, sweat, toil and tears. But they are statements of position, ways of exchanging ideas, and ways of helping the actors forward, with stronger commitment and more harmony. The ideas in these pages are offered in that hope.

Many of the statements made here are political. That is difficult. There is a fiction, convenient to holders of power, that the job of the conservation movement, like the job of religions and philosophies, is to offer ideas which the leaders of the nations and their advisers can then take up and turn into action within their own political settings. To a degree, that is right. But if we accept the concept of 'caring for the Earth' and the belief that we need a new ethic of sustainable living, we cannot just stop there. Acceptance of those beliefs leads directly to political action – action to create a society which lives according to that ethic, in harmony within the world of nature, and offering a life of good quality for all people.

This book is one step in a progression that has no precise beginning, but reached public awareness with the United Nations Conference on the Human Environment held in Stockholm in 1972, and was trumpeted more loudly around the world with the UN Conference on Environment and Development in Rio de Janeiro twenty years later. That progression has been signposted by many books. In 1972 Barbara Ward and René Dubos addressed the fundamental questions in *Only One Earth: the Care and Maintenance of a Small Planet* (Ward and Dubos, 1972). In 1987 the World Commission on Environment and Development published their report, *Our Common Future* (WCED, 1987), with the first and best-known definition of sustainable development – 'development that meets the needs of the present without compromising the ability of future generations to meet their own needs.' In 1992, Sir Shridath Ramphal, then President of IUCN, wrote a background book to the Rio Conference entitled *Our Country the Planet*

(Ramphal, 1992). In between, the way has been paved by volumes and meetings (McCormick, 1989; Adams, 1990).

IUCN and its partners, the United Nations Environment Programme (UNEP) and the World Wide Fund for Nature (WWF) have made their contribution to that pavement. The *World Conservation Strategy* of 1980 was of outstanding importance because it emphasized for the first time that the conservation of nature and natural resources was an essential foundation for development, and that development to meet human needs was an essential context for conservation. In 1987 the social dimension of conservation was emphasized at a conference IUCN organized in Ottawa, the message being caught neatly in the title of the proceedings, *Conservation with Equity* (Jacobs and Munro, 1987). In 1991 came the second world conservation strategy, *Caring for the Earth: a Strategy for Sustainable Living*. In 1994 the 19th Session of the IUCN General Assembly, held in Buenos Aires, Argentina (IUCN, 1994a), set out to review what had been done to convert the proposals in *Caring for the Earth* into practical action. The present book grew out of that debate.

The General Assembly also reviewed the role of IUCN in today's world, and adopted a new mission statement (IUCN, 1994b), which is, in many ways, a *missionary* statement: 'to influence, encourage and assist societies throughout the world to conserve the integrity and diversity of nature, and ensure that any use of natural resources is equitable and ecologically sustainable'.

The key is the recognition that world bodies – whether intergovernmental, like the United Nations system or largely non-governmental, like IUCN – can only work through others. For IUCN this means influencing, encouraging and assisting the world's community to build a sustainable society, based on conserving the natural systems and resources on which we all depend. That in turn means going out and proposing the actions that should be taken at levels from the General Assembly of the United Nations to the households of the remotest village. Such action must be based on scientific understanding of natural processes, and an awareness of the long history of human interaction with the other species that share this planet.

Commitment to sustainability also creates a basis for judgement. It follows that actions that measurably advance sustainable living are 'right', and actions that degrade the Earth, impoverish nature, create inequity in the use of natural resources, and are ecologically unsustainable are 'wrong', in both a practical and an ethical sense. The IUCN mission statement, *Caring for the Earth* and similar documents provide a yardstick for evaluating the validity of political actions.

It is easy (and naive) to argue that this should not present undue difficulties, because the world's leaders signed up, in Rio de Janeiro, to a declaration and to an agenda for action, *Agenda 21* (Robinson, 1993), the values and approach of which closely follow the thesis of this book. The main messages have therefore already been accepted (in principle) at the highest political level. In practice, there will be a great deal of difficulty.

For the change to sustainable living is revolutionary, in the sense that it demands major changes in how people live and how communities operate. It is revolutionary for developed countries, because it calls upon them to cut back on over-consumption of material resources and energy, and this will impinge on the whole culture of consumerism and the advertisement that impels it. The challenge is to transform a high-consumption society, with a linear flow of materials from rocks, soil and factories through households or offices to waste tips or the sea, to a low-consumption, conserver society in which materials flow in closed loops. And, of course, to do all this without lowering people's quality of life or aggravating already severe problems of unemployment and under-employment.

It is revolutionary also for the developing world because it is likely to demand a reversal of many of the political decisions taken in the past fifty years. For example, it will call for abandonment of the social assumption that the countries have to make themselves as like 'the West' as possible. It will force communities to debate what kind of future (within the envelope of the possible) they really want. It will call for many detailed reforms – for example in the land tenure systems of many states.

Sustainability will demand changes in governance at all levels from the global to the local. It will demand new recognition that the power of international bodies like the United Nations lies in their ability to work for worldwide political consensus, a consensus of equity, which can only be turned into action through others. It will demand recognition that the sovereignty that so many nation states guard so jealously is being eroded, and will be further undermined, by two parallel processes – the emergence of supranational groupings and worldwide organizations and communications links on the one hand and increasing decentralization to sub-national and local groups on the other.

The purpose of development is to enrich the lives of people. It is about quality of life, not material standards of living. It follows that the welfare of individuals, communities, and the environments in which they live are the building blocks and measure of sustainability. Governments and governance systems must help sustainability to happen, and shield those on the ground against exploitation and appropriation. The cult of consumerism and redundancy: the quest for cost-effectiveness that has no social-welfare yardstick, and the application of economic value systems that ignore or underrate the environment must all be measured against the indicators of sustainability, and are likely to fail the test.

In both developed and developing countries sustainability will involve giving local communities and groups real power to manage the land they live on. It will mean the entrenchment of community rights to the local environment and its wildlife. It will mean protecting local communities against the kind of large, central, investment and development schemes many governments and international financial agencies favour because they show well in GNP, even though they externalize social costs – that is, load the costs on the poor, who lie outside the formal economy.

Recent years have seen the collapse of political systems that were over-centralized and assumed that the machinery of the centralized state is skilled enough to plan the future with precision, and altruistic enough to act as the champion and defender of the people. The danger is that we will swing to unbridled individualism, and unchained market forces, in which individual quests for wealth and power will be permitted without safe-guards for other people, other communities, or the environment.

Traditional socialism and traditional capitalism both fail the test of sustainability. We need a new political theory, tied to a new ethic, and expressed in new governance, new economics and new laws. In contemporary jargon, we need a new social paradigm – defined by Fridjof Capra (1986) as a 'constellation of concepts, values, perceptions and practices shared by a community, which forms a particular vision of reality and a collective mood that is the basis of the way the community organizes itself'. We need a new social paradigm of sustainability, and new social structures and practices based on it. I doubt whether many of the leaders who endorsed the Declaration of Rio, and the action plan of the Earth Summit, *Agenda 21*, appreciated the full implications of their actions.

This book begins, in Chapter 1, with an overview of human history as our species has expanded to engulf the Earth and dominate its ecological systems. Today, pressures continue to mount and we face the urgent need to guide the process we call development into sustainable channels. The question is how – and that is the question the book as a whole addresses.

Chapter 2 takes a brief look at how the environmental conscience has been awakened, especially over the past forty years. Action to deal with pollution in industrialized countries and to protect great landscapes and wildernesses has broadened into concern to safeguard biological diversity, to re-think development and to move towards sustainable living. Many action plans and strategies have been prepared, but we have come to see that these are of little use unless they inspire action at the individual level, and in local communities. The conveyor belt of time leads to an uncertain future, and all sections of the community have to join together if there is to be a hope of success.

We have said all that before. Some plans and strategies – like *Caring for the Earth* and *Agenda 21* – set out long lists of proposed actions. How far have these been followed through? Chapter 3 takes stock, using the 132 actions, under 17 headings, proposed in *Caring for the Earth* as a checklist. The conclusion – mixed. The good news is that the world community has clearly accepted the need for sustainable development, and that some of the indicators are positive. The bad news is that many are not.

Why not? What are the barriers to success? Chapter 4 examines the gaps between concept and action. It concludes that there are six key areas to address. We need new ethical and economic values. We need to communicate better across cultural divisions and recognize the wisdom that is to be found among people of diverse traditions. We need better public information and education. We need to understand nature better and use its resources more wisely. We need better governance, giving communities and people the power to act. And we need new partnerships and alliances to make action possible, at all levels from the local to the global. We need to plot the steps from knowledge to action, taking one realistic step at a time and recognizing that what will emerge as global success will be the aggregate of many separate advances taken locally, on the smallest of scales.

What people do depends on what they believe. Ethical values are of immense importance: living sustainably depends on accepting a duty to care for all people, now and in future generations, and for the natural world on which we all depend. Ethics, however, has to lead to action: to guidelines for building a sustainable society. The judgements of the world community are immensely influenced by economic valuation – what worth we attach to what in money terms. Environmental resources have been degraded because we have tended not to value them adequately, and this needs to change. Chapter 5 covers this ground and suggests the guidelines and principles to follow.

But unless people are informed, educated, motivated and led to feel that their personal actions matter, we shall not get very far. This is where the biggest single obstacle, the deepest block between concept and action lies. Chapter 6 therefore looks at the role of education and communication. What makes people behave as they do? What is the situation of environmental education around the world, in both developing and developed countries? How can it be improved, and who should take the vital steps?

Chapter 7 comes down to earth, recognizing that success will depend on understanding the characteristics and limits of nature. There are natural laws that determine the pattern of life and the diversity and functioning of ecosystems, and we ignore these at our peril. These principles govern the resilience of ecosystems and the carrying capacity of different regions for different kinds of human society. We can derive certain indicators of sustainability, and certain ground rules for sustainable living from this analysis.

Many of these turn on how we use natural resources, and the sustainable use of nature is the theme of Chapter 8, which draws heavily on knowledge gathered in IUCN. It analyses how we can make farming and forestry more sustainable; how we should use the production of 'wild' ecosystems like fisheries and natural forests, and how we can balance the conservation of nature and its use for human benefit.

Action has to be built from individuals to communities, and Chapter 9 looks at how this can be done. We need action that gives people more control over their lives. We need to help them meet their needs in sustainable ways. We need to help them conserve their environments for the future. Much of this comes together in what has been termed primary environmental care (PEC), just as primary health care is the first essential in medicine. The chapter looks at case studies from many parts of the world, and why some have worked and others have not. It ends by trying to relate the local to the national – PEC to national strategies – and asks how the latter should change.

No community, no nation and no government can succeed on its own. Alliances and partnerships are vital, and Chapter 10 looks at these, again with especial reference to case studies of what has worked and what has not. Successful partnerships have certain key features. These include openness, commitment and confidence among all partners that they have a real prospect of contributing and benefiting. They can be helped or hindered by the formal framework and governance of society.

So, we come to the future. How can we learn from the past and move forward with greater confidence? Chapter 11 looks at the elements of action. It begins with individuals, and suggests five ways in which people can advance sustainable living, and incidentally further their own interests. Then, communities. Again, actions in neighbourhoods, districts, villages and firms are examined. What makes a sustainable company? What should a non-governmental organization do? What actions should be taken at the level of the city, state or canton? What about national level? And, finally, how can the international systems – intergovernmental, commercial and non-governmental – facilitate the advance to sustainable living?

Success is possible, but only with vision and personal commitment, and a refusal to accept disappointment. This book appears at the start of what is bound to be a slow and uneven process of transition. If it has a central message, it is, maybe, that the overriding need is to watch and listen to one another, and to share experience. People, in the midst of much tragedy, poverty and disaster, are finding new ways. There are signs of hope and examples of success. Some have happened because we have listened again to the voices of tradition, which for decades had been swept aside by the brash assertions of cultures and knowledge systems that thought themselves superior. Some have happened because people have taken power over their own lives and their communities. What we need to do now is to apply the test of sustainability, and ensure that we do not allow positive movements to be stifled, or negative actions to be tolerated.

From that will come a book of hope, through example. And from example, and the sharing of knowledge will come increasing acceptance of the imperative for sustainable living, and the adoption of those changes which clearly improve both personal quality of life and the future of societies. It is unrealistic to expect the world to change overnight, or in a decade, or a single generation. But we can look for the diffusion of new beliefs and actions, and a widening change for the better. The crucial need is for this to happen fast enough: for protection and rebuilding to overtake degradation.

This is, let me emphasize, a personal book, despite its origins in an IUCN General Assembly. For as I began to write, so it became clear that another official volume, with a text agreed between IUCN, UNEP and WWF, and based on edited summaries of the proceedings of the ten IUCN General Assembly workshops, was unlikely to break new ground. I was therefore asked to take my own line, and have done so. At the same time, I have stood by the original intention to take *Caring for the Earth*, *Agenda 21* and the papers presented in Buenos Aires as points of departure. They are quoted at many points. But the quotation is selective, and I apologize to those whose contributions are not mentioned because they stand to one side of my main argument.

The preparation of this volume has been helped by a grant from IUCN, on behalf of the three partners in the World Conservation Strategy and *Caring for the Earth*. This support is acknowledged with warm thanks. I am grateful also to all those who criticized successive drafts and helped me to get the text into shape: to my son, Dr David Holdgate, for assistance with the diagrams, and to my wife Elizabeth for a characteristic blend of encouragement and forbearance.

Martin Holdgate
Cambridge, July 1995

THE HUMAN TIDE

The rulers of the Earth

Human beings have evolved within, depend on, and are part of, the world of nature. It is nonsense to speak of people and of nature as separate entities – and many of our problems come from this fallacy, and the attendant conceit that we can 'conquer' nature and make the whole global ecosystem subservient to human will and purpose.

But the human species is what we call 'pan-dominant'. That means that its impact is everywhere on the planet, and there is no place – not even the heart of the Antarctic ice-cap – where the traces of humanity cannot be found.

No species in the history of the Earth has enjoyed such dominance. No other single species has altered the composition of the atmosphere in ways that threaten to change the global climate. No other species has appropriated to its use so large a slice of the productivity of the Earth. On the credit side, no other species has been able to analyse and debate its impact – and consider how it can adjust it so that future generations can live in harmony within the world of nature of which they are bound to remain a part.

This book is about that process of adjustment. It is useful to begin by considering where we are now, and how we got there.

The rise of humanity

Modern humans have been around for some 40,000 years – and the earlier branch of our species, the so-called Neanderthal Man, for maybe 100,000 years longer. Human evolution appears to have been centred in Africa for at least 2 million years. The first hominid to spread outside that continent, our immediate predecessor, *Homo erectus*, appeared around one and a half million years ago and colonized much of Africa, Europe and Asia as far east and north as China (Leakey, 1981).

These early people probably spread slowly. But as Richard Leakey has pointed out, even if the range were extended by as little as 20 kilometres (12 miles) per generation, it would take only 20,000 years to expand from Nairobi to Beijing. Early people lived at low population densities, were hunter-gatherers, and ate a mixed diet of meat, seeds, fruits and other plant material. The coastal zones, with abundant shellfish and seabirds, may have been a favoured habitat.

People first reached Australia between 65,000 and 40,000 years ago. They got to the Americas from Asia around 40,000 years ago, when the seas were lower during the last ice age. Later waves of immigration over the dry bed of what is now Bering Straits took place around 15–20,000 years ago. By 10–15,000 years ago, humanity had reached the southernmost parts of South America, no doubt as the result of another slow process of extension of range, in which the best habitats would be occupied and much unattractive environment in between would be left to nature. By 1000 years ago virtually all the larger land masses in tropical and temperate zones had been occupied (New Zealand being the last to be settled, from AD 750 onwards), and many small islands also had their human populations.

There is controversy over the environmental impact of early peoples. But there is evidence that from very early times – long before *Homo erectus* gave place to *Homo sapiens* – our ancestors successfully hunted large prey. In Africa they killed a now-extinct giant baboon as big as a female gorilla, though we do not know whether they hastened its extinction. In Asia, evidence of bone damage suggests that people had to learn by trial and error that it is imprudent to eat too much of the liver of some kinds of animal (notably bears), because they contain poisonous amounts of vitamin A. It is also clear that they had to learn the hard way about living in balance with the animals on which they depended. As human hunter-gatherers, equipped with weapons and fire, spread over the Earth, many large mammals and birds disappeared. This is especially evident in North and South America, Australia, Madagascar and New Zealand, and it continued into recent years on islands like Mauritius, Reunion and Rodriguez, where large, endemic, flightless and defenceless birds like the Dodo and Solitaire (all descended from ground-feeding pigeons) did not long survive the advent of hungry sailors and settlers. To quote Jared Diamond (1989) 'it is now clear that the first arrival of humans at any oceanic island with no previous human inhabitants has always precipitated a mass extinction of the island biota'.

The evidence for the relationship between extinctions and the arrival of human hunters rests on the fossil and sub-fossil record (and especially on the dating of remains by radioisotope techniques) (Martin and Wright, 1967). In Australia, several giant kangaroos, a marsupial predator the size of a lion, and the 'marsupial rhinoceros', *Diprotodon*, did not long survive human arrival. In North America, mammoths and mastodons (smaller elephants with a more southerly distribution) were common after the last glacial period around 15,000 years ago, and remains of both are found together with the distinctive fluted spear and arrow points of hunting peoples. Mammoths vanish from the record some 10,000 years ago, and mastodons about 4000 years later, and the human hunters switched to dependence on bison, with which they achieved a balance that endured into modern times. In the same period horses and camels were lost, and none remained in North America at the time of European contact. Big predators (like sabre-toothed cats, which may have preyed on the elephants) went at around the same time, probably as a result of the loss of their prey rather than direct human impact. By the end of the late-glacial epoch some 40 genera of large mammal had been lost from North America.

In Eurasia, the northward spread of humans appears to have coincided with the disappearance of the woolly rhinoceros, *Coelodonta*, the giant elk, *Megaceros* and mammoths (a small sub-species hung on on Wrangel Island off Siberia until as recently as 4000 years ago). Both there and in North America these extinctions coincided with major ecological changes following the end of the last glacial epoch. In this process vast tracts of herb-rich 'steppe-tundra' grasslands in which mammoths and woolly rhinos lived were replaced by coniferous forests at about the same time as human hunters moved north. We do not know whether habitat change reduced the habitats available to the big herbivores, and human pressure finished them off, or whether the replacement of steppe-tundra by forest was a consequence of their extermination.

In South America, the record is less clear-cut, but the arrival of people in the far south of the continent appears to have coincided with the loss of horses and of the last giant ground sloths, *Mylodon*, about 9000 years ago. In New Zealand, before people arrived in around AD 750, there were some 27 species of flightless moa, including *Dinornis maximus*, which stood some 10 feet tall. The bones of 22 species have been found in association with human artefacts and remains. It seems clear that even if climate change played some part, moa-hunting people were largely responsible for the extinction of these birds, which had been in New Zealand since the late Miocene period. Indeed, it seems clear that a distinctive moa-hunting culture established itself, and progressively killed out the prey on which it depended. Few moas remained when the ancestors of the modern Maori people arrived in around 1350, although the dated records suggest that a remnant survived until around 1700 – not long before European contact. Many other New Zealand birds, as well as lizards and frogs, died out at the same time as the moas, probably due to habitat destruction or to the impact of species introduced by the Maoris (Diamond, 1989).

Madagascar has a similar history. There is no evidence of an extinction spasm until around 1500 years ago. The remains of seven genera and 14 species of extinct lemurs, most of them larger than any of those that survive, a pygmy hippopotamus, two kinds of giant tortoise and between 6 and 12 species of large flightless birds resembling ostriches or moas have been dated to the same period as the relics of early human occupation. Charcoal associated with pottery and iron hooks shows that people were well established by around AD 1100 – a time when one of the giant birds, the Elephant Bird or roc, *Aepyornis maximus*, the largest bird ever recorded, was still common.

There is a theory that because people evolved in Africa the catastrophic upheavals that followed the advent of well-armed and skilled hunters in other continents were somehow replaced there by a more gradual process of adaptive change. This is very debatable. The extinction wave simply seems to have happened earlier. Some 50 genera of large mammal disappeared during the Pleistocene period, and those we see in Africa today represent only 70 per cent of the complement 60,000 years ago (Martin and Wright, 1967).

The destruction of large animals – prey, enemies or competitors – seems, in fact, to have been the earliest major human impact on the natural world (Figure 1). It went hand-in-hand with the alteration of habitats, especially by fire. Again, the scale of such impacts has commonly been underestimated. In the Americas – where there were probably between 40 and 80 million people at the time of European contact in AD 1492 – there was substantial vegetation change early in prehistory. Regular burning may well have created extensive grasslands within the prairie belt and made the forests of north-eastern North America discontinuous. Over Latin America as a whole some 40 per cent of the forest is thought to be secondary and most of the rest to have been altered by human impact. There are few parts of Amazonia where charcoal from prehistoric burning is not visible in the soil (Denevan, 1992). About one third of New Zealand lowland forest is said to have been altered by burning between AD 750 and 1800. And human impacts were certainly superimposed upon natural variations, especially following the end of the last ice age around 15,000 years ago. The post-glacial period has been one of rapid alteration in climate, which could have been further affected locally by the modification of vegetation by people.

The causes of extinction are clearly complex, but they fall into two main groups (Marshall, 1988). The first is the direct impact of overkill by hunters (defined as cropping at a rate exceeding the reproductive capacity of the prey species). The second is habitat modification by fire, or by the impact of browsing and grazing mammals introduced by people to places like oceanic islands, where the vegetation developed in the absence of such species. Ecosystems have also been upset by the introduction of predators (like cats, rats, dogs, foxes and pigs). But some species have particular attributes that make them especially vulnerable. For example, they may have a low reproductive rate, depend on one or two particular food plants or prey species, be confined to a specialized habitat or small geographical area like an oceanic island, or lack defence mechanisms against predation.

What is clear is that the belief – almost an article of faith among some modern environmentalists – that early people with a simple lifestyle lived in some kind of instinctive harmony with nature is a myth. People have been destructive whenever they have come into contact with a new, available prey whose use permits rapid human population growth. The trait persists to this day. It took only 50 years from the discovery of the largest dugong, Steller's Sea Cow, in 1741 for it to become extinct through predation for meat by European sailors. In the early 19th century the tiny new colony (some 10 people) on the mid-Atlantic island of Tristan da Cunha fed itself and its pigs on elephant seals, *Mirounga leonina*, so that they were quite quickly eliminated from the vicinity of the settlement and became rare elsewhere in the islands (Wace and Holdgate, 1976). The history of sealing, whaling and oceanic fishery has followed the classic pattern of human overkill, distinguished only by the increased sophistication and power of the hunting methods and the fact that the animals were taken for traded products rather than subsistence.

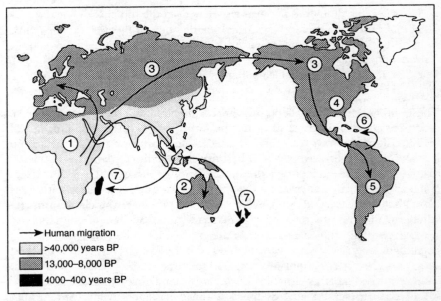

The sequence of human movement and major extinctions in the Pleistocene. The shading indicates main periods of extinction. 1 Africa and Southern Eurasia, 2 New Guinea and Australia, 3 Northern Eurasia and Northern North America, 4 South Eastern North America, 5 South America, 6 West Indies, 7 Madagascar and New Zealand.
Source: Martin, PS, 1971, in Detwyler, 1971

Figure 1 The global sequence of extinction

The more harmonious relationship with their prey now characteristic of indigenous peoples like the Inuit of the Arctic and many North American nations and tribes is the result of hard-won wisdom. That relationship often includes the protection of females and young, the placing of some quarry species off-limits to some sections of the human population for which they are sacred, and a ban on hunting species during their breeding period. The combination of simple hunting tools and extensive hunting ranges reduces the risk of overkill. And the peoples concerned treat their quarries with respect, believing that animal spirits are reborn when their bodies are taken to nourish people – whose own bodies, in the end, go to sustain other parts of the web of life (Kemf, 1993). This value, and the associated rituals, is a constant reminder that the prey species are also sentient beings. Such adaptive cultures, based on generations of knowledge of animal and plant species, are giving valuable insights to those seeking to build sustainable lifestyles today.

However, adaptation can easily break down when social pressures alter, or new technology arrives. Indigenous peoples have been vulnerable to culture shocks, as when the introduction of firearms made it possible for them to kill many more quarry animals than before, or when money and trade goods were offered for furs. As Farley Mowat (1954) wrote of the caribou hunters of northern Canada:

> The rifles that destroyed the deer also destroyed the Indians who held the rifles, as surely as if men had turned the muzzles on themselves. For not even those immense herds could withstand the slaughter they were subjected to, and as the deer's ranks thinned, so were the ranks of the Idthen Eldeli thinned by the meat starvation which was the aftermath of the great slaughter.

These direct impacts undoubtedly altered the biological diversity of an area. And their indirect impacts must not be forgotten. Take an elephant out of an ecosystem and you transform that ecosystem profoundly. The trees, no longer subject to browsing that at best affects individual plants and at worst can devastate wide tracts of habitat, are likely to increase. Other browsers (such as giraffe) may increase – but in North America and Eurasia it seems likely that there were no alternative species to take over the elephant niche when the mammoths and mastodons had gone. Species of plant whose seeds depended on passage through the gut of a large herbivore in order to germinate may well have vanished. Predators like the big sabre-toothed cats, and their dependent scavengers, followed their prey to fossildom. Competitors – notably smaller herbivores, omnivores and scavengers – would have increased, just as there is some evidence that recent human destruction of the great whales in the Antarctic oceans has led to an increase in the numbers of the crab-eater seal, *Lobodon carcinophagus*, and the chinstrap penguin, *Pygoscelis antarctica*, which eat much the same diet (Holdgate, 1967).

It is also untrue that hunter-gatherer peoples live among pristine wilderness. Forests in many parts of the tropics have been altered a good deal by the deliberate selection of species useful to people for food, fibre, wood or other products. In Kalimantan, Dyak peoples have created forest gardens which look to the casual eye like just another stand of tropical forest, but in practice are assemblages of useful trees (Brookfield, 1993). In the Amazon basin, where many dozens of forest products are used by people, the make-up of stands has also been altered by selection. To quote a fascinating analysis by William Denevan (1992), 'large expanses of Latin American forests are humanized forests in which the kinds, numbers, and distributions of useful species are managed by human populations.' Even in western

Europe, the use of the southern English 'wildwood' from Neolithic times onwards appears to have altered a lime-hazel-oak forest into one with oak as the main big tree (useful for timber and yielding acorns important as livestock feed) with hazel as an undercrop, yielding fuelwood, woven branchwork and nuts (Rackham, 1986).

Development: the ladder to dominance

Agriculture appeared about 10,000 years ago in the 'fertile crescent', which runs from what is now Israel, Palestine and Jordan northwards through Syria and south-eastern Turkey, and south through the Tigris and Euphrates valleys of Iraq and Iran. This is the habitat of wheat and barley, which were no doubt first cropped in the wild. It has been shown that a family, using a 9000-year-old stone sickle, could harvest enough of these grains in a period of a month to carry them through the winter (Leakey, 1981). No doubt sowing of surplus grains in spring developed as a natural way of increasing food supplies – and selection of more productive strains again emerged opportunistically. From those origins, agricultural peoples carrying early wheat (einkorn) and barley, and with goats and sheep, spread progressively through Europe and Asia.

There were parallel centres of agriculture in the Americas, where there was cultivation in what is now Mexico 5000 years ago. Indeed crop-growing probably sprang up at many points over the world, when surplus seeds or fruits began to germinate, and people had the idea of scattering them in a suitable and accessible location rather than destroying them.

The point for us is that this was the start of what we now call 'development'. In its crudest form, this is simply the process by which people modify the environment so that it is more favourable as a human habitat, supporting more people with a higher quality of life. It has many components, but commonly involves enhancing the productivity of food and other renewable resources, improving the microclimate in which people live (by creating shelter), giving reliable access to safe water supplies, improving health by safe disposal of wastes, supplying energy for cooking and heating (originally as fuelwood, and later through fossil fuels) and providing for supplies of non-renewable resources including minerals and metals. The making and using of tools, and the transfer of knowledge from group to group and generation to generation are the keys to the process.

Over history, people have 'developed' by the improvement of agriculture, and the establishment of villages, towns and cities. This has in turn increased what biologists term the 'carrying capacity' of an area. At its most basic level, this is simply the ability of an area to support people (or rabbits or cattle or any other species). The American ecologist HT Odum (1967) pointed out many years ago that a square kilometre of rain forest, of East African rangeland and of Indian monsoon-zone farmland – all with much the same input of solar energy – could support, respectively, two or three hunter-gatherers, around 25 pastoralists, and 230 farmers (and in the latter case the marketed surplus could also support about 30 people in a town). Under intensive North American or European cereal farming the same area could support 60 people on the land and around 2000 in the city.

Of course such statements need interpreting with caution. The sites are not interchangeable. The figures can be challenged – many tropical forests can support more people. And modern intensive agriculture is not self-contained: it relies on inputs of industrial energy on top of what comes from the sun, as well as on fertilizers, pesticides, tractors and other implements. As Figure 2 demonstrates, the relationship between increase in effort and increase in return is not a simple one. Beyond the optimum, the return falls away, and at the extreme increases in effort may actually bring a diminishing return, as we see very clearly in today's over-exploited fisheries (TIE, 1971).

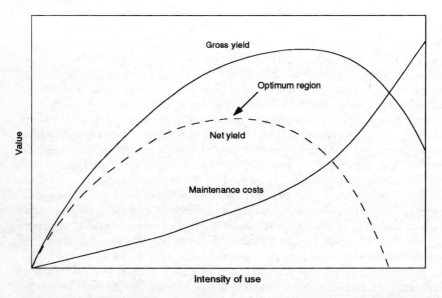

The relationships between intensity of use of an environmental system and the value of the return. High intensity systems have high gross yields and high maintenance costs; the sustainable optimum is likely to lie well below the theoretical maximum yield.
Source: TIE, 1971

Figure 2 The relationship between effort and return

Development was, at least initially, based on farming but as it has progressed a smaller and smaller proportion of the community has been tied to the land. Urbanization began at least 5000 years ago, made possible by the steady increase in agricultural production which allowed people to turn to other crafts and industries (Tolba et al, 1992). Today, in many developed countries, under 5 per cent of the population has direct connections with agriculture. In 1950, over half the population of developed countries was urban, and the proportion was growing, while it was accelerating dramatically in the developing world. The United Nations predicts that by the year 2025, 80 per cent of people in developed countries and 57 per cent of those in the developing world will live in cities and the ultimate balance could well be that in a world of 10 billion, 8 billion will be in the towns (Hardoy et al, 1992; Tolba et al, 1992).

Development has been accompanied and assisted by the evolution of governance. All communities have systems of social order – as, of course, our pre-human ancestors did, as studies of our near relations the chimpanzees and gorillas make plain. In the beginning human groups, like theirs, will have centred on dominant individuals leading in hunting, foraging and inter-group rivalries. The process of development has been one of group enlargement from the extended family to the village, the city state and the nation.

The precise pattern is not important. What is important is that throughout history human societies have increased in complexity. And development has also given societies a greater power to dominate one another. The craft of metal-working allowed the making of harder, more lethal weapons as well as better cooking pots. Iron replaced bronze, just as the latter had replaced stone. People remained mobile, and have imposed their governance systems on one another as they moved. Migration took the Indo-European peoples westwards across Europe millennia ago, and that continent became a complex mingling of languages, cultures and folk-memories as each wave dominated those that went before. Roman imperialism set an administrative and legal stamp on the continent that remains potent to this day. Africa, Asia and the Americas have seen similar waves. The most recent, and the one with greatest impact on today's environment, is that of the European peoples, some 50 million of whom migrated worldwide between 1820 and 1930 taking their land-use patterns, their laws, their governance systems, their livestock and many of the plants and animals of their homelands with them, and dominating the Americas, Australasia and New Zealand (Crosby, 1986). Their ecological impact has been profound.

One direct impact was the destruction of pre-existing cultures, the extermination of some peoples and the decimation of others. Sometimes the extermination was deliberate – as with the Tasmanian and Fuegian native peoples, hunted by immigrants who desired their land. Sometimes it came through disease. Sometimes both. Between 1492 and 1650 the population of the Americas was reduced by about 90 per cent, largely by imported diseases. This catastrophe largely preceded European settlement and use of the land. The result was that the environment, and especially the forests, became wilder and this gave rise to the myth that the Americas prior to European settlement were an empty, pristine wilderness (Denevan, 1992).

The indirect impact of the expansion of European culture and colonial power may have been even more profound. For it imposed certain patterns of governance very widely, on communities that used to do things very differently a century or so ago. Local units were commonly welded into hierarchical administrative systems, district authorities reporting to provincial and they to overlords in central capital cities. Such structures often forced previously independent communities with different ethnic, cultural and religious composition into new states, making a unit, for example, of such diversities as India, Zaire, Russia or Brazil. Economic unification is reinforcing many such pressures today. Many nations make little environmental or social sense – indeed some are almost designed for conflict, with frontiers cutting across environmental resource units like river catchments, bisecting seasonal migration pathways, fragmenting ethnic groups and forcing different cultures together. Fear of unleashing cultural turbulence and dispossessing ruling groups that have built their power base on these distortions underlies the worldwide resistance to the re-drawing of frontiers, and the almost hysterical protestations against any erosion of national sovereignty, yet the fact is that the processes of today are undermining, and will continue to undermine, many artificial units of governance and many cultural tragedies are unfolding in the process. Over-centralized, over-authoritarian governance systems are also coming under pressure from the trend towards decentralization (labelled in Europe by the unlovely word 'subsidiarity'). The quest for sustainable development must incorporate hard thinking about what makes for comfortable, creative and sustainable governance.

The success of development

Judged objectively, development has been – for the human species – an overwhelming success (and even subordinated species might assent to the word 'overwhelming'!). The recent critics of the environmental movement are in that sense quite right. Look at some of the indicators (Tolba et al, 1992):

■ there are now 5.8 billion people in the world – and more people live more comfortably than ever before;
■ in all continents except Africa, food production per head has more than kept up with population growth;
■ the exchange of crop plants between continents has greatly increased the quality and variety of people's diets;
■ medicine has brought death rates down almost everywhere;
■ life expectancy has doubled in the developed countries, and increased by fifteen to twenty years in many developing ones;
■ education is becoming more and more universal, and literacy rates have been growing steadily;
■ human knowledge, skills and technical achievements have grown in a manner that would have seemed incredible a century ago;
■ industrial technology has become better at making more goods with less raw materials and energy, and with less pollution and wastes.

Consider the world population situation (often, and with some reason, taken as proof that humanity is on a collision course with its environment). Development, especially in agriculture, has been the enabler of human population growth. More reliable food supplies enhanced survival, and the creation of food surpluses allowed communities to diversify. Better shelter and clothing, cooking (killing parasites), reliable water supplies, and other features of good settlement reduced mortality. Trading systems, facilitated by the development of sea-going boats (an invention thousands of years old, in several different cultures), reduced a community's dependence on its local soils and hence its vulnerability to famine.

In Europe and North America population increased slowly over the period up to around 1800, but then grew rapidly, favoured by the agricultural and industrial revolutions and by advances in medicine. Birth rates rose while death rates, especially in infancy, fell and expectation of life increased. For about a century populations increased steadily, and the growth was accompanied by major migrations like those from western Europe to other regions (Crosby, 1986). Then, as social factors made people less dependent on their children as a support in age, as birth control became practicable as a consequence of new medical and technical advances, as more women obtained the chance of their own careers, and as cultural changes made large families less desirable, birth rates began to fall. In the developed world we now have a broad balance between birth rates and death rates, and in many countries populations are nearing stability. We call this process of change from high birth rates and high death rates to a new balance in which both are low 'the demographic transition'.

Worldwide, total human numbers rose from around 1 billion in 1800 to 2 billion in 1930, 3 billion in 1960, 4 billion in 1975 and 5 billion in 1987. The projection is that they will pass 6 billion by the end of the century. But while the total population continues to mount, the growth rate is beginning to slow. The demographic transition has been completed in parts of eastern Asia, notably China (with Hong Kong and Taiwan), Singapore and Thailand, where a steep decline in fertility has followed an earlier reduction in death rates. In many other developing countries, including Indonesia, much of southern India, Sri Lanka, Tunisia, Colombia, Costa Rica and Panama mortality has fallen rapidly and fertility is now falling too, although it remains well above replacement level. The demographic transition is gaining ground throughout South America. Even in Africa, the only major region of the world where population growth rates were higher in 1985–90 than in 1960–65 (Figure 3), there are the first signs that birth rates are beginning to decline, as death rates did a few decades ago. Indeed developing countries are moving through the demographic transition faster than developed ones did. It took over a century for the slow decline in death rates in much of western Europe to be followed by a fall in birth rates and for a new balance to be reached. In parts of the developing world, the transition is being achieved in around 30 years (Holdgate, 1994c).

The tide is clearly turning. UN projections in 1993 suggested that world population would stabilize at between 10 and 14 billion, some time around the end of the 21st century. In the run-up to, and at, the UN Population Conference in Cairo in September 1994 there was some optimism that the demographic transition would go faster than that, with stability at around 8.5 to 9 billion by soon after 2050. Indeed, if the 20-year Programme of

Action before that Conference is implemented, the world population could be nearing stability at around only 7.8 billion in 2050 (Johnson, 1994).

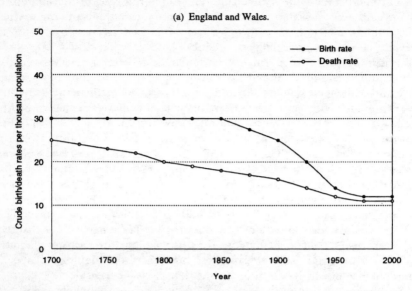

(a) England and Wales.

The steady fall in death rate (lower curve) since 1700 was followed by a falling birth rate after 1850, reaching a balance in 1950.

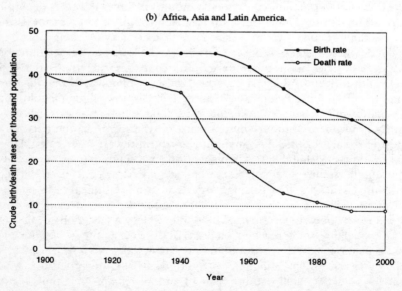

(b) Africa, Asia and Latin America.

The death rates (lower curve) in all these regions have been declining, especially since the 1940s. Birth rates began to fall in the 1950s, and are now declining steadily except in parts of Africa.

Source: Ness, 1994

Figure 3 Demographic transitions

Whatever projection proves true, it is evident that there will be great dif-ferences in human numbers from region to region. And this is crucial from an environmental standpoint. For the key issue is not whether human num-bers will stabilize – they are bound to, like those of any other animal species on a planet of finite size with finite productivity and an ultimate limit to car-rying capacity. The issue is at what level, giving what quality of life, and with what kind of balance between humanity and the systems of the living world on which we depend. There are fears that development, great though its achievements have been, has been profligate and cannot go on as it now is. This is the reason for the calls for change, towards sustainability. We should look at the reasons why doubts have arisen.

The impacts of development

The primary concern is one of scale. All development has an impact on the environment (as we have already seen, it was profound even when human-ity was at the hunter-gatherer stage). That impact has three forms, although they interlock: direct biological changes (like the overkill of prey species); physical transformations (because people alter their environments by clear-ing forests, draining wetlands, opening up grazing lands for livestock, min-ing rocks and metals and building cities and transport networks), and chemical changes (a polite name for pollution).

Over most of history these impacts, even in aggregate, have been rela-tively small and localized – or, even where widespread, scarely constituted a threat to the natural systems of the living world. That is why economists, when creating their discipline, treated most natural resources as external to the human socio-economic system, and as 'free goods'. They were effec-tively limitless, and apparently invulnerable to human impact. No more. As human populations have grown, agriculture has taken more and more land, cities have spread and industries become more complex, impacts have become universal. And today's industries have synthesized and released substances to which the world of nature has never been exposed in all its evolutionary history. Pollution is now a global problem.

The sceptics point out, however, that past predictions that humanity may be coming up against natural limits have proved wrong. Malthus argued that such a collision was inevitable because populations grew faster than agriculture: over recent decades this has not been the case, despite an increase in human numbers he could scarcely have imagined. As Richard North (1995) has pointed out, a consequence (to quote the World Bank) is that 'famine disappeared from Western Europe in the mid-1800s, from Eastern Europe in the 1930s, and from Asia in the 1970s.' The Club of Rome Report *Limits to Growth* (Meadows et al, 1972), which caused a green-storm at the time of the 1972 Stockholm Conference, projected that if pol-lution continued to rise unchecked, it would have a serious impact on human numbers. It has not done so. The monumental Global 2000 Report to the President of the United States (Barney, 1980) made a wide range of projections, of widely varying accuracy. The conclusion? That human societies do have adaptive capacity, and that adjustments in the direction of sustainability are possible.

This is not to say that there has not been a great deal of waste and misuse of natural resources, or that some development and economic growth have not followed the wrong track. They have. As preparation for analysis of what needs to be done, it is useful to review briefly what has happened and is happening to world ecosystems, world cities, world pollution and world governance.

Changes in world vegetation

Figure 4 summarizes what the extent of the world's main habitats would be likely to be without the impact of agriculture or human settlements (Tolba et al, 1992). It is not an exact reconstruction of history because human expansion took place at a time of rapid climate change, following the retreat of the last major ice sheets. But it suggests that before people began the process of transformation, closed forests probably covered over 46 million square kilometres, 13 million of them in the tropics. There were in addition 15 million square kilometres of open woodland and 13 million square kilometres of shrubland. Grasslands, deserts and tundras together covered 57 million square kilometres. Simple cultivations in the pre-agricultural era are likely to have affected under 1 million square kilometres.

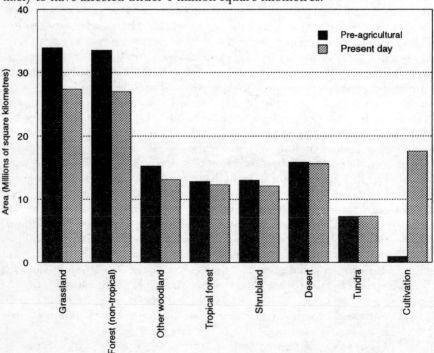

Source: Matthews, 1983, cited in Tolba et al, 1992

Figure 4 Vegetation types before and after the era of worldwide cultivation

The pre-agricultural vegetation held a lot of carbon: perhaps in the range between 800 and 1100 billion metric tonnes of it. The figure 100 years ago was nearer to 700 billion tonnes, and had fallen to around 600 billion tonnes by 1980, as forests were destroyed. One estimate in around 1980, by JS Olson and collaborators (Olson et al, 1983), put the total carbon pool in all forests and woodlands at 400–550 billion tonnes, with only another 5–15 billion tonnes in wetlands and coastal marshes, 17–30 in croplands, 20–50 in grasslands and shrublands, and 10–40 in tundra and arid lands. The ocean biota were thought to contain only some 3 billion tonnes of carbon (though this figure is highly uncertain, and estimates have ranged from as low as 1 to as high as 45 billion tonnes). Hence the importance of life on land, and especially of forests, in holding carbon is obvious – and it is equally clear why forest clearance has been releasing around 2.5 billion tonnes of carbon a year to the atmosphere, not very much less than the estimated 5.5 billion tonnes from fossil fuel combustion. Even more carbon is held in the organic soils of the world and in the waters of the sea, its sediments, and the air (Bolin et al, 1994).

The pattern of primary production – the yearly addition of living matter per unit area – is somewhat different. Olson and his colleagues estimated that all the world's forests, woodlands and interrupted woods (such as savannas) together probably fix some 50 billion tonnes of carbon a year. Croplands fix about 25 billion tonnes, grasslands and scrub another 17, and wetland and coastal habitats a further 8. Hence while conversion of forests to other systems inevitably reduces the total pool of carbon locked up in the system, it does not necessarily mean that biological productivity falls – and under intensive agriculture it may increase.

In the period up to 1980 some 16 million square kilometres of natural vegetation, mostly in forest and grassland zones, were converted to human use, especially cultivation. By 1970 about 15 per cent of the original forest and woodland had been destroyed. Much of the clearance of closed-canopy woodlands was in temperate regions (6.5 out of a total of 7 million square kilometres). The forests of central and western Europe, many of which only re-established themselves after ice retreat some 10,000 or fewer years ago, began to be cleared on an extensive scale some 3000 to 7000 years afterwards. In Britain, about half the original 'wildwood' had gone by the early Iron Age (Rackham, 1986). In North America humans began clearing lowlands at least 12,000 years ago. In contrast, in New Zealand, only settled by people in around AD 750, forest clearance is a recent phenomenon – but even so, about a quarter of the lowland forests had been destroyed by the time of European colonization. That colonial process was accompanied by a great deal of physical change to the vegetation in many regions – in the USA, for example, some 60,000 square kilometres of forest were cleared by 1850 and the total reached 660,000 by 1910. In Canada, Australia, New Zealand and South Africa, about 400,000 square kilometres of forest went by the early 20th century (Crosby, 1986).

But the tropics were not immune. In some rain-forest areas, including parts of the Amazon basin that now lie within Peru, changes may have begun as long as 23,000 years ago (Denevan, 1992). In Bangladesh, over 90 per cent of the original forest had gone by 1980. In that year the world's total area of closed forest was probably around 36 million square kilometres, and the pace of clearance in the tropics had accelerated whereas in temperate zones it had slowed, and was more or less offset by re-growth and new plantation. The most authoritative figures suggest that clearance affected about 11.3 million hectares (0.113 million square kilometres) a year in the late 1970s, 7.5 million of them in the tropics. In the 1980s the rate of loss appears to have increased: 87 tropical countries studied by the UN Food and Agriculture Organization appear to have lost a total of about 16.9 million hectares a year between 1981 and 1990 (Tolba et al, 1992).

In 1976–1980 shifting cultivation accounted for 45 per cent of the losses in the tropics as a whole, and 35 per cent of the destruction in Latin America, 70 per cent in Africa, and 49 per cent in Southeast Asia. In Rondonia, Amazonia, in the late 1970s some 5000 new settlers arrived every month. Much of this immigration was from desperate necessity rather than choice, although in Brazil at this period it was also encouraged by economic incentives (now withdrawn). The result, in many areas, was environmental disaster. Tropical forests support about half the species known or calculated to exist on Earth – yet they occupy only about 6 per cent of the planet's land area. Clearance inevitably brings considerable loss of biological diversity. Moreover, despite their lush appearance, many tropical forests grow on soils of low fertility and much of the nutrient is locked up in the 'standing crop' of trees. Clearance, especially if the logs are removed and the branches burned, disperses the carbon into the atmosphere, and many other nutrients into the air or run-off. Harvests on the poorer soils decline rapidly, leading to replacement of cultivation by cattle ranching, sustainable in many areas only by economic subsidy. Clearance for cattle ranching has also been a major cause of deforestation in parts of Central America, where it is more economically attractive (Tolba et al, 1992).

Charcoal and fuelwood production are other causes of deforestation, especially in the tropics and subtropics. In 1980 fuelwood accounted for over half the energy consumption in Africa, 17 per cent in Asia and 8 per cent in Latin America. Around towns and even some villages, cutting far exceeded the regrowth capacity of the forests. Despite all the publicity, logging for commercial timber uses rather less forest than fuelwood, and far more of the timber sold on the world markets comes from developed than from developing countries. In 1989 some 1760 million cubic metres of 'roundwood' was used for fuel (including charcoal) and a slightly smaller amount (1670 million cubic metres) was marketed as timber, with a further 504 million cubic metres traded as 'sawnwood'. Eighty-five per cent of the fuelwood and charcoal was produced in the developing world, but only 26 per cent of the traded roundwood and 28 per cent of the sawnwood originated in central America, South America, Africa and Asia.

None the less, in many tropical countries and regions, cutting of forests for timber exceeded the regenerative capacity of the woodlands – in Sarawak by perhaps a factor of three – resulting in the denudation of up to

40 per cent of the logged forest land. The process, moreover, is wasteful with more trees broken or damaged than are cut for extraction. And shifting cultivators tend to follow the loggers, using the roads built to take the timber out. They seem to use plots in cleared forests much more intensively than they do when working in undisturbed forests – giving the land only about one eighth of the time to regrow and restore the fertility of the soil. Fire is commonly used to clear vegetation or consume cut branches, and it can easily get out of control and ravage the adjacent woods. As a result, degradation is reducing the carrying capacity of the land in many such areas, even while population pressures mount. Better use of the forested regions of the world must be one goal of sustainable development – and it is discussed in Chapter 8.

Deforestation is only one of the ecological transformations wrought by people. The drainage of wetlands has also been very extensive. Statistics are less complete than for forests (and there has been a lot less fuss over the loss, perhaps because people view wetlands as unaesthetic, useless and mosquito- and disease-ridden). But it is estimated that the United States has lost about 54 per cent (or 87 million hectares) of its original wetlands, while in Europe between 90 per cent and 60 per cent have gone. About 10 per cent of France's wettest areas, and 60 per cent of those in the United Kingdom and the Netherlands had been drained by 1970. Agriculture is a major cause of clearance, along with flood prevention and the canalization of rivers like the Rhine and Mississippi for navigation. Many estuarine and coastal marsh systems, some important as natural sea defences, have also been damaged or removed in parts of Europe and the Americas (Tolba et al, 1992).

In tropical developing countries, rice cultivation occupies some 1.3 million square kilometres, much of which would in nature be wetland. Coastal wetlands have suffered less severely than those inland, but two-thirds of the mangrove forests in the Philippines were destroyed between 1920 and 1980, and 40 per cent of those in Thailand have gone. Much of this clearance has been for shrimp-farming and other kinds of mariculture, which have been locally destructive also in parts of India and Malaysia. There have been other major losses in parts of mainland Asia and Africa. Large areas of floodplain have been submerged following dam construction on major rivers in several developing countries. About half the wetlands of international importance in Asia were recorded as threatened in 1989. While wetlands are not so rich in species as forests, they support many distinctive species (some of which are migratory) and are the habitats of some commercially important species (like wild relatives of rice). They also have a major role as regulators of water flow, and drainage brings an increased risk of damaging floods. In the sea, coastal zones and coral reefs are especially rich in species, and the reclamation of marshes, cutting of mangroves, taking of intertidal areas for fish and shrimp farms, and destruction of reefs by dynamite fishing and quarrying have all had a major impact (Ambio, 1993). Such damage also exposes coasts to erosion and flooding.

Misuse of rangeland is another physical cause of land degradation – a better term than 'desertification', for the land is generally not transformed into vast tracts of shifting dunes. Over 40 per cent of the land area of the world is technically defined as 'dryland', in that the evaporation of water from the ground greatly exceeds rainfall. These systems are fragile and easily damaged by over-exploitation, whether to grow crops or through overgrazing. About 70 per cent of the potentially productive drylands – or a stunning total of 3.6 billion hectares (36 million square kilometres) – are threatened by this process of degradation. This is about a quarter of the land area of the world, and one sixth of the world's population is affected. Degradation has already removed an area almost as big as India from productive use and rendered three times as great an area far less productive than it should be. Figure 5 shows the extent of the problem, and demonstrates that Asia is the continent worst affected (especially in north-west China and Mongolia, Pakistan and the Middle East), and that, despite all the publicity about disasters in the Sahara and the Sahel, North America has a higher percentage of degraded rangelands than Africa (Tolba et al, 1992).

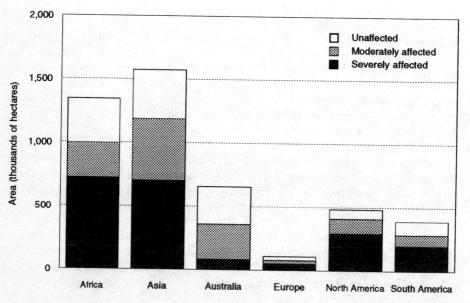

Source: UNEP, 1991a, cited in Tolba et al, 1992

Figure 5 Degradation of the rangelands within the world's drylands.

Irrigation has been seen as the key to enhancing production from drylands from very early times. Indeed, the techniques were pioneered in the 'fertile crescent', and especially in the Tigris and Euphrates valleys, before recorded history. As early as 3700 years ago, some of the cities of that region were being abandoned because of the problems of salt accumulation and waterlogging that are all too common today (Earthscan, 1984; Whitmore et al, 1990). There were 43 million hectares of irrigated land in the dryland zones in 1990, where the soil had been degraded by waterlogging, salt accumulation or alkali contamination. It is estimated that the world is losing about 1.5 million hectares of such land a year from these causes.

There is a good deal of emotional argument as well as scientific debate over whether deserts like the Sahara are getting bigger. Satellite pictures suggest that what happens is that the boundaries of such deserts – which are zones of transition rather than sharp edges – oscillate and that over a few decades the variations in rainfall and other conditions may shift the limits of a particular land use by as much as 130 kilometres. But the underlying trend in Africa between 1931 and 1990 was of increasing dryness, with a decline in rainfall of maybe 30 per cent in some parts of the zone south of the Sahara, increasing the areas classed as arid and very arid by as much as 50 million hectares. Other evidence suggests, however, that the first part of the present century may have been unusually moist and that what we have witnessed has been a return to more 'normal' conditions. What is clear is that in the Sahel zone (the semi-arid zone along the southern edge of the desert) agricultural production has actually increased despite these changes (IUCN, 1991a; Deneve, 1994). The key to dryland production – whether on irrigated or rain-fed cropland or pasture – is human use and misuse, and the degradation that affects so much land clearly results from poor management of irrigation, attempts to grow crops in unsuitable places, and overgrazing. As human pressures increase, so these difficulties will be exacerbated.

Loss of habitats means loss of species and of genetic diversity. That is inevitable. But on what scale? The actual calendar of recorded extinctions is relatively small – we have lost only about 2 per cent of mammals, 1.2 per cent of birds and 0.15 per cent of vascular plants in the period since 1600. Many of these have been island endemics, which are especially vulnerable because of their restricted distributions, and their evolution in isolation from mainland predators or competitors (Table 1) (Whitmore and Sayer, 1992). Habitat destruction is, however, thought to have been responsible for only 36 per cent of those animal extinctions for which causes have been assigned. The impacts of introduced animals account for 39 per cent. The European translocation of predators like cats, rats, dogs and foxes, and of herbivores like goats, cattle, sheep and pigs – to say nothing of the many birds, mammals and plants they took with them to make their new environments 'more like home', and the pests and weeds they trailed inadvertently in their wake – has had profound impact especially on isolated land masses like New Zealand or Australia. A further 23 per cent of animal extinctions is estimated to have been caused by hunting and direct persecution (WCMC, 1992).

However, these recorded extinctions are only the tip of a large iceberg. They relate to well-known and highly visible species like mammals and birds. The issue is how far other extinctions have occurred unnoticed, and how far other major losses of genetic variety are taking place within species which are not yet in danger of extinction but may have their long-term viability reduced by this erosion. A further issue is prediction – what will happen if we do nothing? All recent analyses suggest that the commitment to extinction as a result of current trends is much greater than that recorded in the past 400 years – even though even in that period the extinction rate was running at 1000 to 10,000 times the natural background. One recent estimate was that in 1992, 9 per cent of plants and 5 per cent of vertebrate animals were threatened (Morris, 1995). What can we do if we want to save as much as possible of the Earth's remaining living diversity? These issues are returned to in Chapter 7.

Table 1 Species numbers, extinctions and threat

Taxa	Approximate number of species	Recorded extinctions since 1600	Percent extinct	Species under threat	Percent under threat
Mammals	4,150	83	1.99%	414	10.0%
Birds	9,200	113	1.23%	924	10.0%
Reptiles	6,300	21	0.33%	1,355	21.5%
Amphibians	4,200	2	0.05%	48	1.1%
Fish	20,000	23	0.12%	320	1.6%
Vascular plants	250,000	384	0.15%	18,694	7.4%

Sources: May 1988, McNeely et al 1990, Reid 1992

The growth of cities

Urbanization is the other obvious form of physical change people have imposed on the biosphere. The sprawling 'concrete jungles' of houses, factories, civic buildings and transport corridors that festoon and divide the natural world today are the cumulative result of at least 5000 years of history. But it is only in the last two centuries – and especially since 1900 – that the impact has become devastating. Today, the number of large towns with over a million residents is growing fast. In 1980 there were 222, of which 103 were in the developed world. In 2025 the projected total is 639, of which 468 will be in developing regions. And the 'megacities' with over 5 million inhabitants are increasing rapidly, again especially in the developing world (Berry, 1990; Hardoy et al, 1992; Tolba et al, 1992).

The migration from rural to urban areas is a dominant social process of our era. It happens because people expect more job opportunities in the towns, together with better health care, education and services. In broad terms they are right – but the growth of the cities is in many regions outstripping the capacity (and wealth) of their governments. Squatter settlements, many rife with crime, sprawl among wealthy suburbs. Many lack access to safe water supplies, and even more are without sanitary facilities. Waste disposal is a severe problem. Factories and workshops, often mingled with housing, still use polluting and hazardous processes, contaminating air and water (Berry, 1990). And the process of improvement which has made life less squalid in many countries by eliminating dull, repetitive jobs and cleaning up the working and living environment has its down-sides. Economic growth and mechanization have brought new forms of pollution, especially in streets jam-packed with traffic. Mechanization has also displaced many people who lack skills from employment and imposed a social cost in the shape of frustration, disaffection, social support, and sometimes crime.

As cities, with their associated industries and communication corridors, have expanded they have had five particular kinds of environmental impact. First, they have taken 'greenspace', and eliminated or greatly reduced its biological production. Second, and as a direct consequence, they have caused local changes in temperature patterns. Third, their output of waste heat and pollution has regional impact. Fourth, they are the main sources of pollutant with global impact (especially greenhouse gases and ozone depleters). Fifth, by their demand for food, water and raw materials – and for disposal sites for their wastes – they dominate resource uses in a wide hinterland and even internationally through trading systems (Berry, 1990; Hardoy et al, 1992). As the urban population of the world increases its numerical dominance so these trends will continue and the rural landscape and its population will become ever more subjugated to the needs and impacts of the towns.

These impacts are (and will be) exacerbated by the fact that many cities are where they are because the land around their centres was fertile. Most are in the coastal zone – broadly defined as the land between the shores and the 200-metre contour. Many are on rivers or estuaries. These locations made good sense when the towns were small. They guarantee good access to water, water-borne travel, and food from both land and sea. But the result is that urban expansion has taken good farmland, placed communities at risk because the cities have encroached onto floodplains, and directly created pollution risks – made worse if industries release effluent to the rivers and estuaries. And inter-urban transport corridors – especially roads, carving through farmlands, forests and natural habitats – increase the risk of unplanned settlement and further urban encroachment along their lengths. The opening up of the Brazilian forests by road systems has been a major factor in forest destruction (Tolba et al, 1992).

The impact of pollution

Despite their great and growing scale, physical changes to the world environment are still mostly direct and localized. But the chemical changes wrought by humanity in the biosphere are another matter. Pollution, originally also a local problem where the sewage waste from a town or village fouled a river or pond, or smoke created choking fogs and blackened the surrounding woods, has now become more global and more dangerous

(Holdgate, 1979; Tolba et al, 1992). Substances never before present in the environment have been synthesized and released by humanity. The stratospheric ozone layer which screens us against damaging ultraviolet radiation from the sun has been thinned by the impact of industrial chemicals which are so inert in the ground-level environment that they used to be thought of as ideally safe. The balance of the global climate is threatened by the accumulation of so-called greenhouse gases.

The first reason for concern over air pollution was as a threat to human health – especially indoors, in factories and homes, and outdoors in cities where smoke and sulphur dioxide, produced especially by burning wood and coal inefficiently in small fires, created acrid, choking, fumes and smog. These problems have, to a considerable degree, been cured in developed countries (although unhealthy, smoky air is still a major health problem in many cities in the developing world). But the solution chosen for many countries – like those in western Europe – substituted one hazard for another. For it involved warming homes and offices by central heating in place of open fires, and the removal of power stations from urban areas to country locations, where the fumes were dispersed through tall chimneys thereby reducing concentrations at ground level. This, however, did not eliminate the problem that all coals and oils contain some sulphur, and that when these fuels are burned the sulphur is released as sulphur dioxide – which, in turn, dissolves in rain to produce sulphuric acid. Similarly, when fuel is burned in the Earth's atmosphere, which is 80 per cent nitrogen, some of that nitrogen is unavoidably oxidised to nitrogen oxides – in turn liable to dissolve in rain and mist and form nitric acid. If these gases are allowed to enter the atmosphere, acid rain is an inevitable product of fossil fuel combustion.

In the 1960s and 1970s there was increasing evidence of the damage that these acids could cause when they were swept from the air by trees, buildings, or even washing on the line, or were deposited in mist and rain on vegetation and into lakes and streams. Where the soils and waters that receive such inputs have little capacity to neutralize the acids, severe ecological damage results. In 1985 a survey showed that some 4000 lakes in Sweden no longer contained any fish, while another 17,000 had reduced populations of those species (such as trout and salmon) that are most sensitive to acids. Acid deposition was also identified as a major factor contributing to the forest damage identified in Europe in the 1970s, partly because of the changes it causes in the soils, releasing aluminium and other metals that damage plant roots. A five-year study indicated that damaging levels of sulphur deposition were being inflicted on 75 per cent of European forests, while 60 per cent were affected by excessive nitrogen deposition. The losses in timber were calculated at 118 million cubic metres a year for the next century (48 million in Western Europe, 35 million in Eastern Europe, and 35 million in the former USSR). In economic terms this meant a loss of around US $30 billion a year.

Such damage and loss are clearly unacceptable. From the time of the 1972 Stockholm Conference onwards, demands for remedial measures have slowly borne fruit, as Chapter 2 explains. In Europe, emissions of sulphur dioxide and nitrogen oxides from power stations are now being reduced, and the trend in total sulphur emissions is downwards (although nitrogen oxide releases are being curbed more slowly, as Chapter 3 reports). Moreover, depositions still exceed the 'critical loads' it is thought that sensitive ecosystems can tolerate. But as the problem is attended to in the developed world, it is emerging in many developing countries where there are also potentially sensitive areas (Tolba et al, 1992). And, as the developed world cures its traditional air pollution problems of smoke and acidity, it is increasingly confronted with more and more oxidant fumes, produced through chemical reactions involving vehicle exhaust emissions. Amelioration is possible through cleaner and more efficent vehicles and more use of improved public transport. But once again, the problem seems certain to transfer itself to the developing world where the population of motor vehicles is growing far faster than that of people.

Recent decades have seen pollution problems enlarge from the regional to the global scale. The first such issue to attract attention was the depletion of the ozone layer. This is now well known to result from the accumulation in the atmosphere of chlorofluorocarbons (CFCs) and related chemicals, which, while they are indeed chemically inert in the lower atmosphere, diffuse into the stratosphere where they are broken down by incoming radiation from the sun. The problem is that this breakdown releases highly reactive substances, especially chlorine, which react with ozone and convert it back into ordinary oxygen. The destruction of the ozone layer was first discovered, and is still most pronounced, in the Antarctic during the southern springtime, where the October level of ozone fell by 30 to 40 per cent in the decade between the 1970s and 1980s. Worldwide, the reduction in ozone is of the order of 2 or 3 per cent (Tolba et al, 1992).

This matters from the point of view of conservation and the sustainable use of natural resources because the ozone screen stops ultraviolet B (UV-B) radiation from the sun reaching the Earth's surface. That radiation can damage plants and animals in several ways. The most important impact (ecologically) is on plants. It is estimated that as UV-B exposure rises, so the fixation of carbon by green plants falls. In the Antarctic oceans there are signs that the microscopic plant life in the surface waters of the sea may already be affected, and that production may be falling by several per cent. Multiplied worldwide, the effects on marine and land plant production, including production in agriculture, could be significant. And the more direct human concern is that UV-B is a cause of skin cancer – most of it non-malignant, but some in the form of malignant melanoma. We can expect other sensitive-skinned animals (such as frogs and other amphibians) to show comparable damage.

Action has, of course, been taken. The so-called Montreal Protocol on Substances that Deplete the Ozone Layer was agreed in 1987 (UNEP, 1987). Under it, CFCs are to be phased out. If this happens universally – that is, if all countries implement the policy – and if all ozone-depleting substances are got rid of, then the amount of chlorine in the stratosphere should get back to the levels at which the 'ozone hole' appeared by between the middle and end of the next century. Meanwhile, the situation will get worse before it gets better. It is likely that there will be additional ozone losses in the next decade, in middle latitudes and the Arctic as well as in southern polar regions. The consequences are bound to be further loss of biological productivity and possibly some damage to biological diversity.

Chlorofluorocarbons and some nitrogen oxides are also 'greenhouse gases', as are carbon dioxide, methane and water vapour. The Earth is about thirty degrees Celsius warmer than it would be were there no water vapour or carbon dioxide as natural components of the atmosphere. In other words, the planet is habitable because of this natural greenhouse effect. The problem is that human action has been increasing the concentrations of four greenhouse gases – carbon dioxide, methane, nitrous oxide and CFCs – and hence accentuating the natural effect.

The carbon dioxide (CO_2) comes from combustion processes, inevitably when any fuel containing carbon is burned in an oxygen atmosphere. When the fuel is wood or charcoal, produced directly from today's living plants, the process is no more than a stage in the carbon cycle which is one of the essential processes of the biosphere. But the carbon in coal, oil and natural gas has been locked up in the rocks for millions of years, and it is now being returned to the active cycle faster than the natural processes that abstract it into plants or deposit it in seabed sediments can cope with. Similarly, forest clearance and wetland drainage are reducing the amount of carbon held in the pool of living matter and peaty soil, and augmenting the amount in the air. In total, we are putting some 8 billion tonnes of carbon into the atmosphere each year, and 3 billion tonnes is staying there and accumulating as CO_2. That is why the natural greenhouse phenomenon is being amplified.

We are also emitting methane and nitrous oxide, which come mainly from agriculture (rice paddies and fermentation processes in the guts of cattle), microbial processes and fossil fuel combustion. And while water vapour passes so quickly through the atmosphere that at any time its concentrations are in equilibrium with current climate conditions, if the climate does get warmer then its concentrations would be expected to rise (adding to the warming) unless cloudiness increases in ways that reduce the influx of radiation.

There are many uncertainties. But the world scientific community considers that the overwhelming balance of probability is that the additional amounts of greenhouse gas in the atmosphere will change, and almost certainly warm, the climate and they may also alter rainfall patterns. Latest analyses (Houghton and Bolin, 1992) suggest that if there is a doubling in atmospheric carbon dioxide, surface temperatures are likely to increase by between 1.5 and 4.5°C. In addition, the expansion of the warmer oceans, and melting of mountain glaciers, would lead to sea level rises of the order of 10–20 cm. Table 2 sets out what could happen by the year 2030 in various regions, on the basis of 'business as usual' – that is, no changes in contemporary energy policies.

Table 2 Projected regional climate changes

Region	Temperature		Precipitation	
	Winter	Summer	Winter	Summer
Central North America	+2 to +4°C	+2 to +3°C	+0 to − 15%	− 5 to − 10%
Southern Asia	+1 to +2°C	+1 to +2°C	–	+5 to + 15%
Sahel, Africa	+1 to +3°C	+1 to +3°C	increase	slight increase
Southern Europe	approx +2°C	+2 to +3°C	slight increase	− 5 to − 15%
Australia	approx +2°C	+1 to +2°C	uncertain	+10%

Source: IPCC, 1990, cited in Tolba et al, 1992

Such changes would have serious implications for the distribution of plant and animal species, vegetation patterns, and agriculture. A one-degree rise in temperature would be expected to displace both natural veg-etation types and the corn belt in the United States in a north to north-easterly direction by 175 km. It would elevate the limits of crop culti-vation by 140m in the United Kingdom, by some 150m in the European Alps and by 200m in the Andes of Ecuador (Parry, 1990). Warming on a larger scale could virtually eliminate the Arctic tundra and permafrost, the coniferous forest advancing to the shore of the Arctic ocean, while it might bring Mediterranean-type vegetation into northern France and Southern Britain, and displace the temperate forests northwards into Scandinavia. But how fast could species respond? Dominant trees like the North American eastern hemlock (*Tsuga canadensis*) have spread at only around 25 km per century since the last ice age. Many such species could experience substantial reductions in range, at least until conditions stabilize and they can 'catch up'. There is clearly a risk that climatic warming will reduce bio-logical diversity, favour new and transient vegetation types dominated by the species that are best at dispersion like fireweed or birch trees, and also disrupt agriculture and land use patterns and undermine human lifestyles just when an increase in global food supplies is most essential.

Chemical changes are also affecting both fresh waters and the sea. While the contamination of some developed country rivers with metals and chemi-cals has begun to decline as a result of tight controls, the situation continues to deteriorate in many developing countries. Agricultural chemicals are becoming increasingly serious contaminants of river systems and coastal seas in Europe and North America. The result is excessive growth of water plants – leading in turn to deoxygenation when the masses of plant matter decompose – and an increased frequency of algal blooms and 'red tides' in the sea. The consequent ecological disruptions are damaging to the ecosys-tems concerned, and again impair biological diversity while reducing the productivity of fisheries.

Most of the world's coastal seas are polluted. The most serious problems arise from the deposition of sediment (a consequence of erosion, in turn arising from poor land use and from vegetation clearance), and the excessive inputs of nitrate and phosphate in sewage and agricultural drainage. The structure of plankton communities is altered, algal blooms become more frequent (and are followed, as in fresh waters, by deoxygenation when the plant matter dies), and the proliferation of toxic kinds of alga can in turn lead to poisoning when seafood is consumed by people. Sewage discharges raise the levels of pathogenic micro-organisms, and hence of disease. Contamination with pesticides, polychlorinated biphenyls and other persistent toxic substances affects the reproductive vigour of seals and other marine species. Taken in conjunction with the physical disruption of the coastal zone through land reclamation, destruction of mangroves, and quarrying of coral reefs, the biological diversity and useful production of many coastal areas is being severely reduced.

All these impacts are bound to damage biological diversity as well as impair the capacity of land and water systems to meet increasing human needs. Some are recognized to be intolerable, both ecologically and socially, and have hence led to responses. But it is clear than even when this has happened, the reversal of the trend and the restoration of the damage will take decades if not centuries. Meanwhile human pressures and demands continue to mount. Demographic momentum is such that we face a near-doubling of human numbers to 8–12 billion in under a century – unless mortality rises because nature simply cannot provide enough to meet needs on this scale. Most of those people will live in cities, exacerbating the problems of urban sprawl and bringing major risks of intense local pollution. The costs to human health and welfare from foul air and contaminated water in such cities in the developing world may well, in aggregate, be far greater at present than the more spectacular global impacts that attract the headlines. So far, the responses of governments and communities have been inadequate. We appear to be 'losing the human race' (ICIHI, 1988).

Changes in governance: the rise of interdependence

Today's governance and trading systems are also changing rapidly. We see the consequences every day. Without thinking about it, we may eat at one meal the products of plants and animals that originated on four different continents, and a household in any developed country (and not a few developing ones) may well include products from twenty or thirty countries. The economic linkages can be subtle, but of wide impact.

For example, there are 15 million people in the Netherlands (Nijhoff, 1994). They live alongside (and on) 14 million pigs, 5 million cows and 100 million chickens. The food for this livestock includes tapioca and soya from Brazil and Thailand. The production of livestock feed can have significant environmental impact in its countries of origin, while the manure produced by all these animals pollutes soil, groundwater and surface waters and contributes to the pollution of the adjacent shallow seas in Europe. But there is over-production of meat in the Netherlands (as a result, in part, of over-subsidization in the European Union). The surplus meat is exported and sold well below cost in Western Africa. Local market prices for meat have been undermined. Local farmers cannot sell their cattle, so herds grow in size and cause overgrazing and land degradation. Some potentially prosperous local chicken-raising ventures have also been destroyed.

These interlinkages mean that sustainable development in the poorer countries can be obstructed by social practices in the richer nations. If subsidies lead to agricultural over-production in Europe and North America, and the surpluses are dumped in Africa at prices which undermine the development there of new agricultural industries, some of the good that development assistance is meant to do is undermined. It may be better for the world as a whole to reduce the use of fertilizers and livestock feed in developed countries, convert some farmland to woodland, energy crops, recreational areas or wild habitat, and spend more on imports from developing countries – thereby reducing the need for aid, and enhancing their own economic growth. It may mean assistance to farmers in Brazil and Thailand to grow alternative crops. It will certainly demand a new kind of support to European farmers, to allow them to contribute to other social goals (there is already a farm woodlands scheme in Europe).

Action to address the obvious environmental problems is increasingly linked internationally, because it is recognized that few nations can make much impression on their own. There are now 121 global Treaties and other legal instruments dealing with environmental issues, with another 265 regional ones (IUCN, 1993a). World trade policy is governed by GATT, the General Agreement on Tariffs and Trade, and following the completion of the latest stage in its development, the so-called Uruguay round, the interlinkages and contradictions between measures to facilitate trade and measures to safeguard the environment are having to be faced. GATT is in process of conversion into a World Trade Organization, which will have a standing Committee on Trade and Environment. At the same time, more and more political decisions are being taken at supranational level – in the Group of 7 leading economic powers, the Organization for Economic Co-operation and Development, and regional institutions like the European Union, or the South American Common Market of the Southern Cone, MERCOSUR. And the world is bound together by instantaneous reporting. People hear of events as they happen. An earthquake, a flood, a war, a refugee tragedy, a governmental crisis, can be on everyone's television screen while the events are unfolding. Humanitarian relief, channelling popular sympathy and concern, can be on the way within days of disaster. The United Nations is now better known for its peace-keeping role than for its work of diplomatic negotiation.

At the same time, nations are guarding their sovereignty with a jealousy that at time borders on the paranoid. At the Earth Summit in Rio de Janeiro, some issues that impinged on (or were thought to impinge on) sovereignty were placed off-limits by a barrage of protestation. The proposed

'Earth Charter', which was to have been a resounding declaration of common purpose and global partnership, was weakened and diluted to become a short declaration that scarcely moves beyond the one adopted in Stockholm twenty years earlier. Biological diversity is not accepted as the common heritage of the world, even though wild species ignore human frontiers. Each nation wants to benefit from its own living resources. The environment of a state is a sovereign possession, even though the actions each state takes affect all other states, and some states manifestly cannot develop sustainably and maintain their future populations on the basis of their sovereign resources alone.

To a substantial degree, this national posturing is a charade. In fact global business, industry and commerce govern the economic development of millions of people, as much despite as because of what governments do. Where governments create the conditions in which inward investment is attracted, economic growth is stimulated and material prosperity (for part at least of the community) follows. This has nothing to do with the political or cultural context, but it has much to do with the ability of a government to create and maintain stable conditions under which investors can reap the benefits of their investments. Private sector finance flows are 20 to 50 times as large as official government-to-government aid, and they are flowing wherever commerce is attracted, for example from Europe and North America to parts of Southeast Asia and South America. In Europe there is a marked flow from the west to the centre (but not so much to the states of the former USSR). On the other hand the flow by-passes a large part of Africa, because such investment is unattractive there, aggravating the difficulties of some of the world's poorest nations.

Another supranational dimension is that of information. Within the past two decades powerful, cheap computers have become almost as universally available as radios and television. They are being linked into new and fast-growing networks. Just as news now flows almost everywhere almost as fast as events happen, so groups with mutual interests are continually interchanging knowledge and ideas along the 'information superhighways'. These networks can immensely strengthen the ability of individuals and groups to do things. And they work with very little government control, and often with no government knowledge of who is passing what knowledge to whom. The situation has parallels with science or the Christian church in medieval Europe, where bonds of common interest and belief, and special direct channels of communication, allowed a fellowship to operate across frontiers and build new concepts with the power to shake the world.

The information superhighway will empower groups and individuals. It is enormously strengthening the business world. It allows vast sums of money to be transferred instantaneously. It allows appeals for help to be transmitted worldwide by the oppressed. It can undermine governments because it weakens their control of information and finance. It is bound to reinforce the trend towards decentralization. And decentralization is a continuing social theme. It is a fact that the care and sustainable use of the environment depends especially on local communities and individuals – farmers, fishermen, foresters, factory workers, health workers, consumers – and the way in which they exercise individual choices. In many communities the development process is being stood on its head in consequence. In place of solutions developed, propounded and imposed by central governments, advised by 'experts' from outside the local communities, the latter are developing their own. New approaches involve learning from the poor, local community empowerment, local initiatives – and a diversity of resource use patterns that maintain local social needs, cultures and environmental circumstances. Development is being seen not as a blueprint but as a flexible, adaptive process. Local groups, if empowered to manage their own resources, can often solve environmental problems without recourse to central government. But the result is that some activities transfer from the formal to the informal economy, and means are needed to ensure that the result is not perversely presented as national impoverishment, when it is truly the reverse.

The modern recognition of the importance of biological diversity is being paralleled by a new recognition of the value of cultural diversity. The arrogance with which the European cultural values, transported worldwide in the most recent of the massive folk-migrations in Earth history, were assumed to be superior, so that colonialism was seen as bringing the 'blessings of civilization' is being replaced by a more humble mode. There is grief, today, for lost peoples like those who 'listening to the white man's talk of peace, found it only in unremembered graves' (Barclay, 1926), and who took centuries of knowledge and tradition with them. The reverence accorded to the 'Chief Seathl speech' – actually a film script written in 1971/72 – which has been described as 'the best statement ever made on behalf of nature' (Anon, 1989) no doubt arose not just because it is, indeed, a text of moving eloquence but because it was published at a time of mounting sensitivity to ancient wisdom and culture, and regret for what has been lost.

What people do depends on their beliefs, and these reflect culture, religion and tradition. Working with the grain of culture, and cherishing its adaptive value, is another key to success. Within that process, new alliances are being developed across the community. For example, business, industry and commerce are being brought into new alliances with the environmental movement – at global level through the work of bodies like the World Business Council for Sustainable Development, and nationally and locally through new partnerships like the Round Tables active in Canada and New Zealand, and a host of other groups.

It is becoming more and more widely recognized that the literal 'bottom line' is the individual. Inspiring, motivating, educating, guiding and empowering people is the key to the achievement of sustainable living. In fact, the image of 'bottom line' is the wrong one: the need is to make individuals the top line in concern, and the indicators of success. This will involve changing patterns of resource use and consumption in both developed and developing countries. It will mean adopting and pursuing a new ethic of care for nature and respect for all people and all life forms. But without such transformations, sustainable development will not happen, and the world will become more polarised and riven by inequity. War, waste, cost and environmental degradation will then ensue.

The challenge of our time, and the challenge of this book, is how to turn recognition of the need to deal with poverty and deprivation, the need to stabilize human numbers at a level which allows everyone a decent quality of life, and the need to care for the natural world as the foundation of the global economy, into real and practical action. All the Agenda 21s in the world are of value only if they are applicable.

Approaching the limits?

The momentum of development is carrying many communities towards – or beyond – the limits of support available from their local environments. This does not necessarily matter if trading systems allow them to get what they need in exchange for whatever they produce. Indeed, it makes environmental sense to use the best farmland for agriculture, wherever it is, and not to deplete the productivity of more vulnerable semi-arid or tropical forest areas. But the problem is one of costs and of ability to pay. That limits the nutritional status of people in poor countries, not the capacity of the world as a whole to produce the food.

But there are concerns that we may approach a biological limit at global level. World annual production of organic matter on land is estimated at around 150 billion tonnes a year. One analysis suggests that already humanity collects, uses or destroys about 39 per cent of that produced by plants on land, and about 2 per cent of that in fresh and marine aquatic systems (Vitousek et al, 1986).

Each year a certain amount of natural habitat is modified – as when forest is converted to pasture, or grazing lands are burned, consuming the biomass. This is calculated as reducing global primary productivity (a technical term for what green plants produce by photosynthesis) by a total of 2.4 billion tonnes a year. Both natural and modified systems are converted for cultivation on a much larger scale, however, and this conversion is estimated to pre-empt or destroy some 8.5 billion tonnes of forest organic matter production, and a further 9 billion tonnes of other production a year, giving a total loss of 17.5 billion tonnes. Land degradation, especially in arid and semi-arid rangelands, reduces productivity by some 4.5 billion tonnes annually, and a further 2.6 billion tonnes goes as a result of the encroachment of the built environment on 'greenspace'. This adds up to 27 billion tonnes, or 18 per cent of world production, lost by human action.

That, however, is only part of the picture. People take most of their food and a considerable amount of other products from croplands, grazing lands, woodlands and plantations that have already been converted to such uses. Croplands are estimated to yield 15 billion tonnes a year of organic matter for human use, and forest plantations 1.6 billion tonnes (not all of which is used efficiently: post-harvest crop losses can account for 40 per cent of what is gathered under some conditions). About 3.5 billion tonnes is taken from forests other than plantations, and about one third (1.3 billion tonnes) of this is estimated to be cut but not used. Livestock consume about 10.6 billion tonnes of plant matter a year. Finally, there is a significant amount of primary production in people's gardens, urban parks and so forth, which is treated as used by people and adds 0.4 billion tonnes a year. This sub-total comes to 31.1 billion tonnes – 20.7 per cent of the whole. Hence the nearly 39 per cent, or 58.1 billion tonnes used or wasted by our impact. Looking to the future, we clearly have scope for great gains in efficiency.

Ecological systems themselves are not, in engineering terms, very efficient. Only about 5 per cent of the sun's energy reaching the Earth is intercepted by green plants, and only 1 per cent of this energy is converted into carbohydrate by photosynthesis (Nobel, 1973). The efficiency of conversion of sunlight into plant food produce used by people is only around 0.05 per cent (Southwood, 1976). When a cow or antelope eats herbage, the maximum conversion rate is about 10–25 per cent and there are similar losses when carnivores eat their prey (Morowitz, 1968) (this double loss between plants and meat-eaters is one reason why a largely vegetarian diet is more efficient, and why, in biological terms, it is incredibly wasteful to harvest a high-protein animal like a fish and convert it to fertilizer, at the very base of the food chain). In some ecosystems the vast bulk of the fixed energy finds its way to the decomposers, or in wetland situations to accumulation in peat.

Clearly, there is considerable room for improvement in our use of the living productivity of the planet. Sustainable development will have to tackle this problem if we are to support maybe twice as many people – and give them a decent quality of life. But it seems unrealistic to assume that current mis-use can be wholly prevented, or that some degradation will not occur. This has implications for the world of nature. Obviously, the area of habitat used to produce human food, and the areas available for nature have both been greatly eroded in past decades and the erosion is continuing. One estimate, in 1987, was that about 200 million hectares of land will be lost from agricultural use during the period 1975–2000, and that another 50 million hectares will be seriously degraded, with yet another 50 million becoming desertified. To compensate, about 300 million hectares of land not now used by agriculture will need to come under cultivation, and much of it will be carved out of the forests or drained from the remaining wetlands. But this is only what happens if we want to stay in the same place. If we are to double world food production over the next century, in order to feed the 5 billion or so more people that will be added to the global population – and lift the millions who live below the poverty line to at least tolerable standards, yet more land may be needed.

Is it available? Certainly there are no great untapped reserves of fertility in some of the countries with the most acute needs, like those in the drier regions of sub-Saharan Africa. The solution is likely to lie in improving the productivity of the lands and waters now used to produce food – in reducing the wastage of 18 per cent of productivity on land and enhancing the efficiency of the production process. So far, over most of the world, outside Africa, improved technology has kept food production ahead of population growth, and farmland is even being set aside in Europe and North America to reduce agricultural surpluses. The 'optimistic' view is that current and new technology can provide what is required – if the technology can be transferred to where it is needed. But on the other hand, there are doubts about the sustainability of the most intensive agricultural systems like those in western Europe, with their high dependence on artificial fertilizers, pesticides and mechanization, and the problems they are creating through the leaching of excess nutrients into rivers, lakes and coastal seas. And the poorer countries are in no position to pay market prices for the products of such sophisticated technology.

The probability is that land degradation and loss will largely be responded to locally – and hence by extending cultivation into lands now forested, or marginal to traditional use. More cultivation may go onto steep slopes prone to erosion. More drylands, capable of sustaining low-density grazing, may be tilled or overstocked and then degraded. And more wild habitats will be taken, mis-used, and degraded – unless new processes of co-operation between local communities and central agencies, and between national and international bodies can be established and transfers of skills and technologies made economically and ecologically sustainable.

The pressures of mounting human need are also likely to call for extension of human use to the marine environment. Today, the oceans and seas provide around 100 million tonnes of fisheries products a year. That is said to be near the attainable maximum – but it is also true that overfishing is depressing yields in many areas, while productivity is depressed in some coastal areas by pollution, the deposition of sediment on coral reefs and the destruction of reefs and mangroves. Sixty per cent of coral reefs in Southeast Asia have already been seriously damaged, and in the Philippines the figure is higher at 70 per cent, while in Indonesia it is 80 per cent. Yet in many coastal areas – such as Eastern Africa – reefs support 70 per cent of artisanal fisheries (which yield 70 per cent of the total catch in those countries), while 80 per cent of shrimp catches come from mangrove areas. Clearly degradation is wasting an immense asset – but equally clearly, more marine and freshwater food is likely to come only through much tighter management, and probably much more aquaculture and mariculture, using new and sustainable methods.

The inevitable consequence of mounting human pressures will therefore be the further loss of wild habitats and living diversity. Meanwhile, pollution is not only damaging resources in the immediate neighbourhood of its sources, but is threatening global systems and world climate. Life-support services which nature has provided as 'free goods' are more and more having to be provided by people.

What is the shape of the future?

First, consider a 'business as usual scenario'. On that basis there will evidently be a major divergence between developed and developing countries.

In the developed world, human population growth can be expected to halt. It is unlikely that there will be a demand to take more land from the surviving areas of wild or semi-natural habitat for cultivation, unless the need to grow crops for energy becomes paramount. Forest areas are likely to remain stable or even increase – but the continuing cutting of species-rich 'old growth' forests will erode their biodiversity and logging may well make large inroads in the former USSR, especially in Siberia, with substantial habitat and biodiversity loss there. The commitment of those countries to Agenda 21 and to sustainability strategies will mean some efforts on their part to remove current over-subsidization of agriculture, to curb excessive fertilizer use and nutrient loss, and to maintain habitats and biodiversity. And if we move from 'business as usual' to positive sustainability strategies, we can expect even more effort to reduce damaging pollution, conserve energy, and cut back greenhouse-gas emissions. Since these countries account for over half of global greenhouse-gas emissions these trends can make a substantial difference and can leave some headroom for increased fossil fuel combustion as industrialization in the developing countries expands.

Meanwhile the trends in many parts of the developing world are adverse and on any conceivable scenario, are likely to impose greater pressures on the environment. The key to minimizing the damage is likely to be a triple one:

- recognition by those countries of the great wealth their environmental 'natural capital' truly represents, and hence of the economic and social loss that pollution and habitat destruction would impose;
- acceptance that their economic future demands swift transfer to sustainability scenarios which combine economic growth with good governance, clean and efficient technology, good social services (including health care and support for birth control), and more devolution of power to local communities;
- international support to make such goals realities.

How the human tide can be channelled into practical sustainability is the central question of this book. But before turning to it, we need to devote more attention to where we are now. Chapter 2 therefore digs deeper into what some have called 'the awakening of the environmental conscience', and Chapter 3 takes stock of where we have really got to in action for sustainability.

ALARM BELLS AND ACTION PLANS

The awakening of the environmental conscience

For most of history, the idea that people could, by their collective actions, disturb the whole natural world and threaten their own global future would have seemed absurd. Nature has always seemed almost incomprehensibly vast to us. Well into the present century, explorers were charting lands and seas hitherto unknown. Even the views of a small, blue and white planet from the moon were hard to relate to the patches of land most of us call home.

Similarly, over most of history, people have not talked about 'development'. They have simply got on with it. They have done whatever seemed most likely to serve their personal or family needs, hunting for food, clearing forests for cultivation, building houses and creating communities, developing trading and transport systems, and gradually weaving the fabric of what we now call 'civilization'. In that process, nature outside the farm fence or the city wall was largely taken for granted. In so far as it impinged on the consciousness it was largely as an enemy: the bringer of storms and droughts, cold and famine. The wild beasts that haunted the forests, raided the crops, or ate the livestock, were foes to be fought. People sought protection from the unpredictable hazards of the world – even today treated by insurance companies as 'acts of God'. Even though salinization and waterlogging may have disrupted the cities of Sumeria over 3500 years ago, and

Plato condemned the soil erosion and deforestation of Attica a thousand years later, at worst these were localized problems (Earthscan, 1984). The idea that global nature might need protection from humanity would have struck most of our ancestors as absurd.

People have, none the less, sought environmental goals with increasing clarity and commitment. Many traditional communities have done so as an expression of deep-seated religious beliefs. In so-called western society, care for the land, and a familiarity with what lives on it, remain deep-seated in rural communities. But the emergence of a conscious, politically active, environmental movement is relatively new. Its origins may be traced in part to the growth of natural history in Europe from the 16th century onwards, for this recruited members of the educated and influential classes to the study – and the defence – of nature. It led on to the emergence of the national parks movement in the 19th century – a movement dedicated to protecting outstanding landscapes from mining or deforestation. It was also fuelled by reaction against damage from unbridled industrialization, which profited by externalizing its costs in the shape of pollution. The intolerable damage from acid fumes produced by the alkali manufacturing industry and smoke from coal-burning furnaces forced the first pollution control laws in Britain in 1863 (Ashby and Anderson, 1981). The invention of ecology as a science by Haeckel in 1868 emphasized the unity of nature, and humanity's inescapable involvement in the natural world, and led to holistic theories of politics (Bramwell, 1989). The elaboration of the concept of the biosphere – the domain of life on the surface of the planet, from the upper atmosphere to the sterile rocks – by Vernadsky marked another step forward, and Lynton Caldwell (1984) has pointed out that this led in turn to new thinking about the interdependence of all life and to the concept of Gaia as a complex, self-regulating system.

Much of the early thinking about ecology, the biosphere and the human phenomenon was academic and intellectual, and touched everyday life very little. However, during the 1970s, 1980s, and now the 1990s, a surge of concern for the environment became a major political force and influenced the central decision processes of governments, at municipal, state and national levels. Disasters accelerated the process – disasters like the first great supertanker wreck, of the *Torrey Canyon* in 1966 (Smith, 1970), the releases of industrial effluent that caused sickness and death at Minamata in Japan and Bhopal in India, the hazards associated with toxic waste disposal at Seveso in Italy, or the release of radioactivity from the reactor accident at Chernobyl in Ukraine (Tolba et al, 1992). These, together with the more insidious effects of toxic pesticides highlighted in Rachel Carson's famous book *Silent Spring* (1963), made people in the developed countries demand environmental protection.

The result was pressure on national and local politicians and on regulatory agencies. It led to tighter standards for pollutant releases from industry. It led to international agreements like the Conventions on the dumping of wastes at sea signed at Oslo in 1971 and London in 1972, or on marine pollution by discharges from coastal outfalls and via rivers, signed in Paris in 1974. It led to international gatherings like the United Nations Conference on the Human Environment, held in Stockholm in 1972, and the UN Conference on Environment and Development in Rio de Janeiro in June 1992. It led to shelf-loads of books and research papers and whole hot-air balloons full of political, scientific and pseudo-scientific rhetoric. These developments have been well summarized by John McCormick in his book *The Global Environmental Movement* (1989) and Lynton Caldwell in *International Environmental Policy* (1984).

These were, however, very much developed country concerns – understandably, for two reasons. First, these were the countries where industrial pollution followed hard alongside the industrial revolution: where 'muck' and 'brass' appeared inseparable. And these were the countries with the wealth, science and technology to take action. In the developing world the chief environmental concerns have been with poverty, and the inability to provide enough health care, housing, water, sanitation, education, industry, employment and economic growth. It was only around the time of the 1972 Stockholm Conference that the areas of interest began to come together, with the recognition that the sustainable development process was much broader than the traditional preoccupations of either group of nations.

The last few decades have seen a sharp increase in action against environmental pollution, mounting concern to conserve the ecological processes and living wealth of the planet (code-named 'biological diversity' or 'biodiversity'), recognition that it is essential to make the best possible use of all the environmental resources we have, understanding that the action has to be based on the human individual, and awareness that we need to re-think the whole concept of development – what it is, and where it is going. There has been an immense proliferation of meetings, debates, laws and reports. International environmental concerns have multiplied. Every week has brought its dozens of Conferences and seminars.

At the same time, the pressure has not all been one way. Criticisms of the waste of environmental resources and the destruction of wildlife, and demands for new policies to avoid catastrophe have been met by assertions that resources are not, and will not be, limiting and that it is too early to take action to prevent climate change – which is not a scientific certainty yet, anyway (Myers and Simon, 1994; Beckerman, 1995). Condemnation of contemporary market economics has been refuted by claims that, given the continuing adjustments of which it is well capable, the market system is readily adaptable for the foreseeable future. While we should not be over-confident, we are reminded that human inventiveness, energy and commitment are immense resources that, if properly used, offer every prospect of a better quality of life (North, 1995). We are now entering into a new phase of debate, characterized by demands for more hard-headed analyses, and above all more commitment to find and apply practical solutions (Cairncross, 1995).

This chapter looks at some of the principal milestones on the highway that has led to our present environmental concerns.

Reaction against pollution

It was almost inevitable that pollution would be the first spur to action in the modern period of environmentalism, because some of the most-publicised catastrophes were the direct or indirect result of chemical contamination of the environment (Holdgate, 1979). The great London smog of 1952, caused by smoke and sulphurous fumes mainly from domestic coal fires, killed between 3000 and 4000 people – mostly elderly victims of bronchitis, emphysema and weak hearts, or the frail young. The outrage these deaths caused meant that the 'London particular' or 'pea-souper' would never again be a subject for nostalgic journalism, and led directly to the British Clean Air Acts (Ashby and Anderson, 1981). In Los Angeles, the first appearance of a different kind of smog – choking oxidant fumes created when nitrogen oxides and hydrocarbons, emitted from petrol-engined cars, react in sunlight – stimulated tight controls on vehicle exhausts, and ultimately the fitting of catalytic converters.

The rural environment had its causes, too. Rachel Carson's seminal work, *Silent Spring*, was about the risk that persistent pesticides, especially organochlorines like DDT or dieldrin, would accumulate in the tissues of birds and destroy them. The evidence against these substances increased during the 1960s. In England, the deaths of foxes from residues obtained when they ate pigeons which had fed on treated crops, caused horror among the fox-hunters of Leicestershire. Pioneer work by the Nature Conservancy showed that the shells of eggs of many predatory birds were thinned as a result of the pesticides they had eaten, and that this accounted for the declining populations of hawks and falcons. Such evidence led first to a tighter screening and licensing process, and finally to the phasing out of the pesticides concerned (Sheail, 1985).

At sea, the two first targets were oil pollution and the dumping of wastes. It seems incredible now, but in 1960 there were no international laws or agreements covering either. The deaths of thousands of oiled seabirds on the Cornish coasts in 1966 (Smith, 1970) led to demands for tighter controls on tanker movement, better ship design, and operational practices to reduce or stop the discharge of oily tank washings. The deaths of thousands more seabirds with accumulations of polychlorinated biphenyls in their tissues led to a halt in the manufacture of these substances. The much-publicized movement of ships sent to dump toxic and radioactive wastes in the ocean led to a flurry of international agreements in the early 1970s. More recently, in the late 1980s, the impact of nitrates and phosphate on lakes, rivers and estuaries, causing eruptions of plant growth, red tides of poisonous micro-organisms, and consequent damage to fisheries and hazards to human health, created demands for tighter controls on agricultural run-off.

Toxic metals were placed high up the 'black list' of substances that must not be discharged to the environment from the outset, when such lists were first drawn up in the early 1970s. The discovery of mercury contamination and its link to human deaths at Minamata Bay in Japan; high mercury levels in Baltic and North Sea fish; cadmium and *itai-itai* disease, also in Japan;

and the link between lead emissions from smelters and petrol-engined cars and a risk to children's mental health were powerful spurs to action against these and other heavy metals. These substances all figured prominently in the doomsters' catalogues (Holdgate, 1979).

As described in Chapter 1, the destruction of fish in thousands of miles of European and North American river and lake systems due to acid rain directly prompted an international Convention on Long-Range Trans-Boundary Air Pollution, under which targets for reductions in emissions of sulphur dioxide and nitrogen oxides were set. Air pollution was also blamed for forest die-back in much of Europe, and since not only acid rain but also emissions from petrol-engined cars were held responsible this sparked action to curb the latter by following North American example and adopting catalytic converters. Not quite in time, for Los Angeles smog, with its attendant asthma and other sicknesses, became a London phenomenon in the 1990s and now plagues an ever-increasing number of cities in the developing as well as the developed world. Similarly, the two issues that now dominate global concern about pollution and its impacts – the depletion of the stratospheric ozone layer and the risk of climate change as a result of human discharge of 'greenhouse gases' – have been addressed through international conventions. What is interesting is that neither of these two major concerns was the subject of serious discussion at the 1972 Stockholm Conference. They are a demonstration that we can still be surprised by our failure to predict environmental problems that with hindsight appear obvious.

The first response to pollution was regulation, at both national and international level. Departments of the Environment, with co-ordinating units and teams or inspectorates charged with action against pollution mushroomed during the 1970s. The United States set up its Council on Environmental Quality and Environment Protection Agency, and the United Kingdom created its Department of the Environment in 1970. National state-of-the-environment reports, national commissions overseeing environmental quality, and national monitoring schemes all expanded. By 1990 virtually all developed countries had ministries charged with responsibility for environmental protection. In developing countries, reflecting the different environmental situation and social priorities, environmental ministries were often charged with responsibility for natural resources, and sometimes also for tourism and wildlife.

Laws also proliferated. In the developed countries belonging to the Organization for Economic Co-operation and Development there were only four major environmental laws adopted between 1950 and 1959, but 20 were added between 1960 and 1969, and 64, in the following decade. Internationally, IUCN recorded that in 1992 there were 121 global treaties and conventions on environmental matters, and 265 such agreements at regional level; many of these deal with pollution (IUCN, 1993a).

The expansion of action has been accompanied by new thinking about guiding principles. The 'polluter pays' principle originated in OECD in 1971. Essentially it means that those making a product or using a process should bear the costs of action taken to clean up effluents and ensure that the environment is not damaged. The community at large should not subsidize the industry by bearing 'externalized' costs, or by being taxed so that government could pay industry to clean up its emissions. The purchasers of the products or services involved should pay the true social and environmental costs of their production. Later the 'precautionary principle' was added: it means simply that if there is a significant risk that an action will lead to environmental damage, that action should not be taken. Most recently of all (as will be discussed later), it has become evident that regulations alone may be less efficient than economic instruments in the shape of taxes and charges, and in the mid-1990s there is much discussion about how to use them most effectively, and how to blend them with essential regulation to deter the economically illiterate or the wilfully perverse (points developed in considerable detail by Frances Cairncross in her book *Green, Inc.* (1995), which I saw just as I was finishing this text). This whole burst of debate over environmental economics is one of the most important developments in the 1990s.

Action to protect areas

The protected area movement is one of the oldest strands in conservation. Laws to protect outstanding landscapes were first enacted in the United States in 1864 (Wirth, 1962). Since then, a diversity of landscapes has enjoyed a wide range of protection on all the continents. The number of sites and total area thus protected have increased dramatically (Figure 6) (WCMC, 1992). The whole continent of Antarctica has been designated as a nature reserve devoted to peace and science, and new and comprehensive conservation measures are being adopted under a Protocol to the Antarctic Treaty. A Strategy for Antarctic Conservation has been published by IUCN (1991b). The whole global strategy for protected areas was reviewed in 1992 at the Fourth World Congress on National Parks and Protected Areas, held in Caracas, Venezuela (McNeely, 1993).

That congress took place against the background of mounting concern to safeguard as much as possible of the world's biological diversity. It also recognized that increasing human pressures, and the imperative of development, made a new approach to the protection of landscapes and habitats essential. Although vast areas of land have been designated for protection in many countries – over 20 per cent of Venezuela, for example – it was also evident that for such areas to be more than 'paper parks', there had to be commitment from the people living there.

The World Congress therefore emphasized that 'the establishment and effective management of networks of national parks and other areas in which critical natural habitats, flora and fauna are protected must have high priority and must be carried out in a manner sensitive to the needs and concerns of local people.' The Caracas Action Plan, adopted at the Congress, called for the integration of protected areas into wider planning

frameworks. It called for more broadly based support for such areas, especially by identifying the products and services they could provide and the
groups with a stake in them. It emphasized the need to recognize the priority concerns of local communities, and to back the groups who had a strong
interest in conservation of particular protected areas. It urged an increase
in capacity to manage protected areas, and in international cooperation to
support such action.

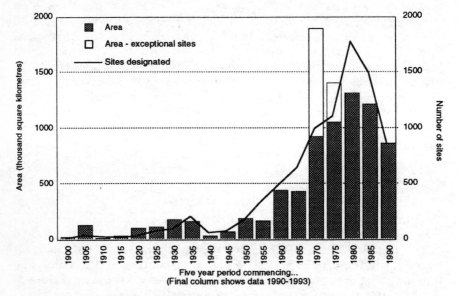

The exceptional sites are the Greenland and Great Barrier Reef National Parks, designated in 1974 and 1979 respectively.
Source: IUCN, 1994e

Figure 6 The designation of protected areas

The national parks and protected areas movement is an important environmental bridge between developed and developing countries. Although the
first national parks were created in the 'North', the great conservation areas
of Eastern and Southern Africa, Asia and Latin America have proved of
even greater economic importance to those countries. Tourism to such
areas is a principal earner of foreign currency. It is very big business
indeed. The result is that protected areas are seen as a priority land use,
and efforts are being made to involve the people who live in or around
them as active agents of conservation and beneficiaries of the employment
and revenue they generate.

All this adds up to a new mood in protected area policy. It recognizes the
need for partnership with all sectors of the community in the countries, and
especially the localities, where parks and reserves are situated. It recognizes
that allowing some sustainable use of the 'products and services' of such
areas wins local allies and establishes a value for conservation. It has led on

to the development of continental strategies for protected areas (IUCN, 1994c), and – remedying a neglect of many decades – a strategy for marine protected areas, as part of a wider effort to conserve marine biological diversity (Kelleher, 1992; Norse, 1993). The convergence of the parks tradition and the more modern biodiversity conservation imperative is another important recent development.

Action to conserve biological diversity

If action to curb pollution was the top of the agenda in the 1960s and 1970s, in the 1980s much emphasis had switched to the conservation of biological diversity. The cause? First, a recognition that there were many more species on earth than scientists had yet described, second a fear that they were being lost at an alarming and accelerating rate, especially as a consequence of habitat destruction, and third a new recognition of the value of biological resources to people, and of the need to conserve them as a foundation for sustainable development.

Since the present system of describing and naming species was invented by the Swedish naturalist Carl von Linne (Linnaeus) in the 18th century, about 1. 7 million have been recorded by scientists – many of them insects, especially beetles ('God', remarked the geneticist JBS Haldane, 'has an inordinate fondness for beetles').

But how many are there really? Only some of the world's habitats have been described. Many have hardly been searched for their smaller animals and plants. We do not begin to know how many nematode worms live in deep-sea sediments. The recent discovery of bizarre assemblages of animals, some belonging to quite new groups, among the deep ocean hot vents or 'black smokers' was both exciting and a reminder of our inadequate survey of our planet. On land, we have reason to know that the tropical forests are our richest habitats, but in what? The classic study by the American entomologist Terry Erwin (1982) relied on clearing the canopies of a series of selected trees with a chemical mist that would 'knock down' insect life without distinction. He found an immense diversity of hitherto unknown beetles and other species. Based on this finding, and the evidence that many of the species are associated with only one kind of tree, and may have a restricted geographical distribution as well, Erwin calculated a world total of 30 million arthropods (mostly insects). This in turn led others to suggest that the world might contain between 20 and 80 million species, most of them in tropical moist forests. Today, 10 million is considered a cautious estimate.

Such estimates clearly mean that our catalogue of species, summarized in Table 1, is inadequate. For while it summarizes the best available general knowledge of the status of plant and animal species, it gives only a partial picture. It lists only plants and vertebrate animals – and so omits the greater part of living diversity. The challenge is to find a method not only for calculating how many species there are on Earth, but for estimating how many occur in each main situation. We need then to refine the analysis to the point at which we can say how much will be lost if we remove so much of a particular type of habitat in a particular region (Table 3).

Table 3 Some estimates of the rate of species extinction

Estimated total loss	Loss per decade, %	Basis for estimate	Source
1 million between 1975 and 2000	4	Extrapolate exponential trend	Myers, 1979
15 to 20% of all species between 1980 and 2000	8 to 11	Species/area curve and forest loss projection	Lovejoy, 1980
2000 plant species per year in tropics and sub-tropics	8	Loss of half species in area deforested by 2015	Raven, 1987
25% of plant species between 1985 and 2015	9	As above	Raven, 1988a,b
At least 7% of all plant species	7	Loss of half the species in 10 'hot spots' covering 3.5% of forest area in next decade	Myers, 1988
0.2 to 0.3% of all species per year	2 to 3	Half of species in rain forest assumed endemic and lost on clearance	Wilson, 1988, 1989
2 to 8% of all species between 1990 and 2015	1 to 5	Species/area curve and forest loss at current rate or 50% greater	Reid, 1992

Source: various sources cited in Reid, 1992

If the losses of rain-forest are assessed together with the known dependence of many species on particular areas and forest components, it can also be calculated that between 0.2 and 0.3 per cent of all rain-forest species may be exterminated each year. Depending on the actual total inferred (or guessed), this could mean losses of between 2000 and 30,000 species a year. Back-calculation, using the same kind of methods, clearly implies that the historic record of extinction must be only a fraction of the losses that have actually occurred. Looking forward, Walt Reid of the World Resources Institute has estimated what the situation might be if the rates of tropical forest loss were cut to 5 million hectares a year, held at 10 million ha, or allowed to run at the high figure of the 1980s (around 15 million ha/year). The results are shown in Table 4 (Reid, 1992).

Table 4 Projected percentage extinction of tropical closed forest species

Period	Region	Low scenario (5 million hectares/year)	Mid scenario (10 million hectares/year)	High scenario (15 million hectares/year)
1990 to 2015	Africa	1 to 3	3 to 6	4 to 9
	Asia	2 to 5	5 to 11	8 to 18
	Latin America	2 to 4	4 to 8	6 to 13
	All tropics	2 to 4	4 to 8	6 to 14
1990 to 2040	Africa	3 to 6	6 to 13	10 to 21
	Asia	5 to 11	12 to 26	28 to 53
	Latin America	3 to 8	8 to 18	15 to 32
	All tropics	4 to 8	9 to 19	17 to 35

Source: Reid, 1992

The implication is that if present rates of closed tropical forest loss continue we would commit between 4 per cent and 8 per cent of the species associated with the world's richest vegetation type to extinction over the next 25 years. Under a high-loss scenario the figure would rise to 6–14 per cent of species. If such forests hold between 50 per cent and 90 per cent of all species on Earth, then we are talking of losing from 2 per cent to 13 per cent of the global total. With around 10 million species on Earth (a cautious estimate) the high figure would mean loss of 20 to 75 species a day or between 8000 and 28,000 species a year.

These extrapolations assume stable climate. But as noted in Chapter 1, there are real reasons for worrying about the impact of human action – and especially the continuing increase in 'greenhouse gas' concentrations in the atmosphere – on climate. Consequent movement of the zones of tolerance for particular species would obviously also affect the distribution of vegetation types and their associated fauna. The fact that the projected rates of change are many times more rapid than the world's flora and fauna has had to respond to in recent millennia, and more rapid than most species seem likely to be able to adjust to by dispersion, complicates the position and makes it look especially grave. We are seeing the rapid destruction of wild habitats in many regions, and in some countries (such as Costa Rica) tropical forests are now almost restricted to national parks and nature reserves. But how far will these areas remain able to support the biological diversity for which they were created? One analysis of 2618 nature reserves in areas that may be affected by large shifts in ecoclimatic zones suggests that around 33 per cent will be likely to change from one climatic zone to another (WCMC, 1992). While the models are still inadequate, such changes clearly pose a further significant threat to the conservation of biological diversity.

Concern about the loss of biological diversity has three particular driving elements. First, there is a fear that it will reduce the capacity of the world's interlinked ecological systems to respond to stress. Evolution progresses by the continuing mingling of genetic material between the individuals in the breeding population, and the production of new individuals that differ in minor genetic respects from their parents. This gives natural selection something to work on – and means that as climate or habitats change, a species is able to respond by producing individuals that continue to function competitively, or other species are able to fill the gap and maintain the integrity of ecological systems. Second, there is a fear that products of immense potential use to humanity will vanish before their value is recognized. Third, there is a deep-seated feeling that this impoverishment of the richness and beauty of nature is morally wrong. These arguments are discussed further in Chapter 7, but all have validity.

It was this concern that led IUCN, with the World Resources Institute and the United Nations Environment Programme, to publish the Global Biodiversity Strategy in 1992 (WRI/IUCN/UNEP, 1992). It was the product of a joint initiative which also involved 45 other governmental and independent partner organizations. It was guided by an international advisory group. The Strategy offered 85 concise proposals for action at local, national and global levels. And it demanded five key, catalytic actions:

- the adoption of a convention on biological diversity;
- the constitution of a global biodiversity forum, as a basis for informal discussion;
- the establishment of an early warning system to alert communities and governments to threats to biological diversity;
- the preparation of national and local strategies and action plans;
- the designation of an international biodiversity decade.

In the same period, from 1990 to 1992, an International Negotiating Conference developed and agreed the text of a Convention on Biological Diversity (Glowka et al, 1994). This was signed by over 160 states in June 1992 at the Earth Summit in Rio de Janeiro. The Global Biodiversity Forum has been established and held its first meeting at IUCN headquarters in Switzerland in October 1993 (IUCN, 1994d). Many biodiversity strategies and action plans are being prepared. There are discussions about the kind of early warning system that will be most useful. Only the idea of the decade has been dropped. The action that is now required is discussed in Chapter 7.

Action to re-think development

The Stockholm Conference of 1972 was a meeting of pathways. From the developed world, came proposals for 'earthwatch': the monitoring of the state of the world, so that nations would be informed about trends in pollution and environmental deterioration, and so have more chance of responding in time. From the South came demands for assistance in order to attack 'the pollution of poverty'. This divergent perspective first threatened to wreck the conference, and then became its chief strength. For the meeting broadened to discuss social needs in developing countries, and this led on to a recognition – developed in the following twenty years – that an integrated approach to the management of land resources and all human activities that affected the environment was essential. The key was a meeting convened by Secretary General Maurice Strong at Founex in Switzerland in 1971 (McCormick, 1989), at which the developing world stated its agenda, and the programme of the conference as a whole was modified.

The basic concept of 'development without destruction' emerged from this dialogue, and was implicit in statements from Stockholm. It is set out clearly by Barbara Ward and René Dubos in the background book they wrote for the conference, *Only One Earth: the Care and Maintenance of a Small Planet* (Ward and Dubos, 1972). They defined humanity's fundamental task as 'to devise patterns of collective behaviour compatible with the continued flowering of civilizations'. How this might be done was discussed in the World Conservation Strategy published by IUCN, UNEP and WWF in 1980. That strategy emphasized that the conservation of nature would be impossible unless it was pursued within a process of development that catered for human needs. But it also argued that such development would be impracticable unless it was conservation-based because of the dependence of all human societies on the natural world.

In the 1970s and early 1980s there was a lot of talk about the goals and practices of development. The word 'development' itself has a simple dictionary definition: 'gradual unfolding, fuller working out', which in turn implies that it is a process of realization of potential. The contribution of the 1980s, and especially of the World Commission on Environment and Development (the Brundtland Commission) was to emphasize that 'development' needed the prefix 'sustainable'. Their widely quoted definition, in their report, *Our Common Future* (WCED, 1987) was: 'development that meets the needs of the present without compromising the ability of future generations to meet their own needs'.

However, the Commission elaborated somewhat, adding:

'It contains within it two key concepts:
- the concept of needs, in particular the essential needs of the world's poor, to which over-riding priority should be given, and
- the idea of limitations imposed by the state of technology and social organization on the environment's ability to meet present and future needs.'

This is a fundamentally different vision from that of the World Conservation Strategy, for it implies that nature has the capacity to meet all human needs, if social and technological deficiencies are remedied. It implicitly rejects the 'limits to growth' philosophy then much in vogue following the publication with that name from the Club of Rome (Meadows et al, 1972). The assertion is that it will be (or should be) possible to abate 'the pollution of poverty' if the environment and its resources are properly managed.

Agenda 21, the action plan adopted at Earth Summit in Rio de Janeiro in June 1992 (Robinson, 1993), essentially followed the Brundtland philosophy. *Caring for the Earth*, the second World Conservation Strategy

(IUCN/UNEP/WWF, 1991), on the other hand, deliberately avoided the term 'sustainable development' because of the contradictions in its interpretation. It discussed some of the confusion in a brief paragraph which said:

> 'Sustainable development', 'sustainable growth' and 'sustainable use' have been used interchangeably as if their meanings were the same. They are not. 'Sustainable growth' is a contradiction in terms: nothing physical can grow indefinitely. 'Sustainable use' is applicable only to renewable resources: it means using them at rates within their capacity for renewal. 'Sustainable development' is used in this strategy to mean: improving the quality of human life while living within the carrying capacity of supporting ecosystems.

It is, in fact, very important to separate 'development' and 'growth', although they are closely interwoven. There are two kinds of model mixed up in these definitions, and they can be expressed in two kinds of graph (Figure 7). Economists mostly talk about growth which arises directly from human creativity and lies within the 'box' of the social order. 'Box'? Yes, for the whole conceptual problem arises from the simple fact that the economic sub-system has grown within the global, natural, ecosystem (Figure 8).

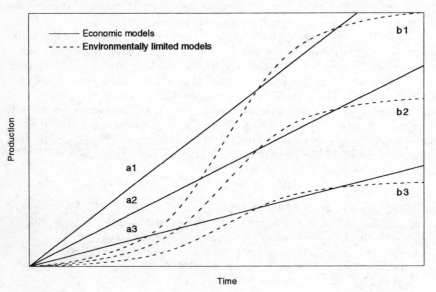

Economic models can generate linear increases without limits, but growth in the production of environmental resources has limits, although these may be increased by technology. Production of environmental systems is also prone to fluctuate due to climatic and other factors.

Figure 7 Economic and environmental growth curves.

The economic sub-system is about the use of resources and energy to produce goods and sustain a growing human population (the growth of which has been made possible by medicine, food security and other components of that sub-system). Growth within the socio-economic sub-system *can* be effectively limitless, because environmental constraints have largely been excluded from it. As human numbers, education, skills and knowledge mount, so indeed does the potential for collective human creativity increase. As Julian Simon has put it (Myers and Simon, 1994) 'the most important benefit of population size and growth is the increase it brings to the stock of useful knowledge. Minds matter economically as much as, or more than, hands or mouths.' In the socio-economic sub-system, the debate over 'sustainability' is therefore mostly about the slope of the curve: the achievement of the fastest rate of growth that will not create economic distortions or overheating.

Ecologists' growth curves, on the other hand, include environmental potential and environmental constraints. They span both the social order and the environmental context, and are S-shaped, reaching some kind of level. Ecologists do accept the inevitability of limits to growth, inherent in the concept of 'carrying capacity'. The debate is over the attainable level: how far technology and good management can enhance efficiency and raise productivity, and what kinds of safety margin are needed, especially to avoid exceeding the resilience of environmental systems at times of stress caused by seasonal and other fluctuations. Many environmental writers would endorse Norman Myers' counter to Julian Simon: 'there is much evidence that human numbers, with their consumption of resources, plus the techniques deployed to supply that consumption, are often exceeding carrying capacity already' (Myers and Simon, 1994).

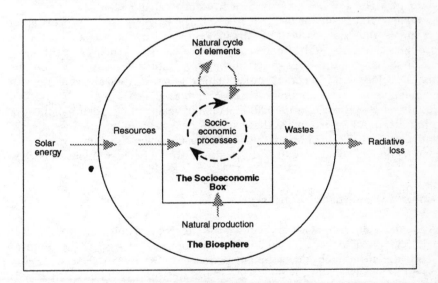

Figure 8 The place of the economic system within the natural world. The relative proportions are crucial.

'With respect' (as civil servants say when they disagree with someone), it seems fairly obvious that the two propositions talk past one another. Yes, of course our aim must be to allow everybody to realize their creative skills, and this is indeed the foundation of social growth. But there are limits. The central issue is how to realize the potential of social and natural resources in the best way. What limits must be respected? What kinds of mosaic of land use and nature conservation are needed to secure the best future for people and for the living systems that sustain us all?

The products of development are social and environmental. In the former category, they must, especially, be people who are healthy, well-nourished, clothed and housed; engaged in productive work for which they are well-trained; and able to enjoy the leisure and recreation we all need. In the second category, they include environmental systems that retain functional integrity – that is, they retain all their essential parts, and work effectively; are biologically productive; are diverse; and exhibit resilience in the face of the changes inevitable in any environment.

One side-debate of the past two decades has been over the indices of success we use. Often these include gross national product (GNP) or gross domestic product (GDP). Many environmental analysts have criticized these measures as misleading, perhaps especially because they appear perversely to add together on the positive side both activities that generate pollution and action to clean it up. But economists have never pretended that these measures equate to the total sum of socially beneficial activity – and it is conceded that they are imperfect instruments. As Wilfred Beckerman has pointed out 'a rise in leisure would reduce GNP but would increase welfare' (Beckerman, 1995). The issue is whether we should seek a new kind of development indicator – a 'beneficial growth indicator' – that really provides a yardstick of progress towards sustainable living.

Clearly, development includes not only the extraction and processing of resources, the establishment of infrastructure and the buying and selling of products, but also, and of equal importance, activities such as health care, social security, education, good husbandry, nature conservation and the arts. Development is a complex of activities, some with social and some with economic objectives. Some are based on material and some on intellectual resources. But the aim is to enable people to realize their potential and live a full life, in an environment that itself remains healthy, productive, diverse and beautiful. The traditional goal of education was 'a healthy mind in a healthy body'. Today we can add the phrase 'and a healthy environment'.

Action for sustainable living

Predictions about how history will see the present are notoriously risky. But it is very possible that the mid-1990s will come to be seen as the point at which the sustainable development process moved from debate to action. We have had our fill of conferences, plans and reports. The issue today is how to turn strategy into action – and to do so in a fashion that caters for the needs of nature, and of humanity within nature, in an equitable way.

As the world leaders recognized in Rio de Janeiro, the world's economy depends on the Earth's ecology. Nature remains vast, but is not infinite – and we live on a very small planet, dominated by our species which can no longer take nature for granted. 'Sustainable development' is about increasing the Earth's support to human needs, by working within the limits of nature. How?

This book is particularly concerned with the second world conservation strategy, *Caring for the Earth: A Strategy for Sustainable Living* (IUCN/UNEP/WWF, 1991). It has two distinctive features, when compared with its predecessors. First, it is a ground-up rather than top-down document. Second, it sets out 132 specific actions. Today, many other action-oriented documents are appearing (this book is one of them). What are the common messages of such statements?

First, it is, I think, generally agreed that action for sustainable living has to pervade the whole of society. Environmental policies are not just, or even mainly, a matter of establishing and maintaining nature reserves as islands of wild habitat in a sea of ploughland and concrete. They are a central area of social policy – to care for the planet and its ecological systems as the foundation of the future for humanity and for all other species. They are about bringing agriculture, forestry, fisheries, industry, economics, health care, settlement design, education, information and all other sectoral activities to a common focus, guided by a common logic. The United Nations Commission on Sustainable Development – the main intergovernmental forum established by the Earth Summit at Rio – has recognized this by endorsing proposals put forward in the name of the UN Secretary General for integrated resource management (UN, 1995a).

Second, we have moved away from over-doctrinaire grand plans. Environmental strategies have to be adaptive, for knowledge is and will remain incomplete and we must be able to change course as we go along. They must enable and support local actions, for the planet is diverse and the strategies and actions needed in the polar zones must differ radically from those of the mountains, coastlands, forest zones or deserts (as indigenous people know well). They must balance local, national and supranational concerns.

The aim has to be to cater for everyone's needs within the limits of the Earth – and to enhance that provision so that the further 5 billion that may be added to Earth's peoples before human numbers stabilize can enjoy a better life than many millions of poor people do today. That can only be done by building more efficient systems of mutual support – including a market that operates equitably, avoiding the barriers of perverse subsidy and tariff exclusions, and facilitating investment that will in turn allow communities to grow in wealth, knowledge and competence.

The need is recognized, and some ways forward exist. Some new alliances are emerging. The economist and the ecologist are in dialogue, seeking an economic theory that is ecologically sustainable (and that is the way the relationship has to be viewed). I myself regard the recent spate of volumes critical of the environmental movement as helpful rather than sacrilegious, for science advances by having its hypotheses tested, and there are enough hypotheses needing testing in the environmental sphere! The United Nations Conference on the Human Environment, held in Rio de Janeiro in June 1992, brought more heads of state and government together than ever before, to debate the fundamental relationship between humanity and the Earth. While much rhetoric has blown away on the wind, the principles set out in the document they endorsed – Agenda 21 – remain valid. Only by a cross-sectoral approach, involving all components of the community and all sectors of the economy shall we succeed.

This need is recognized, at least in part, in Agenda 21 itself (Robinson, 1993). Its 40 sections are arranged very much in a social context. It begins with 'Social and Economic Dimensions':

- international cooperation to accelerate sustainable development in developing countries;
- combating poverty;
- changing consumption patterns;
- demographic dynamics and sustainability;
- protecting and promoting human health;
- promoting sustainable human settlement development;
- integrating environment and development in decision-making.

The second section, on 'conservation and management of resources for development' is more sectoral, with chapters on protection of the atmosphere, oceans and freshwaters, managing fragile ecosystems, conserving biological diversity, combating deforestation, managing toxic chemicals, sewage, and solid, radioactive and other hazardous wastes and promoting sustainable agriculture and rural development. In this section there is also a chapter on the need for an integrated approach to the planning and management of land resources. And the social theme reappears in the third section, on 'strengthening the role of major groups':

- global action for women;
- children and youth in sustainable development;
- recognizing and strengthening the role of indigenous people and their communities;
- strengthening the role of non-governmental organizations;
- local authorities' initiatives;
- strengthening the role of workers and their trade unions;
- strengthening the role of business and industry;
- involving the scientific and technological community;
- strengthening the role of farmers.

And, finally, Agenda 21 gets down to a consideration of the means for action, reviewing financial resources and mechanisms; the transfer of environmentally sound technology; science for sustainable development; promoting education, public awareness and training; national mechanisms and international cooperation; international institutional arrangements; international legal instruments and mechanisms and information for decision-making.

Action within communities

These areas of action, and the emergence of new ideas about people's relations with nature, address the big scene: the blighted landscapes, the polluted and stinking rivers, the holes we are tearing in the web of life. They address industry, or government. Such action has its roots in the very origins of ecology, for Haeckel created political theory as well as ecological science (Bramwell, 1989). But the big picture, like a half-tone block, is made up of innumerable little dots, which are individual actions, and another major feature of the past decade has been the increasing emphasis on the individual and the local community, as the unit of action.

Most people try to win as comfortable a lifestyle as possible and this has meant choices about where and how to live. The very poor have been constrained by their lack of power to live their dreams, even at the most basic level, but in richer countries the public demand for cleaner air and water, access to green space, and some form of development control especially applied to industry are manifestations of collective decisions based on personal commitment. As concern for the environment has grown, so the need to influence people's individual behaviour has become more pressing. The active environmental campaigners have always relied on their power to mobilize a much wider spectrum of society, and to press the political system because so many voters flock to the banner.

Most people's decisions about their lifestyles, and their use of the environment and its resources, are made almost automatically, in response to experience, to the social and cultural traditions of the group they belong to, to their educational background (and the continuing process of informal education which is co-terminous with life), to the momentum of present circumstances, and to the influence of a small group of other people who may range from immediate family and colleagues (or bosses) at work to those who write advertising copy and media columns. Often there is no sense of deciding: people just do what seems inescapable.

As people get older, so the relative importance of the different influences changes. Education, experience and information through the media may erode the early, formative influence of parents, culture and tradition. Sometimes deliberate attempts are made by political leaders, or by those who rule over economically dominant sectors of society, to draw people away from their traditional beliefs. The problem is that these dominant processes, setting out to mould people's views and guide their decisions, rarely have anything to do with sustainable lifestyles. They are more likely to seek to inculcate politically and socially conformist behaviour, or the purchase of consumer goods. The environmental movement of the 1960s and 1970s was seen as at best cranky, but harmless, and at worst as downright subversive, by many in the mainstream of industry and politics. There were reasons for such attitudes, for the environmental non-governmental movement in central and eastern Europe was indeed one of the breeding-grounds for the new thinking that ultimately swept the old social order away.

The problem with that environmental movement was that it did not lead to a balanced or integrated decision process. Indeed, some of the demands for conservation action were counter-productive in that they had little sense of relative priority or value for money, in a world where there is never enough human or financial resource to do everything. Some campaigns were, frankly, damaging to the interests of indigenous peoples (like Inuit, unable to market sealskins taken from a stock that could certainly be managed sustainably). Some pressed for extreme margins of security against relatively minor risks (with all respect, and, yes, appreciating the gravity of the disaster at Chernobyl, some of the standards demanded for disposal of low-level radioactive waste appear to me to be in that category).

All this has been summed up well in the United Nations Environment Programme's review, *The World Environment, 1972–1992*, (Tolba et al, 1992). That study suggests that during the 1980s there were three major strands in the evolution of public awareness and attitudes in developed countries.

The first was alarm over widely publicized tragedies and threats, which had a direct impact on public attitudes, particularly to the acceptability of nuclear power. The second element was the increasing recognition that development is essential, and that conservation and development have to be part of the same process. The third strand was the recognition that concern for the environment was not some peripheral green fancy or additional sectoral element among the many preoccupations of governments, but a demand that the real wealth of nations be cherished. In this third area, the convergence of environmental science and economics had its beginning.

Public concern was stirred by the media (and waxed and waned as environmental incidents caught the headlines). Opposition to nuclear power, for example, leaped after the Chernobyl disaster (Figure 9). Public opinion polls revealed that environmental issues had been lifted to the top of the 'agitation agenda'. In the 1980s they suggested that people were especially worried about air and water pollution and waste disposal, followed by species extinction and natural resource depletion. But this was not a passive worry: they were angry about the perceived inadequacy of action to protect the environment by the relevant authorities.

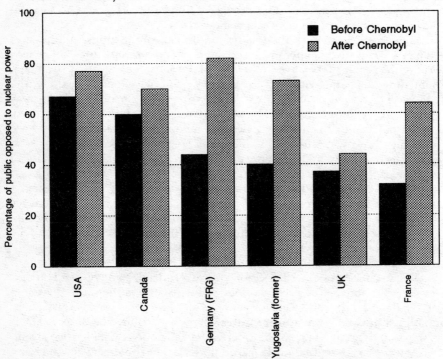

Public opposition to nuclear power rose dramatically after the Chernobyl accident. Black bars represent the percentage opposed before the incident, and stippled bars after.
Source: redrawn from Tolba et al, 1989

Figure 9 Public attitudes to nuclear power

At that time many polls suggested that people favoured increased government regulation and spending to control environmental degradation, even if it meant higher taxes or prices (the richer the country, the more this feeling prevailed). And the sense of frustration with what was perceived to be the slow response by those taking decisions on behalf of the community as a whole led to a credibility gap between populace and government. In both Europe and North America the government (and the scientists and officials working for it) were not trusted to tell the truth about nuclear power whereas environmental groups and TV programmes inspired more trust, and people living near to nuclear installations inspired most of all.

This whole area is one in which (to follow Eliot's lines quoted in the Introduction) a shadow is evident between concept and reality: between recognition of a problem and action to resolve it. While governments had, by 1992, adopted some good general principles to guide their collective action, such as the polluter pays principle, agreed in the Organization for Economic Co-operation and Development in the mid-1970s and the precautionary principle, endorsed at the end of the 1980s, these and the mass of international conferences and agreements were widely regarded as too little, too late. In fact, a dichotomy is evident. Most of the publicized decisions were by central authorities (governments, or their agencies responsible for environmental protection). Many of these were tempered by the perceived need to protect economic activity, and especially employment in industry. Sectoral departments in government tended to champion their areas of interest against environmental concerns that were the primary responsibility of a department of the environment, perceived as a rival sector. Environmental protection was often seen as a cost imposed on the wealth-creating sector of the community. Departments of commerce and industry – supported by finance ministries – fought to minimize such costs while departments of the environment championed tighter controls.

The dichotomy is, of course, false, and its incorporation in the structure of government almost guarantees inefficiency. Environmental resources are part of the wealth of a country – its 'natural capital' (Pearce et al, 1989), and they are the foundation of agriculture, forestry, fishery, tourism and many other industries. A healthy environment is also wealth-creating because it avoids loss and misery through ill-health. No sane community doubts the need to safeguard these things. Setting up a protectionist environment ministry as a counterweight to 'productionist' ministries distorts the picture. It perpetuates the illusion (which may, possibly, have been fostered by the fact that in many countries environmental concerns grew out of nature conservation and landscape protection) that the environment is a kind of green fringe on the real, serious business of nations. It would be better to make environmental audits as universal as financial ones, and for all sectors of the community – from individuals to nations – to apply them side by side.

Public concern – and demand – have had an impact. Industry has learned the need to present itself as environmentally aware (and some firms have genuinely become so). The pressure to meet new environmental standards led many firms to apply their technical inventiveness to the development of new processes which were less polluting – and in this process many found that 'pollution prevention pays' in terms of savings in energy and raw materials and the marketing of by-products that used to be discharged as wastes (Royston, 1979). But at the same time there was understandable reluctance to incur costs that eroded competitiveness. Hence the demands for the 'level playing field' or equality of the control burden.

Some companies were big enough to create this for themselves (it is often forgotten that the world's top 20 multinational corporations have annual financial turnovers greater than that of the world's 70 poorest nations). They tended to adopt uniform standards for environmental protection, in whatever country they operated, and through collective dialogue like that in the two World Industry Conferences on Environmental Management (WICEM) (Sallada and Doyle, 1986; Willums, 1991) and in the Business Council for Sustainable Development, pursued the cause of 'eco-efficiency', realizing that it was a necessity for the future and moved with the tide of social demand (Schmidheiny, 1992). The International Chamber of Commerce produced a 16-point Business Charter for Sustainable Development (Willums and Golucke, 1992).

However, despite these initiatives it remains true that, by and large, the dominant engine of economic change in today's world – business, industry and commerce – was largely responsive rather than pro-active during the recent decades of environmental activity, and hence was not centrally involved in deciding the action communities should take. This is quite a different thing from recognizing the need to be environmentally responsible (or at least to 'speak green' when necessary), or to hold conferences like the two WICEMS. Moreover these latter initiatives started outside industry – in the Paris Industry and Environment office of UNEP. Similarly, the Business Council for Sustainable Development was the brain-child of Maurice Strong, Secretary General of the Rio Conference, who hand-picked an outstanding leader, Stephan Schmidheiny, and then worked with him to recruit 50 key chief executives. While many firms have moved in the right direction, many more have continued to look on the environment as a constraint, to be met where action is unavoidable. Many companies still externalize environmental costs – still dump pollutants in the environment – when they think they can get away with it. The need for social and environmental sustainability has been accepted by a widening circle of leaders of industry, but the world of business, industry and commerce has yet to take on the role of leadership that it could and should have in shaping national and international action for sustainable living.

Another problem arises because people treat action as the responsibility of someone else (usually central or local government or industry itself), and when it appears inadequate, take refuge in indignation. What they do not do (at least not generally) is recognize that in the end it is their own choices and actions as individuals that decide the outcome. The 'polluter pays' principle is often endorsed naively, in the expectation that wicked industry will be made to pay for the remission of its sins, without any costs falling on the purchasers of its products. When this fails – as when domestic water consumers in the United Kingdom found their bills escalating because the utilities supplying them had to modernize their sewage treatment plant to clean up coastal seas and beaches – some sectors of the community and the media start questioning whether environmental health is so important after all.

The opinion polls demonstrate the gap between the recognition of the need for action and individual willingness to pay for it. In 1990 a survey for *Time International* in the United States found that while 94 per cent of people agreed that protecting the environment was very important, and 63 per cent supported stronger laws and regulations, when it came to money only 48 per cent were willing to 'go full speed ahead' with expenditure on environmental protection while 47 per cent 'believed that given other national problems, it would be better to go slow'. Nearly two-thirds of those surveyed admitted that they were not themselves doing enough to protect the environment. And 80 per cent agreed that 'there are so many contradictory things being said about the environment that it is sometimes confusing to know what to do' (Tolba et al, 1992).

There are signs that this questioning mood has been getting stronger. In the United States, there has been a 'green recession'. It is often forgotten that in the 1960s and 1970s the USA pioneered many environmental advances. It announced stringent standards on motor vehicle emissions, with some years lead time, amid howls of protest and prophecies of bankruptcy from manufacturers who pronounced the standards unattainable – and met them well on time. It set tight standards for water and wastes, allowed major developments to be held up so as not to imperil lowly creatures like the snail darter (a small fish), and shook the insurance world to its foundations by allowing massive damages to victims of environmental contamination. Now, following the 1994 congressional elections in particular, a more critical mood is evident. The economic cost of action to safeguard people and the environment is again under scrutiny. The scientific case for that action is being demanded – and challenged. Anti-green books are appearing, some with inflammatory titles.

In my view, such debate is healthy if it is indeed honest debate rather than an attempt to achieve undercover objectives. It is may well be true that the environmental case has sometimes been over-stated. Sometimes people have been told about disasters they simply do not perceive when they look at the world for themselves. But there is a baby in the bath water, and it needs cherishing. The need is to inform people better, and involve them as individuals and small groups more effectively in the decision process. Not only will this most rapidly advance sustainable living, but it will provide a positive feed-back loop into the processes of decision by government, and make the actions of states more determined. Chapter 9 picks up these key issues.

Action plans for nations: strategies for sustainability

Agenda 21 and *Caring for the Earth* both also call for *strategies* for sustainability to be developed, especially at national level. These are not new: IUCN alone has advised governments on the production of around 50 national conservation strategies, many of which have a strong developmental flavour, over the past twenty years. It has recently produced a handbook for their planning and implementation (Carew Reid et al, 1994). The World Bank has promoted national environment action plans in at least as many states and has moved recently to make these a condition for some of its loans (World Bank, 1991). Regional networks of people with experience in such endeavours have been set up in South and East Asia, East and Southern Africa and Latin America, and they have exchanged experience gathered in more than 40 case studies. All sorts of problems have emerged, and one major objective of a workshop at the Buenos Aires session of the IUCN General Assembly in 1994 was to examine what had worked, and what had not.

What *are* 'strategies for sustainability'? They have been defined (in rather heavy officialese) as 'participatory and cyclical processes of planning and action to balance and integrate economic, ecological and social objectives'. They can be international, national, provincial or local. They can focus on particular kinds of situation (such as protected areas). Often within one region all types are evident.

The aim of sustainable development strategies has been clearly stated by Walter Arensberg of the World Resources Institute (Arensberg, 1994):

> to bring about a permanent shift in the way things are done. Strategies should deliberately seek to strengthen the capacity of a country's institutions to develop and implement policies, plans (and strategies) for sustainable development on a consensus basis. This will require flexible and timely action to facilitate an institution's ability to understand issues, express its interests, negotiate and reconcile conflicts, and forge consensus around common courses of action.

Such strategies are expressions of social decisions about how to achieve sustainability. They involve balancing social, environmental and economic objectives; balancing present and future needs; allowing for uncertainties (because nature has a great gift of the unexpected) and acknowledging and building on local differences, so that the result is optimal use of natural resources everywhere.

A great diversity of strategies has been undertaken in different regions. In Latin America (Imbach, 1994), they are proposed or being developed in Costa Rica, Nicaragua, Cuba and Peru; regional strategies have considered various development zones like that of Peten in Guatemala and Sierra Maestra in Cuba; others have addressed regional conservation and sustainable development, like those for Bocas del Toro in Panama or San Martin in Peru; while yet others have considered protected areas and their surroundings (Tortuguero in Costa Rica or Beni in Bolivia), hydroelectric schemes (Maje, Panama) or areas where the interests of rural and indigenous peoples are paramount (Kuna Yala, Panama and Santa Marta, Colombia).

In Asia (Chitrekar, 1994), Nepal began its National Conservation Strategy as early as 1982, while Bangladesh, Bhutan, China, India, Indonesia, Laos, Malaysia, Myanmar, Pakistan, the Philippines, Sri Lanka, Thailand and Vietnam have all undertaken such an exercise during the past decade. There has been a flurry of national reports, national environmental action plans, national strategies for sustainable development and other documents. Sub-national and village-level strategies have also begun in some regions (in Nepal, the Annapurna Conservation Area Project, and IUCN's work on village-level strategies are good examples). The issue is whether these have proved worthwhile when it comes to advancing action on the ground.

The region of Oceania is distinct, for it is a vast tract of sea, dotted with small islands (Boer, 1994). The most important part of Agenda 21 for this great region is Chapter 17, on the Protection of the Seas and Oceans. This chapter notes the particular problems of sustainable development in small islands because:

They are ecologically fragile and vulnerable. Their small size, limited resources, geographical dispersion and isolation from markets place them at a disadvantage economically and prevent economies of scale. For small island developing states the ocean and coastal environment is of strategic importance and constitutes a valuable development resource.

National Environmental Management Strategies (NEMS) or their equivalent have been prepared, or are being prepared, for twelve Pacific Island developing countries, including Cook Islands, Micronesia, Tonga, the Marshall Islands and the Solomon Islands. The emphasis has been on practicality (recommendations to address top priority environmental issues), ownership (making the strategy 'belong' to government and people), catalysis (using the strategy to stimulate awareness and action), sustainable development and partnership. The stress is heavily on integration of environmental concerns in economic development, improving environmental awareness and education, safeguarding natural resources, and improving waste management and pollution control. Implementation is being emphasized – so that (to quote the Strategy for the Federated States of Micronesia) the NEMS do not share 'the fate of many other planning documents gathering dust on some forgotten shelf'. Legal reviews form an important part of the overall exercise.

The situation in developed countries can be illustrated by reference to Canada, Norway, the Netherlands, France and the United Kingdom (Hill, 1994). Initiatives in these five states span the period from 1989 to 1994. They have four features in common – participation, integration, linkages, and monitoring and evaluation. There are cross-government committees or steering groups in most cases. Canada has pioneered the 'round table' approach both nationally and in the provinces. In Norway, there is a Committee for Sustainable Development chaired by the Prime Minister and the Environment Minister and attended by ministers in charge of the departments with the potential to have major impacts on the environment, together with heads of major businesses and trade unions, the country's largest conservation NGO, and the Association of Local Councils. Comparable machinery is being developed in the UK. These cross-sectoral committees provide a main means for linkage in the countries concerned. Monitoring and evaluation is provided for by the publication of regular reports: the UK, for example, publishes an annual digest of environmental statistics and has also reported annually since 1991 on the implementation of the national environment report. It is establishing machinery for monitoring the implementation of its strategy for sustainability (a kind of national Agenda 21), produced in 1992, and the first report appeared early in 1995 (Tickell, 1995).

In Australia (Cotter and Boer, 1994) a whole series of local conservation strategies, state conservation strategies and a national conservation strategy have been produced, and there is now a Local Agenda 21 programme. In the latter, emphasis has been placed on involving all sectors of the community in partnerships, enhanced communication and public awareness, better reporting, and an understanding of how Australia interacts with the global community. A national strategy for sustainable development has been produced, based on the inputs of nine working groups. The details of this strategy are interesting: it has a goal, three core objectives, and seven guiding principles (see box).

**Goals, objectives and guilding principles of the Australian
National Strategy for Sustainable Development**

Goal	Development that improves the total quality of life both now and in the future, in a way that maintains the ecological processes on which life depends.
Objectives	To enhance individual and community well-being and welfare by following a path of economic development that safeguards future generations.
	To provide for equity within and between generations
Guiding principles	Decision-making processes should effectively integrate both long and short-term economic, environmental, social and equity considerations.
	Where there are threats of serious or irreversible damage, lack of scientific certainty should not be used as a reason for postponing measures to prevent environmental degradation.
	The global environmental impacts of actions and policies should be recognized and considered.
	Cost-effective and flexible policy instruments should be adopted, such as improved valuation, pricing and incentive mechanisms.

Source: Data from Cotter and Boer (1994)

Trends and inertia: the conveyor belt to an unsustainable future

The one thing we know about the future is that it will not be the same as the past. The second thing we can be fairly certain about is that it will not conform to our predictions. Prophecies in the secular world have the habit of coming unstuck. As noted in Chapter 1, the 'limits to growth' predicted in many press articles following the Club of Rome volume of that name which appeared in 1972 (Meadows et al, 1972) envisaged that pollution and resource scarcities would interfere substantially with human population growth and be likely to bring about a collapse within 150 years: today, pollution does not seem likely to have the direct effect some projected. Others have speculated that the AIDS epidemic would devastate human populations: re-evaluations suggest that while it will indeed kill millions of people the effect will be to impede the pace and magnitude of the growth in human numbers, but not prevent it. Yet other extrapolations imply the disappearance of most of the accessible tropical forests – at least outside strictly protected national parks – by some date in the first half of the next century, and overall stability in forest cover at one seventh of the world's land area by around the year 2020: the real situation seems certain to be far less extreme. There are, indeed, some grounds for optimism (North, 1995).

Yet the world community is moving on the conveyor belt of time assuming that the past *is* a reasonable guide to the future. As Lester Milbraith (1989) has pointed out, 90 per cent of investment decisions assume continuity. Climate change, if it stressed the socio-economic system beyond its limits of resilience, could cause collapse, the disappearance of people's savings (mostly held in computers rather than vaults filled with gold), and social disintegration on a vast scale. While the simple extrapolation of trends is not a helpful exercise, it is also unwise to assume that (for example) just because oil and mineral prospectors have so far found new reserves as fast as current ones are depleted, this will always be the case. We need a hard-headed look at the probabilities of change. But it is clear that if present trends were to continue, land degradation would become a devastating problem in some of the countries that will have most new mouths to feed, deforestation would take away much of the world's living diversity, and climate change could threaten agriculture and coastal communities in many regions. If these trends are not to lead towards disaster, the causative mechanisms will need to be addressed, and these lie within human societies: they are about how we value our natural resources, and how we decide on their use.

People tend to be traditionalists, clinging to the systems and processes of the past because they are used to them and 'know they work'. But many people argue that those systems – called by Milbraith the 'dominant social paradigm', or by others 'business as usual' will not work well enough. Today's reliance on market systems is a recognition that these can indeed adjust fast and efficiently when it comes to sharing out resources and meeting short-term needs. But markets are limited. They cannot readily plan for the future or be relied on to deliver 'social goods'. They cannot correct injustices, and they are dedicated to maximizing wealth rather than quality of life. They commonly under-value nature and natural resources, which in turn leads them to neglect or turn an indulgent eye to pollution, over-exploitation and unbridled consumption of non-renewable resources. They are not designed to care for the weak: today's society is indeed designed to allow people to rise in power and dominance through competitive interaction.

To deliver long-term sustainability, markets and wealth-creating businesses will need to be guided, and at times constrained, as will the individual pursuit of power (Cairncross, 1995). The substitution of another system, however, will only be feasible if people demand it, and if it builds progressively from the strengths of today so that for the majority at least, there is a 'win–win' gain at every step of the way. We have to pursue adaptive policies that start where we are now, and use (and adjust) the machinery of current society (Holdgate, 1995b).

Caring for the Earth set out 132 actions that would, if taken in the right place and on the right scale, move the world towards sustainable development. *Agenda 21* amplified many of these and added more. As a step towards evaluating what works, and what does not, and the reason why, it is useful to review these actions and develop a kind of checklist of failure and success. That is the subject of the next chapter.

A QUICK CHECK
ON ACTION

Compiling a balance sheet of sustainability

There are many reports on the state of the environment. Some are very good – like the *World Resources Reports* published every second year by the World Resources Institute (WRI, 1986; 1987; 1990; 1992), and the two major volumes on the world environment by the United Nations Environment Programme, covering the first decade after the Stockholm Conference of 1972 and then the twenty years between Stockholm and the Earth Summit in Rio de Janeiro (Holdgate et al, 1982; Tolba et al, 1992). Other reports, such as the Earthwatch Institute's *State of the World Reports* (Brown et al, 1984–1994) focus on problem areas, while yet others (such as those from OECD) (1985; 1991) deal with a group of countries. There is also a mass of national reports and digests of statistics.

Yet selective reporting is almost universal in the environmental literature. It is inevitable, because the information is uneven and there is no consensus on what indicators tell us most, what should be measured, what models should be used, or how the reports should be written. And although the world is awash with environmental data, good time-series – records of trends – are far more limited.

Many of our evaluations are therefore dictated by the availability of data. For example, there is good information about climate, stratospheric ozone, and concentrations of pollutant gases in the air. So statements about the condition of the atmosphere are possible. We have patchier data about acid rain and air quality near the ground, but enough to deduce that in Europe at least, acid sulphate deposition is now falling, although acid nitrates remain a problem. We can also infer that the situation in some industrial regions of the developing world, such as north-east China, is getting worse and will deteriorate further. Smoke from coal fires and sulphur oxides no longer causes problems in city air in Europe and North America, but pollution with oxidants, nitrogen oxides and hydrocarbons from traffic emissions remains a serious problem, and air quality is deteriorating in many third world cities (Tolba et al, 1992).

Similarly, there are some reasonably authoritative statements of trends in the oceans from GESAMP, the Group of Experts on Scientific Aspects of Marine Pollution (1990). There is also a good deal of information on river quality (albeit in only some rivers, mainly in developed countries), vegetation cover (thanks especially to satellite surveillance), the provision of services like clean water and sewerage, waste production and disposal and so forth. On the other hand, data on species distribution and on the extent to which sustainable development is happening on the ground are far more limited. And even where there is a reasonable amount of information there may be problems of interpretation.

This is familiar when we consider trends in world temperature. We have reasonable grounds for stating that there has been an overall warming of half a degree Celsius since the 1880s – although there has been a great deal of oscillation from year to year and decade to decade, and the trends in all the regions of the world are not in precise step. But what is the cause? There is no proof that the trend is due to the increasing concentration of greenhouse gases in the atmosphere, although the change is about what would be expected if this were the cause. It could be a manifestation of natural variability in climate, for it lies within the historic range of variation (Bolin et al, 1994). This in turn leads to argument that action to reduce greenhouse gas emissions should be delayed, because the uncertainty means that there is a risk of wasting investment.

What we really seek is a balance sheet of sustainability. Are we winning or losing? The environment is, in many areas, almost submerged by the human tide – but are there signs of hope that the situation is becoming less hazardous, as the need for sustainable living is recognized?

This chapter reviews the actions taken to implement policies, rather than the state of sectors of the physical environment. The actions are the 132 listed, under 17 headings, in *Caring for the Earth* (IUCN/UNEP/WWF, 1991). These have been chosen partly because this book has been written as an element in the follow-up to that strategy, but also because they are convenient units. Moreover, they cover much the same ground as *Agenda 21*, endorsed at the highest level by heads of state and government in Rio in 1992 (Robinson, 1993). It may be assumed, therefore, that there is broad political acceptance of the need for action on many at least of these fronts.

Building a sustainable society

Caring for the Earth included only one action under this heading - 'develop new strategies for sustainable living'.

By the end of 1991, 52 countries had prepared, or were preparing, national conservation strategies, 18 (many the same) had national environmental action plans, and 68 had national state of the environment reports. Table 5 sets out the position in the developing world, as it was in June 1992 (Tunstall and van der Wansem, 1992). More reports have appeared since then, especially as a consequence of the Earth Summit and the commitment to *Agenda 21*. That document calls on all governments to:

> seek internal consensus at all levels of society on policies and programmes needed for short- and long-term capacity-building to implement its Agenda 21 programme. . . .The national planning process, together, where appropriate, with national sustainable development action plans or strategies, should provide the framework for such cooperation and assistance.

Table 5 Numbers of various categories of National Environmental Reports published and in preparation at the end of 1992.

Continent	Type of report			
	National Environmental Action Plan	National Conservation Strategy	State of Environment Report	National Report to UNCED
Africa	7 published 11 in preparation	14 published 3 in preparation	8 published 2 in preparation	37 published 6 in preparation
Central America Caribbean and South America	12 in preparation	2 published 10 in preparation	5 published 4 in preparation	15 published 4 in preparation
Asia and Oceania	2 published 15 in preparation	9 published 11 in preparation	15 published 4 in preparation	31 published 5 in preparation

Source: Tunstall and van der Wansem, 1992

The UN Commission on Sustainable Development is charged with the task of considering 'information provided by governments, including, for example, material in the form of periodic communications or national reports regarding the activities they undertake to implement Agenda 21'. By March 1995, 16 developing countries, 15 developed countries, one country in transition and the European Union had submitted such information to the UN Secretariat (UN, 1995c). These and other reports were considered by the Commission at its meeting in May 1995. If the test is met by volumes of paper, progress has been considerable.

At sub-national level, in developed countries, there has also been a lot of activity. For example, two cities in the United States (Jacksonville in Florida and Pasadena in California) have used 72 and 112 indicators respectively to monitor quality of life. These include such areas as the environment, health, drugs, education, the economy, housing, arts and culture, recreation and open space, transportation and community safety. At state level, Minnesota and Oregon are among the states using indicators and setting numerical targets: the Minnesota programme includes 20 general descriptive goals and 79 indicators for which annual, quantitative, targets have been set, while in Oregon 272 indicators pertaining to people, quality of life and the economy have been defined and tracked (Corson, 1994). A systematic examination of the process of measuring and evaluating indicators has recently been provided by Hammond and others (1995).

The issue is whether this activity is sound in principle and effective when it comes to application. In particular, are these *new* strategies, and are they challenging enough? *Caring for the Earth* urged that all strategies should give effect to its basic principles – respect and care for the community of life, improvement in the quality of human life, conservation of the Earth's vitality and diversity, minimal depletion of non-renewable resources, keeping within the Earth's carrying capacity, changing personal attitudes and practices, enabling communities to care for their own environments, providing national frameworks for integrating development and conservation, and creating a global alliance. A recent IUCN *Handbook for the Planning and Implementation of Strategies for National Sustainable Development* (Carew Reid et al, 1994) makes the same basic point – it defines such strategies as 'processes of planning and action to improve and maintain the well-being of people and ecosystems'.

The new wave of strategies does, by and large, address this kind of agenda. It is true that *Agenda 21* jibs somewhat at the behest to 'minimize the depletion of non-renewable resources'. There was some complicated manoeuvring in Rio by the petroleum-exporting states who saw such calls, and those for a switch to energy efficiency and new and renewable energy sources, as a threat. There is also hesitation in *Agenda 21* over the precept 'keep within the Earth's carrying capacity', perhaps understandably because this is hard to define. But generally, governments do seem to be working towards implementing the first action precept in *Caring for the Earth*, and the question is no longer whether such strategies will be produced, but how effective they will be in detail and how readily they will be carried from words to deeds. This is the heart of the matter. For sustainability will not be achieved simply by government pronouncements. The new strategies will need to provide for adjustments in the working of societies and economies, and for that reason they must involve individuals, community groups, businesses and official institutions alike.

Respecting and caring for the community of life

Four actions were listed under this heading: the development of the world ethic for living sustainably; its promotion; its implementation in all sectors of society; and the establishment of a world organization to monitor that implementation and prevent or combat serious breaches in its observation.

'The world ethic for living sustainably.' It is becoming much more fashionable to talk about ethics today – which is good – and one of the most important things about *Caring for the Earth* is that it starts with an ethical principle. It is that we should accept a duty of care for other people and other forms of life, now and in the future:

> Development should not be at the expense of other groups or later generations. We should aim to share fairly the benefits and costs of resource use and environmental conservation among different communities and interest groups, among people who are poor and those who are affluent, and between our generation and those who will come after us.

The strategy calls on the world community to develop the ethic. This has gone rather slowly. Some commentators have singled out this area for criticism on grounds of lack of realism, and because they feel – rightly – that any attempt to dictate people's basic values would be wrong. That, however, was never the intention. It is clear that while common human values are emerging, anything in the form of a set of codified, universal ethical precepts – a new set of commandments carved on tablets of stone from a holy mountain – is out of the question.

Yet there is a convergence of values, and this is apparent in the Rio Declaration and *Agenda 21* even if neither speaks directly of ethics (Brown and Quiblier, 1994). The documents are people-centred, committed to equity and the involvement of all sectors of society in decisions about the development process, urge the abolition of poverty and enhancement of the quality of life, recognize the inter-dependence of environment and development and the need to care for the Earth's living diversity, urge full community participation in decisions and action and admit the need for an equitable international economic and trading system, with genuine alliance between nations. The underlying premises of the world ethic are therefore visible in the action plans and statements, even if ethics as such are not addressed.

One concern is that few leaders of religions, philosophers or poets have said much about these things. There have, of course, been some meetings between religious groups – like the interfaith ceremony organized by the World Wildlife Fund (as it then was) at Assisi in 1986, and the Conference on Christian Faith and Ecology held at Canterbury in 1987 (Gosling, 1990). Some religious groups have issued statements about their position on the agenda for Earth Summit or (notoriously) the World Population Conference, and attempted to adjust their liturgies to reflect new environmental insights (Gosling, 1992). *A Sourcebook for the Community of Religions* has been published, setting out the essential elements of the different faiths and their teachings about the human situation (Beversluis, 1993). But surely this is the wrong way round? It is not the business of the religions to make inputs to secular debates, but to take the high ground of vision and lead people in faith and commitment. This they have largely failed to do. The most prophetic utterances have come, instead, from 'deep ecologists' like Arne Naess (1973; 1986) or world statesmen like Shridath Ramphal (1992).

Intergovernmental statements do have an important part to play even though few can be called inspirational. The Stockholm and Rio Declarations and the World Charter for Nature certainly were important advances, providing moral leadership to the international community (Hassan, 1994). But they do not go far enough. One of the failures of Rio was its inability to agree on an Earth Charter that would catch the vision of the world community and state the commitment of all nations to one another, to future generations and to the planet. New attempts are being made by the Earth Council and the Green Cross to fill this gap. Meanwhile, the IUCN Ethics Working Group is continuing to examine ethical principles as a basis for global advance (Engel, 1994). IUCN is also considering how the ethic can be translated into action, partly through a Covenant on Conservation and Development (see Chapter 5). This would transform the 'soft' law of the charter and declarations into a legally-binding treaty. Great efforts have been made to ensure that it is 'an ethically sound document which should enhance the development of a world ethic relevant to the 1990s' (Hassan, 1994).

Another idea floated in *Caring for the Earth* was the creation of a world organization to monitor implementation of the ethic and deter breaches of it. This draws heavily on the idea of an 'environmental amnesty' analogous to Amnesty International, originally proposed by former IUCN President Dr Monkombu Swaminathan. But the action now seems likely to take a different shape. Through the initiative of the Secretary General of both the Stockholm and Rio Conferences, Maurice Strong, a new body, the Earth Council, has been established with headquarters in Costa Rica (Earth Council, 1994). Earth Council will provide an independent global non-governmental forum to examine environmental issues and respond to concerns raised anywhere in the world. Requests for authoritative evaluations and rulings are likely to be met through the commissioning of expert studies which will then be discussed in public hearings. Those who raise issues of concern could themselves provide a documentary base for such a hearing. In the light of the debate, the Council could rule on an issue, and publicize its judgements. This offers machinery which, at least in principle, would allow breaches of the ethic and of the general principles of sustainable living to be brought to the attention of national and global communities.

If it is true that what people do depends on what they believe, and that a gramme of inspiration is worth a kilogramme of argument, then the lack of progress at this deep level may prove limiting to the whole movement towards sustainability. The test will be how far nations and communities really apply the guiding philosophy – and especially the principles of equity, full participation, and reverence and care for the community of life – in action. The words are all there, in *Agenda 21* and elsewhere: the problem is that talking about ethics is intellectual, but living according to them demands commitment. The key is likely to be how far individual people feel gripped and inspired by the new vision, and this will mean bringing concepts down to the human level, and getting them across much more clearly, influencing the deepest levels of belief as well as pervading public information and education. We cannot be sure that the process of social learning (Milbraith, 1989) will go swiftly enough to outpace the slide to unsustainability.

Improving the quality of human life

Caring for the Earth has six recommendations under this heading. They are, quite frankly, a bit of a rag-bag. They call for increasing economic growth to advance human development in lower-income countries; adjusting national development policies and strategies to ensure sustainability in upper-income countries; providing services that will ensure a long and healthy life; providing universal primary education for all children, so reducing illiteracy; developing more meaningful indicators of quality of life and monitoring their implementation; and enhancing security against natural disasters.

Economic growth has been very uneven in recent years. Among countries with an average GNP per head of under US$1000 in 1989, real gross national product increased during the decade 1979–1989 by over 10 per cent per annum in Botswana, and between 5 and 10 per cent in Cape Verde, Congo, Egypt, China, India, Indonesia and Pakistan. But in most lower-income countries the growth was in the range between 1.5 and 3.5 per cent, and there were falls in Madagascar, Niger, Nigeria, Nicaragua, Bolivia and Guyana. In many countries economic growth dropped behind, or barely kept pace with, population growth (WRI, 1992). Many of the poorer countries are not attracting private-sector investment, and government-to-government aid is insufficient to bridge the gap.

In 1989, 41 countries were identified by the World Bank as having an annual GNP per head of less than $580, and 12 had per capita GNPs of under $250. Using the United Nations Development Programme's index of human development (which takes length of life and literacy into account as well as national income), 63 countries were placed in the 'low human development' category (UNDP, 1991). They were concentrated in sub-Saharan Africa, but included Haiti in the Caribbean and several states in Southeast Asia, including Indonesia, Vietnam and Papua New Guinea. Some countries did move up the ladder of development, with very rapid economic growth – Singapore, the Republic of Korea, Argentina, Costa Rica, Chile, Venezuela and Malaysia have already made the transition to fully developed status and China, Mexico, Thailand and many other states are climbing rapidly up the scale. Generally, however, it is clear that human development is not at present being helped by sufficient economic growth in many countries, and some of the growth that is occurring is not environmentally sustainable. And, in personal terms, income is very uneven. Twenty-three per cent of the world's people, in the developed countries, dispose of 85 per cent of its income. The number of poor people is increasing. Even in the rich countries, the discrepancies are great: in Australia, the USA and the UK the top 20 per cent of households have incomes 9.6, 8.9 and 6.8 times as great as the poorest 20 per cent (UNDP, 1991).

While most upper-income countries have maintained steady, if unspec-
tacular, economic growth they are only tinkering at the margins with the
transition to sustainable lifestyles. There are signs of hope: the rise of 'green
consumerism', the increasing environmental awareness among many industries, and the increasing commitment of governments to strategies for sustainability and biodiversity conservation among them, but the fact is that no
developed country has yet emerged through the 'sustainability transition' to
a high-income, high quality-of-life which consumes low amounts of energy
and resources and generates little waste or pollution. There is still a gap
between rhetoric and action, and a failure to enlist the wider community in
partnerships for change. Many of the essential ingredients for action are
becoming clear, and will be addressed in later chapters, but there is still a
long way to go.

Life expectancy remains badly skewed. The low-income countries, combined, have a life expectancy of 63 years (only 55 if China and India are
excluded), whereas the rich countries average 75 or more years. In some
poor African countries life expectancy at birth remains below 50 years and
the impact of the AIDS epidemic has reduced it in a number of states so
that in the four worst-affected countries, Malawi, Rwanda, Uganda and
Zambia, the projected figure for 1990–1995 is 44.2, 46.2, 41.8 and 44.1
years. Without AIDS the figure would be 49.0, 50.5, 50.0 and 55.1 respectively (World Population Report, 1992). In Rwanda, of course, the tragedy
of civil strife makes any forward projection impossible at present. In many
poor countries the 'services that will provide a long and healthy life' are
simply not in place, and under present circumstances there is little prospect
of their being brought up to an adequate level. Equally, worldwide, there
are signs of improvement. Life expectancy generally is improving (although
in some countries, including Russia, it is moving the other way). Many
countries are re-structuring their health services and making them more
efficient (particularly by switching to decentralized grassroots services, paying particular attention to preventable infectious diseases, and using lower-
cost generic drugs).

Education is slowly gaining ground. The proportion of national education budgets going to primary schools increased during the 1980s in 15 out
of 22 African countries surveyed, and there are also advances in South
America and parts of Asia. Literacy rates rose between 1970 and 1990
among males in all of the 82 countries for which rates are quoted in the
World Resources Report, 1992–1993 (WRI, 1992). Among females it rose in all
countries except Cambodia – where the 1 per cent decline is unlikely to be
statistically significant. Female literacy lags behind male, especially in the
poorer countries, and remains under 10 per cent in Burkina Faso and
under 20 per cent in Chad, The Gambia, Guinea, Niger, Sierra Leone,
Somalia, Sudan, Afghanistan and Nepal, but the fact that rates are rising
rapidly in many of these countries from a very low base is a sign of hope (in
Senegal, for example, the rise has been from 5 to 25 per cent in 20 years,
and in Niger from 2 to 17 per cent). The target of universal primary educa-

tion is now effectively met in most of South America, much of Central America and the Caribbean, and an increasing part of Asia.

Efforts are being made, by IUCN and others, to develop more meaningful indicators of sustainability (Trzyna and Osborn, forthcoming). This is also a goal of *Agenda 21* and while it has some way to go, the direction of effort is right and there is more monitoring by governments and more international reviews of the degree to which some of the indicators are being attained. As for security against natural disasters, clearly this can never be absolute: earthquakes can strike the richest as well as the poorest countries, as events in California in 1994 and Japan in 1995 have emphasized. And natural and social disasters often march hand in hand: drought spells hunger and migration, which can lead directly to the collapse of social support systems and to strife. As the first World Disaster Report, published in 1993 (IFRC, 1993) puts it 'the disasters of today involve economic dislocation, drought or floods, the collapse of political structures, violence ranging from banditry through civil conflict to all-out international war, famine and mass population displacements'. International efforts for support in such circumstances have, however, increased both through the United Nations, the established humanitarian non-governmental organizations (notably the Red Cross and the Red Crescent), and the new Green Cross organization that is being established.

The conclusion must be that the world is making slow but inadequate progress in this whole area of endeavour. The good news is that some of the best progress arises where initiatives for better health and education are being devolved to local communities. The bad news is that inequity, avoidable death, acute poverty and illiteracy still stalk the world and waste life and deprive us all of the contribution that hundreds of millions of fellow humans could make.

Conserving the Earth's vitality and diversity

Caring for the Earth, not surprisingly, placed great emphasis on this area of endeavour, proposing no fewer than 14 actions. The first group was concerned with pollution, and called for the adoption of a precautionary approach and the reduction of emissions of sulphur dioxide, nitrogen oxides, carbon monoxide, hydrocarbons and greenhouse gases (surprisingly, ozone-depleting substances were not specifically mentioned). The second group included adoption of an integrated approach to land and water management, maintaining as much as possible of each country's natural and modified ecosystems, taking the pressure off nature by protecting the best farmland and managing it in ecologically sound ways, and action to halt net deforestation. The third group focused specifically on the conservation of biological diversity, covering the establishment and maintenance of a comprehensive system of protected areas, improving plant and animal species conservation, improving knowledge of species and ecosystems, using *in situ* and *ex situ* conservation in combination to safeguard species and genetic resources, harvesting wild resources sustainably and supporting the management of such resources by local communities, increasing incentives to them to conserve biological diversity.

This has been a busy area, although action has to be described as uneven. The precautionary approach to pollution is endorsed in the Rio Declaration (Robinson, 1993) which states:

Nations shall use the precautionary approach to protect the environment. Where there are threats of serious or irreversible damage, scientific uncertainty shall not be used to postpone collective measures to prevent environmental degradation.

The precautionary approach is also written into the United Nations Framework Convention on Climate Change, and is implicit at many points in *Agenda 21*. Although there remains a wide gap in many countries between adopting the principle and implementing it, it can be concluded that the first action is therefore now at least in process in national and international policy.

In the developed world, emissions of sulphur dioxide have been reduced markedly over recent years: in the United States from 28.4 million metric tonnes in 1970 to 20.7 million tonnes in 1989, and in western Europe from 39.2 million tonnes in 1980 to 22.1 million tonnes in 1989. In the European part of the former USSR the decline was from 12.8 to 9.3 million tonnes in the same decade. Some countries have made particularly dramatic progress: the Netherlands and Norway have achieved 75 per cent and 73 per cent reductions in their emissions, while the former Federal Republic of Germany brought its discharges down from 3.2 million tonnes in 1980 to 1.5 million in 1989, and France from 3.5 to 1.5 million. The European Union is now adopting a target of 80 per cent reduction from the 1980 level by 2010. On the other hand, the trend has been sharply upwards in Asia, Africa and South America (Tolba et al, 1992), and in 1987, some 70 per cent of the world's urban population lived in cities where SO_2 concentrations reached or exceeded the World Health Organization guidelines. In some major developing-world conurbations the situation was getting worse.

The position for nitrogen oxides (Figure 10), particulate matter, carbon monoxide and hydrocarbons is less clear-cut. NO_x emissions rose in the USA, Germany and France between 1970 and 1985, but have fallen since then. In the UK there was a fall between 1970 and 1985, but then a return to 1970 levels. Nitrogen oxides and ammonia are now as important as sulphur emissions as a source of the acidity in European rain, mist, streams, soils and forests. Carbon monoxide emissions fell somewhat in the USA and Germany, but have risen in Italy and the United Kingdom. Particulate releases from domestic fires have fallen generally in developed countries, but those from diesel-engine road vehicles have been rising. Hydrocarbon emissions fell in the USA and many European countries but rose in the United Kingdom. New commitments to curb all these pollutants are now being agreed in the European Union, but the fact is that while the northern

countries of the developed world have made some progress there is a long
way to go. Curbs on hydrocarbons and nitrogen oxides are especially
important because it is these pollutants, reacting chemically in bright sunlight, that generate the ozone that at low levels in the atmosphere is an
important cause of damage to forest trees and other plants as well as an irri-
tant to human lungs. There is mounting concern in many cities over the
increasing prevalence of asthma, linked in turn to high levels of pollution,
much of it originating in motor vehicle exhaust. In the developing world,
action against these pollutants is only beginning, but unless they are tackled
they could pose serious problems in newly industrializing urban areas. The
problems are already acute in China.

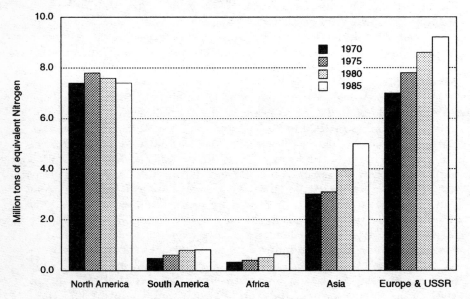

Source: Hameed and Dignon, 1992, cited in Tolba et al, 1992

Figure 10 Trends in emissions of nitrogen oxides, 1970–86

There has been progress in getting rid of chlorofluorocarbons, which are
both greenhouse gases and the chief sources of the chlorine that is attacking
stratospheric ozone. In 1989 an estimated 580,000 metric tonnes was none
the less emitted, 22 per cent of it from the USA and 16 per cent from
Japan. Under the Montreal Protocol to the Convention on the Protection of
the Ozone Layer and its 1990 Amendment a programme first for reducing
and then for phasing out many CFCs and related substances has now been
adopted, but the test will be the speed of its implementation and the extent
to which newly industrializing countries abide by it. The international
agreements do include a technology-transfer mechanism to allow such
countries to make use of substitutes, and so avoid this form of pollution.
    Under the Convention on Climate Change, the bulk of the world's
nations have undertaken to stabilize greenhouse gas concentrations in the

atmosphere at levels that will not significantly disturb the climate. Developed countries are to take the lead because they emit most of these gases (at least on a per head basis) (Table 6) (Tolba et al, 1992). They will also help developing countries to industrialize without aggravating the greenhouse effect, notably by technology sharing. The first targets adopted are for carbon dioxide – the most important greenhouse gas, and the most controllable (apart from CFCs). In Europe the aim is to return emissions of all the major greenhouse gases to 1990 levels by the end of the century. A number of countries, including the United Kingdom, have published detailed statements of how they intend to achieve this goal (UK, 1994a).

Table 6 Carbon emissions for selected countries in 1988

Country	Total emission (million tonnes)	Emission per person (tonnes)
Brazil	55	0.4
Canada	119	4.6
China	610	0.6
France	87	1.6
India	164	0.2
Japan	270	2.2
Mexico	84	1.0
Poland	125	3.3
United Kingdom	152	2.7
USA	1310	5.3
Former USSR	1086	3.8

Source: Marland et al, 1989 and Trends 90, 1990, cited in Tolba et al, 1992

There is a dilemma here. Many developed countries (including those in Europe) clearly favour economic instruments, such as taxes on motor vehicle fuels, as an incentive for energy conservation. But high energy costs bear hard on the poor (who are also least able to invest in making their homes energy-efficient), and hamper industrial growth and employment. The former concern stimulated the furore that led the UK government to abandon its proposal to raise value added tax on domestic fuel from 8 per cent to 17.5 per cent in 1994. In fact, world oil prices in 1995 are lower in real terms than they have been at any time in the past 20 years. Such low energy prices will help development in the newly industrializing countries, but undermine economic incentives for energy conservation. None the less, it is clear that efforts are being made to implement the four actions in *Caring for the Earth* to reduce common atmospheric pollutants. Progress is clearly uneven, and the real question is whether the scale and rate of response is sufficient to safeguard health and the environment, and avoid mounting damage costs.

Integrated land and water management, using drainage basins as units of management, is a feature of many national strategies, and Chapter 12 of *Agenda 21* calls for national sustainable land-use plans and sustainable management of water resources. The Commission on Sustainable Development, meeting in May 1995, endorsed the development of such programmes, emphasizing that they must involve all sectors of the community and all stakeholder groups (UN, 1995b). Progress on the ground is, however, exceedingly hard to monitor, and is likely to be slow because sectoral thinking remains dominant in so many countries. As to protecting the best farm land – the evidence is of continuing encroachment in many countries, notably from sprawling towns, while soil erosion and land degradation remain very serious problems. China has all three, on a substantial scale. Food production has been increasing, but production per head has barely kept pace with population increase in Latin America and West Asia, and has failed to do so in Africa. Net deforestation has not been halted: world estimates in the 1992–1993 *World Resources Report* (WRI, 1992) are of losses of 16.9 million hectares a year, 5 million in Africa, 6.8 million in tropical South America, and 3.6 million in Asia. In North America, although reforestation exceeds clearance by a large margin, losses of old-growth forests of high biological diversity continue.

Caring for the Earth has been criticized for its perceived failure to address the loss of biological diversity as a consequence of human use (and mis-use) of natural resources (Greene, 1994). There is a central issue here which, indeed, the strategy side-steps. It is how far sustainable development depends on the maintenance of biological diversity. There is practical evidence that the two are not inseparable. A managed forest, or a farmland, may well contain fewer species than the natural ecosystems that formerly grew at that site, but this does not mean that the modified systems are not sustainable. The carrying capacity of the land for people, and the quality of human life, are likely to be greater as a result of such changes. The issue is what pattern of change in biological diversity is acceptable within sustainable development. To demand no change and no loss is wholly unrealistic – there were such changes when, for example, there were only 40 to 80 million people in the whole of the Americas (Denevan, 1992). How to strike the balance is a challenge discussed in Chapter 7.

There has been a steady increase in the number and extent of protected areas, although the rate of increase slowed somewhat in the 1980s (Figure 2.1) (WCMC, 1992). In the world as a whole, 4.8 per cent of the land surface had some kind of formal protection in 1992 but the proportion varied very widely from continent to continent and from one biogeographical realm and biome type to another. There were also wide national variations, from 37 per cent in Ecuador, 22 per cent in Venezuela, 19 per cent in Bhutan and 17 per cent in Botswana to 0.1 per cent in Guyana and Libya and zero in Cape Verde, Comoros, Equatorial Guinea, Solomon Islands, Barbados, Cambodia, and a number of Middle Eastern States.

This variation in no way reflects the importance of biological diversity in these countries. Moreover, even where areas are designated the degree of protection varies considerably. For example quite large areas of many European countries have some special status – 19 per cent in Austria; 27 per cent in the former Federal Republic of Germany; and almost 19 per cent in the United Kingdom – but the bulk of these areas are 'protected landscapes' subject to multi-purpose use, with conservation of biological diversity as one only among the goals. And the world series is far from comprehensive if judged against the range of variation in the world's ecosystems. Finally, it is grossly inadequate where marine areas are concerned: there were, in 1991, 977 such sites, totalling 211 million hectares, as against 6931 sites on land, totalling 651 million ha. A strategy for marine biodiversity conservation was not published until 1993 (WCMC, 1992; Norse, 1993; IUCN, 1992).

There are advances to report. The adoption of the Convention on Biological Diversity in 1992 and its entry into force in 1993 is a major step forward, and new efforts are being made to link *ex situ* conservation in botanic gardens and zoos with conservation in the wild. Botanic Gardens Conservation International maintains a network of contacts and aids information flow in the botanic gardens community (IUCN/BGCS, 1989). The World Zoo Organization has published its own conservation strategy (IUDZG/IUCN, 1993), in partnership with the IUCN SSC Captive Breeding Specialist Group, and is cooperating to breed endangered species in captivity and restore them to the wild. This has been done for the Arabian Oryx, Pere David's deer, the North American black-footed ferret and the South American Golden Lion Tamarin, among others. Knowledge and understanding of species and ecosystems is certainly growing, not least at local community level as several projects reported in this book demonstrate. Although there are glaring examples of mis-use, some wild resources are being harvested sustainably, and the value of such resources and the need to plan and manage them as assets has been recognized. And the effort to devolve responsibility to local level is gaining strength. These good features are, however, very much exceptions to the rule: movements against the tide of loss in biological diversity and habitat, and wastage of natural resources. The conclusion: there are enough examples to show that the actions in *Caring for the Earth* can be implemented, but not enough to show a swing from net loss to net gain.

Keeping within the Earth's carrying capacity

Caring for the Earth lists seven actions under this heading. They begin with making people aware of the need to stabilize resource consumption and population, and to address these issues in national development policies and plans. They go on to actions to develop, test and adopt resource-efficient methods and technologies, tax energy and other resources in high-consumption countries, encourage 'green consumer' movements, improve maternal and child health care and double family planning services. These are, quite frankly, only some of the things that need to be done, and as a list they already look a little out of date.

There was much condemnation in the press and the environmental movement of the perceived failure of Earth Summit to get to grips with population issues. Some of this criticism was misplaced. Rio *did* address population, and *Agenda 21* has some fairly strong language about it (at least, strong for an international consensus document produced by a bureaucratic process). Its Chapter 5 emphasizes that there is a close relationship between population trends and development. It argues for:

> full integration of population concerns into national planning policy and decision-making processes. Population policies and programmes should be considered, with full recognition of women's rights. . . . Governments should take active steps to implement, as a matter of urgency, in accordance with country-specific conditions and legal systems, measures to ensure that women and men have the same right to decide freely and responsibly on the number and spacing of their children.

It also urges the development and enhancement of reproductive health programmes (Robinson, 1993). Since then, the United Nations World Population Conference held in Cairo in 1994 has carried the discussion forward and adopted a consensus statement miles ahead of anything seen before (Johnson, 1994).

Although rarely publicized in the environmental press, the fact is that the 'demographic transition' in which both death and birth rates fall from high initial levels to much lower and balanced values has been proceeding apace in much of the developing world – indeed proceeding faster than it did previously in the developed countries. As Chapter 1 explains, it took about a century for countries like those in western Europe to attain the present situation in which fertility rates are near or below replacement levels. In China (with Hong Kong and Taiwan), Korea, Singapore and Thailand the transition has effectively been completed in thirty years, even though total populations are growing because of the number of young people still to complete their families. In many other Asian and Latin American countries mortality rates have declined swiftly and fertility rates are falling, and even in Africa, fertility rates are beginning to follow mortality downwards although both have a considerable way to go (see Chapter 1 for details).

More than 90 per cent of the developing world is now ruled by governments that support population control policies. Birth control facilities, health care and education in this field are expanding. Infant and child mortality rates are falling (although they remain far too high in many countries) (Tolba et al, 1992). Moreover, despite the much-trumpeted condemnation of some religious groups for their opposition to 'artificial' birth control practices, the evidence is that their preaching is having little real impact: people *are* limiting their families for good personal, social, and economic reasons, and squaring their actions with their consciences and beliefs. Indeed, in many developed countries, birth rates are now below replacement levels, and unless immigration increases these countries are entering into a period of population decline. Although many environmentalists still speak of world population problems as if they are insoluble and ignored, the evidence is that action is being taken even though there remains a real need to increase the availability of health care and family planning services in many regions.

In contrast, the world is still skirmishing around the issues of resource consumption and action to make lifestyles more sustainable. Some economists are contending with some asperity that there is, in fact, no justification for action to curb current uses of materials or energy – although they do support more direct action to stop environmental damage (Beckerman, 1995). The rich countries are still driven by rampant consumerism, fuelled by advertising, and when recession strikes there are calls for reflation of the economy, with consumer spending – especially on motor cars – taken as a sign of national economic health. No solution is in sight to the problem of loss of traditional labour-intensive employment, leading to personal despair and social unrest among an unacceptably large number of unemployed. Taxes on labour rather than on materials and energy provide an incentive to employers to reduce their workforce and substitute machines – 'externalizing' social cost which is then borne by the community at large in welfare or by the individuals in terms of increased poverty. There are few demands for action to 'internalize' the social costs of unemployment in a way that environmental pollution costs are being internalized: were this done, it might well become clear that 'labour saving' electronic and other automation systems are not cost-effective alternatives to systems based on higher use of human skill, albeit under more stimulating conditions that prevailed previously in developed countries and still prevail in many newly industrializing ones. Our apparent inability to find a social path that uses and rewards human individuals and gives then a quality of life based on satisfying occupation remains the largest single barrier to sustainability.

There is a broad view that while economic growth is essential, not least to generate the resources to invest in new, sustainable, industries and better social systems, it needs to be adjusted in order to protect air, water and human health and reduce damage to the living world. Even those who attack 'green extremism' endorse such an approach. Today's fashion is to work through adjusting the market so that it generates the solutions. This means setting more precise values for environmental resources, charging for their use, setting prices that reflect the true cost of making a product or delivering a service, and imposing taxes for the use of communal assets. For example, charging users of energy the full social and environmental cost of its generation, supply and use is seen as a way to ensure economy and efficiency, and so reduce pollution. Taxes on emissions of carbon and sulphur are justified in the same way.

These things can work – provided people are informed about the choices before them and can afford to alter their lifestyles (for example by insulating their homes, buying efficient light bulbs, demanding fuel-efficient vehicles and so on). But many poor people are locked into lifestyles where capital outlay is impossible, and higher energy prices mean an aggravation of poverty: the incentive to save energy may be there, but the means and knowledge are not. Similarly, if carbon taxes are reflected in higher prices for essentials, the problems of poverty are again aggravated. And market factors do need reinforcing with regulation. As Frances Cairncross (1995) points out 'the market alone will not necessarily deliver a cleaner environment'. This whole area is one of challenge largely unvoiced in *Caring for the Earth* and *Agenda 21*, and must be addressed in the future. It is considered further here in Chapters 4 and 11.

Changing personal attitudes and practices

In *Caring for the Earth* there are only three actions under this heading: ensuring that national strategies for sustainability include action to motivate, educate and equip individuals to lead sustainable lives; reviewing the status of environmental education and making it an integral part of formal education at all levels; and determining training needs for a sustainable society and planning to meet them.

We have gained understanding since *Caring for the Earth* was written. We have asked more probing questions about *how* changes can most effectively be brought about. It is clear that the way ahead is to inform and empower people to take action that they see will improve their lives and give their children better prospects. This in turn means giving them the opportunity to benefit from sustainable economic growth. It also means involving them in wider community and group partnerships. But there has to be consensus in those partnerships, reached through dialogue. That is where information and motivation comes in. As Chapter 8 shows, there is increasing recognition that without the commitment of individuals, action for sustainable living will not happen. What is needed begins at the level of personal understanding and belief. Education, information and training are all important, but they have to be linked to the actions to develop and promote the underlying ethic, and they have to form part of community dialogue and community understanding. The whole process adds up to one of social learning – and social demand for a new paradigm and a new approach (Milbraith, 1989).

Most if not all national strategies for sustainability *do* include action to involve individuals (Carew Reid et al, 1994). Those that did not are being reviewed, with participation as a new dimension. The message of the first of the actions noted in *Caring for the Earth* does therefore seem to have been generally accepted. It is evident in *Agenda 21*, Chapter 36 of which comments 'Education, raising of public awareness and training are linked to virtually all areas' (of action). . .'and even more closely to the ones on meeting basic needs, capacity-building, data and information, science and the role of major groups' (Robinson, 1993). The actions called for in *Caring for the Earth* are therefore generally accepted as essential, although levels of implementation are uneven between countries and communities – often because of resources. They are seen, however, as insufficient, and their success depends critically upon their social context as well as their detailed content. We still have to work out social pathways to sustainability that will not be rejected because they make too many people worse off in the short term.

Enabling communities to care for their own environments

This section lists six actions: giving communities and individuals secure access to resources and an equitable share in managing them; improving exchanges of information, skills and techniques; enhancing participation in conservation and development; developing more effective local governments; ensuring that there is care for the local environment in every community; and providing financial and technical support to community environmental action.

All these figure among the criteria for success discussed in Chapter 9, but the emphasis there is again on the 'social chemistry' that will make these necessary activities practicable. As to implementation: it must be admitted that there is resistance in many communities – in the developed as well as the developing world – to giving local people secure access to, and an equitable share in managing, local resources. Some of the opposition comes from powerful interests like major industrial corporations, who are nervous of the 'not in my back yard' (NIMBY) syndrome, and believe that it is far easier to get a central government to decide on the more controversial aspects of resource use such as where to site a major power station, a nuclear waste disposal facility or a recycling plant. Other opposition comes from central government itself, nervous of losing revenues and even more frightened of losing control. Another obstacle is political dogma, expressed in the belief that the state must own the land and manage it for the people – an attractive concept in theory, whose failure in practice has undermined the economies of a number of states and created much personal misery.

Hence while there are visible moves towards empowering local communities, many of them noted in Chapter 9, progress is uneven and beset by pitfalls. But there are some remarkable successes – like the return of autonomy and control to indigenous communities in northern Canada, Greenland, New Zealand, Australia, and increasingly in developing countries. And some of the other actions called for – like enhanced information exchange, transfer or sharing of skills and techniques and more participation – clearly have gained ground. Effective local governments have not yet emerged in many regions of the world, but there are some, and in some countries alliances between local governments, industry and the non-governmental sector are actually by-passing obstructions in the central government machine and advancing sustainability willy-nilly. There is certainly not yet care for the environment in every community, but there is more than there was, and some outstanding demonstrations are noted in this book. Financial and technical support is another area of unevenness, but where local communities are enabled to benefit from the use of natural resources (as, for example, in the Zimbabwe CAMPFIRE project) (Child, 1994; Maveneke, 1994a,b), it is clear that sustainability can become self-funding. So there are many, widely scattered, signs of hope: the issue is whether positive change can be accelerated so that gains come to exceed losses. If so, there will be positive feedback to motivate individuals and change their attitudes and practices, for nothing is more infectious than success.

Providing a national framework for integrating development and conservation

This is a major thrust of *Caring for the Earth*, with ten action proposals. The first demands the adoption of an integrated approach to environmental policy, with sustainability as the overall goal. This is also the central thrust of *Agenda 21*. It has received worldwide political acceptance, in principle, and the emergence of new national strategies for sustainability is evidence that many governments are seriously attempting to carry it through into action on the ground. What action? The second one urged by *Caring for the Earth* is the development of strategies for sustainability, to be implemented directly and through regional and local planning, and the third calls for proposed development projects, programmes and policies to be subjected to environmental impact assessment and economic appraisal. These, too, are widely accepted in principle, although it is now appreciated that *no* strategy can really be implemented directly – all demand partnerships across sectors of society, and all demand regional and local action. And while environmental impact assessment and economic appraisal are important, these are tools among many others to be applied to test the soundness of a proposal, rather than some magic philosopher's stone that can make an ill-considered idea work in a society and community that is not ready for it.

Three legal actions are called for as part of the national framework: the establishment of a commitment to the principles of a sustainable society in constitutional or other fundamental statements of national policy; the establishment of a comprehensive system of environmental law and its implementation and enforcement; and a review of the adequacy of legal and administrative controls and of implementation and enforcement mechanisms 'recognizing the legitimacy of local approaches'. Well and good – but again these are parts of the action, not ends in themselves. The first may be held to be partly satisfied by the number of speeches of acceptance of the principle of sustainability by heads of state and government in Rio, by the Rio Declaration, and by the national strategies for sustainability that are emerging. Few states, however, seem to consider it appropriate to amend their constitutions to incorporate the principle, nor is such action really essential if the policies and practices are there. A test will come when the Covenant on Conservation and Development being prepared in IUCN is ready for adoption, for it will provide a general statement of legal principles which will, effectively, bind those who ratify it not only to the general goal of sustainability but to a number of more precise undertakings as well

(Hassan, 1994). The second and third areas of action are edging forward, but few countries have used Earth Summit as an opportunity for the kind of comprehensive review implied by *Caring for the Earth*.

There are three economic actions which are seen as complementary to the legal ones: ensuring that national policies, development plans, budgets and decisions on investments take full account of their effects on the environment; providing economic incentives to sustainable use; and using economic policies to achieve sustainability. Many environmentalists would greet claims by governments that they are implementing these actions with hollow and mocking laughter. Lip-service is widely paid to the inclusion of environmental criteria in appraisals of investment decisions. Some countries have indeed insisted in reviewing the environmental implications of national budgets, and of the spending plans of major departments of state: Norway is a good example, where a committee co-chaired by the Prime Minister and Minster for the Environment looks across the whole budgetary field in this way. But most have not, or have done so superficially. In the same way, many countries accept the need to place proper value on natural capital, to internalize costs through application of the 'polluter pays' principle, to get rid of perverse subsidies on energy and agriculture – and also food price controls that deter small farmers – and to develop economic incentives for more efficient use of energy and resources. In practical terms, actions have lagged behind concepts. Precise measurement is difficult, but few economic instruments are in place and proving their worth in advancing sustainability, and (as already noted) it remains uncertain whether such instruments can be adopted without bearing unduly heavily on the most vulnerable members of society.

The last action under this heading is 'Strengthen the knowledge base, and make information on environmental matters more accessible'. There is no doubt that the volume of information about the environment has increased enormously – and that it is slowly being brought to a more common statistical base, and providing more useful support to those who take decisions. There are more and more information reports, and their coverage is expanding. The 1991/1992 UNEP *Environmental Data Report* (UNEP, 1992) contains 153 tables under headings ranging from environmental pollution through climate to natural resources, population and settlements, human health, energy, wastes, natural disasters and international cooperation. It is noteworthy, however, that the pollution sector is by far the fattest, with 48 tables, natural resources coming next with 21, and health following with 19. There are relatively few tables on socio-economic aspects and none on education or law. The 1992/1993 *World Resources Report* (WRI, 1992) is also dominated by information about environmental sectors and activities. But there is an increasing capacity in expert centres like the World Conservation Monitoring Centre to use a Geographical Information System to relate basic topographic, climatic and habitat features to ecological and land-use patterns. The United Nations Environment Programme is leading in a Global Biodiversity Assessment. And there is a real effort to expand data and information services to decision-makers in developing countries.

Overall, the conclusion has to be that this action proposal is being taken seriously, but there needs to be more dialogue to ensure that the needs of the users are more clearly specified so that the information they want can be supplied in the form in which they want it.

Creating a global alliance

The last general chapter of *Caring for the Earth* included nine actions: to strengthen existing international agreements to conserve life-support systems; to conclude new agreements to help achieve global sustainability; to develop a comprehensive and integrated conservation regime for Antarctica and the Southern Ocean; to prepare and adopt a Universal Declaration on Sustainability; to write off the official debt of low-income countries and retire enough of their commercial debt to restore economic progress; to increase the capacity of lower-income countries to help themselves; to increase development assistance and devote it to helping countries develop sustainable societies and economies; to recognize the value of global and national non-governmental action and strengthen it and to strengthen the United Nations system as an effective force for global sustainability.

The result is like the legendary egg in front of a very junior member of the English church establishment, on a breakfast table presided over by a very senior one. 'I'm afraid you've got a bad egg' boomed the host. 'Oh, no, my Lord' came the reply. 'Parts of it are excellent.'

Parts of the action are excellent. There has been a strengthening of international agreements for sustainability. Judged by the number of global and regional legal instruments on environmental topics, progress has indeed been dramatic. As noted in Chapter 1, IUCN has published a list of 121 of the former (including protocols and amendments) and 256 of the latter that existed in 1992 (although they had not all entered into force) (IUCN, 1993a). About half of the major ones date from after the Stockholm Conference of 1972. Some of the more important – like those on the protection of the ozone layer, prevention of long-range transboundary air pollution, prevention of dumping of wastes at sea, or control of trade in hazardous wastes – have been progressively strengthened at successive meetings of their contracting parties. In addition, several important new agreements have been agreed very recently. The UN Conference on Environment and Development in Rio de Janeiro saw the adoption of a declaration, an agenda for action (*Agenda 21*), a series of guiding principles on forest management and two international conventions on climate change and on biological diversity (Robinson, 1993).

IUCN published its *Strategy for Antarctic Conservation* (IUCN, 1991b) in 1991, and in that year the Consultative Parties to the Antarctic Treaty agreed on a Protocol on Environmental Protection which, when ratified by all of them, will implement the action proposed in *Caring for the Earth* by putting a comprehensive and integrated conservation regime in place for the continent and the seas south of 60 degrees South latitude. The Convention on the Conservation of Antarctic Marine Living Resources provides a basis for such action further north and the recent decision of the International Whaling Commission to adopt a sanctuary for whales in most of the sea areas south of latitude 40 degrees South is a further substantial conservation measure.

There is, as yet, no universal declaration on sustainability, at least under that title, although the Rio Declaration adopted by some 150 countries goes a little way towards that goal. The Covenant on Environment and Development now being prepared by IUCN will, if adopted, substantially meet the action objective. The Earth Council is continuing to work on an Earth Charter. Such a short, clear, statement committing the whole world community to equitable, sound, sustainable development was intended to be a product of the Earth Summit in Rio but the medicine proved too strong for the world's leaders, who ended with a Declaration that fails the test of vision as much as it does that of literary quality.

Progress on these general fronts has therefore been fairly good. On the other hand, the economic measures have not been followed through with sufficient vigour. Some governments have written off much of the official debt of lower-income countries, but the retirement of commercial debt has not been sufficient to restore economic progress. Indeed the situation got worse during the 1980s. In the three years between 1980 and 1982, there was a net flow of US$49 billion from the richer to the poorer countries (Figure 11) (Keating, 1993). Between 1983 and 1989 the flow went the other way, with a staggering total of $242 billion passing from the poor to the rich – much of it to service the burden of debt, incurred in the hope that the development the loans financed would deliver a profit. Since 1989, when 107 countries surveyed in the *World Resources Report, 1992–1993* (WRI, 1992) had a total, and increasing, debt of $1.15 trillion, the situation has only improved slightly. In that year, debt servicing had a cost equivalent to 81 per cent of the total earnings of exported goods and services in Uganda, 71 per cent in Algeria, 52 per cent in Madagascar and over 30 per cent in Argentina, Bolivia, Brazil, Burundi, Colombia, Côte d'Ivoire, Ecuador, Ethiopia, Ghana, Guinea-Bissau, Indonesia, Kenya, Mexico, Morocco, Niger, Pakistan, Papua New Guinea, São Tomé and Príncipe, Somalia, and Turkey.

Moreover, despite the rhetoric of Rio, official development assistance has been falling in recent years as recession deepened its impact on the economies of many Northern developed countries and as the European nations in particular diverted some of their resources to assisting the reconstruction of the nations in the central and eastern parts of that continent. The economic gulf between the affluent and the poor nations remains one of the major barriers to global sustainability, exacerbating the problems of many countries that have substantial pressures on their natural resources, widespread land degradation and desertification, rapid population growth and wholly inadequate social services.

Earth Summit and *Agenda 21* do recognize the value of non-governmental actions and a number of steps have been taken to strengthen the partnerships between the governmental and non-governmental sectors: some of these have already been reviewed. The High Level Advisory Board to the Secretary General of the United Nations has emphasized the need, stating (UN, 1994a) that:

> the United Nations system, either alone or in alliance with State Governments, cannot achieve sustainable development. There is a substantial community consisting of non-governmental entities which needs to be accepted into partnership with the United Nations system and/or with Governments in order to enhance progress towards sustainable development.

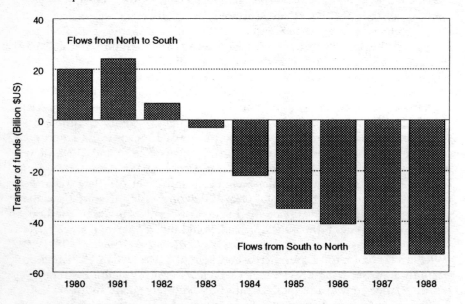

Source: UNDP, 1992, cited in Keating, 1993

Figure 11 Debt-related net transfer of finance, 1980–89

A number of cogent proposals have been made, some discussed later in this book. A number of governments are involving their non-governmental sector in round tables and partnerships and these operate at many levels, down to the local and the grassroots. However, the UN system is in something of a dilemma. The need for such alliances is accepted very widely, but the practice is moving very slowly, partly because many governments do not want to open up their discussions to outside influences. Nor do the UN agencies, and the bureaucracies that serve them, feel altogether happy about opening up their debates to the sometimes unruly delegations from the non-governmental sector. The non-governmental movement itself has some way to go to equip itself for partnership at the highest level.

The United Nations system emerged from Earth Summit in Rio de Janeiro strengthened in the sense that its essential role was recognized, and because new coordinating machinery to integrate its work on environment and development was reflected in the creation of the new Commission on Sustainable Development. But the test will come in the products of that system, discussed in Chapter 11. At present, the need to make the action called for in *Caring for the Earth*, and echoed in *Agenda 21*, work is generally recognized, but the resources to make it happen are not yet being provided. The only new money on the table after Rio has been in the Global Environment Facility, a US$2 billion fund administered by the World Bank in partnership with UNEP and UNDP, to support action on global environmental problems especially relating to climate, biological diversity, and sustainable land use.

Energy, business, industry and commerce

These two sections of *Caring for the Earth* contain 11 actions. All of the five concerned with energy are being addressed in some countries, especially in the developed world. Many of these nations are developing explicit energy strategies. Some are trying to reduce the use of fossil fuels, wastage in energy generation and use, and pollution from commercial energy generation. There is mounting interest in the development of renewable and other non-fossil-fuel energy sources. Efficiency campaigns are seeking to reduce the waste of energy in homes, industry, business and transport. There is publicity for energy-efficient products. But these actions are uneven and in many newly industrializing countries they are barely visible. Commercial energy consumption worldwide continued to rise slowly in developed countries over the two decades 1970–1990, but increased dramatically, albeit from a much lower base, in the developing world (WRI, 1992). Energy intensity (energy used per unit of GNP), however, fell in the developed world. The real test is how far these countries can continue to cut back their use of fossil fuels, and share advanced technology so that the industrializing world can avoid exacerbating pollution and climate change. The only verdict here at present has to be 'not proven'.

The same goes for the other actions in the industrial sector. Yes, some firms and governments are seeking a dialogue for sustainability: examples of this action are quoted in other chapters. Yes, environmental performance standards in industry have been rising, especially in the major multinationals and those based in the developed world. The Business Council for Sustainable Development has provided a ringing declaration of need (Schmidheiny, 1992), and the International Chamber of Commerce and many individual businesses have committed themselves to sustainability and environmental excellence (Willums and Golucke, 1992). Much has been done to reduce the risks from hazardous industries (although each month brings some glaring exceptions to light). National and international systems for waste management have been advanced and the curbs on international traffic in hazardous waste under the Basel Convention have been an important step forward. Some industries that are based on the use of natural resources are seeking economy in their use, but clearly this is unlikely to work for those that are actually marketing such resources, whose profitability depends on the volume of sales. In general the only verdict has to be that we have the knowledge to enhance the sustainability of industry greatly; that clean, non-waste and energy- and materials-efficient processes exist in many sectors, but that in many parts of the world there is an immense way to go to make the best practices universal.

Human settlements

There are only four actions under this heading – all rather self-evident, and even taken together falling far short of what is needed. They call for the adoption of an ecological approach to human settlement planning (whatever that means). More effective and representative local governments, committed to caring for their environments, are demanded. So is efficient and sustainable transport policy. Cities, we are told, should be made 'clean, green and efficient'. So what?

A city is an organic entity. It is, as the examples of Seattle and Curitiba, described in other chapters, illustrate, a living system of interaction between people and their physical setting. Since *Caring for the Earth* was published, a great deal of discussion about how we can build the sustainable city has gone on (Hardoy et al, 1992; Mitlin and Satterthwaite, 1994). It is clear that designing a sustainable city starts with a look at the whole context of life in that particular settlement: location, size, living conditions, health, social activities, urban–rural interactions, resource-use patterns, waste management, transport, employment and so forth. It is also clear that we have to consider the social structure and local communities within the cities, and explore people's needs, perceptions and values. We have to enlist them in partnerships for action.

The provision of a host of enhanced services which meet people's needs without polluting or degrading the environment, or eroding its capacity to serve future generations (which is what the ecological approach comes down to) is certainly essential. It is a part of primary environmental care, described in Chapter 9. Transport policy is clearly a part of that action, but doctrinaire assertions about specific formulae are not helpful. A 'clean, green and efficient' city is a desirable goal but the statement itself is a slogan, not an action point. And while local governments should indeed be representative, effective, and committed to care for the environment this is only part of what they should be (they should, for example, be open, approachable, accountable, and not corrupt). Finally, it must be recognized that the sustainable city must grow within a sustainable context: cities cannot be sustainable alone. External support – for investment of many kinds – will often be essential.

The conclusion here is that some cities and townships are making genuine progress, but that the actions listed in *Caring for the Earth* are not sufficient yardsticks against which to measure progress. The sign of hope is that there are real examples from which we can cull clearer blueprints for action, and many will be discussed in later chapters.

Farmlands, rangelands and forests

There are 24 actions under these headings. They range very widely. The problem with them is that not all are applicable everywhere. For example, a national strategy for sustainability (the first action) is certainly needed, and called for in *Agenda 21*, but it would be a mistake to tie this simply to farmlands and rangelands or to forests although these sectors must be a part of it. The call to protect the best lands for agriculture is sound, but cannot be universal: there should be a presumption that any responsible country or local community will protect its irreplaceable croplands and try to build its cities on sites of lower value, but there will be occasions when this is not feasible. Much the same goes for the other actions under the 'farm and rangelands' heading: the call to promote effective soil and water conservation through better husbandry; to reduce the impact of agriculture on marginal lands; to encourage integrated crop and livestock farming and increase the efficiency of fertilizer use; to increase the productivity and sustainability of rain-fed farming; to promote integrated pest management; to control the use of fertilizers, pesticides and herbicides through regulations and incentives; to promote action to conserve genetic resources; to try to increase non-farm employment for small farmers and the landless; to promote primary environmental care by farmers and to switch from price supports to conservation supports.

Very well. Yes. Of course. Most of these actions are accepted in principle in many areas and being followed in some. But they are not in themselves the starting point for action to secure sustainable farming or rangeland management. That has to begin on the ground, in the community, with a review of local needs, opportunities, current practices, aspirations, traditional wisdom and all the other ingredients. Different approaches will be needed in developed and in developing countries, in different climatic zones, and in different cultural circumstances. The actions in this section of *Caring for the Earth* are best treated as a checklist for communities to consider when they take stock of the options open to them locally. Many are being implemented, some are not; but the key indicators of success are likely to be more basic and relate to such matters as productivity, soil integrity, erosion rates, salt levels and so forth.

The same holds for the actions on forests. *Caring for the Earth* calls on countries to establish a comprehensive system of protected forests, with priority to the types that are most important in terms of the national centres of biological diversity. Action for such conservation has moved forward in a number of countries, although the losses of old-growth forest in temperate zones and diverse tropical areas continues. An adequate permanent estate of modified forest is also important because it is likely that much of the national need for timber can best be met by the sustainable use of secondary forest. Some (but rather few) countries have taken action in this area.

The area of planted forest is being increased in many countries, but the situation remains volatile. National capacity to manage forests sustainably does need enhancement, and is not yet sufficient, one problem being the debate over whether we yet know how to manage tropical forests sustainably for timber production, whether or not in combination with the supply of non-timber products. Certainly community management of forests should be strengthened (and is being in some areas). Forest genetic resources should be conserved (and are being, but on an inadequate scale: this is a challenge to the Convention on Biological Diversity). The call to 'create a market for forest products from sustainably managed sources and use wood more efficiently' is widely echoed, but has proved very difficult to translate into action. Setting prices to reflect timber's full value and discouraging exploitation of stands of marginal commercial value comes up against basic questions of market intervention: who should do it, on what scale, and how will international trading systems work to improve sustainability? It is right that the capacity of lower-income countries to manage forests sustainably be increased, and that international cooperation in forest conservation and sustainable development be improved, but this calls for development assistance especially for planning and training, and the scale of such assistance has been reduced lately.

Overall, the actions listed in *Caring for the Earth* in these sections are extremely difficult to evaluate. Some are being undertaken, in some places, but as part of rather wider programmes of action. There are gaps in understanding – for example about the resilience of soil in many parts of the world and the optimal balance between resource use and the maintenance of biological diversity. The most effective approach is likely to begin with an assessment of need and opportunity at local and community level, with a judgement about which kinds of action are best to accomplish those goals. The checklist in *Caring for the Earth* may help in such analysis, but not all the actions are likely to be right in all places. These issues are considered further in Chapter 8.

Fresh waters, oceans and coastal areas

These two sections of *Caring for the Earth* contain 23 suggested actions, and again these range widely, from the strategic and national to the specific and local. Many are echoed in *Agenda 21*. At strategic level, there are calls for a cross-sectoral mechanism for integrated water management, greater emphasis on the drainage basin as a unit of water management, development of a national policy on the coastal zone and ocean, establishment of machinery to coordinate the planning and allocation of uses in the coastal zone and the use of 'an ecosystem approach' for the management of marine resources. Some of these actions are indeed being pursued within national strategies for sustainability, and in administrative reforms, especially in developed countries, but it is difficult to give any overall estimate of progress.

Another set of actions is directed at social policy. States are called on to improve the information base for sustainable water management; to conduct information and education campaigns that will raise awareness of issues and promote sustainable use; to promote interdisciplinary research and information exchange on freshwater and marine ecosystems and on how to use both sustainably; to provide training in the management of human demands and impacts on the water cycles; to ensure efficient and equitable allocation of water among competing users; to establish a cross-sectoral mechanism for integrated water management; to give local communities greater control over the management of aquatic resources; to allocate marine user rights more equitably, with more weight to the interests of local communities; and to give local communities greater control over the management of aquatic resources and enhanced capacity to use them sustainably.

All these actions are sensible, indeed important. They are being pursued largely in the context of national sustainability strategies, and particular projects for resource management. It has to be said that progress appears very uneven. International and inter-sectoral competition to apportion water rights goes on, often impelled by short-term vision. There are few effective international regimes. Even in developed countries such agreements as that for the Rhine have moved forward slowly. There are a number of agreements on the management of shared coastal seas, and some have achieved action to curb pollution, but agreements on fisheries management have notoriously failed to deal with the global problem of over-fishing, essentially because they have not started with an ecosystem approach based on potential production and carrying capacity, and then tackled established social rights of use: the tendency has been for the impetus of past use to prevent the cuts in fishery that are environmentally essential. There has, indeed, been extraordinarily wasteful over-subsidization of fishing industries, and unseemly squabbles between states over resources which they know they cannot harvest at the rates they demand.

More progress is visible with the actions on pollution – which, however, were not really highlighted in *Caring for the Earth* although they are prominent in *Agenda 21*. Priority is being placed in many countries on cleaning up polluted watercourses, reducing marine pollution from land-based sources, and implementing international agreements including those on the dumping of wastes. Action to reduce the risk of pollution from ships has also been advanced under the auspices of the International Maritime Organization. Oil spills from tanker accidents – one of the most visible, although far from the most damaging, form of marine pollution – have declined. The UN Convention on the Law of the Sea has now entered into force, although several major developed states have yet to sign and ratify it. International cooperation on marine protection has increased.

Implementing the strategy

Caring for the Earth concludes with ten actions regarding its follow-up. Recipients are urged to study the Strategy and consider its implications. This has happened fairly widely, although the strategy was overtaken swiftly following its launch in November 1991 by the negotiation and adoption of *Agenda 21*. There is really little point, now, in trying to analyze the follow-up to these documents separately because of their wide overlap. The good news is that the main issues both raise continue to be the scene of global attention, not least in the Commission on Sustainable Development. It is not that governments and communities are unaware of the implications of the Strategy and Agenda, but that the next stage is moving slowly.

The second follow-up action is to evaluate the implications of the Strategy for the policies and approaches of citizens' groups, NGOs, local communities, governments and international bodies. The third is to promote it through broadly based national and international publicity campaigns, and the fourth to promote it within government. Such action is not being taken directly – in the sense that the actions advocated in *Caring for the Earth* are being checked off by the various groups as they review their policies. What is happening is that the approaches to sustainability strategies and more specific policies and projects have undoubtedly been greatly influenced by the thinking that has fed through from the *World Conservation Strategy* and *Caring for the Earth* into *Agenda 21* and its follow-up. Rio saw the start of much new dialogue and analysis in many contexts, and this is likely to prove a more effective way forward than any slavish adherence to the action agenda of a particular document. If any such is to dominate, however, it will be *Agenda 21* – rightly, because this is the world agenda, adopted by an unprecedented number of governments.

There has been considerable progress with several of the remaining actions. Communities are taking, and being given, opportunities to prepare local strategies for sustainability. The emphasis on the local level has been one of the principal and encouraging features of recent years, counteracting the unduly 'top-down' thinking that characterized the Stockholm Conference of 1972. That was a period when the world community seemed to assume that once governments had been enlisted, action would happen. We now know better. But it is true that government agencies need to be organized to implement action for sustainability, and many are being as a result of Rio. National and sub-national strategies for sustainability are being prepared by an increasing number of states. The global alliance is being developed, albeit slowly and imperfectly, with major challenges to the financial and economic systems, and to world trading machinery: these defects and needs are addressed in Chapter Ten. The transition to sustainability indeed needs funding, and *Caring for the Earth* argued that the action required would cost $77 billion a year in 1992 rising to $161 billion by 2001. New funds on this scale have not been forthcoming, and it seems clear that they will not be available from governmental sources. The chief hope is that private sector financial investment in the developing world will increase and help pull through the process of sustainable development. The chief negative sign is that expenditure on armaments – identified as the principal area of wasteful investment, from which resources could be transferred – remains almost as high as ever.

An overview of progress

It is clear that progress with the 132 actions of *Caring for the Earth*, and the 40 chapters of *Agenda 21* has been very uneven. The good news is that the world community has accepted the crucial need for development that is based on care for the planet, and the sustainable use of its natural resources. There has been progress in some areas, and some countries. Some of the global indicators are positive. Others are adverse.

One of the most disturbing things, however, is the gap between rich and poor countries. In terms of education, science, research, and the supply of services like radio and telephones (indicators of information availability), it has widened. Income disparities have become greater, too: in 1960, the richest 20 per cent of people had 30 times the income of the poorest 20 per cent, but this ratio rose to 45 times in 1980 and 59 times in 1989. As already noted, despite official development aid, in much of the 1980s large amounts of money actually flowed from the poor to the rich countries. While poverty fell in Asia, the one major region where development clearly took off, it increased markedly in Africa, and to some extent in other regions of the developing world. And it is a sombre comment on the seriousness with which nations view their commitments, entered into at Rio, that the volume of development aid passing from the richer to the poorer countries actually fell during 1993.

It is good that although global human population continues to increase, the rate of increase is slowing and the demographic transition has clearly advanced in many parts of Asia and is well underway in Latin America. On the other hand, in Africa it has scarcely begun, and the conjunction of rapid population increase, increasing poverty, falling food production per head, and severe land degradation in many regions is bound to increase the sense of foreboding. AIDS is having its most severe impact on this continent, and while it seems clear that the pandemic of this disease will not of itself halt population growth, it is reducing expectations of life, and adding immensely to human misery. Moreover, it is causing severe losses in the educated sections of the population, which are a vital human resource for the future. And ethnic and civil strife – in Rwanda, Somalia and elsewhere – add a new dimension of hopelessness, destroying social infrastructure and human resources alongside those of the environment.

There are clearly signs of advance in some actions to protect the biosphere – like the phasing out of ozone-depleting chemicals and the tightening action against other air pollutants including greenhouse gases and the precursors of acid rain. These actions, of course, are largely being taken by the developed countries (and rightly so, for they have been the main cause of the problem). Likewise, rivers and coastal seas in such regions are an increasing focus of action. But the real test for such countries is whether they can make the transition to sustainability without intolerable stress on societies that have become used to high-energy, high-resource, high-waste, advertisement-led consumerism.

The needs identified in 1980 in the *World Conservation Strategy*, in 1991 in *Caring for the Earth*, and in 1992 in *Agenda 21* remain pressing. There are some signs of hope, but they are like faint lights shining in an encircling gloom. The real issue is how to move forward and multiply those lights. There can be no perfect prescription. But we should perhaps start by probing deeper into the causes of the gaps between statement and action; idea and reality. That is the task of the following chapter.

C H A P T E R 4

THE BARRIERS TO SUCCESS

The gap between concept and action

Judged by the mass of documents on the shelf, we should be winning the environmental race. The world is replete with national conservation strategies, national environmental action plans, world conservation strategies, blueprints for survival, state of the world reports, world resources reports, state of the environment reports, plans for this city or that rural hinterland or nature reserve (see Table 5). We have over 120 international treaties and conventions on environmental matters, and over 250 such agreements at regional or local level.

Yet Chapter 3 demonstrates that, at best, progress is uneven. There are many signs of unsustainable development and of the waste of natural resources. And there is a paradox. The world community is well aware that this misuse of environmental resources aggravates the immense difficulties that confront the nations of the world, where a billion people live in poverty, where social and environmental catastrophes increase from year to year, and where – unless those catastrophes bring mortality on an intolerable scale – we shall have at least 2 billion more people to feed fifty years from now. Yet we know, in scientific and technical terms, how to reverse many of these adverse trends. The knowledge base is massive and there are many examples of good practice, including traditional processes, which if followed more widely would solve many problems and enhance the human condition.

The problem is not, as we used to think, getting the leaders of the nations to talk about the environment. It is not even about getting them to agree to actions plans. Over twenty years ago, in Stockholm, a declaration and framework for action was agreed by the representatives of many nations. Had that plan been put into speedy effect, we would have escaped many problems that now constrain the human future (Holdgate et al, 1982). In Rio de Janeiro twenty years later, the largest-ever gathering of heads of state and government adopted, in the 40 Chapters and 630 pages of *Agenda 21*, the most comprehensive action plan for sustainable development ever produced (Robinson, 1993). Since then, things have gone rather quiet in many countries. Yet the need for prompt and effective action has never been greater.

We should not be surprised that all the plans, reports, and agendas seem to lack expression in action. In central and eastern Europe national politics revolved for decades around imposing central three- and five-year plans adopted in the planned economies, and the targets they set for implementation. National statistics, based on theory rather than practice, purported to show that success was being achieved. Of course, for that was an article of faith. We now know that the whole thing was an elaborate sham, and led to disaster on the ground, whether measured in terms of human quality of life or the productivity and health of the natural environment. Scientific papers in themselves achieve nothing. They provide knowledge, and a basis for action, no more. Central – or local – plans in themselves achieve nothing.

Discussions in 1992, 1993, and 1994 in Stockholm (Ambio, 1993) on just how to secure action concluded that, first, the most important need is to transfer of knowledge to those able and willing to apply it in action. Second, social practices are at the heart of both problem and solution, and if people are either unconvinced of the need for action, or distrust the arguments addressed to them, or have different priorities, or simply lack the power to act, nothing will happen. Third, changes in social behaviour have their roots in public attitude, and therefore if there is to be change, it must be built on informing the public and convincing them that the change is necessary, will benefit them and their grandchildren, and is morally right.

The fundamental question today is how far sustainability demands a radically new approach. How far can the dominant social paradigm (Milbraith, 1989) of today – the social thinking and market system of the 'Northern' developed nations – achieve sustainability? That paradigm has been exported from western Europe and the United States to lands as far distant as Australia, Argentina, Chile, New Zealand and South Africa, and is also growing vigorously in the soil of Japan, China, Singapore and Thailand, despite their very different traditional cultures. It is the assumed model for the leaders of many developing countries, educated in Northern universities.

The assumption is that human life is best advanced by giving people, and the companies, cities and states to which they belong, ever more commercial energy, fast transport, manufactured goods, diverse foodstuffs, sophisticated medicine and information technology. Development is equated with economic growth, in turn measured largely in terms of expenditure. The social system accepts fierce competition between individuals, companies and political factions, using the skills of modern communications to promote their interests. While it no longer accepts the externalization of costs in the shape of damage from pollution, it tolerates the externalization of social costs in the shape of unemployment, in the name of efficiency. It is a dominator society, in which small groups (mostly of male gender) have a disproportionate influence on what is done. Nominally democracies, because all adult citizens have a right to speak their minds, and to vote every four years or so to elect the elite that governs in their name, such societies are in reality oligarchies – ruled by that elite, allied with other power groups that run major companies or institutions (including academic and scientific ones).

To be fair to the system, it works. It is not normally repressive. It creates a climate of stability and opportunity. It has brought steadily increasing material benefits, health, nutrition, education, entertainment and travel. On most of these indicators, the world has made good progress in the past 50 years, as Chapter 1 and the data in the UN Development Programme reports on human development show (UNDP, 1991). Critics of the 'green movement' like Richard North (1995) or Julian Simon (1994) are right to point out that for many people life has been getting better. But (as Chapter 3 showed) development has been uneven, and today there are also more poor people than ever before.

And the economic and technological growth of the developed world has had a cost. It has appropriated a large share of the material resources of the planet, and generated much of the pollution. Mahatma Gandhi is said to have commented that it took half the resources of the world to build the prosperity of Britain in the 1930s: where could India find four worlds? While that was an exaggeration, we cannot gear the whole world up to the United States. Equally obviously, we cannot gear the United States and Europe down, in terms of quality of life. The benefits that modern technology has brought must be retained, but the footprint of the developed world on the world of nature must dig less deeply. This demands change – and it will be hard to get those who feel well off as things are to accept it, even for the sake of global equity. At present, most of them are just not convinced of the need – while the poor need help tomorrow, not sustainability thirty years hence.

Some writers, including Lester Milbraith (1989), argue that whatever the comfort people find in today's world, the divergence between human demands and the capacity of the environment is becoming so great that we must have a 'new environmental paradigm', or new basic philosophy and socio-economic system. There is certainly a strong case for change. But I believe that such a new approach can only be introduced progressively, starting from where we are now. If there are to be new goals – and especially a sustainable world society – people have to see that these can be achieved more or less smoothly and painlessly. The process of adaptation has to be self-evidently sensible, with benefits along the way. People demand a 'win–win' approach, as far as possible.

The issue, therefore, is how we can adapt and adjust the development process so that it is more efficient (or 'ecoefficient', if we follow the terminology of the Business Council for Sustainable Development), and brings people into a stable and enduring balance with the natural systems on which we all depend.

One obvious fact is that we do not all start in the same place. So the paths of development have to converge, rather as the drivers in the Monte Carlo Rally used to converge on their goal from starting points in several parts of Europe. I think, however, that all the paths from concept to action are likely to have to meet eight particular needs. They will require:

- a clearer vision of the world we want;
- recognition that the sustainability process must respect and fit a wide range of traditions, beliefs and social practices;
- better communication across cultural divisions;
- better public information and education;
- new economic values, leading to sustainable policies, practices and goals and to a market that works for rather than against sustainability;
- better understanding of nature, and wiser use of natural resources;
- better governance, avoiding sectoralism and over-centralization, and giving communities the power to act;
- partnerships and alliances to make sustainability possible.

In the following sections, these areas are reviewed in turn, the obstacles are assessed, and a rough quantitative (but wholly subjective) estimate is made of the 'index of impediment'. An index rating of 10 implies a massive blockage: one of 2 or 3 that the problems are not too difficult. The steps towards action are then elaborated in the chapters that follow.

The need to see more clearly, and share a vision of the way ahead

'The power of man is as his hopes', wrote John Masefield. When people have seen their goals clearly, and when the vision has been widely shared, they have often succeeded in making their dreams come true.

The trouble is that not all visions meet the test of abiding value. 'The dreamers of the day are dangerous men,' wrote TE Lawrence (Williamson, 1942), 'for they may act their dream with open eyes and make it possible.' History is studded with the stories of civilizations led astray by visionaries. There was a vision in the Crusades, that took a mixed crowd of villains, saints and opportunists across Europe nine hundred years ago to treat their perceived enemies with great inhumanity in the name of their God. There was vision in colonialism. Some at least of the conquistadors genuinely believed that they were bringing salvation to the indigenous peoples of Central America. There was a vision in Nazism, put across with the power of compelling oratory. Visions are easy: the hard test is of the value they enshrine.

Humanity's judgement of visions is clearly deeply flawed. And we have a dreadful tendency to dilute even our greatest visions as they are turned to action, and destroy them through factional squabbling. Great religions that began with a clear and direct revelation have been riven into sects each claiming sole authority for the partial truth they guard. Some people – some other groups of visionaries – have seen this as proof that there is a force of evil in the world, 'the devil, like a raging lion, seeking whom he may devour'. Setting such arguments aside, we should learn from history that humanity erodes its greatest insights. If we believe that we can and must make the dream of harmony between people and the natural world an abiding truth – then we must also recognize that there will be strong forces undermining that process at every step.

Such a vision starts with odds against it. Many people still look on nature as limitless, or even hostile. The whole process of development has been one of conversion of the wilderness to the garden and city. The dream of harmony with nature appears to many people like an image of paradise, with blessed humanity sustained by the bounty of subservient plants and animals.

The real world is not, and cannot be, like that. Harmony with nature means letting some parts of the natural world dominate human action, for there are real limits in nature and we have to live within them. Harmony also means respecting nature, and accepting that other forms of life have their own value and importance. They, after all, are the foundation of tomorrow's life, as the process of natural development unrolls alongside that of human societies.

Success will come only if the clarity and integrity of the vision are maintained. And this means that we have to go on putting the ethical dimension first. What people do depends on what they believe. They will respect nature and demand sustainable resource use if they feel that this will bring them benefits, if it is essential for the welfare of children or grandchildren, if it alleviates visible human suffering, and if they are satisfied that it is morally right.

This last is a factor of immense importance. Although western society, at least, is less influenced by religion than it was, beliefs are still universal and have a major impact on individual choices. It was no accident that IUCN, UNEP and WWF began *Caring for the Earth* with an ethical principle – 'respect and care for the community of life' – emphasizing that it is the root of action. We need 'to secure a widespread and deeply-held commitment to a new ethic, the ethic for sustainable living, and to translate its principles into practice'. The ethic of care for the Earth, and for other communities and future generations, is the moral foundation of sustainable development. It needs to be emphasized.

Is a lack of such an ethic limiting at present? Clearly the answer depends on society and circumstance. I believe that the ethical base exists in many societies, but its expression is often impeded or distorted. In some it is submerged by the oppression of poverty. In other tragic communities, as in Rwanda and the Horn of Africa (Hutchison, 1991), it is crowded out by strife. In yet others, it is stifled by greed. We used to speak a lot about 'the pollution of poverty', but it can be argued that the 'pollution of affluence' can be just as deadly. Indeed, the societies that may be most impeded by a lack of the ethic of care for the Earth and its peoples are the advanced, affluent, consuming societies which have also lost their original religious guidance and have yet to find a new social consensus of values. As Chapter 3 commented, the religious community is itself moving too hesitantly. At the very highest level, there is a lack of ethical principles to guide the operation of world institutions. This may be one area where the Commission on Global Governance (1995), the Earth Council (1993), or the Parliament of Religions (Beversluis, 1993) can help advance world society.

Sir Shridath Ramphal has summed the situation up in the final paragraph of his book *Our Country the Planet*, written for the Earth Summit in Rio de Janeiro (1992):

> The war for human survival is unlike other wars. It is not a matter of winners and losers. Each must lose, so that all may win. Only to the extent that individual nations accept limits and thresholds can there be collective victory. It is not a war of man against man, nation against nation, but rather a war of humanity against unsustainable living. It is the only war we can afford. Only through enlightened change can humanity hope to triumph.

I think that the lack of a clear, widely shared vision, itself rooted in a strong ethic, and of visionaries committed to making it work in political and practical action, is one of the greatest obstacles we face and may be the most difficult to overcome. I give it an impediment index of 8, and am not confident that we have enough torch-bearers. Chapter 5 goes more deeply into possible ways forward.

Communication across cultural divisions

Cultural barriers remain a severe obstacle to global action for sustainable living. Chapter 1 touched briefly on the problems created by colonialism and the superimposition of values – and frontiers – on one people by another. I believe that such barriers, and especially those between the systems of Europe and North America on the one hand, and the developing world on the other, still do not receive enough attention.

Until recently, western European culture, including its science, was dismissive of the traditional knowledge of people who had not codified their understanding in our kind of way. Our 'experts' transferred scientific and technical knowledge without trying to discover whether the communities in the recipient areas had their own knowledge systems and without considering that indigenous tradition – for example in agriculture – might be better adapted to the region than the ideas from outside. We now know that many rural communities have large assemblages of knowledge. We are sending western botanists to work alongside the indigenous botanists of Panama and Amazonia, and tap their vast knowledge of plant properties and uses. We are recognizing that the key to sustainable development is to involve and empower local communities. We are realizing that people are not necessarily ignorant because they are illiterate, and that the poor may yet be wise.

The resulting attitudinal change is well summed up by Robert Chambers (1993):

> We, who call ourselves professionals, are much of the problem and to do better requires reversals of much that we regard as normal. The challenge is to upend our thinking, to turn values on their heads, to invent and adapt new methods, and to behave differently. The frontiers are personal and professional requiring changes which are radical but quite surprisingly practical; to question our values; to be self-critically aware; to see simple as often optimal; to offset our spatial and seasonal biases; to help rural people do their own analyses; to stay in villages and learn from and with rural people; to test and use participatory approaches, methods and procedures; to encourage decentralization and diversity; to put people before things and poor people first of all.

Perhaps it goes even farther than that. For the cultural transfers go beyond rural land use – agriculture and forestry. They extend to the basic culture of industrialized society: its faith in technology and the engineered solution, its centralized governance, its economics and its ethics. The basic assumption that 'development' is the substitution of the manufactured for the natural, the extension of cities, the construction of roads and railways and airports, mechanization, computerization and the replacement of large unskilled work forces by much smaller groups of highly trained employees is – questionable. For these are processes, whereas development is the realization of potential. Human and environmental potential. If the goal is a community of people with healthy minds in healthy bodies in a healthy environment, the goals of development must be stated in human terms. The ways to development must be judged by their efficacy in achieving those goals.

We know already that the world cannot simply export the Northern consumer society in its present form to the countries that at present have low standards of living and low incomes. At present, the quarter of humanity that lives in the rich countries generates more greenhouse gases and more ozone-depleting chemicals than the atmosphere can tolerate. It is evident that if everyone started to use energy and natural resources at European or North American rates – at ten to thirty times the consumption levels of the people of Bangladesh, or rural India or China – things would choke or grill to a halt. So we have to find new pathways to the social goals that development must pursue.

The techno-fix dominates the adaptive strategy of the industrialized world. We seek cleaner, more energy-efficient, less wasteful industries. Fine. Such progressive adaptation and substitution is likely to be an important way forward for the already-industrialized nations. But are there other ways for communities with other cultures and beliefs? Could we find more sustainable pathways in systems that, for example, place a higher value on employment even if some of it is manual? Many apparently simple communities are in fact a mosaic of skills and crafts, where everyone has a part to play, and where respect and fulfilment result. Is that a better model?

At least we need to look at the whole of human cultural diversity and recognize that there are likely to be adaptive features in unlikely places, that could hold promise just as genes in unlikely habitats hold the promise of crops adapted to tomorrow's climate. But if we do recognize this, there is a major political implication for the developing world.

Cultural arrogance has already been imported to the developing world by many 'experts' from the Northern, developed nations. Often it has been transferred quite innocently, by sincere and capable professional educators, scientists, agriculturalists, or engineers, who are simply expressing their own training in a new setting. As Robert Chambers has commented, the need is to train such people to listen, study, and participate in the communities they go to, thereby blending the best of the cultures and helping the recipients to develop in the way that they want.

This has implications for the funders of development, for most of those institutions also have their roots and cultural assumptions in the North. Lending agencies like the World Bank, or the Regional Development Banks, and those concerned with investment by major Northern firms, inevitably apply the scientific and economic judgements of the North. They seek developments that march with their cultural assumptions. They often seek developments that will reinforce the financial flows from the recipient to the investing countries. This may in part be inevitable. But it, too, needs looking at.

Finally, cultural assumptions have often been transferred through the education system. I am writing this book in Cambridge, England, seat of a great and ancient university. Many leaders of the developing world were educated here. The problem is that while they undoubtedly took many benefits away with them, they also took a risk of acceptance of the western norm as the social goal for their own countries. They seek development that mirrors the North. When they go for loans to the World Bank and other agencies, they tend to favour engineering schemes – dams, hydroelectricity, irrigation works, coastal barriers – and 'modern' methods of agriculture and forestry. But they may be able to do better than that – may have to do better than that if they are to lead sustainable development. The solution may lie in looking also at the traditional values and strengths of their own communities. Mahatma Gandhi thought so.

We have to share our cultural values and insights, and look with open minds at the different systems that have brought sustainability to some places and disaster to others. Certainly we must not be dismissive of any particular value system or resource management practice, until we have taken the trouble to understand it. In much of the developing world, the cultural and intellectual differences, if not arrogance, displayed by Western and Northern experts is a major obstruction to sustainable development. It has been aggravated by the gulf between some national leaders in developing countries and their own rural poor. This in turn has been a major hindrance to the success of Northern institutions that have worked at central government level – for example the World Bank. I give this area an impediment rating of 8, and fear that it is only falling slowly.

The special culture of science

The cultural divisions between scientists and non-scientists have also been made much of by some writers. They remain of some practical significance.

The culture of science breeds misunderstanding. Scientists codify their knowledge in formats designed to be readily transferred to people with similar training in other countries, despite differences in social conventions and language. They use highly structured language, often with a large mathematical component. They are not good at communicating their insights in everyday speech – which demands generalization and simplification that in itself distorts. Again, the approach of science is to refine descriptive hypotheses and models through continual challenge – an intellectual replica of the evolutionary process. The consequence is that any statement made in science should be regarded not as a certain pronouncement but a hypothesis for testing. All scientific theories get refined, and many get radically altered as knowledge grows. This does not mean that the original theories were weak, but that they were first approximations, to be altered as new facts arrive.

The mere fact that science seeks universal conceptual transferability means that it also tries to step outside the cultural and political context of the individual scientist. When this is prevented, whether by religious or political influence, as when the medieval Church tried to block the insights of Galileo or Soviet dogma imposed the genetic theories of Lysenko, the result is bad science and a halt to human progress. But politicians and other decision-takers in society have to stay embedded in the national, and often local, cultural context. Unless they understand the mind-set of the scientist – and vice versa – communication is often difficult.

Scientific hypotheses – and policy responses – are of two broad kinds. The first assumes that an event is likely, and therefore that there will be change. Research then seeks to refute the proposition, usually by monitoring whether predicted changes are appearing. Policy meanwhile demands action to counter the threat of change – or to adjust to it if it is unstoppable. The second kind of hypothesis assumes that there will be no change, and research again tests the hypothesis by watching to see how valid that proposition was. Policy here tends to defer action, because no risk is forecast. Paradoxically, the actual risk of damaging change may be the same in both cases! However, if the first kind of hypothesis is put forward, the 'precautionary principle' leads to action, and the hypothesis then proves wrong, there is a cost in terms of wasted effort, whereas when a 'no-change' hypothesis is wrong the costs are incurred through unexpected damage – and belated action. It follows that we have to be clear in each case what kind of hypothesis we are adopting, and what the implications of action or inaction are (Shrader-Frechette, 1994).

Politicians expect their scientific advisers to be precise – and this allows some at least of the responsibility for decision to be transferred. The public expects scientists to be authoritative, if not infallible (at least, they used to: they are getting wiser). They are perplexed at the diversity of scientific opinion which is part of the evolutionary process of refinement through challenge. They may also feel that science is wasteful, expending so much money and human effort on gathering information yet able to deliver so little certainty at the end of it. For their part, scientists are often irritated by the demand for more certainty than is possible, and accuse politicians of intellectual superficiality and of being blown this way and that with every wind of public emotion. The caution of the scientist, moreover, sits uneasily beside the confidence with which many economists predict the outcome of decisions.

These conceptual barriers between scientists, economists, industrialists and politicians can be a serious obstacle to sustainable development. The inevitable uncertainties in science are often paraded as excuses for deferment of action – implying acceptance of a 'no change' hypothesis, with the attendant risks should it prove wrong. The diversity of views that is an inevitable consequence of how science works is paraded as a disqualification of any such views from attention until consensus emerges – at the point where the parallel lines meet. Some of these dismissive arguments are based on short-term self-interest: it pays the manufacturer of persistent pesticides, ozone-depleting chemicals, greenhouse gases or tobacco to argue that there are still uncertainties about their impact. Others are based on a reluctance of scientists to step outside their own culture and debate with economists – for example – the true limits and values of nature. Yet others are a natural consequence of the economic assumption that money today has greater value than money tomorrow and that investment to avert future risks may therefore be less prudent than waiting until the investment is proved necessary.

I think we understand one another better than we did, but must go further. Earth Summit did establish, for politicians and other decision-takers, that the world's economy depends on the world's ecology, and more and more laws and policies attempt to be well grounded in ecological science. What we need now is a better communication service. I give this problem area an impediment index of 5, reducing.

Better public information and education

Everyone may have insight and vision of a kind, and yearn after a better world, but these feelings need feeding, usually by the support of a group of like-minded people – which is why faiths need temples as well as hermitages. Action for sustainable living likewise depends on reinforcing the vision at its heart. But the process has to be practical, and information, education, and guides to action are all key ingredients.

People know that we have environmental problems. They want to do something about them, as many opinion polls show (Tolba et al, 1992). But they are rarely presented with the opportunity to act (except by protest). Much of the information we get about the environment is concerned with global problems like ozone depletion or climate change, or continental ones like acid rain, or events far away like the poaching of rhinoceroses. For many people these are remote, or even theoretical, concerns rather than practical realities that they can do something about. You cannot see the ozone hole, or the greenhouse gases, and their effects are not easily detectable except by those unfortunate people who are suffering skin cancers as a result of increased ultraviolet penetration. You, as an individual, are likely to believe that nothing that you can do will make any difference. People feel angry, upset and powerless (which reinforces concern, but not commitment to action other than protest). Even water pollution with sewage effluent is commonly presented as a failure of a government or municipality rather than the collective impact of individual actions.

Another problem is that a good deal of the information people receive is not accurate. The extreme situation makes the headlines. For example, the slaughter of African elephants by ivory poachers was indeed wasteful, illegal and inhumane. It was right that governments in the countries concerned were encouraged and helped to stop it. But it was not an immediate threat to the survival of the African elephant – of which there were over 600,000 even after the poaching crisis reached its peak. In fact, the Asian elephant is considerably more endangered than the African, which is increasing in some countries, including Botswana and Zimbabwe, and creating serious problems because of depredations on cultivated land. Yet people who read the newspapers and the advertisements in Northern developed countries could be pardoned for believing that the species hovered on the brink of extinction. When they find out that a case like this has been over-sold, there is serious danger that they will conclude that environmental arguments as a whole are exaggerated.

Much public concern, moreover, is a reaction to what has already happened. It is aroused by obvious abuses, like foul air, stinking rivers, the destruction of beautiful landscapes by motorways, or the tragic spectacle of victims of famine and strife. It demands clean-up and humanitarian aid. But prevention is really far better than cure. Sound environmental management, and sustainable development, are branches of preventive medicine. If we are to avoid disasters we have to live and work within nature's limits – and this is what sustainable development is all about. The problem is that you cannot see sustainability. When it is happening, things look all right. People tend only to notice when sustainable living breaks down. People need, therefore, to be informed, educated and helped to demand the actions that will prevent disaster, and they need access to monitoring that will allow deviations from the path of sustainability to be detected, and adaptations to lifestyle set in hand.

Public opinion polls show that people do take an interest in their environment and want to see it safeguarded. But they need to be informed about what the problems are on their own ground, and what they as individuals can contribute to both problem and solution. They need to be involved in an interactive mode – not just fed information but told where they can go to get more, and of the kind they want.

Here there is another contradiction. Despite the volume of press comment on environmental issues, much public information in the developed world is actually hostile to sustainable development. The media tend to treat evil things as 'news', while leaving reports of good ones in the editorial waste-paper basket or cutting room. For some reason, people are keener on buying papers, or watching programmes, that stimulate envy and portray antagonisms. The vision of sustainable living – or the case studies of success that appear later in this book – are unlikely to get much prime time on television when there is war, massacre, scandal or political sleaze to report. Moreover, newspapers and commercial television depend on advertising. Much advertising is designed to accelerate the linear flow of materials throughout society. Belatedly, recycling and reducing pollution and the waste of materials and energy have become a selling point and object of advertisement. But true sustainability will demand real improvements in the efficiency with which energy and raw materials are used in developed countries – and the question is whether this can be compatible with consumer society information habits.

There is a real difference between 'information' and 'education'. Information is an *input* to people: education is a *drawing out* of their abilities. They should, however, be mutually reinforcing. TV, radio, books and newspapers have (or could have) a powerful, informal, educational role. Both informal and formal environmental education are defective in many countries. *Agenda 21* emphasizes the importance of new action to strengthen them.

There are some encouraging examples in both the formal and informal sectors, from developing as well as developed countries. There are new curricula, new books, and good information programmes at local as well as national levels. These efforts need strengthening. But we also need to recognize that in many countries we have allowed a sectoral split to appear. Governments are very concerned with formal education in schools and universities and rightly seek to set minimum standards and define curricula. But informal education is left to the media, which are often driven by commercial motives. Yet evidence shows that for most people the informal sector has the most telling influence. People can be motivated to demand action and this can close the loop in the decision process – but very commonly they do this on the basis of distorted information and biased priorities (Palmer, 1995).

Maybe the 'information superhighway' can help drive a path through the intellectual slums that the information systems of many societies have constructed. It could do so by strengthening the links between the groups working for practical action on the ground, sharing knowledge and strengthening capacity. Certainly the environmental movement in its widest sense needs to look again at how well it is using the new networks that link the world.

I give this whole area an impediment index of 5. There are major forces pulling it in both directions. Perhaps the most important need is to persuade at least some of the leaders in the informal sector – joining some enlightened television and newspaper proprietors and editors that have already made a start – to commit themselves to promoting sustainability, and to draw up criteria that they will apply to these endeavours. They could then lead a movement within their own profession, as leaders of other professions are seeking to do.

New economic values, leading to sustainable policies, practices and goals

Ethics and economics interlock. For the former is about the basic values and principles that should guide action, and the latter is about the apportionment of finances, which are the active vehicle of power. Some features of today's global economy appear unethical, if judged on any yardstick of shared human duty for people everywhere. Over the past decade, financial flows have been from the poorer to the richer countries, aggravating their poverty and hampering their development. The market is better at delivering weapons of war than investments in environmental and social security.

Some of the reasons are rooted in the past – errors of judgement by governments, which sought loans for ill-conceived development, especially of large civil construction projects like dams and highways, or mechanized fisheries or the wrong kind of industrial expansion. Many such schemes did not deliver the hoped-for prosperity, but still have to be paid for. The same goes for weaponry which has not fired a shot in the defence of the nations buying it. Blaming the lenders for making such loans, when they were asked for by the recipients, is not wholly fair. Blaming the lenders for not entering into dialogue, and not understanding conditions on the ground in the recipient countries may be. Blaming the recipients for getting it wrong is also a doubtful judgement. The right course is to note that the whole process was clearly badly flawed on both sides and that a new approach needs to be found, with sustainability and social advantage as the yardstick. Easier said than done.

Economic valuations dominate social and political decisions in all countries. Finance ministries dominate the decision systems of governments, and financial considerations govern the decisions of industry. Fear of neighbouring countries, or of enemies within, remains a potent force driving investment in so-called security. We have reaffirmed our social and cultural belief that the free operation of the market is the best means of optimizing our use of resources. The problem is that the market has at times worked in fashions that appear perverse – destroying local cultures that are in sustainable balance with their environments, and destroying long-term assets for the sake of short-term goals. Sustainable development depends on putting the right values into the market, and making it work properly.

Nothing much, short of true democracy and stronger international guarantees for peace – a topic returned to in Chapter 11 – can help curb over-investment in weapons of destruction. But coming nearer to our environmental home, if the market is to work for sustainability it must not be distorted by false values in the economic equations. At present what David Pearce and other economists (1989; 1991; 1993) have called 'natural capital' is not yet correctly valued in most economic appraisals. Some environmental systems are left outside the economic model on the grounds that they are effectively limitless and unaffected by anything people do. This has been the attitude to air, water, the capacity of the seas to receive wastes, the yields of fisheries, the renewal of oxygen by green plants, the availability of wild crop relatives as sources of genes for improving cultivars, and many other essential components of our life-support system. It made sense to leave these components outside the calculations, when the socio-economic 'box' (see Figure 2.3) was small in proportion to the natural world. Our impact has now expanded so much that these 'goods' can no longer be treated as limitless or freely self-renewing.

Nature remains the human life-support system for people and all other species. For we are inextricably linked to, and dependent on, the processes of the biosphere – the thin layer of atmosphere, ocean, and land surface and substratum in which everything on earth lives. These processes are driven by the sun's energy, and by the energy of the earth's rotation. Within this complex, it is helpful to group environmental assets in three categories, from the vast to the immediate (Holdgate, 1995a). At the largest scale, they consist of global life-support systems: the second level is that of more direct life-support systems, while the third, smallest-scale, category is that of ecological products.

The first category includes those features of the biosphere which determine the habitability of the planet. They operate across national frontiers, and are not capable of direct regulation by our actions (although they increasingly need protection against them). They include the stratospheric ozone layer, screening out damaging ultraviolet radiation from the sun; the processes that maintain more or less stable concentrations of oxygen and other gases (including carbon dioxide) in the atmosphere and the cycles of the essential elements – carbon, nitrogen, oxygen, phosphorus and sulphur, together with certain metals; the fixing by green plants of the sun's energy, to produce carbohydrates which are the base of almost all food chains; the cycling of water, essential to all life on land; and the maintenance of a sufficient diversity of life forms to allow evolution to proceed.

The direct life-support systems include components of the environment which operate at regional or local levels and are the basis of processes which directly or indirectly sustain people. They all depend on the global processes and support the generation of ecological products. They include:

- soil fertility, obviously essential to plant production, whether in wild habitats, managed forests or farmlands;
- the flow characteristics and water quality of freshwater streams, rivers and lakes, which in turn determine their richness as habitats for all forms of aquatic life, and their production of fish, and other things useful to people;
- the quality of marine waters, essential to maintain the diverse life of the sea and the production of fish and other products important to people;

- the coral reefs, mangroves, salt marshes and other coastal systems which protect the shores from erosion, support fish and other food sources and are important to human enjoyment;
- the integrity and biological diversity of a range of natural and semi-natural 'wild' habitats and vegetation types on land, with their dependent species.

The third category of ecological products includes resources derived from the wild and from managed habitats in aquaculture, agriculture or forestry. The two categories overlap: all fish-farming is of wild species (although already both trout and salmon are undergoing transformation as a result of selection and culture techniques) while some 'ranched' species like crocodiles and turtles are taken from wild breeding stock, and genetic material is taken continually from the wild to develop new strains of crop plants. A wild wheat strain from Turkey, of no commercial value in itself, gave disease resistance to commercial varieties worth $50 million annually in the USA alone (UN, 1995d). Other short-straw genes boosted rice and wheat production in the 1970s by several billion dollars a year. And today people are also raising more and more wild animal species in captivity. Ostriches, deer and wild boar are all farmed in Europe, as are the llama, vicuna and guanaco – all members of the camel family – in South America. Crocodile ranching has been a growth industry in the 1980s.

Some of these resources are already within the commercial economy because they are harvested by fisheries, forestry or agriculture or by collection from 'wild' ecosystems (Brazil nuts, rattan canes, and latex are examples). Others lie outside the formal economy but are often used extensively by local and indigenous peoples. For example, in Botswana over 50 kinds of wild animal are cropped; in Ghana 75 per cent of the population depends for much of its protein on wildlife, fish, insects and snails; in Nigeria wild animals provide about 20 per cent of the meat eaten in rural areas (and two giant rat species alone yield 100,000 tonnes a year), and in Zaire 75 per cent of the animal protein consumed comes from wild sources (UN, 1995d; McNeely, 1988). Such resources have obvious economic, social and cultural value, and could, in aggregate, be as valuable as the harvested products that do show in the statistics, yet because they lie outside the formal economy they are disregarded in national accounts.

Consider a tropical forest. Table 7 lists 32 kinds of product taken from forests in Papua New Guinea (Hamilton and King, 1983; Holdgate, 1993). In Ecuador, a study showed that indigenous peoples used as many as 224 plant species and knew some 2000 species and varieties altogether. The Chacoba people of Bolivia and the Ka'apor of Brazil use 75–80 per cent of the woody species in their forests (UN, 1995d). Traditional medicine, mostly based on wild plants, is the mainstay of over 2 billion people in developing countries. Some 40 per cent of all drugs traded across North American counters are said to be derived from wild plants (although many of the active ingredients are now synthesized in laboratories) (Prescott-Allen and Prescott-Allen, 1986). The retail value of plant-derived drugs was calculated at US$43 billion in 1985, and herbal drugs could command a market

Table 7 Minor forest product uses in Papua New Guinea

Use	Example
Abortifacients and contraceptives	*Caldesia parnassitolia*
Artifacts	'Galip nuts' for tourists, wood in mask shields etc
Bark cloth	Beaten *Ficus* sp for 'tapa' cloth
Basketwork	*Kygodium* sp
Beverages	Palm wine, sap from vines and creepers
Bird bait	*Melanolepis multiglandulosa* fruit attracts cockatoos
Condiments	*Zingiber* sp; *Amomum* sp
Containers	Bamboo and gourds for carrying water
Cooking and eating utensils	'Kwila' bowls (*Intsia bijuga*), bamboo stems, coconut shells
Decoration and ornaments	Seeds of *Coix lacryma-jobi* in necklaces, and leaves of *Celosia* and *Olearia*
Drugs	*Areca* nuts
Dyes	*Bixa orellana* (red), *Curcuma longa* (yellow) *Leucosyke* (black)
Exudates	Guttapercha (rubber)
Fibres	*Gnetum gnemon* and *Althoffia pleiostigma* for net bags
Fish intoxicants	*Derris*
Food	Many species
Glazing	*Celtis* for glazing black paint among the Abelam
Gums	*Artocarpus* for caulking and bird traps
Insecticides	*Pyrethrum*
Juices and saps	Toddies and stimulants such as *Anamirta* and kava (*Piper methysticum*)
Medicines	Many species
Musical instruments	*Pterocarpus indicus* for 'kundus' and *Vitex coffasus* for 'garamuts'
Oils	Tree oil from *Campnosperma* and *Pandanus* oil seed
Poisons	*Derris*, *Gnetum catifolium*
Resins	*Parinari* (the kusta nut)
'Rope'	*Calamus* for 'kanda' and *Lygodium* for weaving masks and baskets
Salt making	*Coix gigantea* among the Baruya and *Eriocaulon longifolium*
Starch	*Sago*, *Manihot* and *Tacca* spp
Thatching	*Sago* and *Nipa* fronds and 'kunai' grass (*Imperata* and *Miscanthus* in the highlands)
Tool making	*Bambusa* stems, *Diospyros* wood
Wearing apparel	*Pandanus* leaf capes and penis gourds
Weapon making	*Caryota* for bows

Source: Hamilton and King, 1983

of US$47 billion in western developed countries by the year 2000 (UN, 1995d). Calculations suggest that the harvesting of this multiplicity of forest products could yield anything from $420 to as little as 75 cents per hectare per year, but that over wide areas the returns could be worth more, each year, indefinitely, than the $150 per hectare that comes from once-off logging and leaves a degraded environment in its wake (Myers, 1988: see also Chapter 8). And recreational values are not to be despised: tourism is the largest foreign exchange earner in Kenya and some other developing countries, and a lion in the Amboseli National Park, on that basis, is said to be worth $27,000 a year (a group of elephants is rather more valuable!) (McNeely, 1988).

If you take the values of the three kinds of environmental asset in turn, it is obvious that the global life-support category is so valuable that it is, effectively, beyond price. The world's economy in this sense depends so completely on the world's ecology that it is dwarfed by it. Beyond price, but not beyond damage. Today vast social and economic costs are in prospect unless the measures to get rid of the chemicals that are damaging the ozone screen succeed, and climatic change resulting from the accumulation of 'greenhouse gases' in the atmosphere can be prevented.

Recently, the demands for urgent action in this latter field have been contested. Wilfred Beckerman (1995) has argued that the concern is misplaced because the projected magnitude of change (1 to 3 degrees Celsius in 50 years) is so small – much less than someone experiences when moving from Canada to California. He dismisses impacts on agriculture because this constitutes only 3 per cent of GNP in the United States and comparable countries, and because the impact would at worst cost only some $10 billion in the USA. The rise in sea level, similarly, would demand only an investment of $100 billion over 100 years to protect all the vulnerable coasts in the United States. The cost of deferring action by a decade until the science is more certain would be far less.

This comes back to the relative merits of hypotheses of change and no change discussed above. And it would be unwise to be too dismissive of the potential costs for two reasons. First, a rise of only 1 degree Celsius in mean temperature would none the less displace the limits of tolerance of crop plants and wild species as much as 100 to 150 kilometres towards the poles or 140–160 metres up a mountain. A 10 per cent change in rainfall could also have major implications for river regimes, agriculture and economies. While humans are good at tolerating wide climatic variations, plants have sharper limits. Moreover, the postulated rates of change are greater than the world's ecosystems have experienced in a short period in the last 10,000 years, and would certainly cause considerable disruptions.

The second reason for concern is that not all countries have the wealth of the USA: proportionately, the environmental changes would have much higher significance in their economies. The USA, Japan, Europe and other wealthy countries may indeed find it cheaper to invest in corrective engineering as problems arise, but developing countries could not fund such efforts and in the worst case of small coral-island states, a rise in sea level of only 20 centimetres could make them much more vulnerable to storms and greatly reduce the volume of fresh water held in their rocks. There is an issue of international equity to consider here. Much of the threat of climate change arises because of the actions of the developed countries. To argue that because they can afford to pay to protect their environments when need arises does not answer the whole case. Will they also pay to protect the environments of disadvantaged developing countries as well? If they do – and a case in equity if not in law exists for making them do so – they may find that prevention is cheaper after all. While it is undoubtedly wise to step action up as scientific understanding deepens, there are 'win–win' policies that it makes sense to introduce now, for example by eliminating subsidies that lead to the waste of energy and making internal combustion engines cleaner and more efficient.

The 'direct life-support systems' have immense value. Worldwide, soil degradation has taken about 295 million hectares of land – an area almost as big as India – out of cultivation, while the equivalent of three Indias has lost a large part of its productivity (Tolba et al, 1992). The World Bank estimates that worldwide, soil depletion is costing between 0.5 per cent and 1.5 per cent of global gross domestic product annually. In Java, on-site erosion is costed at $323 million a year. The destruction of sea defences is also costly (over half the coral reefs in Asia have been destroyed or severely damaged). In the United States, the natural salt-marsh defences of Boston Harbour are estimated to save $17 million year in flood protection works, while a hectare of natural marshland is valued at $72,000 a year if its role as a fish nursery grounds is also taken into account (McNeely, 1988). Air pollution has been estimated to cost the OECD countries – the western market economy countries – around 3 per cent of GDP a year.

These things do not show in the economic statistics, for several reasons. First, the major life-support systems have traditionally been treated as a 'free good'. Second, there are indeed some things on which it is almost impossible to put a price tag. The notion that people can own the sky, the free wind, the mountain tops or the sun's warmth strikes many as absurd, if not downright blasphemous. 'How can you buy or sell the sky, the warmth of the land?' Hoax or not, the words put into Chief Seathl's mouth in that 1970s film script ring true (Royston, 1979). More succinctly, to quote the title of a modern book, many believe that 'ecology into economics won't go' (McBurney, 1990). But while major social decisions are taken on the basis of economic calculations, it seems better to insist that those equations do include the best available valuations we can put on natural systems.

This is the aim of a good deal of new economic effort. This seeks to state the value of 'natural capital' as precisely as possible, to provide a new methodology for calculating its importance in the wealth of a nation and guiding its use, and to calculate such things as the marginal opportunity cost of resource depletion.

But there are problems. First, it is quite obviously easier to value some kinds of environmental asset than others (Holdgate, 1995a). Products harvested from the wild that enter the conventional economy can obviously have a price tag applied. It is possible to look at the revenues derived from cropping wild species, as in the CAMPFIRE project in Zimbabwe, alongside what pastoral use of the same land to graze cattle might provide (Child, 1994). That is the basis for decision in the villages concerned to stay with the harvest of multi-species wildlife rather than turn the land into cattle pasture. But it is much more difficult to estimate what the undiscovered wealth of medicinal plants in a tropical forest may be worth, while some elements in nature, like the warmth of the sun, are effectively of infinite value. Without the sun, there would be neither ecology nor economy on Earth.

Another problem is – valuable to whom? We commonly slant investment decisions in favour of central enterprises delivering directly to national accounts, and showing clearly in GNP statistics. As a corollary, we often undervalue the resources used by people – especially poor people – outside the formal economy. The multi-product harvest of a tropical forest may well support local communities, and be essential to their future. But the displacement of such forest dwellers by logging gangs, destroying the long-term biological productivity of an area for the sake of commercial sales that benefit the central exchequer of the country (and help to service its foreign debts) may make apparent sense in a capital city. And those who do the logging are not concerned with the sustainable use of the resources: when they have devastated an area, they move on. Very similarly, in many countries coastal communities have lived sustainably for centuries on the fish and other produce of the local seas. But it may make apparent sense to governments and aid agencies to invest in offshore commercial fishing fleets that catch more, and bring their catches to city markets or for export, even if the local artisanal communities are destroyed (IUCN/UNEP/WWF, 1991).

A third problem is – who can buy what? For example, in most developed countries individuals or groups (like companies) can acquire indefinite rights in land, but in many developing countries all land is vested in the state. From colonial times onwards, and through the reaffirmation of state ownership at the independence of many formerly colonial territories, the process has led to the dispossession of many indigenous and local peoples (often in flagrant disregard of treaty rights and social agreements that were entered into in earlier times). Such action deprives local people of an incentive to conserve and develop their areas and makes them vulnerable to expropriation by wealthy entrepreneurs who can buy concessions from government, or by the enterprises of central government itself. Giving the people who live on the land a stake in the land – or coastal fishing communities a legal stake in the resources they use – is proving the best incentive to sustainable use today, and demands the reversal of many deeply entrenched policies (and the rejection of a good deal of political dogma). In economic terms it may also demand entry of social values and costs into the equation. Dispossession of forest dwellers or coastal communities may seem less attractive economically if the social costs are made explicit and charged to the enterprises that cause the displacement. Such a policy would be no more than a social counterpart to the 'polluter pays principle'.

The challenge of sustainability is one of getting the economic equations right in ecological, economic and social terms. Development has to serve the goals of the society, and the ethical component is important here. Clearly some of the land tenure systems and consequences of current economic process are not ethical.

Development depends on analysing what an area of land or water could produce, both sustainably and through short-term destructive exploitation, looking at the true costs and benefits involved to all sectors of the community, and seeking a rational judgement. In the course of that process some fundamental issues have to be faced. Economists are addressing these kinds of issue, but there are plenty of examples of bad investment, externalizing costs in terms of pollution and social disruption. I give this area an impediment index of 7, and consider it needs to be worked on hard.

The need for better understanding of nature, and wiser use of natural resources

Science has been around a long time. The description of the natural world, and the derivation of the principles that govern the way it works – 'the laws of nature' – have absorbed thousands of specialists for several centuries. We now have more scientists than ever, and more information than we can cope with. It is virtually impossible to keep up with the flood of scientific and technical literature (Tolba et al, 1992).

The problem is, in part, that the information has not been gathered systematically, for a clear purpose. We have not defined what we need information for. We have not set out – until quite recently – to monitor change in the environment in ways that will make action easier. We have very uneven coverage of data, with a lot known about the developed countries (where compendia of national statistics and national state-of-the-environment reports are now the norm), but very inadequate coverage of the developing countries where many problems are most acute.

Another problem lies in the gap between information and understanding. Environmental systems are so large and complex that models that describe their behaviour are a recent development, and still have a long way to go. The global climate models being used by the Intergovernmental Panel on Climate Change (Houghton et al, 1990) employ the world's most powerful computers, but still fall short of being able to predict how greenhouse gas accumulation will lead on to changes in temperature regimes and rainfall patterns at national level. Models to describe the behaviour of ecosystems are even less perfect. Prediction is not a precise skill in environmental science.

Uncertainty remains evident. Almost all the major environmental alarms of recent years have taken both the scientific and lay community by surprise. The impact of the apparently safe 'wonder' pesticide DDT, and its structural relatives, startled everyone (Moriarty, 1975). The metal mercury was considered safe to discharge to the sediments of the sea bed, in small quantities, for it is not very toxic in that form – but nobody had worked out that it would then be transformed by bacteria into methyl mercury, taken up by living organisms like fish, and cause the tragedy of 'Minamata disease' (WHO, 1976). Chlorofluorocarbons were hailed as ideal chemicals for they were invaluable in refrigerators, aerosols, foam-making and fire-fighting and appeared so unreactive that they had no ecological impact at ground level. They diffused up to the stratosphere where, tens of miles above the ground, sunlight broke them into simple molecules – that destroyed the ozone screen (Tolba et al, 1992).

Ozone depletion took us by surprise. True, the process was predicted before it was proved to be happening – but in 1972, at the time of the Stockholm Conference, the finger of suspicion pointed at high-flying aircraft like Concorde and military jets rather than at the decomposition products of CFCs, and it was expected that any impact would show as a worldwide depletion of a few per cent (Holdgate et al, 1982). The localized but intense 'ozone hole' over Antarctica in the southern springtime, with near-total loss of ozone at certain altitudes, was not expected. Its discovery through the long-term routine observations of the British Antarctic Survey gained added piquancy when it became clear that it had also been observed by satellite-borne instruments, but that the observations had been rejected by the computer as they diverged so much from the norm that they 'had to be' error. Similarly, although climate change due to human augmentation of the greenhouse gases in the atmosphere was predicted by the Swedish scientist Svante Arrhenius nearly a century ago, it has become a matter of serious concern only in the past twenty years.

And so on. Uncertainty also affects the ecological world. We still remain uncertain as to the number of living species in the world, and the science of taxonomy – of classifying and naming new species – is so unfashionable that it would be totally impossible to deal with even a tithe of the millions of species we calculate remain unknown to science. We remain uncertain about the relationships between the age and history of a habitat and its biological diversity. We are far from agreed about the causes of extinctions. The rates of extinction going on around us are, as Chapter 2 showed, being calculated by extrapolation rather than observed. The relationship between the diversity of an ecological system and its functional integrity and resilience in the face of stress is another 'grey area'. 'Carrying capacity' is a self-evident concept, but not something that can easily be calculated for a defined area, under defined patterns of use.

Such uncertainties have two implications. First, it is very difficult to predict what the impact of a particular pattern of human action and resource use will be. Sustainable development cannot, therefore, be designed by science like a five-year plan. We have to work by best estimate, and monitor nature's response to our actions as we go along. We need to leave room for error and adjustment. Safety margins are crucial.

However, the solutions are, in essence, straightforward. We need to see scientific study of environmental problems as one input to the action process. We do need to put more effort into the development of models of environmental systems, and to monitor those variables that are most likely to show whether the real world is working as the models indicate. Above all, we need to recognize that action for the environment has to be a continually adaptive process. Action for sustainable development is, in essence, a hypothesis: we do this because we think it will achieve a better pattern of resource use. We will make mistakes in our use of natural resources. We will have to learn by progressive approximation.

Inadequate science still casts a shadow, but is not a severe obstacle to progress. In many areas, we know enough to get on with action for development that will be more sustainable than today's model. I give ignorance an impediment rating of 4.

There are many illustrations of failure to use nature sustainably, and of destruction of resources for short-term gain. Most fish stocks have been 'mined' by competitive over-cropping to well below the optimum size so that yields are less than they could be (Holdgate, 1994a; James, 1994). Catches in all 17 of the world's main fishing areas have either reached or exceeded their natural limits. In nine they are in serious decline. Multi-species cropping of tropical forests for a wide range of products ranging from meat and medicines through fibre, latex and timber to musical instruments and ornament has been replaced by one-off logging even though there are economic calculations which suggest that the latter yields, once only, little more money than sustainable management of the intact forest can derive every year for an indefinite future. Cattle are displacing wild animals on African rangelands that are more productive, biologically and economically, and cost far less to maintain, if the wildlife is cropped instead. Agricultural subsidies are distorting the land-use patterns of much of western Europe. And so on.

Sometimes these problems arise from genuine ignorance. Sometimes they reflect distortions in economic valuation, considered earlier in this chapter. Sometimes they result from the export of ideas and approaches to areas to which they are ill-suited. For example, forestry practices in many of the developing world countries that were once colonies were based on the export of European ideas, dominated by German and British practices (Holdgate, 1993; Cassells, 1994). In those countries, as in others in Europe, the original natural forest was altered centuries ago. Oliver Rackham (1986) has suggested that the initial southern English 'wildwood' was dominated by lime, hazel and oak – but that it was selectively altered by people to a forest with oak as the dominant canopy tree and hazel as an underscrub. About half the wild forest had been cleared for agriculture by Roman times, 2000 years ago, and in the early mediaeval period the remaining woods were intensively used to yield timber (mainly oak) and wattle and firewood (mainly from coppiced hazel), with nuts and acorns as valuable extra products that fed people and pigs respectively. The forestry schools of the 19th Century, in contrast, looked on forests essentially as timber production systems. This attitude was exported to the developing world, regardless of the immense diversity of products people there had been used to take from their forests.

Agricultural assumptions were also exported. Where land could be cultivated in the European mode, it was. In Australia, large areas of fragile soil in a semi-arid climate were cropped for cereals or grazed by imported livestock with little understanding of the sensitivities of the environment. In South America and Africa, ranching of cattle and the growing of northern crops followed European colonization. Tea in Kenya, coffee in South America, bananas in Central America and the Caribbean, maize in Africa – all are the consequence of crop-plant transfers to areas that originally depended on other staples (Crosby, 1986).

In all cases, the need is to learn the central lesson: that the prescription for the use of a natural resource has to start with a study of the resource itself, and of ways in which it has been used – sustainably or otherwise – by those people who have depended on it for centuries. Their approach may provide the insights needed for sustainability. Changes in resource use – and the importation of alien systems – should be undertaken with the greatest caution, and monitored and adapted as we go along. Chapter 8 expands on these matters.

We know and understand much more about all this that we did, but we have a long way to go. I give this area an impediment index of 5, and consider that the shadow is lifting slowly.

Better governance, avoiding sectoralization and over-centralization

Sectoralization in government has been a universal Aunt Sally in recent years. It is argued that having the business of the state parcelled out among departments of this and that – finance, industry, agriculture, transport, defence, tourism, the arts, science, and so on and so forth – is inefficient. It makes public administrators narrow, for virtually their whole career may be spent in one department. It breeds rivalry and commitment to a narrower good than that of the community as a whole. The criticism has some truth. There does tend to be a departmental culture. Doing down other departments, especially when it comes to wringing money out of the finance ministry has become a special skill, almost elevated to an art form.

The environment does not fit easily in a sectoral system, for it quite obviously deals with joint resources – the 'natural capital' of the nation. The environment is influenced by the actions of all the sectoral departments. Since many are custodians of (and advocates for) forms of development that squeeze the natural world in favour of the built environment, tensions between a department of the environment and other sectoral departments are inevitable.

It is in the nature of things that environment departments can easily find themselves continually on the defensive. For they seek to maintain natural resources – either conserving biological diversity and its habitats, or championing the true value of natural assets like salt marshes and coral reefs, or arguing against the intrusion of transport corridors or defence installations into national parks, or trying to make industry observe proper standards of pollution control. In many countries the development control process tilts power to the would-be developer, who is free to present a case for building a housing estate or a highway as often as he or she likes, regardless of past rejections. The champions of the environment are continually reactive. It is rare for a country truly to set an area of natural environment 'off limits' to change.

The recognition by governments in Rio de Janeiro that the world's economy depends on the world's ecology offers a new way forward. For human communities are comfortable with development as a concept: it implies human activity for future human benefit, whereas 'environment' and 'conservation' often raise visions of 'hands-off' protectionism in which nature is seen as more important than people. Protectionist conservation is, of course, necessary in some areas – like national parks and centres of biological diversity, or the habitats of rare, endangered and cherished species. But conservation within a framework of sustainable development is easier for most people to accept as a mainstream social activity. And sustainable development is self-evidently cross-sectoral, involving agriculture, forestry, fisheries, nature conservation, land use planning, water resource management, transport, pollution control and so forth.

Although sectoralization has been assailed on many sides in recent years, there are good reasons for it and it will endure. It breaks the business of government – or of learning – down into manageable and relatively homogeneous themes. It makes sense to have special agencies concerned – say – with agriculture or transport or energy. It would be totally impracticable to manage government in an amorphous, multi-disciplinary, mass. Even when regional or local units are the primary subdivisions, they in turn generally bring the familiar sectors in as the next level of subdivision. The issue is, therefore, how environmental care and sustainable development should be treated in an essentially sectoral government structure, and apportioned between central and local authorities (Tolba et al, 1992).

One administrative solution could be to place responsibility for overseeing the care of the environment, and the wise use of its resources, in some cross-cutting department (such as the finance ministry or the office of the prime minister and cabinet). That solution has not been favoured, although it is common for countries to have authoritative commissions or councils on environmental resource policy with direct access to the head of government. What is more normal is the construction of cross-linkages between sectors of government, able to draw together policies for the environment and examine the impact on them of sectoral goals and practices.

Another model is to establish a high-level interdepartmental committee chaired by the head of government, or a very senior minister, and charged with examining the policies and spending plans of all departments of government annually from an environmental standpoint. Another is to establish consultative and coordinating committees, round tables and cross-sectoral agencies. National environment strategies are commonly compiled through such machinery. In the United Kingdom a Panel on Sustainable Development is charged with advising the prime minister on progress in implementing the national sustainable development strategy, and it is flanked by a consultative round tables (a device perfected in Canada) and a special forum for non-governmental bodies. Some policies are also designed to cross sectors – the requirement to apply environmental impact assessment to major developments is one such.

At international level sectoralization has been a persistent problem in the United Nations, whose specialized agencies have focused on special themes such as food and agriculture, health, population, labour, telecommunications, meteorology and, through the linked Bretton Woods organizations, economic affairs. The UN agencies are somewhat broader in scope than many national departments, but they share the feature of strong indigenous cultures and great autonomy. The United Nations Environment Programme was established after the Stockholm Conference to provide a coordinating and catalytic influence, and after the Rio Conference the Commission on Sustainable Development was established as a further bridging and unifying force, whose success has yet to be demonstrated. Meanwhile, what might be termed 'supracentralization' is emerging as a new force. The nation state is, in a sense, being squeezed between the pressures to devolve more power to local level and the emergence of powerful supranational groups like the European Union or the Group of 7 leading economic powers.

The need to treat the environment as a cross-cutting element in national and international governance is now widely appreciated. I give sectoralism an impediment rating of only 4, although, that being said, I am aware that departments of environment still fight continual battles against other departments that champion particular industries and think that they serve them best by allowing them to externalize all the costs they can get away with. But I assign a much higher rating to over-centralization.

Over-centralization is a form of sectoralism. In many countries there is an unending tension and competition for power between central and local governments. In Germany, in the 1960s, central government used the rise of concern for the environment to take powers to coerce the provincial (*Land*) governments. In Australia, where land use management is a state concern, the Commonwealth Government has used its responsibility for international affairs, and therefore for treaties, to impose central thinking on the States and Territories. In many other countries, the tension between central and local authorities has hampered the power of local communities to decide what should be done with their environments and resources.

Devolving power, and re-establishing security, at individual and local community level, is, however, a key to effective action. The environment becomes real only when one lives in, or stands on, it. It is changed – sustainably or not – at local level. Many problems have arisen because people in the richer countries – and rich communities in the poorer countries – have enlarged the circles of their world. In past times, people depended on what they could grow in their own neighbourhood. They hunted, fished, cut fuelwood and timber, gathered nuts and fruits, grew crops and vegetables, gathered medicinal herbs, raised livestock, carded and spun their own wool, cured their own leather and ate such surplus meat and milk as their livestock could provide. Many communities enlarged their local 'carrying capacity' by a bit of trading, and even a bit of raiding, but they were essentially locally dependent. They still are in the vast majority of villages around the world.

Today one of the major differences between the developed and developing worlds is that people in the former no longer have to live within their immediate environmental carrying capacity. They have universalized their foodstuffs – we eat potatoes from South America, bananas from Asia, maize from central America and fruits from all the continents, imported out of season by air. The result is that it matters far less than it did if a town sprawls over the fertile floodplains that used to feed its people, or if air pollution blights the nearby orchards, or if some entrepreneur buys up what used to be a communal resource. This has, in turn, eroded the control local communities have over the resources on which many still depend. It impedes local decisions about how the communities will live. The need to reverse this process comes through *Agenda 21*, and is discussed further in Chapter 9.

The need for decentralized action has only gained general recognition recently. The environmental movement in the period between 1970 and 1980 focused especially on global or national issues. Look back to Chapter 2. Alarm bells rang at Stockholm and Rio over global pollution issues and other problems – pesticide impacts, metal toxicity, ocean dumping, ozone holes, deforestation, desertification, climate change, population growth, unsustainable resource consumption, debt, economic barriers to development, trade distortions and inequity between groups, genders, cultures and generations. Look at the themes of UNEP's annual *State of the Environment Reports*, or the two major volumes on the world environment, for 1972–1982 and 1982–1992 (Holdgate et al, 1982; Tolba et al, 1992). Look at the responses – the Montreal Protocol on eliminating chlorofluorocarbons; the Conventions on Climate Change and Biological Diversity; the Basel Convention on the international movement of toxic wastes; the World Conservation Strategies; *Agenda 21*. They are global. But such general approaches need decentralization to local level if they are to work. How?

The traditional route is via governments (with or without secretariats of international conventions, UN agencies or international NGOs as intermediaries, interpreting the agreements, monitoring progress, and bringing pressure to bear on the laggards). Governments in turn create documents – national strategies for conservation or sustainable development or action plans for implementing commitments on pollution reduction and the avoidance of climate change. They have good powers of convening, and readily create round tables, forums, panels, consultative meetings and the like. The assumption is that if discussed enough among the dominant oligarchies and publicized enough to the community at large, the issue will then take fire among the constituents of the nations and somehow consume the obstacles in its path. 'Light blue touch paper and stand back to safe distance'. Often the result is just a splutter or a fizzle.

There is an immense gap between strategy and action. This book is really yet another attempt at explaining why the rocket remains grounded, fizzling faintly. Chapter 9 in particular looks at the other end of the process – the community – and how it can be fired to action.

What we are learning is that communities often do not move, not through ignorance or lack of will, but through lack of power, resources, and support. To quote a new pun, they are not 'response-able'! Given the ability, many do then get busy. Some get the action wrong. They need to monitor, and adjust, their actions – with outside help where necessary. Some appear perverse, but are following their own wisdom. Whichever the situation, the need for 'subsidiarity' (loathsome word), devolution, decentralization, 'power to the people' or whatever the favoured catch-phrase, is now evident. We need machinery to transfer resources from the central structures to specific local action. I give the barriers in this area an impediment rating of 8, and consider that along with the barriers imposed by cultural arrogance they are the most serious of those that confront us.

Partnerships and alliances, to make action for sustainability possible

The notion that only governments can achieve sustainable development is clearly nonsense. It is also untrue that governments and industry are inimical to sustainability and that only the non-governmental community can be the custodian of sound environmentalism. There is yet another fallacy that the United Nations machinery is all-powerful and all-sufficient. The fact is that sustainable development demands partnerships that involve all sectors of the community, from the individual and the small local action group through industry to local and central government.

What is a partnership? Essentially, a coming together of groups from the various sectors of society, at international, national or local levels, or a mix of all of them, to support one another in the shared goal of sustainable development. How to build them has been much discussed recently. A whole conference in Manchester, England, in September 1993 debated it (DOE, 1994). Some of the conclusions appear in Chapter 9. In essence they say that partnerships must have focus – clear objectives. All participants must be willing to listen to one another and share their perspective of the problems to be addressed. There must be mutual trust. There must be information about what each prospective partner wants to contribute. The partnerships must have transparency. There must be good communication.

Given all these things, the mechanistic details like who will do what, how resources are to be obtained and shared, how the solutions are to be made appropriate to the needs of the community, how work is to be planned and managed, and how capacity is to be built are secondary, albeit crucial.

Unless there are better alliances that bring together all the components of society, sustainable development will not happen. Making these partnerships easier is one objective of good governance. Nationally, this is the best use of the government's power of convening, and of the round tables, commissions, committees, councils and the like that it can so easily create. But such devices only work if the right people come to the table with the right commitment to a common goal, rather than a wish to score debating points or make other groups the scapegoats for failure. Governments have to be committed to making their structures work.

The non-governmental movement and the business sector have an immense amount to contribute. They are repositories of great expertise, resources and commitment. Religious groups, media, the arts, the sciences, education are all important partners. All, however, have to be ready to adapt and some groups – like the environmental NGO movement – have not yet worked out how to change from a mass of often discordant pressure groups to a structure with which other major groups like the United Nations can work. Partnerships demand adaptation, adjustment and compromise.

But there is also need for better partnerships between governments. The 'tragedy of the commons' (Hardin, 1968) has arisen because governments have permitted the resources that lie outside national jurisdiction – especially in the sea – to be exploited as a free-for-all. The destruction of fur-seal and whale stocks that resulted is well documented. Today it is oceanic fish stocks that are in deepest trouble (James, 1994). More and more ships are chasing fewer fish, and trying to expand their share by using destructive mass-catching methods like big drift nets. Governments subsidize this foolishness on a scale that may well exceed the economic value of the catch.

The only solution is to create intergovernmental partnerships that work, where catches are regulated below sustainable yield and where there is an equitable sharing of the resource. So far, fishery agreements have proved no more able than the International Whaling Convention to create such a regime (as Chapter 8 demonstrates). The refusal of several major industrial nations (including the United States and the United Kingdom) to ratify the 1982 UN Convention on the Law of the Sea because they did not want to accept international regulation of deep-sea mining is another failure to establish a partnership where one is clearly right. International conventions in some other areas – like global pollution, Antarctica, and conservation – provide more hopeful signs, but international partnerships clearly have a long way to go before the world's international resources are used sustainably.

Very similarly, wasteful investment in munitions occurs largely because governments feel vulnerable to aggressive neighbours. Although the United Nations' role as a peace-keeper has helped to ease the bitterness of conflict in some 17 local wars, it has become obvious that it cannot stop war between determined adversaries. Finding a way of deterring such waste and tragedy and substituting some kind of binding adjudication, is a priority. It will no doubt be debated in connection with the report of the Commission on Global Governance (1995).

At the moment many artificial barriers block partnership. They include suspicion, competitive manoeuvring between groups within society, bad communications, and a lack of essential finance. Internationally, the machinery to link governments and non-governmental sectors is defective. In the United Nations, the Secretary General himself has emphasized that there must be partnerships with the scientific, educational, business and environmental non-governmental sectors if the work of world governments is to be enhanced. The dialogue is beginning, but has a long way to go. I give this whole area an impediment index rating of 7.

Conclusion: the steps to action

Our task is to plot the steps from knowing to doing. We can only operate within a political context. The theories and insights of science, the need to re-estimate our values and re-design our economics, the essential improvements in information and education systems, and the removal of barriers in the machinery of governance have to be addressed in the real world of humanity and human society.

We must be progressive – in the sense of taking one realistic step at a time. We cannot expect instant, total, universal solutions. We need to ensure that action involves the people on the ground, empowers them, informs them, and is guided by their perceptions, traditions and goals.

Universal success is unlikely, and the best probability is that we shall edge forward in some areas and slip back in others. One reason why we may appear not to be making progress is that we focus our attention on the global dimension, whereas all logic indicates that success has to be looked for first on the smaller scale, just as global problems are the aggregate of a multitude of local ones. It may even be that sustainable development will emerge as a patchwork, a slow transformation, enhancing human life and environmental quality in some places just as others visibly deteriorate.

But the barriers listed here have to be addressed. What that means is the subject of the following chapters.

C H A P T E R 5

DEVELOPING NEW VALUES

The ethic of care for the environment

People do what they believe is right, advantageous, necessary or unavoidable. As Chapter 4 noted, we are all guided by a vision, and one problem of today's world is that the visions are often blurred, while expediency has become stronger than principle in many societies. As we seek practical action, we have to look again at the principles that should guide it.

The heart of the message of *Caring for the Earth* is that development has to be people-centred and conservation-based. Conservation is a social policy with care for nature, and the sustainable use of natural resources as its objective. We need development that provides a real improvement in the quality of human life and at the same time conserves the vitality and diversity of the Earth. We shall only get it – we shall only get the kind of community action we need, and the kind of strategies we need – if individuals are convinced and move forward together.

For this very reason *Caring for the Earth* begins with the ethical principles for a sustainable society. To quote some key sentences:

Living sustainably depends on accepting a duty to seek harmony with other people and with nature. The guiding rules are that people must share with each other and care for the Earth. Humanity must take no more from nature than nature can replenish. This in turn means adopting life-styles and development paths that respect and work within nature's limits.

One founding principle provides the base for all the others. It is:

<u>Respect and Care for the Community of Life</u>

This principle reflects the duty of care for other people and other forms of life, now and in the future. It means that development should not be at the expense of other groups or later generations. We should aim to share fairly the benefits and costs of resource use and environmental conservation among different communities and interest groups, among people who are poor and those who are affluent, and between our generation and those who will come after us.

All life on earth is part of one great interdependent system, which influences and depends on the non-living components of the planet – rocks, soils, waters and air. Disturbing one part of this biosphere can affect the whole. Just as human societies are interdependent and future generations are affected by our present actions, so the world of nature is increasingly dominated by our behaviour. It is a matter of ethics as well as practicality to manage development so that it does not threaten the survival of other species or eliminate their habitats. While our survival depends on the use of other species, we need not, and should not, use them cruelly or wastefully.

The question is how we can change attitudes so that this principle is accepted at all levels of society, and is translated into personal, social and national policy.

The environmental ethic is founded on a belief in people as a creative force, and in the value of every human individual and each human society.

An ethic is important because what people do depends on what they believe. Widely shared beliefs are often more powerful than government edicts. The transition to sustainable societies will demand changes in how people perceive each other, other life and the Earth; how they evaluate their needs and priorities; and how they behave.

We need to re-state and win support for the ethic of living sustainably because:

■ it is morally right;

■ without it the human future is in jeopardy; poverty, strife and tragedy will increase;

■ individual actions are, perhaps for the first time, combining to have global effects.....;

■ no major society yet lives according to a value system that cares properly for the future of human communities and other life on earth.

Developing this theme, *Caring for the Earth* emphasizes the need for support from the religious community, because they have spoken for centuries about the individual's duty of care for fellow humans, and of reverence for divine creation. It equally emphasizes the need for support from secular groups concerned with the principles that should govern relationships among people, and with nature. It points out that an ethic defines both rights and responsibilities. And it calls for a series of actions, first to develop the world ethic for living sustainably, second to promote it at national level, third to implement it through action in all sectors of society and finally to establish a world organization to monitor implementation of the world ethic and to prevent and combat serious breaches in its observation.

Chapters 3 and 4 have criticized the slow pace of action. But a wide-ranging discussion continues. The needs were debated at the IUCN General Assembly in Buenos Aires.

Developing the ethic

Environmental ethics is a relatively new subject despite having its origins in classical Greek thought, and no doubt thinking of similar antiquity in other cultures. In recent attempts to address the fundamental basis for social action, the ethical approach has begun with an analysis of the factors that produce attitudes – and ethics has been treated, according to Professor RJ (Sam) Berry (1994), 'not as a branch of academic philosophy but in the fundamental sense of expression of moral understanding, usually in the form of guidelines or rules of conduct, involving evaluations of value or worth.'

Professor Ron Engel, Chair of the IUCN Working Group on Ethics, leading the discussion in Buenos Aires, stressed the need to find a middle way between a universalism which is culturally imperialistic and a relativism which denies any universally shared values and principles. He commented (Engel, 1994) that:

> Over the course of the past several decades there have been many calls for a world ethic that will bring into one common discourse and practice our duties to one another and to the earth, Some call it a 'global ethic', others an 'earth ethic', others an 'ethic for survival', others an 'ethic of living together worldwide', and others an 'ethic of global solidarity'.

Ethics is not something imposed by one group, class or profession on others.

> In fact, it is precisely the opposite. It is the one activity that most self-evidently makes us equals. Most simply put, ethics is the ability to distinguish good and evil, right and wrong, in our relationships to one another, and in our relationships to all of life. Thus we are all ethicists...
>
> But ethics is not only our inherent birthright: it is also embedded in culture; indeed it is primarily by means of culture that moral values are transmitted, criticized and transformed. Ethics are taught, thought about, practised, reformed by means of religions, by means of national and local traditions, by means of family life and educational institutions, by means of art, ritual and sacred places, by means of law, philosophy, politics and also, as many would hold, by the sciences.

Chatsumarn Kabilsingh of Thammasat University, Thailand, discussed the elements of a sustainable world ethic from a Buddhist perspective (Kabilsingh, 1994). Recognizing the deterioration in the world environment, he had a simple and clear diagnosis:

> Governments at national and international levels are trying very hard to cope with all these impossible crises. More often, they try to make some sincere amendment at the bottom line, and not at the root cause of it. Surprisingly enough, the cause of all these troubles are here within our hearts, and not to be sought outside.

> Let us try to understand the basic and simple truth of man (and woman). We consist mainly of two parts – mind (or spirit) and body. It is an utter necessity that mind must be the master to control and order the physical body. The crucial point is – one must have a trained and righteous mind so that the person can direct the body in the right direction. This is the basis for global ethics.

> People with righteous minds must be peaceful within themselves as individuals and they must be peaceful with the world outside. But how can they remain peaceful when the world is exploited to the point of threatening humanity's own survival?

Buddhists (like followers of many other faiths) emphasize that humanity is part of nature, and when nature is exploited or harmed, so are people. We do not stand apart or above, and attempts to conquer nature are vain. Buddhists do not believe that the world is a creation from the mind of God, but the consequence of certain fundamental laws, in whose unfolding human beings originated as divine, spiritual entities that came down to the world, were attracted by it, and became a part of it. As such, their conduct can significantly affect the courses of nature. When people are righteous, nature itself runs aright: when people are greedy and destructive, whether through ignorance or deliberate choice, things go wrong.

This contrasts, of course, with the Christian, Judaic and Islamic view that the world of nature and all living things, including humanity, are created beings: the works of God. Clever Tabaziba (1994) of Zambia set out this perspective in Buenos Aires when he said:

> The divine presence of the spirit in creation binds us as human beings together with all created life. We are accountable before God in and to the community of life, an accountability which has been imaged in various ways (as servants, stewards and trustees, as tillers and keepers, as carers for creation, as nurturers, as co-workers). This calls for attitudes of compassion and humility, respect and reverence. Creation protests its treatment by human beings. It groans and travails in all its parts. Ecological equilibrium has been severely broken through misinterpretation of our faith.

The need for a spiritual rebirth has been emphasized by writers and thinkers outside orthodox religion, including Dag Hammarskjold and André Malraux. Looking through the statements of essential belief in 14 different religions, summarized by their adherents in the *Source Book for the*

Community of Religions published in 1993 (Beversluis, 1993), what stands out is that in all there is an awareness of a spiritual being who stands above and beyond the world (and is usually seen as its creator), an affirmation of the spiritual nature of people and of their importance to the creative being, and a strong emphasis on our responsibility to care for one another and for the world. In contrast to modern secular statements which emphasize human 'rights', religions emphasize duties – to worship, to help others, to be of service to all living beings, to pursue peace. Most recognize the need for change in a world where self-seeking has become dominant, but many also emphasize that change is easy – if it is led by the spirit. This same conclusion is evident in the essays on ethics and *Agenda 21* compiled by the UN Environment Programme (Brown and Quiblier, 1994).

All concur in the belief that there is integrity, unity, in the creation and that the establishment of justice, peace, and harmony between humanity and the rest of creation is an essential goal for the world. As Pope John Paul II (1994) has put it 'there is only one community, and it consists of all peoples. . .Men turn to various religions to solve mysteries of the human condition which today as in earlier times burden people's hearts.' This leads to the practical conclusion that any environmental ethic must tackle the linked themes of unity and diversity. We are global citizens. We inhabit a shared Earth, and an increasingly interdependent world civilization, and if it is to survive that civilization must be guided by shared values. Moreover, there are no global values that are not local values: the foundation for global agreements and the basis for their implementation lie alike in attitudes and ethical approaches in many places and cultures. Each person's ethic will be guided by each person's deeper beliefs.

The environmental ethic we need is universal but diverse. It should draw on various faiths, principles and forms of expression in a mutually creative way. It isn't that 'anything goes' – but that the diverse inputs should come together to build a whole that is greater and richer than the sum of the parts. Translated to the secular world, it should lead to equity in law. This was emphasised by Lothar Gundling of the IUCN Environmental Law Centre in Bonn, who commented (1994) that: 'equity is a basic principle of any normative order. As such, equity is not a new subject in law. It is often linked to the common law legal system where it exists to supplement established common law rights and duties. . .In essence the idea of equity is universal.'

Summing up the discussions in Buenos Aires, Nigel Dower and Richard Tarasofsky (1994) concluded that:

a world ethic may mean one or more of the following three things:

a) an ethic whose **content** is global: that is, one that incorporates specific principles, values and rules that are to be accepted by and applicable to people generally throughout the world;

b) an ethic that specifies the **scope or domain** of obligation and responsibility as worldwide: that is, a person accepting it accepts some responsibility to promote or protect what is of value anywhere in the world, or takes the state of the world as a whole as an object of practical concern;

c) an ethic which is fairly generally, if not universally, **accepted** by people throughout the world.

Dower and Tarasofsky emphasized that:

it is important to link global obligation with global responsibility. Whatever may have been the case in the past, the idea of responsibility needs now to be closely linked to patterns of causality flowing from our acts, and must therefore take into account the effects of our actions, individually and collectively, outside our country, outside human domain, and beyond the present time.

Other key conclusions were:

- the search for a world ethic will fail if the test is universal acceptance: even general acceptance is unlikely at present – 'What one can do is try to build a world ethic on the basis of consensus', recognizing that there is a long way to go;
- the acceptance of a world ethic will not eliminate conflicts in many particular situations. Even where people accept the same guiding principles, there will be debate over the reliability and meaning of stated facts, and over the probability of different outcomes;
- ethical obligation depends on a sense of contract: a sense of obligation by the human individual to others and to the natural world;
- it is important to develop and publicize a clear statement of principles or premises upon which global and national action is to be based;
- these principles must represent a convergence of ideas involving the whole nature, properties and management of the Earth;
- the principles must describe responsibilities rather than define rights.

Policy based on, and expressing, the ethic needs to express a global sense of obligation and responsibility, a commitment to care for the Earth, and a strong linked commitment to social justice both between groups of people alive today and between generations.

From ethics to action: the building of a sustainable society

Clever Tabaziba (1994) spoke of two major problems confronting humanity – that of social justice and of environment. But he emphasized that:

pursuing justice requires us to learn new ways of paying attention to all creation (of the land, water, air, all people, plant life and other living creatures). Any world ethic should integrate our interdependent ecological, social, economic, political and spiritual needs. We must say as forcefully as we can that social justice for all people, and eco-justice for all creation must go together.

This echoes the Code of Environmental Practice drawn up after the conference on environmental ethics convened in Brussels in 1989 under the auspices of the Economic Summit (G7). The Code (Berry, 1994):

> was based on a deceptively simple statement: *an environmental ethic involves stewardship of the living and non-living systems of the earth in order to maintain their sustainability for present and future, allowing development with forbearance and fairness.* Health and quality of life are ultimately dependent on this.

We need to listen to various traditions and streams of thought. Whatever our personal belief systems, we must listen with respect to those of others and 'reject nothing that is true and holy' in their religions (Pope John Paul II, 1994). Women's experience is indispensable. The poor 'teach all of us things we must know for an adequate theology of creation' (Tabaziba, 1994).

Precious insights can be learned from dialogue between different faiths and cultures, and from the heritage of indigenous peoples and non-western cultures, 'especially those who have retained their (sense of the) spirituality of the land and the sacredness of all life'. Scientists are keepers of the most powerful tools for understanding nature, and have discovered things that deepen our awe and wonder. Those of different abilities have much to teach us.

Tabaziba suggested six ingredients for an ethical and sustainable approach:

1 those with enough material goods beginning to live with less, replacing their 'idolatry of consumerism' with a new care for others;
2 those with economic and political power making decisions based on the needs of all creation, and especially the poor, leading to a fuller life for all;
3 local communities being empowered to resist the many threats to their survival;
4 the integration of the needs of all creation in the workings of governments and international business, so that economic and commercial processes do not spell danger, hunger and environmental degradation for the poor;
5 the development by industrialized countries of new patterns of energy consumption, so slowing the dangerous process of global warming; and
6 the application of the resources of scientific and technological research and economic analysis to serve all creation.

This analysis has much in common with Lester Milbraith's call (1989) for a 'new environmental paradigm' that: places a high value on nature; is suffused with compassion towards other species, other peoples and other generations; is advanced through careful plans and actions to avoid risk; accepts limits to growth; and builds a completely new society, guided by new politics which emphasize consultation, participation, foresight, and planning.

Many obstacles block this path – personal quests for wealth at the expense of others, ideologies and political economic thinking dominated by consumption; the dominance of society by elites with a strong stake in 'business as usual'; the gulf between industrialized and non-industrialized, rich and poor nations; the burden of international debt; the potential mis-use of biotechnologies; and especially the lack of democracy in the management of world resources. Another obstacle has been the lack of consensus on the need for responsible parenthood, and of recognition that the further the world population rises above the present 5.8 billion the more difficult it will be to achieve sustainability.

Tabaziba has proposed nine elements in a strategy for sustainability which would also ensure a just and equitable distribution of resources and the liberation of people from all forms of bondage. They are:

1   local self-empowerment;
2   reform of the international economic order;
3   new economic thinking;
4   education and the building of a new conscience and spirituality, recognizing the unity of all creation;
5   clearer assessment of needs, as a first step toward equity and sustainability;
6   debt forgiveness;
7   more involvement of non-governmental organizations in international and national action;
8   agrarian policy that ensures food security, food distribution and ecological sustainability; and
9   a switch from militarism towards security, including environmental security and peacekeeping.

This vision of the agenda for change parallels an analysis by the late Josef Vavrousek, former Minister of Environment for Czechoslovakia, of the values inherent in Euro-American culture, imposed by colonialism on a far wider range of cultures, and still dominating global economic and trading processes. He contrasted the reality of the present situation with the approach that was needed for sustainability (Vavrousek, 1994).

In 'western' cultures today, he argued, people have a predatory, exploitative, relationship to nature, treating it as a limitless resource. The relationship between the individual and society involves, on the one hand, an emphasis on individualism and competitiveness, manifest in extreme market systems which have encouraged explosive economic growth but undermined the sense of personal responsibility for others and for the common good. The alternative pattern, manifest in some systems of 'real socialism', in theory subordinates the interests of any individual to the collective whole, but in practice has concentrated power in small groups and undermined individual commitment and power to participate in decisions. This is what Milbraith (1989) called the 'dominator society'.

The concept of continuous economic growth has, Vavrousek went on, become an obsession, and growth in GDP and in personal wealth are taken as the measure of success and of development. Consumer lifestyles, where the main goal is achieving higher and higher comfort and greater satisfaction of material needs have become dominant. Success is equated with wealth and luxury consumption. There is a one-sided emphasis on human rights and freedoms, and an erosion of recognition of personal responsibilities. (This is expressed even in the environmental field with insistence that everyone has a 'right' to an environment of high quality – something which can only be won by human restraint, understanding of nature and responsible cooperation). Arrogant over-confidence in the extent of our knowledge and capacity to 'conquer' nature and foresee future situations, leads to over-reliance on technological developments and solutions.The human instinct of self-preservation has weakened, and no longer alerts us to actions which threaten our futures through allowing environmental or social deterioration.

Short-term goals are preferred to the long-term, and future generations are threatened through the over-exploitation of natural resources and the dissemination of pollution. There is little respect for other opinions and cultures, racial intolerance, and a reliance on force and violence to resolve conflicts. The assumed superiority of the Euro-American culture makes its members ignore or underestimate the values and knowledge of other societies. People have resigned responsibility for decision-making in the community to others, allowed political and economic power to be monopolized by small groups, accepted foreign ideas uncritically, and so weakened the capacity of their communities to decide their collective futures. The obstacles that this creates were touched on in Chapter 4.

Vavrousek's solution had echoes of Milbraith's 'new environmental paradigm'. He argued that the need is to rebuild a community aware of nature in all its forms, with respect for life, and using natural resources within the limits of sustainability. Such a society must balance its treatment of individuals and the collective community, emphasizing the value of every person but also the place of everyone within the human family. Emphasis should be placed on love, solidarity and altruism, and competition should be constrained and supplemented by cooperation.

The development goals of such a society must centre on improvement in the quality of life and human relations, and on the development of human creativity, expressed in culture, science, spiritual and intellectual life and the cultivation and use of people's abilities. Quality of life must be emphasized, and modesty and a denial of superficial things cultivated.

Guiding principles would include the establishment of a balance between rights and freedoms on the one hand and responsibilities to other people (in this and future generations) and to the rest of nature on the other. The precautionary principle would be adopted, the need to allow for uncertainty recognized, and more support given to the development of new systems of thinking that link the natural sciences and the arts, and to research. Awareness would be built, especially through education of the widest character, of the human activities that pose a threat to personal or social survival, together with an understanding of the actions to take. The need for responsible parenthood and voluntary birth control would be emphasized.

Internationally, the sustainable society would develop mutual tolerance and attempt to learn from the experience, knowledge and wisdom of other cultures. It would also develop political, economic and other global mechanisms which enable different peoples to cooperate, preserving their uniqueness and autonomy and allowing them to enrich global society. Participative democracy which supports the creative role of all citizens would be built, and would ensure decentralization of powers while maintaining effective coordination and feedback mechanisms.

Josef Vavrousek emphasised that the alternative, sustainable society so described does not demand new values. The approach has its roots in the Greek-Roman-Judaic-Christian foundations of European civilizations (and, of course, counterparts in many others). The need is for rediscovery and incorporation of such values as effective guides to the lives of individuals and communities. There are flavours here of 'deep ecology', codified especially by Arne Naess (1973; 1986). This holds that human and non-human life alike have inherent value, that the richness and diversity of life forms are valuable in themselves as well as contributing to the flourishing of human life, and that humans have no right to reduce living diversity except to satisfy vital needs. In consequence, a decrease in human populations is needed in order to guarantee alike the flourishing of human life and of human cultures. Present human interference with the natural world is considered excessive and must decrease. Policies must therefore be changed. A new ideology must be based on life quality rather than material standard of living and those who accept these beliefs have an obligation to work to change society in the required direction.

The challenge is two-pronged. First, these values need to be developed into a coherent, practical, programme of action that can really be implemented within, and progressively transform, today's societies. Second, we need programmes to make people aware of both the need for, and practicality of, new policies for sustainability: the need for a process of social learning.

The roots of the problem: the natural world and the socio-economic box

One of our major problems is that our value judgements, our dominant social assumptions, and our governance systems all distort the relationship between the natural and the man-made. We favour the replacement of traditional ways of using nature by built, engineered, and human-dominated systems.

This happens because (as noted in Chapter 4) we live in a socio-economic box. We have wrapped the built world around us, as a defence against the wilder hazards of nature. As societies, especially in the developed countries, have grown further and further away from the natural world, and larger and larger in proportion to it, so certain myths about our relationship with that wider world have become current. Many people still behave as if they could make the environment their own possession, and could conquer nature. They seem to assume that nature will sustain them whatever they do.

All these are fallacies. We never 'possess' nature, even when we fence bits of it off and give ourselves legal documents constituting ourselves owners. All that we do is establish personal rights against other people within our own community – rights to have exclusive use of an area of land or water, rights to plant and harvest crops or trees, to hunt, or to take pleasure in contemplation. The fertility of the soil is maintained, still, by the myriad organisms that live there, and the productivity of the plants is governed by sunlight, water, and atmosphere – parameters we can alter, but do not create.

We cannot conquer nature, for nature is not an adversary but our own life-support system. We climb mountains, but the 'conquest' is over ourselves: the mountain remains unchanged when we have gone away, and frequent tragedies remind us of our slight powers compared with those of storm, precipice and ocean swell.

And nature will not sustain us whatever we do. Pollution, degradation, ozone holes and erosion demonstrate that human mis-use can reduce carrying capacity, and is doing so just when we need the natural life-support system more than ever. We can alter carrying capacity, but substituting built environment-protection systems for natural ones is generally more costly in terms of money and effort. All common sense dictates, therefore, that we study and adapt to make the socio-economic box compatible with the wider biosphere. This is an essential task for science, which will need to improve the accuracy of its analysis and help societies to balance their choice of risk and investment in an uncertain world (Brown and Quiblier, 1994)

There are two particular ways in which we need to address this relationship. We need to review our personal ethic of care for the environment, and the way we then take decisions about how we use it and share its resources with others – now, and in future generations. And – as stated in Chapter 4 – we need to see that our economic models and processes of development are realistic, and compatible with our ethics and nature's limits. We need to see that economic values are subordinated to ethical and cultural ones, rather than the other way about.

Moving towards change: introducing new values

Such dramatic changes cannot happen all at once. They have to be incremental. The essential levers moving change forward have to include education and public information, the empowerment of people and communities to follow their beliefs and goals, the adoption of clear policies for sustainable development and a clear declaration of global objectives, backed by a global alliance to achieve them.

There are already signs of change in how people approach their environment, although the overall movement for social reform is weak and fragmented. One recent manifestation of personal environmental decision-taking, in developed countries, has been the rise of 'green consumerism' (Tolba et al, 1992). This has taken several forms, including increasing concern with local schemes to improve the environment, a demand for better facilities, especially for the recycling of wastes, a demand for products that are 'environment-friendly' and insistence that the true social costs of producing a product are made clear so that consumers have an informed choice.

The rise in green consumerism has been dramatic. A 1990 survey in the USA revealed that 83 per cent of people returned cans or bottles to a store or recycling centre, while 84 per cent shopped for environmentally safe products, 64 per cent saved newspapers for recycling, 77 per cent bought products made from recycled materials, 54 per cent tried to avoid the products of companies with poor environmental records and 48 per cent gave money to environmental groups.

A number of conferences and publications have reinforced this movement. The Asia-Pacific Consumer Conference in Omiya in 1989 revealed that people not only look for price, quality, durability, performance and after-sales service, but also asked three environmental questions (Tolba et al, 1992):

■ Is the product ethical (ie does the producer maintain high environmental standards regardless of lax laws or social and environmental regulations in some countries where it operates, and also avoid any taint of malpractices like bribery and corruption)?
■ Is the product ecologically sound (ie does the production process avoid harmful impact and damaging wastes, and is the product or service itself environmentally benign)?
■ Is the production process equitable (ie does the producer take account of the traditions and welfare of local communities and vulnerable sectors of society, and where they are involved in production, make sure that they get a fair return for their produce and labours)?

New guidelines for environmentally benign products are now being developed. These specify that the product or the process by which it is made must not endanger the environment or human safety, must not cause environmental degradation when its raw materials are extracted or refined; must not waste energy; must not generate avoidable waste either because of over-packaging or too short a life-span; must not use material derived from threatened species or environments and must not have a damaging impact on other communities, especially in the developing world. The point, of course, is that environmental problems have to be averted, and greater efficiency in the use of materials and energy facilitated, 'upstream' at the design stage. Recycling of materials is economically marginal, and on its own achieves little (North, 1995). It is the total process that counts.

Although still especially prominent in developed countries, actions for environmental protection are gaining ground in many developing countries also. Here, of course, there is a strong tradition of recovery of useful products from waste, because economic circumstances give value to things that are thrown away in more affluent societies. In Metro Manila, the Council of Women Balikatan Movement now involves over 20,000 women in recycling dry household wastes (Camacho, 1994). The basic system is simple, and depends for its success on delivering a benefit for all the participants all along the line. Households are paid a small amount for the wastes they segregate – bottles, papers, cans, plastic and compostable food waste. The children who collect these materials and take them in push-carts to junk shops pay the households and are themselves paid for what they bring to the shops. The shops are paid by factories the organizers have enlisted to receive and recycle the materials. In 1993 the system was working in 21 villages in the San Juan district, with 25,000 households, made up of 250,000 people, separating 50 tonnes of materials daily – 18,000 tonnes a year. The income generated is $15 a year for the poorer, and over $50 for the richer families, while the junk shop owners average about $1000 a month profit and the collectors ('eco-aides') average $100 a month.

People are more likely to decide in favour of sustainable action if they can see it working, are involved and gain benefit. Another example of a positive outlet is the Groundwork initiative in Britain (Davidson et al, 1994). Groundwork Trusts are local charities, and there are now 33 of them, mostly in areas degraded by former industry. They involve local government, local industries, and a wide range of community groups and interests. They get people together to discuss what they want to do to improve their environments, seek funds from government, industry and local communities, and help to design and guide solutions – which take many forms. For example, primary school children have re-designed their playgrounds and incorporated natural areas; derelict industrial sites have been made into country parks; waste spoil heaps have been smoothed and re-vegetated to serve as public open space; factories have re-landscaped their surroundings; and woodlands have been re-created in areas denuded of trees.

Groundwork has stated three golden rules for securing the cooperation of business and industry. First, 'it is vitally important to secure the interest and involvement of business leaders. That doesn't mean passive membership or donations but active involvement from the top, able and willing to deploy their influence.' Second, 'it is absolutely vital to develop and sell services that are relevant to industry.' Third, 'it is essential to provide long-term support to business, to help it solve its problems.'

In many countries and communities around the world, efforts have been made to create 'sustainable citizenship'. The 'Partnerships for Change Conference', held in Manchester, UK, in September 1993 (DOE, 1994) reviewed examples from Seattle in the USA, Curitiba in Brazil, Manila in the Philippines, farming communities in Australia, and towns and villages in Scotland, as well as dozens of other places described in interactive workshops. Many of these are described in fuller detail in Chapter 10.

In Seattle, the key to change was the rejection by groups of citizens of the leadership of their city! To quote their Director of Planning (Lawrence, 1994):

Recycling in 1988 was born out of the frustration of our citizens that the elected leadership was not giving them a chance to make sustainable decisions. The leadership in the city was pressing ahead with a waste incineration programme but the citizens said that in no circumstances were they going to allow the city to burn its garbage. They organized themselves to force the city to take them at their word. We are more than delighted that the result has been better than anyone's expectations.

What happened? The early argument led to four separate efforts that have merged into a common effort to build a preferred future for Seattle. First, recycling of wastes – using economic incentives and public education to persuade people to change their ways. Second, the convening of groups within the community to discuss and agree on their priorities, and develop an environmental action agenda. Third, a comprehensive plan covering land use, transport and urban design. Fourth, a citizen effort (called 'Sustainable Seattle') to agree on indicators of progress, and a monitoring and feedback process.

In Curitiba (Taniguchi, 1994), the key has been the development of a master plan to guide the development of the town and its transport system. A well-planned integrated public transport network has led to saving of about 25 per cent in fuel consumption – and hence in pollution. Curitiba is one of the few places in the world that has turned the familiar cry to get people out of their cars and back onto public transport into reality – and they have done it by making the latter clean, efficient, and comprehensive – and backed by the people. In rural Australia, the Landcare Programme (Campbell, 1994) is based on the premise that 'better systems of land use and management will only be developed if those people who actually live on and manage the land are involved'. The focus has been on stopping land degradation – itself the result of the uncritical introduction of European land management processes. It has been done through getting groups of farmers together with technical experts on soil and water management, to work out new ways of looking after the land that are sustainable – and profitable for the farmers. Two particular findings are noteworthy: that women have been the leaders in pressing the process forward, and that a major obstacle has been institutional cultures within public agencies. National Landcare Facilitator Andrew Campbell vividly described a widespread problem when he said:

> We still have people who think that public consultation means writing a strategy document, sending it out to the people who you think need to read it, giving them six weeks to respond, and calling that public consultation. We are battling against that sort of ignorance, but we have found that it is not always malevolence that causes this sort of mind set. Our natural resource management agencies lack people who are actually trained in conflict resolution, facilitation techniques, participatory processes and what consultation means.

In Scotland (Wright, 1994), they began by defining 'sustainable citizenship' as: 'a way of living in family and community which enhances the quality of life, is sensitive to present and future needs, and empowers the citizen to influence and participate in the economic, political and social changes necessary for sustainable development.' They focused on three roles of the citizen – as a consumer, as a member of the community, and as a co-partner in taking decisions about the future. In each case the emphasis was on information, dialogue, and active cooperation in turning ideas into actions. They developed 'Pledges for the Planet' as quite specific promises by people to change their lifestyles in the areas of energy use, product purchase, recycling, transport (especially use of cars), caring for nature and supporting community action. In the latter area they identified five keys to success:

- action must start where people are, with their priorities (like damp houses, poor energy use and consequent high bills);
- the people must act together;
- they must be confident that they can change things – and a good way to build confidence is to publicize success;
- the efforts of such groups must be recognized by more powerful decision-makers;
- connections must be made between the different kinds of action that build the community's future, and the actions of different communities.

These threads run through several chapters of this book. They demonstrate that many people are keen to take decisions, and inject effort into action for sustainable living, if they are educated, informed and empowered to put their knowledge into action. They also demonstrate that people usually do know what should be done in their local circumstances, and have expertise that is often more relevant than that of the highly qualified specialist from outside the community or country. It all adds up to a challenge to established wisdom and the established professions – in a real sense to turning the decision process around: 'to up-end our thinking, to turn values on their heads, to invent and adopt new methods and to behave differently' (Chambers, 1993).

Guiding principles for sustainable development

Sustainable development – or, better, sustainable living – is about staying within nature's limits. Many principles to guide it were set out in *Caring for the Earth*. They have been analysed further by David Munro (in Trzyna and Osborn, 1995). They include acceptance of a duty of care for other people (including our neighbours in time, in future generations), acceptance of a duty to conserve the living diversity of the Earth, in its own right as well as a resource for the future, measures to maintain harvests within the renewal capacity of the life forms that are used and measures to minimize the depletion of non-renewable resources.

It is clear that the application of these principles involves social, ethical, economic and ecological judgements. Social sustainability demands that a development process either conforms with the established social norms of the communities concerned or does not stretch them beyond the community's tolerance of change. Such social norms are based on religion, tradition and custom: they may or may not be codified in law. They have to do with ethics, value systems, language, education, family relationships (including the roles assigned to men and women, young and old), class systems, castes and hierarchies – and a host else. Such standards and beliefs are, of course, subject to change, but they limit very clearly what kinds of land use and development patterns are likely to be both tolerable and practicable in a community.

The displacement of one group (such as indigenous forest dwellers) because another group (for example, timber concessionaires) decides to impose a development pattern that disregards such norms and sweeps the human rights of the local people away, is not ethically acceptable. Moreover, it is unlikely to lead to sustainability. There are many demonstrations of the superior effectiveness of development processes that are rooted in local tradition and knowledge and move with the grain of culture. Among many traditional societies, high values are attached to the environment, or to features of it such as the land itself, water, fish, or the animals taken for food. In many communities some or all of these resources are regarded as common property, and while traditional user's rights may be respected, the resource itself is considered inalienable. Indigenous peoples have now re-established their rights to much land that was treated as ownerless by European colonialists because it appeared empty and unused (Kemf, 1993).

Sustainability depends on many factors. Many are only partly understood, poorly defined, and hard to predict. But the world is now committed to sustainability, and if it is to happen there has to be a methodology for defining nature's limits and fixing a strategy for living within them. We need a protocol for assessing sustainability. What might it contain? A checklist of key questions has been put together by the Department of Environmental Affairs in South Africa (Trzyna and Osborn, 1995). It has 12 general and 34 specific headings. They span the environmental and the social.

The general question is 'Could the proposed development (or activity, programme, policy or law) have a significant impact on, or be constrained by....?' The environmental objects of the question include river flow, the dispersal or influx of pollutants, the survival of rare or endangered species, the rate of soil erosion and sediment deposition, and the quality of the landscape. In social terms, attention is devoted to the distribution of income, job creation, economic opportunity, the incidence of disease, the adequacy of facilities for primary health care, and the stability of culture or lifestyle. The list has much in common with the 'indicators of sustainability' mentioned (and criticized) in Chapter 7.

The problem today is that 'sustainability' is much more a concept, with a few examples of its translation into success, than a well-established process. As the economist Paul Ekins has observed (Trzyna and Osborn, 1995):

> there is literally no experience of an environmentally sustainable industrial economy anywhere in the world, where such sustainability refers to a non-depleting stock of environmental capital. It is therefore not immediately apparent that, on the basis of past experience only, the term 'sustainable development' is any more than an oxymoron.

Denis Goulet asserted in Buenos Aires (1995) that it is impossible to decide whether development is sustainable until two prior question have been answered – what constitutes genuine wealth and what is authentic development. Wealth should not be equated with the accumulation of material or economic goods. Genuine human riches may lie elsewhere. Wealth lies in the value attached to something, and especially in the power to sustain or enrich life. And spiritual as well as material goods are important: wealth also resides in an internal freedom to use material goods to meet needs and as a springboard for cultivating the higher values that bring deeper satisfaction – virtue, friendship, truth and beauty.

One rediscovery of our age is that a community can be wealthy, in terms of true quality of life, without being affluent. Many island peoples know this, treasuring the freedom that their isolation brings, their right to use the products of their lands and seas, and the enrichment that comes from being part of a tightly-knit community, where everyone relates personally to everyone else. People in the villages of the developing world are never alone. They can be rich spiritually, while lacking consumer goods and material wealth. The message from the indigenous peoples is the same. The emphasis on basing development on the individual, on touching personal values, and on decentralization of power over environmental resources to local level stems from this fundamental point – for it recognizes that communities should set their own development goals on the basis of their own cultural values. It is implicit in the call for a new environmental ethic, and for changes at the individual level, based on true understanding of human need.

One of our problems is that the global measures of sustainable development still equate it too much with open-ended economic growth – creating a 'bigger economic pie' – partly by widening the base of useful production and partly by using technology to increase productivity. Such a programme is essentially an adjustment of the developed world's 'business as usual', allowing markets to operate much as before, within a new framework of constraints set to prevent unacceptable environmental damage or wastage of resources. Of course economic growth is essential, not least in order to fund investment in education, health care, new employment and cleaner and more sustainable industry. But the nature of the growth and the way it is measured are all important. It is essential that the pattern of growth is adjusted to deliver real sustainability. Otherwise it may simply defer the need for more radical change, and make it harder to achieve.

This is likely to involve interference in, or constraints on, the market, for financial power can create serous problems. For local people are vulnerable to rich entrepreneurs, especially if they have central or local government backing. In parts of southern Asia, for example, such people have bought out local community rights in coastal rice paddy, watered by freshwater springs, and created shrimp ponds flooded with salt water. The shrimp industry is lucrative, at least for a period, but it displaces communities from their roots and alters the whole basis of land productivity. Should the market be allowed to operate in such a way? What constraints should be imposed on ethical grounds?

An alternative approach is social, with equity as the key. It is very much the message set out in the declaration of the World Summit for Social Development in 1995 (UN, 1995e). However, because it is socially unpopular to base policy on redistribution, taking from the well-endowed to ease the lot of the poor, in many countries the strategists who plan development for equity also demand high economic growth and pretend that in the best of all possible worlds nobody will be worse off. The issue here is whether the socio-economic and environmental cracks are too deep for such papering. In Germany, the investment needed to bring the eastern provinces up to the standards of the west could not be financed without imposing some costs on the richer sector of the community, and political unpopularity followed. In Sweden, the electorate voted in 1994, for political change that would involve some redistribution of wealth within a community that has placed high value on social equity. But these examples are at present exceptional: not many countries have faced up to the possibility that the transition to sustainability will impose extra costs in the short term, for the benefit of future generations.

Many countries, of course, have more pressing needs. For them, the priority is simply meeting basic human needs – at least alleviating appalling poverty and deprivation – and the best indicator is the extent to which such needs are met. Economic growth and enhanced use of natural resources are likely to be essential elements in such strategies, and the danger the whole time is that short-term imperatives will undermine long-term sustainability. The pressure to over-use environmental resources for short-term benefit is strong, and there are many examples of this destruction in action.

There are many other approaches. We could start with the value systems of a particular society, including its traditional beliefs and customs, and work out how to enhance life quality without jeopardising those values. Some Islamic communities are trying to follow this path, insisting that their laws, economics and social systems enshrine the fundamental tenets of their religion. Clearly there is no universally accepted 'best path', because different people have different needs, values, and environments. What is evident, however, is that a nihilistic approach to development, based on demands for no further human encroachment on the world of nature even if it means accepting poverty or lowered standards of living in regions that have retained high biological diversity is wrong in principle and doomed in practice. The BANANA syndrome (Build Absolutely Nothing Anywhere Near Anybody) is an expression, largely, of selfish exclusion of change by those whose own interests are vested in the status quo. The need is for a new path, not a full stop.

But are there ingredients of satisfactory development, from which universal indicators could be derived? Some people have argued that we should seek a value-neutral definition of development, permitting consensus among people with different values and perspectives. But is this practicable? Denis Goulet (Trzyna and Osborn, 1995) argued in Buenos Aires that any adequate definition of development must have six components:

- economic, dealing with the creation of wealth and improved conditions of material life, equitably distributed;
- social, measured as well-being in health, education, housing, employment and other components of life;
- political, embracing human rights, political freedom, legal enfranchisement of people, and some form of democracy;

- cultural, recognizing that cultures confer identity and self-worth on people;
- ecological soundness, because unless development is ecologically sound it cannot endure; and
- a 'full-life' dimension, which includes beliefs about the ultimate meaning of life and history.

Sustainability must be assured in four domains – economic, political, social and cultural. Long-term economic viability depends on using resources without depleting them irreversibly. Political viability depends on giving all members of a society a stake in its survival. Social and cultural viability demands the protection of the foundations of community life and its values and beliefs. Vavrousek's and Milbraith's views of an ethical new western society accord with this approach.

Clearly, the narrow view of 'sustainable development' as an economic process is invalid. But so is the view that it can be defined solely in ecological (or scientific) terms. Sustainability is not a technical problem to be solved, but a vision of the future focusing our attention on a set of values, and moral and ethical principles to guide our actions. Yet (said Goulet), 'the ecological imperative is clear and cruel: nature must be saved, or we humans will die'. Ecology does impose constraints – outer limits – defining the size and shape of the socio-economic box. And the more that the functions of nature outside the box are eroded by human pressure, the more those social goals will be at risk.

It is also clear that there must be solidarity between groups of people – at least expressed in terms of strong mutual interest in cooperation and in determination to end poverty and hunger. The development process and pathway will not be the same everywhere, but competitive jostling to grab as much as possible of the Earth's wealth must stop. At present, such an approach has dehumanized millions.

In seeking alternatives, Steven Viederman (Trzyna and Osborn, 1995) suggested that we should start with some questions, such as:

- How can we design an economy that honours economic security, democracy and ecological integrity?
- What can be done to help indigenous peoples (and many other groups) to preserve their lives and cultures as well as their habitats?
- Can we develop technology and products with human needs (and environmental tolerances) foremost in our minds?
- What systems of valuation of work and wealth are most compatible with sustainability?
- What makes individual people live in an environmentally sustainable way? Does it depend on confidence that societies are equitable and just?
- How can we attain sustainable agriculture and forestry? What are the best ways of measuring production?
- How can we live in peace and achieve that solidarity and sense of community which is needed if we are to oulaw competitive strife?

There are some social principles which can guide policy:

1   The precautionary principle: avoid actions which clearly could undermine sustainability, or at least weigh them cautiously and thoroughly before proceeding, and monitor what actually happens.
2   The protection principle: make development activities as impact-free as possible. Avoid spreading damage costs around other people's environments by releasing pollution, altering the flow of shared rivers, damaging sea defences and the like.
3   The reversibility principle: avoid irreversible actions – unless there are overwhelming advantages, in the long as well as the short term.
4   The preparedness principle: the unexpected may well happen. All development processes should be adaptive, and able to be adjusted when the original plan proves to be wrong.
5   The partnership principle: there must be active co-operation in science, technology, economics, trade and many other activities if we are to achieve that mosaic of interlocking regional, national and subnational sustainabilities which we need.

There is debate over whether genuinely sustainable development (called, unhappily, by some 'Sustainable Authentic Development' or SAD) is compatible with today's economic and commercial world. The demand for free markets, minimal regulation and worldwide free-trading systems is seen by many as incompatible with the need for a community or nation to defend itself against commercial activities which may harm its environment. However, if we are serious about building all six components – economic, social, political, cultural, ecological and 'full-life' – into development, then world trading and economic systems must be constrained by the need not to undermine the other elements. Free trade and free market economics are social devices and means to an end – which has to be authentic development, evaluated in human and environmental terms. We have to move towards new economic styles. These will involve new models, will include natural capital, in national accounts, and will demand a reform of familiar economic indicators like gross national product (GNP) or gross domestic product (GDP).

The criticisms of the latter have already been noted. The indicators are widely used as measures of the market value of goods and services produced in an economy in a given time. They are, as Fulai Sheng (Trzyna and Osborn, 1995) pointed out in Buenos Aires, supposed to measure true income – the maximum amount that can be consumed without eventual impoverishment. On this basis they should be another measure of sustainability. But they are not good measures of sustainable development because they cannot capture social or ecological aspects – and indeed they may appear environmentally perverse if the expenditure on industrial activity and the expenditure on cleaning up a damaged environment are both regarded as positive contributions to the total level of economic activity. Household medical spending due to exposure to air pollution represents a source of revenue for hospitals, and is entered as income in national accounts. If there is an oil spill, and the government spends money to clean up the coasts, that shows as expenditure on goods and services, but the damage to the marine environment and its income-generating potential is not counted at all. Leisure contributes to quality of life, but reduces GNP, unless it is spent to support the tourist industry. Moreover, the indicators fail to capture the large volume of economic activity that lies outside the formal sector – such as subsistence farming or household work. In Bangladesh, 40 per cent of the population is engaged in these informal sectors: in Papua New Guinea subsistence fishing, which amounts to 13 per cent of GDP, is normally excluded from national accounts.

This kind of distortion explains why it may appear economically sensible to destroy environmental capital, for example by commercial logging of a rain-forest or construction of an offshore fishing fleet which undermines traditional fishery by coastal villages. Clearly the indicators are therefore dangerous. They give an illusory picture of the true wealth of a country, and lead to unsound judgements about public policy. They need reform, if the processes of economic evaluation – which are a fundamental part of the decision process in many countries – are to lead to sound and sustainable development based on the care of the environment, and conducted within nature's limits.

There are ways of altering the system. The cost of defending the 'natural capital' of the environment against damage, and the economic value of depleting that capital (if this is happening) can be calculated, and clearly should be charged against national income, not added to it. Some first – though insufficient – steps have been taken in the direction of environmental and resource accounting by the UN Statistical Division and the UN Development Programme (Abaza et al, 1992). But this does not directly alter the system of national accounts, or prevent the existing indicators being used – with the existing distortions. It provides, instead, a kind of extra, or parallel, assessment.

Something more radical is needed. But the obstacles should not be underestimated. To start with, correction would reduce GNP for many countries – and although the result would be more honest, it might not look good politically. For example, recalculation for Indonesia suggested that growth in GDP in 1971–1984 was actually 4.0 per cent instead of the 7.1 per cent claimed under the traditional system. In Costa Rica, in 1970–1989 the depreciation of national environmental resources exceeded GDP – so that the country actually declined economically in that period. In the Philippines the annual depreciation of forests and dryland farm soils totalled 5.8 per cent of GDP. Significant reductions in calculated national income resulted from application of new valuations in the Netherlands, Papua New Guinea and Mexico (Trzyna and Osborn, 1995).

The wider need is to balance economic, social, political, cultural, ecological and 'full-life' elements in guiding development. It is not proven that it can be done – that we can live within the tolerances of nature – but if we are to do so, it is through the development of social strategies that are environmental-adaptive. As CS Holling (1993) has commented: 'there is an inherent unknowability as well as unpredictability concerning these evolving managed ecosystems, and the societies with which they are linked. . .[so that]. . .uncertainty and surprises become an integral part of an anticipated set of adaptive responses.'

The emphasis on moving with the grain of culture does not mean that we should be locked into traditions. Such a rigid approach would, self-evidently, prevent the adaptability we need. Yesterday's way of life of some indigenous peoples may have been sustainable and adaptive, but it also delivered material poverty and vulnerability to extremes of environmental change. As Hassania Chalbi of Femmes-Environnement-Developpement in Tunisia has emphasized (1994), many cultures depend on the role of women as resource managers, but do not recognize their knowledge, or draw on it in an explicit way when it comes to social decisions. Yet the women in the community (for example in North Africa) often play a central part in the process of domestication of plants and animals, choosing the seeds to be sown and the individuals to be added to the breeding stock. They have a central role in the management of cultivation systems, including delicately balanced ones like those of desert oases and traditional irrigations. They need to be involved as partners in the process of sustainable development, building on and adapting their knowledge.

Mathias Finger of Columbia University, New York, described this social adaptive process as 'learning our way out' (Trzyna and Osborn, 1995) – the same process as the 'social learning' advocated by Milbraith (1989). Finger argues that the problems of unsustainability are aggravated by intellectual inertia – governments, industry, economists, academia, the media and even some Northern environmental NGOs see the solution to the problems of under-development in much of the world simply in terms of new industrialization. While that may indeed be part of the solution, the way ahead must be chosen through a collective effort between all sectors of the community, which begins at the conceptual level and leads on to action (an approach discussed further in later chapters of this book).

The social indicators of sustainability must clearly be developed further. Mathias Finger suggests that these could measure three broad elements: first, the involvement of the various sectors in planning and executing action for sustainability; second, how far the various sectors are collaborating; and third, whether the various sectors are themselves being transformed into sustainable units (Finger, 1995).

Conversely, not only are the various manifestations of environmental degradation negative indicators, but so are social ones such as poverty, inequity, oppression, militarization, violent conflict, individualism and cultural erosion

The role of universal principles: a covenant on conservation and development

The quest for a declaration or set of principles, enshrined in law and adopted at the highest political level, has been a recurrent feature of major conferences on the environment. Such a document has value in setting out the global consensus and allowing those nations that perversely walk the other way to be reminded of their obligations. The Universal Declaration of

Human Rights has served just such a purpose. Such a series of 'Legal Principles for Environmental Protection and Sustainable Development' was annexed to the report of the World Commission on Environment and Development, and has been used as a basic text by groups preparing draft Codes of Environmental Practice with a strong ethical base (Berry, 1994). Such a code is likely to incorporate the following attributes, which are, in a sense, common to good citizens, states and corporations everywhere:

■ *freedom* – to leave the widest range of environmental choices open to both society and future generations;
■ *justice* – for individuals of all nations, recognizing that some carry environmental burdens which may require help from the more privileged;
■ *truthfulness* – in seeking the causes of environmental problems and dealing with them in open and honest debate;
■ *sensitivity* – to the interdependence of ecological systems on which we depend for our survival but manage for our own ends;
■ *awareness* – that quality of life depends on our interactions with our environment and is distinct from, and only partly dependent on, standard of living;
■ *responsibility* – to strengthen good management so that no irreversible damage is done, or unacceptable risks imposed on current or future generations;
■ *integrity and decisiveness* – recognizing the special responsibilities of environmental scientists and decision-makers, the need for education, and the fact that restraint may be needed where knowledge is incomplete, but that action is often essential before scientific certainty is attained.

IUCN has been preparing a draft International Covenant on Environment and Development for many years (Hassan, 1994). Ten fundamental ethical principles underlie this document, which forms a component of the action discussed in Chapter 11.

1 'Environmental conservation and sustainable development are essential for human health and well-being on a planet with finite resources and carrying capacity.' The Covenant, like the Stockholm Declaration or the Rio Declaration, is a human document about human management of the environment as a basis for human survival. It is important that any such prescription recognizes the need to live and work within nature's limits.
2 'Nature as a whole warrants respect; every form of life is unique and is to be safeguarded independently of its worth to humanity.' This echoes language in the World Charter for Nature, endorsed by the General Assembly of the United Nations.
3 'The global environment, both within and beyond the limits of national jurisdictions, is a common concern of humanity, held in trust for future generations by the present generation. All persons have a duty to protect and conserve the environment: each generation has a responsibility to recognize limits to its freedom of action and to act with appropriate restraint, so that future generations inherit a world that meets their needs.'

4 'To achieve sustainable development, environmental protection and management must be an integral part of all development effort.' This echoes language used at the UN Conference on the Human Environment in Stockholm and the UN Conference on Environment and Development in Rio de Janeiro. It leads on to the affirmation that 'States have, in accordance with the Charter of the United Nations and the principles of international law, not only the sovereign right to their own resources but responsibility towards them.' They should protect the environment within their jurisdiction and control; ensure that activities within their jurisdiction or control do not cause damage to the environment of other states, or to areas beyond the limits of national jurisdiction; work with and collaborate in good faith with other states and competent intergovernmental and non-governmental organizations, minimize waste in the use of all natural resources and develop and use environmentally safe technology.

5 'States and people should cooperate in promoting health, social well-being and environmental quality by striving to eradicate poverty.' This demands action to eliminate unsustainable patterns of production and consumption, and also action to help bring human populations into stable balance with the environmental systems on which they depend.

6 'States have a responsibility to anticipate, prevent and minimize significant adverse effects of human activities on the environment: lack of full scientific certainty must not be used as a reason to postpone action to avoid potential harm to the environment.' This is the precautionary principle, routinely endorsed in political statements, but regularly evaded in practice.

7 'States shall take all necessary measures to ensure that the full costs of prevention or compensation for environmental damage, as well as the costs of restoration of the environment, are borne by the person or organization whose activities give rise to such damage or the threat thereof, unless such obligations to bear costs or restore the environment are allocated elsewhere by national or international law. States have the right to be protected against, or compensated for, significant environmental harm caused by activities outside their jurisdiction.' This is the polluter pays principle, expanded to the 'developer pays principle' – something which again needs strengthening in many national and international documents.

8 'States should require environmental impact assessments for all proposed activities likely to have a significant environmental effect and should include the full social and environmental cost of all environmental impacts within the calculation of those effects.' This principle is an explicit linkage between the method of environmental impact assessment and the precautionary principle, as a guide to the process of sustainable development.

9 'States shall establish and maintain a legal, administrative, research and monitoring framework for environmental conservation, giving full and equal consideration to environmental, economic, social and cultural fac-

tors.' This can be done through regular review of policies on the integration of planning and development activities; the development of mechanisms to involve groups within communities, and communities at local and provincial level, in decision-making; and generating means to ensure that the full social and economic costs of using natural resources are made clear and the benefits from such use assigned equitably. Chapter 10 considers the needs for such partnerships, and how they work.

10 'Justice, peace, development and environmental protection and management are interdependent and indivisible, and vital to the integrity of creation. States have a responsibility to work towards an environmentally aware citizenry that has the knowledge, skills and moral values to protect and preserve the environment and to achieve sustainable development.'

There are heartening signs that the world's leaders are moving towards such a position. The United Nations convened a World Summit for Social Development in Copenhagen in March 1995. In his overview report to the first session of its Preparatory Committee the Secretary General stated the underlying issue starkly:

There is a moral crisis at the level of the individual and an ethical crisis at the level of the society when rights are no longer balanced by obligations and guided by responsibilities: when the search for individual satisfaction became an end in itself: and when the search for identity, either at the individual or group level, is pursued at the expense of others (UN, 1994b).

The Declaration from the Summit (UN, 1995e) contained some telling phrases:

We acknowledge that our societies must respond more effectively to the material and spiritual needs of individuals, their families and communities.

We share the conviction that social development and social justice are indispensable for the achievement and maintenance of peace and security within and between our nations.

We are deeply convinced that economic development, social development and environmental protection are interdependent and mutually reinforcing components of sustainable devlopment, which is the framework for our efforts to achieve a higher quality of life for all people. Equitable social development. . .is a necessary foundation for sustainable development. We also recognize that broad-based and sustained economic growth. . .is necessary to sustain social development and social justice.

The Declaration goes on to commit the signatories to the creation of a framework for action which places people at the centre of development, and the economy at the service of human needs. The Programme of Action covers a wide spectrum of social development based on equity, and including the empowerment of people to strengthen their own capacities. The specific commitments will, if implemented, emphasize the enabling role of governments. Chapter 11 considers how these detailed prescriptions may be carried forward through partnerships in the global community.

Beliefs and actions: where are we getting to?

The overwhelming impression is of a very wide range of initiatives and thoughts which are distilling slowly into cohesion but have some way to go. There does appear to be consensus that changes in lifestyle toward a more sustainable and equitable approach are not only technically feasible but ethically right. Indeed, it seems clear that the painful transition to sustainable living will only be accomplished if people believe that it is morally right as well as a practical necessity.

Even so, progress will not come through preaching or through Summit Declarations, however enlightened. *Caring for the Earth* has been criticized in several articles as impossibly utopian. The Social Summit Declaration is likely to receive the same treatment (the Summit itself was widely condemned as a non-event, even by some participants). The criticisms are valid, in that we still have no clear path to follow towards universal (or majority) sustainable living, and until we see communities at large moving down that road, the sustainable future will be a concept rather than a construct.

Debate must go on, and some of the mechanisms are discussed in the remaining chapters of this book. But it does appear that some guiding values are apparent, and that they seek to link what strikes at the mind and heart as ethically sound principles, with the mind's fears of what may happen otherwise, and with our calculations of personal and group advantage. The universal themes are a recognition that long-term sustainability must be an object of policy now, that equity between peoples and nations in their use of, and impact on, the finite resources and vulnerable systems of the planet must be improved, and that personal obligations to other people and to the world of nature need to be codified and communicated.

It is also clear that we need to learn from the hopeful actions that are being taken, so that practical pathways to sustainability are established, in a manner that maintains equity along the road and does not expose those with altruism and the long view to being undermined by those only concerned with profit today. Education and communication are clearly central to this process, and another need is clearly to link them to the deeper analyses of values and the development of the road-map to the sustainable future. For education and communication will only have positive benefit if they are part of this wider process, and help humanity down the road. Ways in which they may contribute are considered in Chapter 6.

EDUCATING AND INFORMING PEOPLE

The need for new understanding

Chapter 2 described the evolution of public concern about the environment. Quite clearly, it has been stimulated in part by direct, personal, observation – people have become alarmed by foam, smell and dead fish in their local river, oiled seabirds on the beach, streams drying up in summer or running red with eroded soil in the winter floods and choking fumes in city streets jam-packed with traffic. But most people, most of the time, are even more influenced by what they learn about events elsewhere. Few people have had the privilege of visiting Antarctica, yet the 'ozone hole' that opens over the heart of the white continent in the southern springtime has been made common knowledge by the world's media. The 'Chernobyl factor' of massive public alarm over an accident leading to environmental contamination is essentially a demonstration of the effectiveness of modern information exchange. And whereas a few decades ago those who read the newspapers only learned of distant horrors weeks after they happened, when the despatches arrived by steamship, now the news is beamed instantly around the globe. We see tragedy unfolding in real time.

This is good, for it brings home to us that we are indeed all citizens of one small planet. It can be bad, however, if it distorts as well as informs. The media are, inevitably, selective – indeed selection to tell an important story, vividly, is an essential skill for any good journalist. But readers need to know how to interpret and react to what they read. This is a particular problem where we are trying to catch the essence of highly complicated environmental systems, and interpret the finding of sophisticated science.

The decisions that people and communities take depend on a wide range of factors including:

- where they are at the start (it is no good preparing the most perfect plan if it cannot start from present reality);
- their values and beliefs;
- the adequacy of the information available;
- their understanding of the choices open to them;
- their power to make the changes they desire;
- the degree to which the community is linked by a common vision and commitment;
- the extent to which other communities will support or obstruct their efforts.

If we are to develop the right pattern of actions, with the best probability of success, we need to help people to understand the world of nature better, and appreciate the impact that millions of tiny, single, individual actions can have upon it. We need to touch people's beliefs and attitudes, and make them want to live sustainably. We need to ensure that they get enough information, and that what they read or hear is reliable. We need to help them to work out what to do. Information, communication and education are the keys to empowering individuals.

'Environmental education' is a broad term, often mis-used. It includes, but is much wider than, teaching children about the world of nature and about people's impacts on the environment. It includes, but is much wider than, college classes and degrees in biology, atmospheric physics, pollution prevention, waste treatment and environmental protection. Such teachings – together with adult classes and vocational courses – constitute 'formal' environmental education. Another whole dimension, 'informal' education, embraces communication and information through newspapers, magazines, broadsheets, newsletters, radio, television, plays and entertainments, and people who tour villages and discuss their environmental needs and problems. A third crucial element is 'training' – perhaps given a better image by the French word 'formation': shaping people's skills so that they can put their desires for a sustainable lifestyle into effect as they cultivate land, manage water, grow crops, care for animals, build settlements, recycle wastes, use energy efficiently and so forth. This chapter is about all of these things.

The role of education and communication

Caring for the Earth emphasizes the need for education and communication at many points. For example, it emphasizes that the world ethic for living sustainably will only be implemented if it is taken up by all sections of the community. In Action 2.3 it calls for:

- parents educating their children to act with respect for other people and other species;
- educators incorporating the world ethic into their teaching;
- children helping their parents to become aware and change their behaviour by explaining at home the new ideas they have learned at school;
- artists in all media using their creative skills to inspire people with a new understanding and respect for nature, and a wish to conserve it;
- scientists improving understanding of ecosystems, their sensitivity to human impact, and their capacity to meet human needs, and at the same time ensuring that findings are communicated accurately and applied responsibly.

In Action 3.4, it demands universal primary education for children, and the reduction of illiteracy. In Actions 4.10 and 4.11 the emphasis is on improving knowledge and understanding of ecosystems, and training people to manage wildlife and natural resources better (needs picked up again in the detailed chapters on the care of sectors of the environment). Action 5.1 demands increased awareness of the need to stabilize resource consumption and human population. Elsewhere there is mention of the need to help people, by information, to become 'green consumers'. Action 6.1 stresses the need for national strategies for sustainability to include action to motivate, educate and equip individuals to lead sustainable lives. The following two actions urge review of the status of environmental education, making it an integral part of formal education at all levels, and the definition of the training needs for a sustainable society and development of plans to meet them. Action 7.2 urges better information to communities so that they can plan the care of their environments. Strengthening the knowledge base, and making information on environmental matters more accessible is seen as an essential component of national frameworks that will integrate development and conservation.

As Marco Encalada of Ecuador (Encalada, 1994) commented to Workshop 7 at the IUCN General Assembly in Buenos Aires, environmental education has become prominent in local, national and international discussions of development and environment, action against poverty, and efforts to achieve peace, democracy, cultural identity and spiritual enhancement. This is because it is accepted that human minds control individual and collective behaviour, and education plays a crucial part in establishing the conditions under which minds evolve and mature. Agenda 21 recognizes this by stating:

> Education, including formal education, public awareness and training should be recognized as a process by which human beings and societies can reach their fullest potential. Education is critical for promoting sustainable development and improving the capacity of the people to address environment and development issues.

All nations are therefore urged 'to achieve environment and development awareness in all sectors of society on a world-wide scale as soon as possible'.

Like *Caring for the Earth, Agenda 21* addresses education and training in a large proportion of its chapters, recognizing that there is scarcely an action for conservation and sustainability which does not require an education and communication component. It urged every country to prepare its own national strategy for environmental education and in Chapter 36 on 'Education, Training and Public Awareness', it presses for:

■ making education on environment and development available to people of all ages;
■ including environment and development concepts in all educational programmes;
■ involving schoolchildren in local and regional studies of environmental health;
■ setting up training programmes to help school and university graduates attain sustainable livelihoods;
■ encouraging all sectors of society to train people in environmental management;
■ providing locally recruited and trained environmental technicians to give communities the services they require;
■ working with the media, entertainment and advertising industries to stimulate public debate on the environment;
■ bringing the understanding and experience of indigenous peoples into education and training programmes.

But in turning concepts into action, three central questions are paramount:

■ How can education and communication be used to change the attitudes and behaviour of people?
■ How can education and communication be focused effectively on sustainability?
■ How can we promote, plan and carry out education more effectively?

Dr Joy Palmer of the University of Durham, UK, who played a leading part in the discussion of these matters at the IUCN General Assembly in Buenos Aires (Palmer, 1994a) and has edited a book (Palmer, 1995) containing most of the papers presented there, has emphasized that since education and communication both deal with 'the transfer or exchange of ideas, information and skills in a two-way process', they inevitably shade into one another:

Environmental education (formal as well as informal) builds the motivation, skills and understanding on which environmental citizenship may be based. . .Environmental communication is aimed at changing practices and behaviour, and inviting participation or action in relation to environmental issues. It has a short-term, action specific goal.

It is aimed at linking specific conservation or environment issues to key actors in the community, because changes in their behaviour will make a real impact on the problem.

Both education and communication have a very different starting point from science and other disciplines, and from research. They begin with the perceptions of their target audiences, and try to improve these perceptions by providing better and more reliable information (much of which comes, of course, from scientific and other research). 'In seeking to change knowledge, attitudes or behaviour, scientific facts and data are in themselves insufficient', states Joy Palmer. They may even be counter-productive. They have to be translated into concepts and messages which make sense to a target audience, and to be relevant to them. 'In many cases, communications experts have proved that knowledge of facts alone is of no consequence when it comes to changing behaviour. Linking information to personal benefit is more important' (Palmer, 1994a).

Action for environmental education and communication has to be integrated into wider policies, and into plans for environmental care and for sustainable resource use. It has to be combined with legal, economic and technical instruments for change. And different kinds of communication and support for education are needed at different stages in the action. To start with, people need to be enthused to join in discussion of the problems and how they may be solved. Then they need to be motivated to join in the action – or at least support it when it is challenged. Programmes of environmental action often go wrong because the vital work of education and communication are left undone.

Any communication strategy must be flexible and adaptive: people learn as they go along, and their new insights must in turn be used to improve policy. Education and communication programmes in fact need a four-phase, cyclical approach leading from research through planning to implementation and on-going evaluation. And educational work must not take place in isolation. It must be tied into the network of community planning and action.

Research itself has to be based on effective communication, involving a two-way exchange of information. All interested people and groups must be involved at every stage of research, planning, implementation and evaluation. People's needs, perceptions and priorities must be understood. Environmental education must be relevant (and be seen to be relevant) to the lives and needs of individuals and communities. So while planning for environmental education needs to have support, and may have to start, at the highest levels in a society it must be guided by feedback from local level, so that its feet remain on the ground.

People need to feel 'ownership' of problems and solutions, and to derive benefits from the new policies they adopt as a result of the programme of education and communication. For information alone does not necessarily lead to changed behaviour: the latter is far more likely if the change will clearly bring personal benefit. This can take many forms, including social acceptance, enjoyment, greater environmental or financial security, and a healthier life for children.

In any programme, a common goal must be established with local residents, the education or communication agency, and conservation groups. The participation of local residents in itself builds long-term sustainability. The closer the links with the community, the more easy it will be to choose and support key actors within it.

Behaviour, social marketing and the environment

What kinds of experience promote environmentally positive behaviour? Joy Palmer (1994a) reviewed a study by Tanner, reported in 1980, and some of her own work published in 1993 which address this question. Tanner analysed 45 replies from people who had chosen to work in conservation and were asked why they had done so. The dominant factor was youthful experience of the outdoors and of wild environments. The conclusion: that children must come to know and love the natural world before they can become concerned with its care.

Dr Palmer looked at a much larger sample of adult environmental educators, in the United Kingdom. One hundred and thirty women and 102 men replied. The study confirmed Tanner's conclusion about the importance of childhood experience of the outdoors. In fact 'outdoors', identified as important by 91 per cent of respondents, embraced three sub-categories: childhood experience, outdoor activities and experience of wilderness or solitude. The second major category of influence was that of education, and here courses taken as an adult had a somewhat greater influence than school courses. The influence of parents and close relatives followed in the order of importance. Contact with environmental organizations, TV and other media, friends, travel abroad, awareness of disasters, and books all had some considerable impact. The conclusion was that giving young people positive experience of outdoor environments is a key to the awakening of care for the Earth. But this must not be abstract: the advantage of outdoor experience is that it identifies people with a particular place or project towards which they can develop a sense of 'ownership' or 'belonging'.

These, of course, are developed country data, and probably (though the report does not say so explicitly) apply largely to town dwellers. In rural areas, and perhaps especially in developing countries, the patterns may develop otherwise. Research into this aspect would clearly be valuable.

The question of how human behaviour is determined, and how it may be influenced, was discussed in some detail by William Smith of the Academy for Educational Development in Washington DC (Smith, 1994). His basic thesis was simple:

> I believe that human behaviour matters to the solution of many problems facing our species today. I believe that human behaviour changes in response to the world. And I believe that it is the obligation of people who care about the environment to use the best knowledge we have to help people adopt more environmentally sound behaviour.

Smith dismissed the antithesis some draw between a 'behaviour change' and a 'participatory' model, arguing that we need, and can have, both. We need the full and conscious participation of the people whose behaviour must change if we are to live sustainably, in a healthy environment, and we need to apply behavioural science effectively if we are to help them change their approach.

The environment presents a special challenge. It involves highly complex inter-relationships. The science of environment is relatively new, and understanding is developing rapidly, but this means that there is less certainty over both problems and solutions. Problems that arise from actions today may not make their full impact felt for decades, so there is a conflict between short- and long-term benefits and costs, and the long-term cost is often disregarded for the sake of short-term gain. Many problems are so vast that they seem remote from people, who come to feel that as individuals they can do very little to help, so that changing their behaviour (and maybe foregoing immediate benefits) makes little sense. And the North–South, rich–poor divide is – divisive:

> In developing countries, policy-makers and the public are offended by Northern insistence that developing people must save the environment at the expense of jobs and rapid industrial development and forego the benefits of consumption practised in the North. The North criticizes the South for irresponsibility, and the South criticizes the North for hypocrisy.

William Smith argued, none the less, that these problems can be overcome. To do so we have to understand what shapes human behaviour. He considers that four factors are of paramount importance:

- *maximized utility* – people want to increase their benefits from any behavioural change;
- *stable preferences* – people have relatively stable values that define what benefits matter to them;
- *optimal accumulation of information* – people spend as little energy as possible on solving a problem;
- *market equilibrium* – people choose among competing options.

In approaching a situation, people are influenced by four social psychological determinants: the perceived benefits from doing something new; the perceived barriers to getting the desired benefit; the social norms that prevail in the community, and by which new behaviour will be judged; and the skills available to allow the individual or group actually to make the change.

With these determinants in mind, the Academy for Educational Development has prepared a framework for applied behaviour change. It seeks to answer three practical questions asked by someone seeking to alter human behaviour – what do I do first?; what do I manage at each stage to ensure a comprehensive programme?; and what milestones do I monitor and evaluate?

The framework (Smith, 1994) has three parts: programme development, social marketing and 'behavioural constellation' (the choice of priority targets). The first is built on the premise that people must shape and control their own transformation, and that this is best done through a participatory process. So it starts by assessing the problem with the community, reviewing current behaviour, knowledge and attitudes. A plan to deliver products, services, messages and support is then developed – by the community involved. The process is pre-tested and implemented, while the circle is closed by monitoring and re-assessment.

The framework looks on social marketing as a broad process of value exchange. It is centred on the target audience and the benefits its members seek though (or in return for) altering their behaviour. The 'product' can be a commodity, service or behaviour. The 'price' is the sum of the barriers an individual must overcome before accepting the proposed product – barriers that can include loss of status, embarrassment and time as well as financial cost. The 'place' is the system whereby the product is delivered, and can include training and other preparatory action. 'Promotion' is the total activity of delivering the message, through advertising, communications or education.

Behavioural science helps managers close the gap between knowledge and behaviour. People do not always do what they know they should do. To quote William Smith:

> Knowledge does not always translate into behaviour. For example, smokers know that smoking is dangerous, mothers know their children should be immunized, and many adolescents know that drugs are dangerous. Smokers, however, continue to smoke; many mothers do not get their children immunized, and many teenagers take drugs. Explaining the knowledge–behaviour gap is the domain of behavioural science.

Based on observation, the Academy suggests that there are six steps to behavioural change:

> *Step 1. Observe the behaviour.* Identify what people are doing, what they like about it, and what they don't like about it. Note who does it and who doesn't. Look at behaviour; count it, record it, don't just ask questions about it. Have a few people do what you want the whole community to do instead of what the community is doing now. Watch the problems they have, and note the things they seem to like.

> *Step 2. Listen to the people you hope will change.* Ask them what matters to them, talk about how your target behaviour fits into their overall life. Get them to talk about incidents, episodes, events that made a difference to them. Look for what they want to get out of the behaviour, and who matters to them.

> *Step 3. Decide what you think matters.* Compare people who do what you want with those who don't. Look for changing trends over time. Describe who you want to change as though they were a character in a novel you wanted readers to know – what are they like, where do they live, how do they act out the behaviour you care about. By this time you should realize that you have several audiences – different segments you have to reach in different ways. Define what you think each segment wants in order to adopt the new target behaviour, and decide how you are going to give it to them.

> *Step 4. Check the generalizability of your thinking.* Take the points you have decided are critical – the benefits you think they care about, the kinds of messages and words you think will work, and the kinds of speakers

and channels you think they believe in. Test your assumptions with a representative survey.

Step 5. Deliver benefits, not information. Solve barriers people face, don't just 'educate' them. This means that you have to plan service delivery and communication together. One has to complement the other. Service delivery has to provide the benefits – but communication has got to help people believe they are real and credible. Persuade as well as inform. Make people feel good about the change. Touch their lives with hope, don't scare them into denial.

Step 6. Monitor effects. You are going to make mistakes. Plan on it. Be proud you found them and fixed them. To find them you need to monitor what's going on. Don't just evaluate your programme when it is all over – but selectively monitor those things you expect to make a difference. Monitor by looking at the behaviours you expect to change – are health workers more friendly, are vaccines more available, are newspaper articles more favourable and accurate, and so on.

These six steps do sound rather paternalistic and 'top-down'. To succeed, we have to listen to communities, work with them, and empower them as leaders in the process of change. 'Experts' whether in behavioural science or conservation have to contribute what the communities concerned need and want. So partnerships, as discussed in Chapter 10, and true community level action, as described in Chapter 9, are alike crucial.

Education in the community: the situation around the world

Progress in establishing environmental education is uneven around the world. Some of the apparent differences are of course cultural adaptations and thus right and proper. But there is no doubt that in developed nations the process has become more institutionalized, and has had stronger political, academic and administrative support. At the same time, education and communication are often separated: formal education is seen as something for the student in schools and universities, while informal education and communication is left to the media and to NGO campaigns and is scarcely recognized as education at all.

The result (as Chapter 4 noted) is a dichotomy in the attitude of government, which commonly seeks to direct and regulate formal education, investing large sums of public money in the process, while regarding interference in what the media teach as somehow improper in a democratic society. Even when the media purvey what are clearly inaccurate, or exaggerated stories, or are driven by profit motives towards entertainment rather than information, governments are reluctant to intervene. Similarly, whatever the importance of outdoor experience in building commitment and understanding, this is rarely supported as an element in core education, and is left far more to non-governmental bodies (like the Scout movement or young people's exploring societies) and to parents.

In the developing world more attention has been given by governments to informal education, in villages and via the radio. Only a small group of countries has developed effective formal and informal systems of environmental education with a reasonable level of comprehensiveness. This may in part be due to lack of resources, and partly to the overwhelming problems, like those of acute poverty, that these countries face. Because of lack of support, such environmental education programmes as exist tend to weakly structured, weakly developed, and poorly supported socially. As a result, a negative feedback loop is all too easily established: environmental education does not pervade the whole educational system, because it lacks high-level institutional support; it is not informed by efficient educational research because the system is not attuned to using the results of such studies; and it becomes discredited further because what is done does not produce useful results.

But there are examples of success in developing countries, including India, Zimbabwe, Brazil, Nepal, Zambia, Ecuador and the Sahel, as well as from many developed countries. They tend to fall into two categories: successful actions for conservation, based on public information, communications and education, and successful action to establish organizational structures for education in the various countries.

Examples from the developing world

Education and public information for action

In the Atlantic coastal forests of Brazil, an educational programme has sought to increase public awareness and commitment to conservation in an area where encroachment on the remaining natural areas threatens outstandingly rich biological diversity and there are insufficient resources to enforce protection through the use of guards. Eighty-two per cent of the State of São Paulo was originally covered by forest, of which less than 5 per cent remains. The last significant remnant is the Morro do Diabo (Devil's Hill) State Park, which has several highly endangered species including the black lion tamarin, *Leontopithecus chrysopygus*, which is the most endangered primate in the world.

The aim of the education programme described by Suzana M Padua (1994) is to involve the communities who live around the natural areas, making them more aware of the richness and value of those areas and gaining their support for conservation. These people are socially and economically disadvantaged, and before the education programme began they were unaware of the importance of the park and its biota. In addition the programme seeks to gain the support of such decision-makers as directors of institutions, landowners, entrepreneurs and political leaders. This is crucial because it is largely through the actions of powerful landowners and political leaders that the reserved area has been eroded from 290,000 hectares to only 34,000 ha over the past 25 years.

The programme follows the PPP (planning – process – product) model, but involves continuous evaluation, thus allowing its effectiveness to be assessed throughout and adjustments made where these will clearly enhance effectiveness. In the first stage the needs, goals, objectives, target public, constraints and available resources were defined. Surveys showed that local people had very little knowledge of this environment. The environmental education programme was directed especially at local students who served also as bearers of information back to their families and other community members. The planning stage also sought institutional support and participation from the park's employees, the Forestry Institute of São Paulo (which administers the park), and other institutions which might be able to help.

The process stage included visits, prepared and followed up by separate stages of activity. Information was provided, nature trails constructed for the use of students, a visitors' centre established and art exhibits, workshops, and local media programmes were all involved. Local high school students and two park employees were trained as nature guides. At the product stage an evaluation programme showed a high level of community acceptance. By the end of the first year, 6000 students had visited the park and the average of the following three years was 8000. Knowledge of the park and its importance clearly increased. Problems of garbage dumping on the edge of the park were solved through local community involvement. Local community action also helped fight forest fires and rallied opposition to illegal logging in an area near, but outside, the park. The programme itself is continuing under a local director, appointed in response to public demand. The park has become a symbol of regional pride. The project as a whole demonstrates the importance of targeting students and reaching out through them to entire communities. And if the outdoor experience is as formative in Brazil as it appears to be in North America and the United Kingdom, the result should be a lasting commitment to conservation and environmental care on the part of a large group of tomorrow's citizens.

In the urban environment of Bangalore, India, described by Shyamala Krishna (1994), serious problems of social deprivation are aggravated by a lack of self-help and cooperation among members of the community. The Centre for Environmental Education's Southern Regional Cell has worked by bringing people together to make them aware of social and infrastructural problems in a city, and of the methods by which the problems can be addressed. Particular attention has been given to community hygiene, waste management, and the protection of greenery. The key proved to be personal contact, although films, slide shows, plays, songs and other media approaches had some impact in motivating people and drawing their attention to particular issues and problems. Once personal contacts have been made, posters, pamphlets and other educational material proved very valuable in maintaining commitment and impetus.

An umbrella committee of organizations and individuals worked out the plan for action, collected information, and developed a radio serial to create awareness. Each 15-minute programme gave the views of scientists, officials, experts and members of the public, followed by suggestions for action and contact points for concerned citizens. The whole aim was to encourage people to participate in the action projects, beginning with one on garbage management. Research established how much waste was produced in the city, where it came from, and how it was disposed of. Communication programmes trained families, shopkeepers, schools and officials to segregate their waste. Land was obtained for composting sites. Corporation workers and waste-retrievers were trained in composting. Educational materials such as films, slide shows, posters, pamphlets, booklets, and notice boards were produced. Volunteers were trained and sent from house to house to spread the message and help households respond. Itinerant waste collectors began to collect (and pay for) the segregated waste (just as in Metro Manila, described in Chapter 5 (Camacho, 1994)). Other approaches were used in communities where there were no established waste collection facilities. Overall, the project not only succeeded in cleaning up a lot of waste but in generating a keen interest in environment among children and their elders.

This study demonstrated that one key to success is to develop materials and approaches that fit the cultures of the people, and their levels of literacy and education. Another need is to document what people are doing, and publicize it, thereby reinforcing their commitment, stimulating them to do more, and leading others to follow their example. A third need is to build from the specific projects into wider community and personal concern for the environment, so that other improvement schemes take off.

In Zimbabwe, the CAMPFIRE programme, also described in other chapters, depends on the voluntary participation of communities and must therefore have a strong education, information and training component. Taperendava Maveneke (1994a) emphasized that it 'is a learning process, through adaptive management, where we utilize what works and discard what does not'. It invests a great deal in training of community workers, 'problem animal reporters' and (recently) professional hunters. The trainees are chosen by the local people, who themselves participate in the training process: outsiders are involved largely as facilitators. Training covers such practical skills as basic bookkeeping, project planning, project implementation, monitoring and evaluation and the handling of meetings. It is emphasized that 'training must be a slow and incremental process that allows the local communities to ask questions and arrive at consensus.' A newsletter provides local people with their own medium to exchange their knowledge and experiences. Experience leads to the conclusions that, first, environmental education must involve all strata of society; second that an environmental education syllabus does now need to be developed; and third that informal linkages through radio must also be strengthened, as an important educational tool.

Raphael N'diaye, Monique Trudel and Ibrahim Thiaw (Trudel and N'diaye, 1994; Trudel, 1994; Thiaw, 1994) have examined the relationship between environmental education and changes of behaviour in Western Africa, and especially in the Sahel. In this region pressures on the environment and problems of land degradation and loss of wildlife are acute, and information, awareness raising, and capacity-building are of utmost importance. It is essential to take account of the target population's basic concepts and perceptions, and the socio-economic and socio-political constraints which bear upon them. The Sahel is a land of old traditions and societies, deeply rooted in history, and is therefore generally very structured. These traditions and beliefs influence perceptions and define the kinds of action which can be taken. Many traditions are positively favourable to sustainable living. Environmental education seeks to raise awareness of environmental problems, analyze them, develop and create appropriate attitudes and behaviour, and develop the skills and actions needed in response. The process must be long-lasting, avoid developing or extending a mood of reliance on social security, improve field techniques and link rural and urban actions.

Both formal and non-formal educational approaches have proved their worth. The IUCN regional environmental education programme, described by Monique Trudel (1994), 'is based on the fact that, in Western Africa, a large majority of the population depends on the use of natural resources, and conservation of natural resources is possible only with the population's assent.' The programme concentrates on school children:

> because they will soon be in charge of their country, and they will have to manage their parents' heritage; their academic standard allows them to understand the interactions between the different elements of the ecosystem and to handle the environment management tools; they are more open to innovations than previous generations; they have a creative potential; and they can be involved in practical environment protection actions.

IUCN has operated a project termed WALIA ('stork' – a lucky animal) in Mali since 1985, and it has since been extended by other projects in Niger, Burkina Faso, Senegal and Guinea Bissau. All focus on conditions in particular areas, and on critical problems in those areas (like deforestation, destruction of mangroves, wood-cutting, over-exploitation of soil, pastures and wildlife, and lack of water). They have to contend with poor educational infrastructure, the need for teachers to take other jobs in order to support their families, high levels of illiteracy (over 80 per cent in many areas) and school systems that do not meet today's needs. But they have to work with and through the educational system, such as it is. The main educational aid 'is an extracurricular report, *How to get a better understanding of our environment*. It is an end-of-term report, free of charge for target schools.' It provides a basis for teaching, meetings led by the children themselves, surveys and contests (in which pupils interview key people in the community and write reports), club activities, and the use of local singers, story-tellers, mask-wearers and other traditional messengers who carry the message to the rural, and functionally illiterate population. The end point is the creation of national teams trained by IUCN, schoolchildren and teachers.

The conclusions from experience, according to Monique Trudel and Raphael N'diaye (1994), are that both formal and non-formal education must be developed in dialogue with the populations concerned; that parents must be convinced of the merits of the environmental education programmes; that partner organizations must be involved at the outset; that the tools to be used must be chosen to suit the people who will use them and the context of their application; and that networks must be built, linking the organizations involved, and spreading information about problems and successes.

Action to establish educational systems

FUNAM (Fundacion para la Defensa del Ambiente – Foundation for the Defence of the Environment) in Argentina has been in operation since 1982. Its goals, summarized by Raul Montenegro (1994), are to work towards the preservation and wise use of the natural environment. It promotes understanding and agreement between the various sectors of the community. It supports a new ethic of humanity in nature, not against nature, and accordingly rejects open-ended consumption, non-sustainable lifestyles, unnecessary waste production, the use of hazardous energy sources and inequities in North–South relationships. It is very much a community-based organization, and uses action campaigns, publications, media and meetings as vehicles through which to change attitudes. It has worked especially through information and education campaigns including a 'Children's Campaign for Peace and Life', for which it issued a series of special publications including an 'Environment Little Defender's Manual'. With the Norwegian Campaign for Environment and Development it has launched a 'Voice of the Children International Campaign' which, in January 1992, was in action in 39 countries. The idea is to give children worldwide an opportunity to express their concerns directly to decision-makers and to adult society generally, through children's consultations, children's congresses, children's appeals and children's hearings with top leaders.

Farther north in Latin America, in Ecuador, Fundacion Natura developed an 'Education for Nature' programme (EDUNAT), which ran for 13 years, between 1981 and 1993. It was described by Marco Encalada (1994). It operated through both the formal and informal education sectors, was aimed at the entire population of the country, and sought to change their knowledge, attitudes and practices. A very wide range of approaches was used, but the emphasis was on establishing communication systems. In its second stage there was emphasis on helping to define environmental problems more clearly, identifying solutions, stimulating people's involvement in changes in decisions and policies, fostering awareness among children and adolescents and making a group of private enterprises interested in environmental education initiatives.

Studies showed that it succeeded in altering people's perceptions of environmental problems and their attitudes to nature, but there was less evidence that this carried through into behaviour. However there have been major changes during the period. In 1984 only 4.5 per cent of a sample of people from all provinces understood the meaning of 'environment', whereas in 1990 80 per cent did so. Awareness of environmental problems increased greatly. In 1990, 95 per cent of the population appeared to understand that economic development would not be possible if environmental damage persisted. National ecology groups have been created. The government has endorsed the need for environmental policies. Groups of peasants and ethnic minorities have requested authority to manage their own environments in their own way. Public demands for action on environmental issues through the media, municipalities and government agencies have increased enormously. Yet while in 1984, 84 per cent of people thought that the population at large should surely be able to do something to remedy environmental problems, even by 1990 only 21 per cent were positive about behaviour to protect the environment at home, and 24 per cent were positive about such action elsewhere. Positive responses were commonest among political leaders, student leaders and professionals, and even these proved on enquiry to focus largely on safe disposal of garbage, discussing the environment, handling food better and saving water.

Nearby, in Venezuela, a National Council for Environmental Education (CONEA) has been established by government agencies, representatives of the media, the universities, and environmental NGOs. Its functions are defined in a national plan for environmental education, and were described to the Buenos Aires workshop by Professor Jose Moya (1994). They include analysis of the environmental content of curricula, establishing co-ordination of formal and informal programmes, holding workshops, conferences, fora, special events and courses to increase public awareness, increasing environmental action, stimulating action among NGOs and creating an information base. Organizations have been created at provincial and municipal level and national networks established. National strategies for both formal and informal environmental education have been adopted. Emphasis has been placed on bringing the process down to the level of the community, where environmental resources are actually used. At all levels, particular attention is being paid to protected areas, biodiversity, climatic change, ozone layer depletion, solid wastes, waste waters, the origins and methods of treatment of all forms of pollution, rural and urban planning, recreation, basic public services, administrative procedures for environmental protection (including environmental impact evaluation), environmental law, and the implications of international treaties including the Rio Declaration and *Agenda 21*.

In Nepal, an environmental education and awareness programme was an integral part of the implementation of the National Conservation

Strategy, and the approach was reviewed by Badri Dev Pande (1994). He commented:

> It is disturbing to note that the increase in literacy rates in Nepal has been accompanied by rapid depletion of natural resources and deterioration of our national heritage. Nepal's natural and cultural environment was in a much better state thirty years ago, when the literacy rate was barely two per cent. Now, with a literacy rate of 40 per cent, we are environmentally a much poorer country. The question is, then, has our educational system failed to respond to environmental conservation needs?

Analysis showed that the curricula, textbooks and associated formal educational materials were indeed inadequate. A new five-year plan (1992–1997) includes provision for environmental education at all levels of formal education, technical education, teacher training, non-formal adult education, in-service programmes and for the use of the mass media to raise the level of environmental awareness. 'A newly-formed Environment Protection Council headed by the Prime Minister is able to issue directives to government agencies and non-governmental organizations to develop programmes directed at environmental education and raising the level of public awareness about conservation needs.' Conferences, seminars and training workshops have been held.

At basic level, environmental education curricula have been developed as components of four main subjects: the Nepali language, social studies, health education and science. Texts, readers, and environmental games and posters have been prepared and tested for their relevance and effectiveness. At secondary level, a new course entitled 'Population and Environmental Education' is being introduced at grades 6–8, and another course on 'Science and Environmental Education' in grades 9 and 10, where environmental education can be chosen as an optional subject. A draft curriculum for grades 6–8 has been discussed at a national workshop, and revised. In addition to formal teaching, environmental camps and environmental art workshops have been organized for primary and secondary schoolchildren, in collaboration with local NGOs. Training and extension programmes have been organized, while the awareness-raising programmes have included radio programmes, a wall newspaper for rural areas, street theatres, video films, environmental games, newsletters, booklets, pamphlets, and many other initiatives. The NGO community has been closely involved in the whole process.

The chief lessons learned have been:

■ environmental education should be integrated within continuing programmes;

■ the agencies responsible for these continuing programmes should take the lead: special project teams should stimulate, advise and support, but play as low-key a role as possible;

■ workshops and seminars bringing all concerned parties together are invaluable;

■ NGOs should be brought into the partnership;

■ good environmental education materials can recoup costs through sales.

A rather similar process has been followed in Zambia, which prepared a National Conservation Strategy in 1985. This emphasized that a comprehensive programme of conservation education would be 'the surest long-term strategy for bringing about sustainable use of natural resources.' However, as Juliana Chileshe explains (1994), this proposal, like many others in the draft strategy, was not followed up at the time. Environmental education was not included in early Zambian national curricula, but in 1993 a review led to the decision to include elements of it in curricula for environmental science, social studies and home economics, with other subjects following in due course.

In addition to the Ministry of Education's role in developing the schools programme, a number of other departments including those for forestry, natural resources, agriculture, health, fisheries, national parks and wildlife, and several parastatal bodies, have environmentally based information and informal education programmes which reach out to communities. A number of NGOs also provide educational materials, newsletters, magazines, readers and posters and the Zambia Environmental Education Programme (ZEEP) for which Juliana Chileshe works has prepared educational material and trained teachers. There are now 20 ZEEP coordinators in different districts of the country. Religious groups have attempted to teach stewardship of the environment. Attempts have been made to involve traditional leaders, especially chiefs and headmen. The media has been targeted, and its coverage of environmental matters has improved. The chief lessons learned are:

- The government needs to set out a clear policy for the environment, and for environmental education. National machinery for co-ordinating environmental education is needed.
- Following *Caring for the Earth* and *Agenda 21*, the main aims should be to create awareness, change attitudes, equip individuals and communities with knowledge of the environment and the inter-dependence of life, equip people and communities to identify and solve environmental problems and reverse degradation, and enlist people's participation in such endeavours.
- Target groups need to be identified clearly, and addressed. Some, including women and young people, are not adequately involved at present.
- The content, techniques, materials and approach to environmental education need clearer definition. Inter-disciplinary and multi-disciplinary approaches are needed to many subjects in the curriculum.
- People need to be trained to teach environmental education at primary, secondary and teacher training levels.
- Environmental education materials need to be developed, printed, and distributed to all educational institutions.
- Substantial funds are needed to support a wide range of environmental education activities.
- Government departments concerned with sectors of the environment need to coordinate their policies on environment and natural resources, and concert their efforts to enhance public understanding.
- Non-governmental organizations also need a coordinated programme for environmental education.

Examples from the developed world

Education and public information for action

The developed countries have also provided illustrations of how education and communication can change personal and community attitudes. Kathleen A Blanchard of the Quebec-Labrador Foundation of Ipswich, Massachusetts, has examined (Blanchard, 1994) the effects of education on attitudes and behaviour towards seabird conservation on the north shores of the Gulf of St Lawrence in Canada. Here the problem was that illegal hunting and disturbance caused severe declines in the breeding populations of several species between 1955 and 1978. Razorbill and Atlantic puffin numbers fell by 85 per cent and 76 per cent respectively, from totals of 18,500 and 62,000 to 3000 and 15,000. But although illegal, the harvest followed tradition. The people had a long history of using seabirds for food and 95 per cent of households considered such harvest acceptable.

The Quebec-Labrador Foundation collaborated with the Canadian Wildlife Service in a project designed to restore the depleted seabird populations, while preserving the integrity of local culture. They sought to improve local knowledge, attitudes and behaviour and establish greater local support for, and involvement in, the management process.

Information exchange alone cannot be relied on to cause durable changes in behaviour. Information on posters or brochures is not necessarily read or applied, and is no substitute for an educational process. The project therefore began with a thorough study of the problem from the human and cultural side. It found a general ignorance of wildlife laws and regulations, unawareness of the legal status of the seabirds being hunted, and a universally utilitarian attitude to seabirds. In response, four kinds of activity were started: youth instruction, leadership training, information dissemination and support-building. The first of these did not preach conservation so much as make children more aware of the birds. Visits to bird colonies were part of the process. The result was to raise questions in the homes about seabird conservation and the need for sound management strategies.

The leadership training process recruited teenagers and adults to take responsibility for conservation. They were trained in field ornithology and teaching methods, and the project helped to build up the capacity of local organizations to sustain the conservation programme. On the information side, a poster, a children's guide to the regulations affecting seabirds, a newsletter for primary schools, a calendar using material from the children's poster contest, and local radio were all employed. As for support-building, study tours for conservation with leaders from across Canada played an important part. The fact that the human communities concerned were small and closely knit was an aid to the whole process.

As a consequence of the campaign, during the period between 1977 and 1988 most of the seabird colonies increased quite dramatically: razorbill and puffin numbers about doubled. There was a marked reduction in egging and hunting. Knowledge of the laws protecting the birds increased substantially, and while the prevailing view remained that birds should be harvested for food, the number of people engaging in it fell, and the average number of birds which were considered necessary by a single family per year fell from 44 in 1981 to 24 in 1988.

It was significant that the educational programme did not focus on stopping poaching so much as promoting more thoughtful and positive behaviour, including legal hunting and bird study. It reinforced a rural culture's own conservation ethic. 'Rather than attempt to convince people that it was wrong to kill birds, the programme allowed the basic cultural norm to remain the same: it is acceptable to harvest birds for an occasional meal, especially if they are needed as food.' To succeed, the programme needed support from individuals and communities. It was helped by the way community leaders supported the message, and by the involvement of community members including children. Overall, the following features were instrumental in its success:

- local residents, the wildlife agency and conservation groups agreed on a common goal from the beginning;
- education was seen as a part of a comprehensive management plan that included research, habitat protection and enforcement;
- the education programme involved the four important phases of research, planning, implementation and evaluation;
- local residents participated throughout the programme, with training to encourage local leadership;
- activities were participatory and hands-on, including fun learning opportunities;
- the programme included both short- and long-term components, and overall has lasted for 16 years, evolving as the situation changed.

Australia is a country with many strong environmental initiatives, and active NGOs. Chris Mobbs of the Nature Conservation Agency's description of the Landcare Programme (also described in Chapter 9) stressed (Mobbs, 1994) the need for information, booklets to explain what is being done or can be done by participants, and the creation of awareness through the media. One key need in securing community action is to target the audience:

> Some of the most successful projects have been those which have targeted specific groups. For example, in South Australia, one project has been aimed at getting rural women involved in protecting native vegetation. Rural women constitute 50 per cent of the owners of most farms, and are either active decision makers or have strong influence over the active decision makers. This project organized workshops for women to meet and discuss activities for protecting remnant vegetation and planting trees on farms.

Another good approach is to involve young people in practical action:

One of the most successful projects with schools has been through water quality monitoring. In New South Wales, the Streamwatch programme has over 120 schools involved in taking water samples and measuring biological and chemical attributes of waterways in and around Sydney. The information gathered by these schools is regularly used by the water authority in determining management activities. Through this participation the students are also bringing the issue of water quality to the attention of their parents, and therefore assisting in changing older people's attitudes.

Donald Alcock (1994), of the Great Barrier Reef Marine Park Authority (GBRMPA) emphasizes that:

> the most important method of managing natural resource areas like the Great Barrier Reef World Heritage Area is by well-designed education and extension programmes, which shape visitor and user attitudes and behaviour. They focus on the area's value and on nature conservation, not by direct teaching but by experience.

The marine park is actually managed largely through public understanding and acceptance of the zoning of use (which is in turn related to environmental sensitivity) and the development of patterns of activity appropriate to each area. It treats all its staff as extension agents, and has an Education and Information Section which concentrates on services in this field. Information kits are produced, and public participation programmes get community groups involved in the development of zoning and management plans. It has been shown that the extensive news reporting on regional television, linked to advertising, increases public interest in proposed new plans. The philosophy is clearly summed up by Donald Alcock (1994):

> The Authority believes that if people help develop management plans for the Reef they will be more committed to support its conservation. An educated community becomes a caring and concerned community. Long-term investment in this philosophy always pays off, with local communities now forming voluntary marine conservation groups.

The Authority produces a lot of books, maps, posters, videos, research publications and brochures, and these are in high demand from educational establishments. The reef is growing in popularity as a subject of study in primary and secondary schools, and specialist curriculum material is now being produced. About 2000 copies of a book for teachers, *Project Reef Ed* have been sold to schools. There is a network of information and interpretative centres for visitors, and training courses have been mounted for tourist operators, including boat skippers, diving staff and resort managers. It is clear from research that the tourist industry plays a significant part in forming positive attitudes to the Australian environment, and as in the UK and North America, 'direct contact experiences in natural settings such as the Great Barrier Reef holds the most power for shaping this public attitude. Direct experience is better than television, films, books or legislation.'

The Authority calculates that the costs of the environmental education programme are offset by the reduction in management effort required: 'Positive community education programmes cost less than legal prosecutions for infringement or repair to damaged coral reefs.' It has been suggested that public education programmes would achieve the same results as fisheries regulations enforcement programmes – at 2 per cent of the costs. As Abraham Lincoln commented: 'With public sentiment, nothing can fail: without it, nothing can succeed.' The challenge for natural resource managers is to design the right mix of education and extension strategies to influence and lead the client groups and audiences.

Alcock concluded with a rhetorical question: 'should emphasis be placed on serving the formal education system using the theory that concentrating on the next generation is most cost-effective in the long term?' He considered that there is no simple answer: a mix of strategies is likely to work best. But the experience of the GBRMPA clearly establishes that an education and information approach is crucial to secure support for conservation, and can save very large sums in operating costs, while without the cooperation of an informed public, conservation is likely to fail.

Action to establish educational systems

Action has been taken to establish or improve environmental education in many developed countries. Examples come from Scotland, Canada, the Netherlands, and Spain.

In Scotland, reviewed by Professor John Smyth (1994), a national strategy for environmental education is being designed in response to *Agenda 21*. Many interests need to be involved in the process, and a working group, with broad representation, is drawing the inputs together. The final report has four main sections: a review of environmental education in its Scottish context; a review of current activities in different sectors (for example, national and local government, school and post-school formal education, industry, urban and rural sectors, voluntary organizations and others); an assessment of present needs and prospects; and the main recommendation for a strategy. Four main areas of essential action were identified: first, the need for an agreed and authoritative statement of intent from government regarding environmental education; second, the need to draw the agencies and influences that guide the development of behaviour towards the environment into a common purpose, through the development of partnerships; third, the need for an information base; and finally, the need for continuity.

Action to coordinate environmental education in Spain has been summarized by Susana Calvo (1994). The initiative stemmed originally from small, active but rather isolated groups of conservationists and educational reformers. They stimulated action, especially from the 1970s onwards, by the government departments responsible for education, environmental management and youth. Today, four ministries, almost all of the 17 regional governments, many local councils, and a growing number of NGOs are involved.

The Law on General Ordinance of the Education System requires that environmental education must be a focus of school work, from primary stages onwards. It is treated not as a separate subject but as an extra-curricular activity that must influence all subjects. Almost all the autonomous communities and many councils now have a department devoted to environmental education. Activities are directed towards school-goers and to visitors to protected areas. There is also substantial activity in the non-governmental sector. Coordination has been sought through meetings and seminars.

The adoption of *Agenda 21*, has given a boost to coordination and to the development, as in Scotland, of an integrated strategy. This is still at an early stage, and at present fact-finding is to the fore. The need now is to draw the various working parties together, define clear guidelines, encourage all sectors of society to join in action for the environment, outline a plan for a more coordinated and coherent approach to environmental education, promote research, define social groups that need preferential attention, and commit resources to priority tasks. The greatest difficulties arise from the complexity of the concepts and organizations involved.

In the Netherlands emphasis is also very much on strategic planning for environmental education, and the actions taken were reviewed by Peter Bos (1994). Environmental education in schools has been stimulated by an education plan, 1991–1994. But in the autumn of 1993 a concept plan was presented to the Cabinet, partly in response to the call for a national strategy in *Agenda 21*.

The overall Dutch strategy has two main features: first, it seeks to integrate environmental education in the core business of public and corporate organizations and citizen's groups and second it seeks to improve communication between the various parties and so provide better planning, more integration and more professionalism. Second, it seeks to influence individuals and so create stronger community support for actions to improve environmental quality; to help people to find ways to combine their leisure activities with sustainable development; to encourage sustainability at work; and to encourage and monitor initiatives for alteration of lifestyles and consumption patterns.

The process involves three key parties – government, NGOs and target groups. Communication is seen as the key to making the process work. Monitoring and evaluation are also essential, and one output will be policy advice. But as Peter Bos emphasized, the current concept plan is no more than the start of a process. It provides a framework for more systematic communication about the development of environmental education in the country. Its important features are, first, that all government departments have committed themselves to participation and second that the improvement of professional standards and approaches is recognized as of paramount importance.

In Canada, according to Christine Hogan of Environment Canada (1994), the Green Plan has established a national objective: 'to secure for current and future generations a safe and healthy environment and a sound and prosperous economy.' This will demand environmentally responsible decisions at all levels of society. Government will not achieve this goal through traditional 'command and control' measures like regulations and economic incentives. All sectors need to cooperate. Voluntary action is essential. In Canada in 1992, 84 per cent of the population stated that they believed that the environment could only be protected if individuals are willing to make changes to their lifestyles. The need is for a culture of environmental citizenship – with voluntary action on environmental issues by an informed and educated citizenry. 'The more Canadians engage in this exercise, the less will we require complicated regulatory and economic regimes, and the more involved will individuals be in the decision-making processes that affect their daily lives as citizens.'

The process begins with improved environmental education, seen as 'the fundamental building block for effective environmental decision-taking'. Various learning materials have been devised – including 'primers' on topics like waste management and water conservation, 'snapshots' which provide critical environmental information in a colourful and easy-to-read format, and daily 'citizenship messages' to convey information and encourage individuals to take action to help deal with a range of environmental problems. Another strand is the enlistment of 'learning partners' who work with Environment Canada to develop guiding principles, training programmes and public education activities.

Conclusions

It is self-evident, as Joy Palmer comments in her summary of the actions to create environmental education and communication at the end of her book (Palmer, 1994b; 1995), that these can be effective ways of bringing about voluntary action for conservation and sustainability. The approach that works depends strongly on the social context: where people and communities are starting from. The needs evolve as communities and actions evolve. There has to be flexibility and adaptation. The audiences have to be well chosen and well targeted.

To be effective, education and communication have to be seen to be relevant, and they have to offer the prospect of an improvement in people's lives. All with an interest have to be involved at every stage of the process of development of the action, for this leads to the essential sense of ownership of the product. Sustainability is built when local residents participate and are trained to take the action they know is required. Individual aptitudes and insights can then move forward as community partnerships.

Governments have a role to promote environmental education and training. That role is, however, essentially enabling rather than directorial. Governments can also demand coordination between Ministries and facilitate cohesion between different sectors of the non-governmental community. They should also ensure that resources are provided as a high priority – for the returns in terms of voluntary social action for a sustainable future, and voluntary implementation of the law, are highly cost-effective.

Education and training are useless unless they lead to action, and governments have a responsibility to facilitate this also. They must ensure that their own agencies behave in an environmentally enlightened manner, or they will undermine the whole educational process. They should promote clear and effective communication, and establish standards for accuracy and accountability in reporting.

The scientific community must recognize that it, too, has a responsibility to communicate clearly and accurately with the public at large (something many scientists are bad at). Barriers between so-called experts and other people need to be eliminated. Likewise, education and communication must look outwards from national societies to a wider world. The understanding of our *Only one Earth*, Our Country the Planet, is essential to all our futures.

C H A P T E R 7

UNDERSTANDING NATURE

All human communities depend on – live off – other components of the biosphere. Sustainable development can only take place within nature, and its success depends on understanding nature's limits, and working within them. The development process inevitably alters the ecological systems of the planet. Most, if not all, actions for development reduce biological diversity. Does this matter? As we move towards further development, essential to support the billions of people who will be added to the planetary population, how do we strike the balance? What are the risks? Are there ecological guides for sustainability?

In Chapter 4, deficiencies in science and in the communication of science were identified as obstacles to action. Specifically, it was argued that:

- while we had gathered a mass of information, quite a lot of it was not useful as a guide to the process of sustainable development;
- models remained inadequate;
- uncertainty had to be catered for, and we had to be prepared for nature to go on surprising us;
- we needed to know more about the basic processes governing the evolution of biological diversity, the relationship between diversity and the integrity and resilience of ecosystems, the true nature of 'carrying capacity', and other key concepts;
- we had to communicate better across the sectoral divides.

This chapter looks especially at the fundamental features of the natural world which need to be taken into account as background to the processes of conservation and sustainable development.

The dynamics of evolution and extinction

The history of life on Earth has been one of steady increase in the diversity and complexity of life forms. It has also seen a great increase in biological productivity. The initial cradle of life was the sea, and for several billion years life appears to have been confined there, and to have been dominated by relatively simple forms (such as the blue-green algae, whose massive globular concretions are among the earliest fossils). But during the past 600 million years the diversity of marine animals has increased greatly, and the land has been colonized by an increasingly rich array of life forms (Figure 12) (Marshall, 1988).

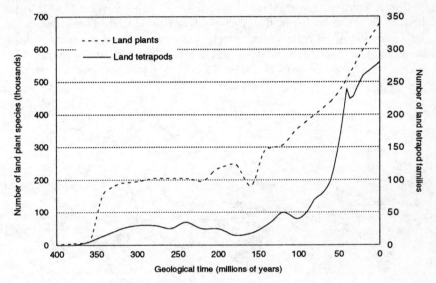

Source: Nixlas et al, 1983, cited in Marshall, 1988

Figure 12 The increase in biological diversity during the history of the land

Organic evolution has not run smoothly. It has been marked by periods of apparently steady diversification of life forms, and periods when extinction has thinned their ranks. The process is evident in Figure 12. Some extinction is a normal and essential consequence of the evolutionary process, and means no more than that a particular habitat has been taken over by a replacement species that suits the conditions of the time better than its predecessor did. If speciation and extinction march forward in a dynamic equilibrium, then nature will be on course.

They need not match one another strictly. Catastrophic events like volcanic eruptions, ice ages, or a rising sea level submerging a low-lying island, will naturally cause extinctions and reduce the diversity of life forms in the affected areas. If species diversity is favoured, as it appears to be on land by warm moist climates, then periods when such situations are extensive are likely to see increases in biological diversity, while periods when these conditions contract will reverse the process.

Over the past 600 million years, warm and moist and cool phases of global climate have alternated about a long-term mean temperature not far from the present (Frakes et al, 1992): the causes of this pattern are not clear, but slow changes in the Earth's orbit, differing arrangements of the continents, variations in volcanic activity, and changes in the carbon cycle (and hence in the strength of the natural greenhouse effect) linked to changes in ocean circulation and heat transfer by the currents have all been postulated. These changes may well be the cause of variation in the rate of increase in biological diversity.

There is reason to believe that something of this kind happened during the Pleistocene Ice Ages in the tropical rain-forest zone. Drier, more arid conditions seem to have led to the retreat of moist tropical forests from what are now the basins of the Amazon and Zaire rivers. The forests were confined to refuges ('refugia' is the technical term) around the rims of those basins (Figure 13) (Lynch, 1988). It has been suggested that the greater biological diversity in the Amazon forests today has arisen because their refugia were larger, and themselves more diverse, than in Africa.

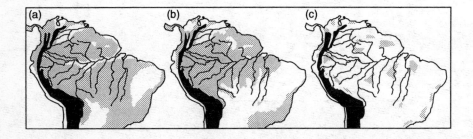

The pattern of distribution of lowland forest in northern South America, (a) at glacial minimum, (b) recently, prior to human deforestation, and (c) at glacial maximum, showing refugia.
Source: Major, 1988

Figure 13 Pleistocene refugia in South America

There do appear to have been periods in the Earth's history when extinctions ran at far above the normal rate, and led to the disappearance, in a relatively short period, of groups of plant and animal that had been domi-nant for millions of years (Marshall, 1988). The most famous of these epochs in the late Cretaceous period, some 75 million years ago, is commonly spo-ken of as the 'end of the dinosaurs'. But there are signs that the dinosaurs were declining in numbers and diversity for some 5 million years before the Cretaceous/Tertiary 'horizon', and that some remained after that horizon (Charig, 1989). The period was, however, one of major biological change. In a relatively short period (we cannot be sure how short) about 75 per cent of the species (50 per cent of the genera and 13 per cent of the families) known to have lived in the sea before that period disappeared from the fossil record. The dinosaurs did not pass unaccompanied into oblivion.

It has been suggested that this, and perhaps some of the earlier major extinction spasms, was caused by a massive, catastrophic, event like the colli-sion with the Earth of an asteroid about 10 km in diameter. This would have made a crater some 100–150 km across, and if it fell in the sea, would have thrown up a wave which, to start with, would have been around 5000m high – as high as Mont Blanc. The wave, declining in height as it went, would have encircled the globe within hours and inundated all low-lying coastal areas. The impact would have released some 100 million megatons of kinetic energy (about 10,000 times more than the simultaneous detonation of all man-made nuclear weapons), and produced a dust cloud which shut out solar radiation (and hence shut down photosynthesis) for 18 months or so. There would also have been other major impacts on atmos-pheric physics and chemistry, and there is no doubt that such an event would have had a catastrophic ecological effect. However, it is by no means certain that this is the explanation for any of the observed 'extinction spasms'. Changes in climate, ocean circulation and the arrangements of oceans and continents may well all have had major influence (Chaloner and Hallam, 1989).

Whatever their causes, about 12 'extinction peaks' have been identified by various scientists who have scrutinized the fossil record of the past 250 million years (Marshall, 1988). Yet it is evident that despite the massive loss of species and genetic material in these events, the surviving gene pool and ecosystems were resilient enough for new diversity to be built afterwards. The world was probably more diverse, biologically, 100,000 years ago than at any time in its previous history. But the most recent of all extinction spasms, at least among the large birds and mammals, appears to have taken place over those last 100,000 years and, as Chapter 1 showed, to be directly related to the rise of humanity to worldwide dominance. It is clear is that human agency is now the chief cause of extinction (Diamond, 1989), and impending rates of species loss today may well be 10,000 times the 'back-ground rate' in the fossil record (May et al, 1995). Does this make this cur-rent spasm any different in kind from the earlier ones? Will it jeopardize the human future because it erodes the ecological support for our own species? We have already adopted a social decision that we wish to bring the new wave of extinctions under control – hence the Convention on Biological Diversity. But what are the realistic limits to that action – what are the key ecological factors we must attend to?

The patterns of biological diversity

Different habitats and situations have acquired assemblages of life which differ widely in diversity. Broadly speaking, biological productivity follows a similar pattern (Brown, 1988):

- the polar regions are poorer in life and less productive than the temperate and equatorial zones;
- high altitudes are poorer than low levels;
- drylands are poorer than areas with abundant water;
- small islands support fewer species than comparable areas on mainlands, although they may be highly productive – they also have a high proportion of endemic species, found nowhere else, as do isolated high mountains;
- sea waters of low salinity have fewer species than the oceans (hence estuaries and shallow seas are less diverse, although they are often areas of high biological productivity). However, diversity rises again as one passes from the brackish transitional zones into fresh water;
- deep marine waters are poorer in life than those near the surface.

All these generalizations require some qualification. For example, the deep seas and oceans are far from being the biological deserts once supposed. Over 800 species, in more than 100 families, have recently been described there, and there are some extraordinarily diverse deep-water assemblages around 'black smokers' (volcanic vents on the seabed, especially in mid-oceanic zones where the crust is spreading, and where warmth and salts are continually supplied). These support at least 16 families of invertebrate animal that were unknown to science ten years ago (Grassle, 1989).

There are whole libraries of theory to explain the obvious variations in living diversity from one region of the Earth to another. In essence they come down to saying that such variety reflects the history of the life form and habitat, the diversity of the habitat and its inherent favourableness (in terms of solar energy, water availability, water composition, soil quality and the like), and the history of interaction between life forms.

The relative impoverishment of the polar zones is probably largely due to the much smaller amount of solar radiation to reach the ground in high latitudes, the immense seasonal alternation between winters with months of continuous darkness and summers of unending light, and the low temperatures at almost all times. The climatic oscillations of the past million years, with alternating glacial and interglacial phases, probably led to further impoverishment, explaining why the northern temperate and sub-polar zones have few distinctive species. The poverty of high mountains arises because of the increasing severity of habitat with altitude. In both polar and montane habitats, species-poverty may also have been increased by the fact that there are large areas of relatively new habitat, exposed because the ice caps and mountain glaciers have been retreating since the last glacial period, only a little over 10,000 years ago (Brown, 1988).

Productive continental habitats support more species because there is simply more energy and nutrient to go round. There is more room for specialist organisms that can take advantage of particular, limited, kinds of resource. Many of the most diverse habitats are not only favourable but old, so that evolution has had time to produce a wide variety of species, parcelling up the total life-support system between them by dividing it into a large number of narrow 'niches'. The more heterogeneous a habitat is, and the longer it has existed under relatively constant conditions, the richer it will be.

Age, area and diversity are important factors. Young volcanic islands, or areas that lost all or much of their flora and fauna during recent Ice Ages, and were then isolated by rising seas before much recolonization could occur, are well known to be poor in species. Today's dominant forest trees and land animals are not good at dispersing across sea barriers, so that even large land masses that have been isolated for a long time may lack dominant groups that evolved recently. New Zealand has no indigenous land mammals except bats and their place was, in pre-human times, filled by a variety of distinctive birds among which the moas – giant ostrich-like species – were the dominant browsers and grazers of the vegetation.

The relationship between species richness and habitat area has been explored with relish by mathematical ecologists, because it is an ideal and intriguing subject for such analysis. But it is the cause of the relationship that matters in practical terms, especially when we set about the task of conserving biological diversity. Habitat heterogeneity may also be an underlying factor in the relationship: it also tends to be greater in larger areas.

Some species, and even higher groups of plant and animal, have a restricted distribution, occurring on one island, one mountain peak, or even one small patch of habitat. Species confined to an area are termed *endemics*. The endemism of an area is defined as the proportion of flora or fauna that is confined to it. Obviously, there will be a relationship between endemism and the size of the area: a continent is bound to have many distinctive species, whereas a small lowland country with relatively monotonous terrain which differs little in its topography, rocks, soil or climate from its neighbours is unlikely to do so. Conservationists are likely to be especially concerned with areas of higher than normal endemism, and with the fit between endemism and national boundaries because that makes a country solely responsible for the species concerned. This has been a particular topic of attention at meetings under the Convention on Biological Diversity. It has been the subject of detailed analysis by the World Conservation Monitoring Centre (WCMC, 1992; Johnson, 1994).

The analysis shows that a large proportion of the species so far described by science are confined to single countries. For example some 45 per cent of the 25,000 species of mammals, birds, reptiles and amphibians are found only in a single country. The proportion is particularly high in reptiles (60 per cent), and lower in birds (30 per cent). About 65 per cent of the 3175 species of vertebrate listed by IUCN in 1994 as 'threatened', and 78 per cent of the 2754 threatened invertebrates are endemic to a single country: for all threatened species the figure is 71 per cent.

Islands usually have more endemic species than comparable mainland areas, and these endemics are of two kinds – relicts which have become extinct outside their island refuges and distinctive new species which have evolved in isolation on the islands concerned. The former are illustrated by lemurs, once widespread but now a special feature of Madagascar, and the unique tuatara lizard, *Sphenodon*, now confined to some small islands off New Zealand. Evolution in isolation on remote islands can create substantial endemic diversity if the habitats are large enough and there has been sufficient time. Under such circumstances initial colonists, which inevitably belong to those relatively few groups of plants and animals that are good at long-range dispersal in air or water currents or with the aid of seabirds, 'radiate' into a whole series of descendent endemic forms which occupy different ecological niches. This happened dramatically in Hawaii, where as few as 26–32 original plant colonists may have given rise to 469 species in 20 genera, and over 3700 species of endemic insects arose from between 233 and 254 initial colonists (Wagner, 1980; Zimmermann, 1948). It was the manifestation of this process in the finches of the Islas Galapagos that so impressed the young visiting naturalist Charles Darwin and set him thinking about the origin of species.

Today's biological diversity is the result of past processes. These have led to a great deal of parallelism in the living world. Pouched (marsupial) mammals in Australia fill comparable ecological niches to placental mammals elsewhere – and where ocean barriers excluded mammals, as in New Zealand, large flightless land birds radiated to fill those niches. There are three unrelated moles in the world. Among plants, the tree growth form has appeared in a very wide range of groups including groundsels, lobelias and heathers that are more familiar as herbs or shrubs. In the far south, on land areas that once formed part of the great southern continent of Gondwanaland, there is a temperate forest complex in which southern beeches of the genus *Nothofagus* are prominent, with a structure, productivity and contribution to biogeochemical cycles very like those of temperate forests made of different species elsewhere. In wet situations in the same southern regions there are peat-forming carpets of higher plants which function much as *Sphagnum* bog mosses do elsewhere. Distinctive insects accompany both kinds of vegetation.

It is evident that today's biological diversity has complex and ancient roots. In each area it reflects the outcome of immigration, speciation, emigration and extinction. Barriers, especially of ocean, have been of great importance. Today, human agency has broken these barriers down and moved many species around – creating new patterns of competition and predation. In biogeographical terms, some loss of biological diversity is an inevitable consequence. It is almost unstoppable. The question is – does it matter?

We also need to recognize that the current extinction spasm is not equally advanced everywhere. As Chapter 1 emphasized, the hunter-gatherer destruction of large mammals and alteration of habitats started over 100,000 years ago in Africa but only reached New Zealand and Madagascar within the past 1500 years, and got to many remote islands even more recently. The spasm associated with deforestation and cultivation reached the Mediterranean region and western Europe around 5000 to 3000 years ago and had a patchy impact in India, China, and central America in the same period. It has only really hit the tropical forest zone since 1970. The spasms associated with industrial pollution have yet to reach much of the developing world. Meanwhile, some countries such as those of western Europe and North America are (or should be) entering a phase of stabilization and ecological reconstruction: their human populations are more or less stable, the value of biological diversity is accepted socially, and there are national and regional conservation programmes.

The resilience of nature

There are three views about the ability of the environment to withstand the impacts and pressures humanity is now piling upon it. They can be labelled respectively 'nature-forgiving', 'nature-unforgiving' and 'nature-resilient'. The first contends that nature can indeed reclaim areas devastated by natural catastrophe and human impact. The second argues that many impacts of humanity are effectively irreversible. The third view is that at least some kinds of environmental shock may even strengthen the capacity of ecosystems to withstand stress and recover.

All three views are of course true, and together compose the whole. The scars of volcanic eruptions heal quickly – in a matter of decades or, at most, centuries. Vast areas in the northern hemisphere that were under ice 20,000 years ago now support forests. In New England, apparently natural woods grow on land that was cleared and farmed in the 19th century. Even industrial wastelands can be retrieved: the Swiss National Park in the Engadine is centred on a valley once devastated by metal smelting.

However, nature was forgiving in these examples because climate and soil were favourable. Where they are not, deserts, once created, remain so. The conversion of tropical forests to poor pasture, with the dissipation of their fertility to air and water, and often with the conversion of iron-rich soils to hard and intractable laterite, is irreversible on any useful human timescale even if a few millennia will indeed, in the absence of grazing, see forest restored. The eroding, peaty moors of northern England were forested once, but rendered semi-deserts by Bronze Age clearance and mis-use.

Even stressed systems like these can be ecologically efficient. Deserts, for example, are occupied by a range of species well adapted to extreme conditions. Australian forests can withstand repeated fires, and indeed fire plays an important part in stimulating the regeneration of component species: the forest type is actually preserved by the fires and in their absence would change to something else. This viewpoint leads on towards the notion of actively managing systems to increase their resilience.

Ecosystems have developed in constant interplay with the factors of the physical world, which select from the pool of genetic diversity those attributes that can best succeed. Change the physical and chemical environment, and new configurations are selected. They may be less diverse in species and less productive, but they will generally display the essential features of ecosystems – a range of plant primary producers, a range of herbivores and carnivores, and a range of decomposers. This is so even in farmlands, where we are the principal herbivore and/or carnivore in the systems we have moulded to our needs.

Our thinking about ecological systems and ecological processes has changed a good deal recently. For many decades we have thought of climax systems as near-stable, semi-closed, self-perpetuating equilibria towards which ecosystems progress through succession. Classical theory implied that a particular type of climax ecosystem was characteristic of a particular region and habitat type (thus oak forest was seen as the climax in much of lowland England and the Eastern United States). Linked was the concept, inherent in Tansley's original definition, that ecosystems are more or less closed and functionally and structurally complete.

It is now realized that these concepts are flawed (Pickett et al, 1992). Many so-called climax systems are neither stable nor in equilibrium, if a timescale of centuries is used rather than the brief perspective of a human life-span. Many actually require disruption (for example by fire), taking them back to a more open and dynamic configuration, if what appeared to be the climax is to be regenerated. (This has been appreciated for many years for formations in dry climates, like Australian Eucalypt forests, but now also appears to hold in temperate formations like New England oakwoods.)

But there is no guarantee that successional processes will always follow the same path: there may be a range of alternative configurations in any area, emerging as a result of subtle variations in process. The climate in western Europe was not vastly different in the successive intervals between the Pleistocene glaciations, but the forest types were very dissimilar. Natural systems are thus seen as far more open than previously believed, and near-equilibria are to be found only in patches within the overall mosaic land-scape, and for periods within the longer time span.

The same holds for biological diversity. The species-richness of an area today is an expression of the ecological and evolutionary past, and is inter-related with the productivity, functional processes, biomass and structural configuration of ecosystems, the physical heterogeneity or patchiness of a region, and the nature of the dynamic processes that exist there. Biodiversity today may be a poor guide to diversity tomorrow – and main-taining present conditions is not a sufficient assurance of the future.

It follows that the aim of conservation is to maintain processes and potentials rather than particular configurations, and ecosystem integrity and resilience are likely to be expressed not in terms of how far a system will 'bounce back' to its initial configuration when stressed, but whether it has within it the capacity to remain diverse, healthy and functional under whatever range of pressures seem likely to be put upon it. This may mean that resilience is indicated by the presence of a dynamic, patchy, pattern. If a particular species, or group of associated species, is to be conserved, the need is to maintain the processes that will guarantee sufficient patches of habitat for them in the overall area at any one time (there are bound to be some patches of unsuitable habitat, as this is part of the overall dynamic process) (Pickett et al, 1992).

It follows that some disturbances, like periodic fires or water-level oscillations in wetlands, may be beneficial to conservation rather than disruptions to be prevented. It also follows that human impact should be taken into account as a part of the overall dynamic process rather than automatically assumed to be deleterious. Moreover, even when catastrophic damage occurs, as through major fires or wind-throw in a forest, it does not follow that human managers should rush in and clear debris or attempt to re-plant. A more judgemental approach is required, for resilience may in fact be favoured by periodic stress.

This does not mean that we should accept all kinds of human impact as part of the evolutionary process, for some are clearly deleterious. But it does mean that conservation managers should re-think the basis of their management, and especially seek to understand the dynamics of the systems they are conserving. Perturbations should, as far as possible, be held within the range that the ecosystems concerned have been exposed to in the historic past and which therefore must have been within the resilience of the processes generating the present configuration. But zero interference and minimal change in habitat conditions are likely to be false goals.

We do have problems both with timescales and our ecological preferences. Humans, with an average life expectancy of between 40 and 80 years tend to think of a decade as a long time. If you watch woodland re-establish itself on abandoned farmland, it generally takes three or four times as long. Moreover, the human observer tends to start with the idea that the proper destiny of land in a formerly-forested region is high, closed-canopy forest. This is the notion of the climax again. Observers tend to think that unless an area of cleared land is visibly on track back to the kind of forest that was present before, something has gone wrong. And they also get fidgety if the process seems to be going slowly, through transitional stages like rough scrub which they do not find visually appealing. A century is really the minimal time for nature to build significant new systems. People used to understand this and plant woodlands for their great-grandchildren. We are more impatient today – perhaps partly because in the developed countries we no longer have land tenure systems and social and occupational continuity that maintain families in the same location for centuries.

But we do need more studies of what makes nature tolerant. We do not clearly understand the ingredients of resilience and forgiveness. And we find prediction difficult. Unless we make progress in these areas, conservation management and sustainable development are both bound to be impeded, for we shall lack knowledge of where a system is headed, and how we can direct it another way (if we want to). We also need new understanding of how much a system can endure before it changes to an alternative system of lower productivity, diversity and resilience.

Resilience, ecosystem function and biological diversity: how do they inter-relate?

All ecosystems can be described in terms of a series of essential attributes. Some are structural, for almost all ecosystems are made up of plant primary producers, herbivores, carnivores, decomposers and microbivores that feed on the latter, although different groups of plants and animals are involved in different situations. Another set of universal characteristics is functional, for all ecosystems fix and transmit energy, and most are based on photosynthesis and the transmission of chemical energy to consumers, while all are also involved in the biogeochemical cycles of water, carbon, nitrogen, oxygen, sulphur, phosphorus and other elements. The third universal set of attributes is diversity, for all exhibit some degree of genetic and species variety and this, indeed, is the basis of their capacity to develop in response to change.

Diversity is thus one attribute of ecosystems – how varied their component life forms are. One of the major current issues is how far diversity, as an attribute, is important ecologically. Analysis is not made easier by the fact that the term 'biological diversity' is being used in two alternative ways in some recent literature (with some ambiguity in the 1992 Convention on Biological Diversity itself) (Glowka et al, 1994). One usage is as a collective noun – the total sum of the genes, species and ecosystems on Earth, and all the variety within them. On this basis 'biological diversity' is synonymous with 'life on Earth' or 'living nature'. It is the sum, not a property, of ecosystems. The alternative use – as an adjective – is more familiar to ecologists. It defines diversity as the variety *within* an ecosystem or a region. As such, it can be set alongside other attributes such as biomass (the total mass of living material in a system), primary production (the amount of carbon fixed in a given time), and the rate of energy flow through such systems. Another important attribute is the resistance of a system to stress (whether from physical or chemical disturbance). All in turn affect its capacity to support people (or some other consumer of its productivity) – and hence its 'carrying capacity'. All are interlinked, but none is paramount.

Analysis suggests that the most diverse ecosystems – forests – also have the greatest biomass. Of the total of some 560 billion tonnes of carbon held in living organisms, 477 billion tonnes is in forests and woodlands (Olson et al, 1983). But the relationship with diversity is not a close one. A tropical forest can be a hundred times more diverse than a temperate or sub-polar one, but the biomass varies only by a factor of around two. Similarly, some diverse systems do have higher primary production than species poor ones, but again the relationship is complex. Some systems of low diversity, like sub-Antarctic coastal tussock grassland dominated by a single species, have net primary production rates as high as some diverse forests. Farm systems are deliberately manipulated towards high productivity.

The fact is that energy flow and biological production in an ecosystem, and its contribution to global biogeochemical cycles do not correlate closely with diversity (Holdgate, 1995c). Some ecosystems of low diversity maintain a wide range of ecosystem functions in an apparently sustainable way. They are distinctive and extremely important in the global scheme of things. They have biological production rates not greatly inferior to those in the diverse tropics. They fix carbon and maintain the cycles of the elements. They regulate water run-off. They support herbivores, carnivores and decomposers. They can provide a range of products useful to people. They have immense local importance. Desert ecosystems, for example, may not contain many species, but they do include some that are highly tolerant of extreme environments and able to maintain productivity, habitat characteristics and energy flow, and hence support human life, over large areas. Conservation must be concerned with maintaining these other attributes as well as genetic and species diversity. Even systems of low species diversity contribute to the total pool of biological wealth. It would be wrong to concentrate conservation effort according to a numbers game that hunts out the areas with the arithmetically-greatest array of life forms.

Diversity can, however, be important in enhancing the resilience of a system. Where an ecosystem is made up of many species, if conditions change in a manner unfavourable for some, others are likely to be promoted so that the overall character, productivity and biomass of the system is retained. Tropical forests, with as many as three hundred kinds of tree in the canopy, ought to be more resilient than species-poor ones, because slight shifts in conditions should lead to many species competing to assume the place of one that is disadvantaged. Moreover, diversity means that a system has the potential to provide a wide range of useful (or potentially useful) products. A tropical forest yields a vast range of these, as Table 4.1 indicates (Hamilton and King, 1983). Its diversity is a measure of its potential, for example, to provide medicines or fruits as well as meat, nuts, fibres or wood. But it does not follow that people will favour retaining all these options in the development process. A boreal conifer forest, for example, may be a better source of timber than a diverse tropical woodland because there are only a few species of tree there, and all provide good logs. That is why people deliberately altered the composition of natural forests from very early times onwards, creating the modified forests of Amazonia, Borneo or southern England (Rackham, 1986; Denevan, 1992; Brookfield, 1993). That is why people plant monospecific plantations rather than multi-species forests.

Natural diversity is the starting point, but sustainable development often means altering it, and quite often means reducing it deliberately, to create a modified system more appropriate to human needs. Weeding is an ancient human occupation. Under some circumstances, moreover, human influence can increase diversity. When the European forests were opened up, many species that were previously confined to patches of open habitat on the coasts or along rivers, or were inhabitants of forest edges, increased enormously in abundance. New habitats became occupied by new assemblages of species – for example creating diverse chalk grasslands. People have also increased diversity by importing useful species – not always to the benefit of the native flora or fauna, as the plantations of exotic conifers in parts of northern Europe, or of Eucalypts in warmer climates abundantly demonstrate. Such altered systems can, however, be perfectly sustainable. We would not be here if they were not, for all agriculture depends on altered ecosystems.

The modern preoccupation with 'biological diversity' or 'biodiversity' can lead some people to conclude that it is the key to sustainable use. That is not necessarily the case. In conserving, managing and developing ecosystems it is important to recognize that several quite different objectives may well be sought:

■ functional integrity – the basic operation of the system, fixing carbon, recycling elements, regulating water run-off, stabilizing soil, shielding coasts and so on;
■ supply of useful products – chosen to met the priorities of the local community or others with an interest in the system;
■ evolutionary potential – to contribute to the global gene pool and to maintain long-term adaptability.

Biological diversity is not equally important in all three sets of circumstance. It may scarcely matter at all in the first, while it may be deliberately reduced in the second to optimize the supply of the chosen outputs. Only in the third is the maintenance of maximum diversity clearly of paramount importance. The selection of the diversity we want from the total array of nature is an ancient and central element in the development process.

The conservation of biological diversity

The conservation of biological diversity, none the less, is an accepted social goal today. Under the Convention signed in Rio de Janeiro, and entering into force in 1993, each state party has a responsibility to survey, evaluate and conserve its own heritage of living resources (Glowka et al, 1994). But not all nations are equally endowed with this heritage. Nor are they equal in conservation capacity. Hence there will need to be international cooperation, and this is provided for by the Global Environment Facility which now has its own secretariat, working closely with the World Bank (which holds the fund), and operated in partnership with the UN Environment Programme and the UN Development Programme.

Caring for the Earth urged action to safeguard the Earth's living diversity, but it did not demand the protection of every species now present in the world, recognizing that this is simply impracticable. The enhancement of agriculture and the improvement of human quality of life in many developing countries will inevitably mean some conversion of wild habitat to farmland, agroforestry or plantation forest, and even to urban settlement. The economic growth and social development that are essential if the world population is to stabilize at around 8.5 billion by 2050 will mean action to enhance 'carrying capacity', which in turn means modification of some natural systems to yield more products important to people. Some wild species are likely to be sacrificed in the process. Conservation and sustainable development are resource-use optimization processes, not campaigns to protect all nature everywhere against the human poor. *Caring for the Earth* therefore called for a mixture of measures to enhance human quality of life and to maintain as wide a range of species and habitats as possible.

Because it accepted that some erosion of wild habitats and living diversity is inevitable in the face of needs to cater for maybe twice as many people as now live on Earth, and improve the quality of life for billions now alive, *Caring for the Earth* has itself been attacked as advocating unsustainability (Robinson, 1993). For some conservationists hold that the loss of biological diversity is a direct measure of unsustainable development. If this is so, the logical deduction is that we cannot create a sustainable world and allow human populations to double, and that sustainability of a sort will only be reachable when our own species has stabilized its numbers, preferably far below the present total. Put bluntly, on this argument we are wasting our time to call for sustainable development under present circumstances: what we shall achieve, until we halt the human tide, is no more than the minimization of damage. Some scientists believe that this is indeed the case. Analysis of energy cycles and the implications of projected energy consumption lead some to conclude that the Earth can sustain only about 1 billion people indefinitely, at a reasonable quality of life (Glasby, 1995).

My own view is that sustainability certainly depends on halting the increase in human numbers, region by region, and achieving a durable balance between people and the life of the biosphere that supports them. But I see no logic in the argument that *any* loss of biological diversity spells unsustainability. The issue is more complicated than that.

However, the loss of biological diversity should never be accepted without question as a part of the price we pay for progress. When a species-poor but highly distinctive system like that of an oceanic island or desert region is destroyed, or replaced by a cosmopolitan assemblage of those species that are humanity's fellow-travellers – universal weeds and highly resilient animals like mice, rats, cats or sparrows – the richness and fascination of the living world is diminished. It is clearly contrary to the ethic of care for the Earth to allow the needless loss of other species.

There are also utilitarian reasons why it matters when a highly species-rich system like a tropical forest is destroyed before scientists have even catalogued the plants and animals it contains, never mind testing their potential value for medicinal or other purposes. It matters when wild relatives of crop plants are lost through the destruction of their habitats. We may well need those wild relatives, and the genes they carry, if we are to help agriculture adapt to changing climates. It matters whenever life forms are needlessly extirpated because we can never be quite sure of their place in the total scheme of things, and once they have gone we deny future generations the chance to find out. So while we may have to accept the loss of some biological diversity, and be glad that this need not undermine the functional integrity of major ecosystems, we should always seek to minimize such losses. At the very least, maintaining living diversity is an insurance policy.

The conservation of diversity is likely to confer resilience against change. In the short term, the resilience of an ecosystem in the face of stress is an expression of the physiology of the individual plants and animals that are there – some more tolerant than others. Here, appearances can be deceptive. A stand of mature trees – or a herd of adult elephants – may appear to put up with drought or disturbance, yet not produce offspring that can survive. They are thus a wasting asset, and if the stress persists, will disappear in a matter of decades. In the longer term, resilience is a matter of genetic potential: of the presence within the gene pool of species and individuals that can tolerate the new conditions, maintain a functioning ecosystem, and provide a basis for continuing evolution. On this timescale, diversity and resilience are closely linked and define the capacity of systems to change in response to altered conditions. Erosion of that diversity may therefore have an effect a long time ahead. It is very likely that the massive destruction of large mammals by early people also led to major ecological changes, and to the disappearance or rarity of plants whose reproduction or dispersal was linked to the habits of the larger fauna.

Loss of genetic diversity in the wild is also a serious threat to human welfare when it erodes the range of characteristics among wild relatives of crop plants, and so reduces the capacity of crop breeders to develop new strains. The problem is aggravated by the progressive replacement of local, traditional, strains of crop plant by widespread 'improved' varieties. In the Green Revolution of the 1960s and 1970s, new varieties of wheat, maize and rice rapidly squeezed out earlier strains. Modern varieties came into use on 40 per cent of the rice farms in Asia within 15 years of their release, and in the Philippines, Indonesia and some other countries more than 80 per cent of farmers now use them. In Indonesia 1500 local rice strains have become extinct in the last 15 years. In Kenya, home of wild coffee, a recent survey showed that all such plants had disappeared from two sites, while three more were highly threatened and six were possibly threatened. Only two were secure.

The increasing genetic uniformity of crops brings dangers, for it increases vulnerability to disease. This was made manifest over a century ago when the potato blight fungus, *Phytopthora infestans*, ran like wildfire through the monocultures of Ireland. Of a human population of 8 million, one million died in the famine that followed and 1.5 million were forced into emigration (Large, 1940). More recently, the genetic similarity of Brazil's orange trees opened the way for a severe outbreak of citrus canker in 1991. A similar blight swept Florida in 1984. In 1970 United States farmers lost $1 billion through an epidemic disease of maize. In 1972 disease played a large part in the failure of the wheat harvest in the then Soviet Union. Since some 62 per cent of the rice varieties in Bangladesh come from a single maternal plant, while the figure is 74 per cent in Indonesia and 75 per cent in Sri Lanka, similar outbreaks could happen there very easily (WCMC, 1992).

There are obvious economic reasons why species whose usefulness is already evident are likely to be at the receiving end of conservation efforts. But today's pressures on the natural world mean that the genetic diversity of many species we do not use is being reduced because the total sizes of populations are decreasing and they are often being split into small, widely separated, sub-groups which cannot inter-breed. This may affect survival and commit a species to extinction even though an apparently substantial number of individuals are still alive. For example, there are only around 50 of the northern sub-species of white rhinoceros in existence. Some 35 of these are in the sole significant wild population in the Garamba National Park in northern Zaire. Their numbers are increasing slowly, but we do not know what genetic diversity the population contains, or how viable it will be if conditions change.

This kind of pattern is replicated in many other species. It has led conservationists to develop ways of conducting population viability analysis as a means of determining what prospects a species has in the wild. It has led also to the recognition that captive breeding in zoos and botanical gardens can play an important part in maintaining a species and ultimately re-introducing a genetically representative sub-population to its natural habitat. This was done with the Arabian Oryx, and more recently in North America with the black-footed ferret, both of which had become extinct in the wild, and in Brazil it is being attempted with the golden lion tamarin, a small and striking monkey of the coastal forest zone. Such action is important because the species concerned play a significant part in the ecosystems to which they belong – and also have their own right to exist. However, it is not as easy as it sounds. The reintroduction of herbivores like Arabian Oryx is likely to be much easier than that of carnivores, whose hunting behaviour is at least partly learned from parents. Today about half the world population of some kinds of tiger is in captivity. It does not follow that these captive stocks could easily be used to re-establish wild populations.

Plant conservation, like that of endangered animals, depends partly on captive breeding and the maintenance of strains in gene banks, and partly on conservation in situ in nature reserves. But seed and gene banks need constant maintenance. One review, in 1980, concluded that between half and two-thirds of the seeds collected in past decades had been lost (Fowler and Mooney, 1990). In 1991 a study of 13 national germ plasm banks in Latin America reported that between 5 and 100 per cent of maize seeds collected between 1940 and 1980 were no longer able to germinate (ASTAF, 1991). Hence there are even dangers in recording the presence of a strain in a seed bank, since false security may be inspired. The only way is regularly to germinate and grow plants from the collection, and save fresh seeds under efficient modern conditions.

We should give great weight to the Convention on Biological Diversity as a means to conserving the living resources of the planet – but we should do so with awareness that it has several goals including safeguarding ecological integrity and the productivity of systems we use, or may want to use. While it is natural that we seek out the areas in the world where biological diversity (measured as species or genetic richness and distinctiveness) is greatest, we must not treat diversity as a be- and end-all, and conclude that the conservation of nature must concentrate on areas with the highest arithmetical total of species. What is needed is to ensure that the range of the world's functioning ecosystems is conserved, and that each is used in ways that do not threaten its basic structure and biological productivity – its 'integrity'.

Carrying capacity and sustainability

Caring for the Earth states the constraints facing us all in unequivocal terms. It says:

> Humanity has to live within the carrying capacity of the Earth. There is no other rational option in the longer term. Unless we use the resources of the Earth sustainably and prudently, we deny people their future. We must adopt life styles and development paths that respect and work within nature's limits. We can do this without rejecting the many benefits that modern technology has brought, provided that technology itself works within those limits.

What does this mean in practice? What are nature's limits? If we are to work within them we have to understand them. We have to know what determines the 'carrying capacity' of ecosystems, and what makes nature resilient.

Carrying capacity can be defined as: 'the capacity of an ecosystem to support healthy organisms while maintaining its productivity, adaptability and capacity for renewal'. Or, in simple human terms, 'how many people can live sustainably, and enjoy a life of good quality, on Earth (or in any region or country on the planet)?'.

The concept is easy to state and grasp, but becomes increasingly difficult and contentious when attempts are made to translate it into hard analysis. The problem is that while the ecological roots of the concept are clear, and derive from the self-evident fact that some factors can be limiting to species health and abundance, the classical models developed by ecologists have their own limitations while the translation of these ecological models into the social sphere has departed a long way from the original notion (and done so in several different ways). And while most people will agree that there must be some absolute limit to the number of human beings the Earth can support, it is difficult to define the basis for estimating it. Indeed, the term is often used in discussion of human population without being defined in any way at all.

Certain conclusions are, however, evident. First, because the concept is essentially about limits, it has to be worked out and applied within a context where limits are really likely to operate. Scale factors are very important. The units and time frames chosen have to make some kind of environmental sense: as Basia Zaba and Ian Scoones commented in Buenos Aires (Zaba and Scoones, 1994), 'most of us have no problem with the notion of the carrying capacity of Botswana, but would be incredulous at the idea of calculating the carrying capacity of Birmingham' – because, indeed, it is incapable of estimation, the city (like all others) being biologically unsustainable without the hinterlands, and sources of traded products, on which it depends. As another IUCN workshop concluded, 'the transfer of resources, people, labour and technology has effectively broken down the spatial and temporal limits to carrying capacity which constrained earlier populations.' It is also essential to apply a time-frame: thanks to continuing improvements in agriculture, food production per head has kept ahead of human population growth, in all continents except Africa, thereby deferring the kind of limit envisaged by Malthus, and re-stated by the Club of Rome (Meadows et al, 1972).

For this kind of reason it is more useful to talk about the carrying capacity of a defined region or resource base, over a fairly short span of time, than to seek to apply the concept to the whole planet and the long term (Toth, 1994). It is of course true that there are ultimate limits to global carrying capacity (though what they are will depend on how efficiently people use global productivity and are able to enhance it). But it is much more useful to talk about how many people can be sustained from a smaller environmental unit (such as the island of Mauritius).

The Sahel is one region where 'carrying capacity' can clearly be limiting. Robert Deneve, Consultant to the IUCN Sahel Programme, has demonstrated that aridity and drought, as such, are not the basic cause of food shortages (Deneve, 1994). A single limiting factor, soil fertility (which however integrates many causal elements), determines the upper limit to agricultural production, and thus ultimately to human population. Carrying capacity is constrained, however, by the economic circumstances of the human community. They cannot afford to buy the energy, fertilizers, or other technological products that would allow them to enhance carrying capacity. To maintain fertility about three-quarters of the cultivable land needs to stay fallow in any year: cropping thus needs to run on a 4-year cycle. And the arable land is only about one-third of the non-desert area. Using traditional farming methods, only about 20 to 25 people can be supported by one square kilometre of land. As it is, population growth is leading to an extension of the area under cultivation, taking in unsuitable soils and causing deforestation. It is also curtailing the fallow period and so reducing nutrient replenishment. The result is a vicious circle of degradation of marginal land, soil exhaustion, massive migration and the creation of large new deserts that do not lack water, but do lack soil fertility. The process is reversible – but not with the resources at the disposal of the community.

If the carrying capacity of an area for people is to be defined, it has to be done at some specified standard of living, from minimal survival to a particular number of calories per head. A 'welfare-referenced' capacity has a different meaning from basic biological capacity. Food and water availability, energy throughput, and economic activity are all used as measures in different studies. In a non-human resource-management situation, much depends on what products are sought: for example the economic carrying capacity of a wildlife area will vary according to whether a high biomass of vegetation is to be sustained, or easy viewing of animals by visitors is to have priority, or meat production is to be maximal. In each case we have to ask what we are trying to maximize when we alter environmental systems to enhance carrying capacity. Coming back to the human situation, is it human numbers or numbers at a particular level of food intake, income and quality of life? Clearly, even if there are ultimate global limits to resource use levels, such 'ecological carrying capacity' ceilings are enormously difficult to measure, and more often debate centres on levels of 'economic' or 'welfare referenced' carrying capacity. Here there are no absolute standards that can be applied to all populations. This type of carrying capacity depends on the objectives of the resource users – ultimately a political, social, economic or ethical judgement (Zaba and Scoones, 1994).

The concept is also sometimes applied to systems like large marine ecosystems (Sherman, 1994). For example, the 'carrying capacity' of the oceans in terms of food production from global fisheries is commonly estimated to be around 100 million to 120 million metric tonnes per year, and most of this comes from 49 large marine ecosystems (LMEs). There are increasing demands for an 'ecosystems approach' to be followed in managing such systems, and this is considered essential for long-term sustainability. The tie between this concept and that of carrying capacity can be succinctly summarized as 'the amount of intervention an ecosystem can have without altering its functioning in a permanent way' (Sprengers et al, 1994). The key is to relate carrying capacity to stress and resilience, and this in turn brings in other concepts like that of critical loads of pollution. It also recognizes that by defining carrying capacity for one species, you incidentally define or influence it for many others. The carrying capacity of the oceans for the blue whale is defined in terms of the productivity of a massive supporting ecosystem.

A third area of possible application is the management of visitors to national parks and protected areas, and to vulnerable habitats such as the Antarctic. Here, the primary aim is to allow people to experience the wonderful natural beauty and wildlife of the areas, while maintaining the diversity and functional integrity of their ecosystems. The term 'carrying capacity' can be used to mean 'the maximum acceptable level of tourist activities, in various defined forms', but it may be more useful to define this as 'assimilative capacity'. In Antarctica the issue is how much physical disruption, scientific activities, logistic support by ships and aircraft (and their crews), tourist activities or chemical contamination the fragile polar ecosystems can tolerate (Dingwall, 1994). On the Australian Great Barrier Reef limits are imposed on the daily number of visitors permitted in certain areas (Craik, 1994). These quotas are fixed on both ecological and amenity grounds. In both areas, value judgements rather than objectively determined ecological tolerances underly the definition of tolerable human activity, and this will be so throughout the conservation world. The term 'carrying capacity' is not generally used in these contexts.

How useful is the concept of carrying capacity in defining nature's limits and in planning for the sustainable human use of natural resources? Clearly it has value in terms of the vivid image it conveys, and the message that there *are* limits to the resilience and productivity of any system for any species, including our own. But at the level of practical detail, is it as useful as two other concepts – productive capacity and assimilative capacity? In the marine realm, for example, the maximum sustainable yield – which is, or should be, the goal of the resource manager – is obtained from populations which are undergoing rapid growth, and these are much smaller than the population would be were it allowed to grow until it came into balance with the whole array of natural limiting factors. The resource manager obviously wants to ensure that the carrying capacity of the *environment* is large – that is, that conditions are favourable for the species being harvested – but will not want the species to attain the theoretical maximum level that some people would take as the true measure of that carrying capacity. Sustainable productive capacity measures how much of a useful product can be taken indefinitely from the environment, and is a more important concept for development purposes. Similarly, assimilative capacity defines, at least in part, the resilience of the environment. It is a measure of its ability to withstand stresses imposed by people. It can measure, for example, the 'critical load' of acidity that a soil or a water catchment can receive without ecological deterioration. Such a measure is useful if one can work back from it to define the emission patterns that can be tolerated in a region. It measures the costs that must be internalized in an industry. True, there remain arguments about whether such tolerances can truly be measured at present, and whether short-term and superficial observations miss subtle effects which could lead to disintegration in the longer term, so that more and more we rely on the precautionary principle to minimize impacts. But clearly such a concept does merit deeper analysis.

The conclusion is that while it is indeed valid to recognize and define the limits that must be set to human demands on the world of nature, the term 'carrying capacity' must be qualified. Carrying capacity of what, for what, under what circumstances? Application of the concept to the management and use of natural resources must recognize the dynamic nature of ecosystems, and the fact that carrying capacity for different components of those systems will vary over time through forces beyond human control, and often beyond human understanding. Management of these systems must be adaptive, and guided by the precautionary principle.

It is not really useful to try to define the ultimate capacity of the Earth to support human populations – and this may even be harmful in diverting attention from more immediate issues. For while such a figure could theoretically be derived on the basis of limiting factors and minimum basic requirements per person, in human terms we are concerned with far more than meeting basic needs. The whole aim of today's quest for sustainable development is to avoid a situation in which human numbers are controlled by density-dependent mortality in a limited environment. And a whole host of value judgements – not the same for all cultures – enter the picture when we start defining minimum acceptable standards for sustainable development. And the use of the word 'acceptable' clearly brings value judgements to the fore.

Respecting the integrity of the natural world

There is an obvious ethical dimension to conservation and sustainable development. It is what makes many people conservationists. The ecologist Aldo Leopold summarized the link between ecology and ethics as: 'That land is a community is the basic concept of ecology, but that land is to be loved and respected is an extension of ethics.'

In *Agenda 21* one goal of international agreements is stated to be to: 'protect the integrity of global environments and the developmental system'. Integrity is also stressed in the IUCN Mission Statement. Integrity in this context is seen as something different from the functional health of ecosystems. One way of defining it is that integrity is assured when the system retains the optimum capacity for development (Westra, 1994). Ecosystem health, on the other hand, is concerned with how the system is functioning at the present time. Thus integrity is about long-term and health about short-term perspectives. In developing *Agenda 21*, particular attention needs to be given to ecosystem integrity. Such a consideration places a higher stress on the maintenance of diversity than comes from a strictly functional demand for maximum productivity now.

There are apparent contradictions in the Rio Declaration in this area. It begins by emphasizing that 'human beings are at the centre of concerns for sustainable development.' But later principles emphasize 'the integral and interdependent nature of the Earth, our home', and the need to protect the integrity of the world environment. These are holistic statements, and Laura Westra (1994) commented in Buenos Aires:

> In fact, if 'they are entitled to a healthy and productive life in harmony with nature', then the first thing we need to accept is that human beings cannot see themselves at the 'centre of concerns' (at least without qualification) as it flatly contradicts the very 'harmony with nature' that is sought. It is for this reason that promoters of biodiversity (such as Michael Soulé), speak of anthropocentrism as an outmoded and dangerous perspective that must be transcended.

The whole thrust of sustainable development and the maintenance of global ecological life-support systems is in fact to adjust human demands and uses so that people live and work within nature's limits. Meeting human needs (and especially those of the poor, and of sufferers from pollution) can only be at the centre of concern if it is accepted that this action is possible only within the wider capacities of nature.

Agenda 21 does however call for some actions that fully uphold the principle of integrity. For example there are demands for integrated land-use planning and integrated coastal-zone management. Chapter 11 on 'Combating Deforestation' demands 'a rational and holistic approach to the sustainable and environmentally sound development of forests'. Very similar language appears at numerous points in *Caring for the Earth*. Laura Westra concluded:

> In essence, the principle of integrity requires that primacy be given to ecosystem integrity, hence to environmental considerations, before other economic or social considerations, on the ground that life (thus life-support systems) ought to be considered primary, before any question of other individual rights, preferences or fairness.

This is not to negate the need for development – that is, continuing environmental change to meet human needs – especially in the underdeveloped countries with their immense challenges in the shape of poverty and environmental degradation. In the developed world, conversely, the need is for more sustainable living, and the restoration of integrity which has so widely been undermined. But unless a significant part of the Earth supports 'wild' ecosystems that are also healthy, and maintains global life-support systems and the genetic reservoir on which future evolution will draw, sustainable development in the South and sustainable living in the North will alike be unattainable.

If this analysis is set alongside that developed earlier, the conclusion that seems to emerge is that we must accept a mosaic of priorities for the use of habitats and ecosystems within the overall, integrated, system of management for sustainability. Some areas must be safeguarded as wild areas with as complete a series of natural systems and as high a diversity as possible. Others may be modified and manipulated to achieve high productivity for human benefit – but with the retention of as much diversity as practicable. Getting the balance right is the challenge.

Development in a healthy environment

Sustainable development is about maintaining healthy people and healthy ecosystems, in an environment that is used optimally. How can theory be converted into action? Clearly, it can only be done on the ground, for each region has its characteristics imposed by climate, topography, rocks, soils, life and history. The world is a mosaic, and originally human needs had to be met largely from the immediate neighbourhood, so that an immense diversity of cultures and lifestyles emerged. The people of the Kalahari or central Australia or the high Arctic took quite different products from nature, but met their needs sustainably as a result of long experience of their environment, and systems of hunting and gathering that had evolved through trial and error and proved sustainable over the centuries.

Such people understood the limits of their supporting ecosystems, and lived within them – the problems arose when outside pressures forced changes that the cultural wisdom of the people could not absorb. Contact with other cultures brought pressure for trade, for example in furs, in exchange for consumer goods some of which (like new clothing or cooking utensils) were beneficial and others (like alcohol) were socially disruptive. But the cultural exchanges were even more devastating, bringing new belief systems and new goals of personal wealth which in turn fostered rivalries and competition to take as much as possible of the tradeable resource as quickly as possible. New firearms greatly enhanced hunting success, in the short term, and undermined sustainability and social adaptation over the generations.

Today, the value of traditional systems of resource use – of traditional development patterns – is being recognized, but there is another issue to face. Many such lifestyles may have been sustainable and given personal satisfaction. Their quality may have been high in spiritual terms. But they did not make for high standards of health or longevity, and those that followed them were poor in material goods. Can such traditional lifestyles provide a better quality of life, while remaining sustainable? Or are they best treated as illustrations of the kind of balance we need to seek, but not models directly applicable in today's world?

It may be wisest to start at the other end, at the environment itself. For any area, it is possible to define the products it can yield indefinitely, in its present configuration, what it might yield, if used differently (for example with the introduction of new kinds of crop, and new systems of management), and how many people it could support, with what lifestyles.

The second of these elements has been of immense importance over the past few centuries. Indeed the movement of crops and livestock around the world has been a dominant human activity that has transformed the lives of many peoples. Potatoes, peanuts, peppers, pineapples, pumpkins and cocoa from South America; maize, beans and sweet potatoes from Central America; wheat, rye, barley, peas and coffee from the Middle East and the Horn of Africa; bananas, sugar cane and tea from east Asia; and many other plants from other places have gone all over the world so that they are now staples of cultures that knew nothing of them a few centuries ago. It is hard to believe that the universal maize of Africa or the bananas of Central and South America are new arrivals there – or that virtually every major crop in Europe originated somewhere else (Crosby, 1986). But it is so, and the result has been an enormous increase in the 'carrying capacity' of the Earth.

Generally speaking, this translocation of crops has increased the capacity of the environment to support people, without overstepping the tolerances of nature. There have, however, been breakdowns in such systems. In Ireland, in the 1840s, the dependency of a poor peasantry on one crop – potatoes – grown on small, intensively cultivated plots, turned to disaster when a blight fungus swept across Europe (Large, 1940). In parts of Africa, maize has become a staple crop in areas that are prone to periodic droughts that it cannot tolerate: famine and migration, exacerbated by social breakdowns and strife – or causing it – are a perpetual risk in many regions today. There is nothing new in these things, of course: great famines in England, for example, were regularly recorded in the *Anglo-Saxon Chronicle* written between AD 890 and 1154.

Such disasters have complex roots, and it would be wrong to claim that transgression of nature's limits: of the sustainable production of the environment is a universal or principal cause. But what is clear is that so long as people ignore ecological limits, or treat them as infinite (which comes to the same thing) the risk of such disasters will remain – and increase as populations grow and demands mount. The majority of people still act as if there were no limits to the tolerance of nature, some justifying their behaviour on the grounds that new technology and resource substitution offer infinite possibilities for cleaning up the environment and enhancing its production.

They confuse the substantial with the infinite. It is a matter of common observation that limits exist. A field can only graze so many cows, and the acceptable stocking density can be calculated on the basis of the present and potential production of the pasture, the ability of the farmer to use some of his profits from the sale of milk to buy in foodstuffs (thus exploiting someone else's pastures), and the severity of the limits placed on the run-off of organic wastes and other nutrients in the drainage from the land. Other limits may come if other products of the land – including the maintenance of biological diversity and recreational use – are demanded. The point is that the calculation is not difficult and that there is some limit.

It is more difficult when the scale is enlarged. The prosperity of many colonial powers in the past was based on the same principle as a farmer who increases his milk yield by buying in cheap fodder – the natural resources of the colonies sustained the wealth of the colonizers. The world economic system operates similarly today, for the poorer developing countries remain largely exporters of primary products like foodstuffs or timber, with relatively low unit prices, determined by commodity markets dominated by the importers. Those same importers maintain high tariff barriers against manufactured products, thereby safeguarding their own industries and economic dominance (Figure 14) (Tolba et al, 1992).

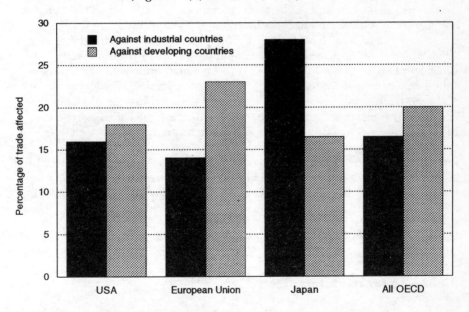

Source: World Bank (1991a) in Tolba et al, 1992
OECD data excludes Australia, Austria, Canada, Iceland, New Zealand and Sweden

Figure 14 Tariff barriers to developing country products in 1986

Even within a developing country, the division of interest between local people and central governments can lead to unsustainable land-use patterns.

For example, the value of the many products a community of forest dwellers can harvest from their local forests sustainably can easily exceed the revenue that same area generates once only, if it is logged for export, leaving an area of degraded habitat and impoverished soil behind it. But (as noted in Chapter 4) the equation is not so simple. The forest dwellers may lie outside the commercial economy. The products they take do not show in national economic statistics. Moreover, the law may vest the ownership of the land in the state, so that the local people have no title to the area even though their forebears may have been there for centuries. The state may have a burden of external debt to service, or an urban redevelopment scheme that it must proceed with in order to industrialize or even to relieve acute poverty. Logging concessions lead to revenues that flow to the exchequer, can service debts, are visible in GNP, and may be used for redevelopment. The social costs of dispossession are absorbed by the local peoples who, if displaced, may become but a part of the swelling ranks of the urban poor. The costs of land degradation only arise in the future, and can be discounted as of negligible importance compared with the money in the bank now.

This kind of separation of interests and priorities can lead to the destruction of resources that are of immense importance to people far away. The global distribution of staple food plants has already been described, as well as the risks that arise if pests, diseases or climatic stresses cause crop failure and famine. Often these risks can be reduced by crop breeding that incorporates drought- or frost-tolerance, or pest-resistance. But the genes needed for these improvements are commonly held in primitive strains of the crop plant or in its wild relatives, in its original homeland. The conservation of a patch of wild potatoes in the High Andes or of wild rice in an Asian wetland, or of cereal grasses in Ethiopia or Iraq may be of global priority. Yet it may seem quite unimportant to desperate local villagers trying to keep alive by cultivating every food-bearing scrap of land, or to their governments who want to build a hydropower scheme. Here the economic interests are reversed – the world community has an immense amount to gain from what should be relatively low-cost investment in conservation on the ground, yet relies on the owners and occupiers of the crop homelands to maintain and supply these essential genes without payment. The Convention on Biological Diversity is intended as a mechanism for changing this situation, and this is one issue on which it will be judged.

Preparing for the future

The limits of nature are constantly changing. The causes are far from clear. For example, while we know that there were four major glacial periods within the past million years, separated by warm interglacial periods many tens of thousands of years in length, we do not fully understand the cause of this oscillation. We know that the Earth is habitable because of the warming due to the natural greenhouse effect – but we still lack firm models to predict how the increases in 'greenhouse gases' in the atmosphere will alter future climates, and hence vegetation zones and crop-plant production. Now we are superimposing on these dynamic and uncertain natural processes large perturbations of our own making.

The only acceptable response to change is adaptation. As we face a future with twice as many people to feed, it is imperative that we adapt agricultural systems, and especially seek to enhance the productivity of crops. We may be able to use new skills of biotechnology to transfer genetic material and so render some plants now confined to the tropics tolerant of cold and able to grow in temperate zones, and others salt-tolerant so that we can grow grain on land that is too saline for present strains. We may be able to enhance disease resistance and increase the efficiency of photosynthesis. We should be able to improve our efficiency: a UNEP report in 1982 suggested that the minimum loss of food after harvest in developing countries as a whole was from 10 to 20 per cent (or 40–50 million tonnes of durable and 50–60 million tonnes of perishable materials, worth around US$10 billion a year) (Holdgate et al, 1982). A reduction in such loses from 10 to 8 per cent would save enough cereal grains to feed 60 million people.

Planning for a sustainable future is being impeded by ignorance of the systems we are trying to manage, and by poor data. If we are to guide development so that people live within nature's limits, we need better knowledge. At present the most telling illustrations are of how not to do it. Richard Carpenter (1994, 1995), speaking to an IUCN workshop in Buenos Aires, quoted CS Holling's analysis (Holling, 1994) of how managers monitor new schemes designed to enhance the useful production of various systems. They usually measure some indicator which is closely related to their primary goal – like how many cattle can be grazed, or fish taken from a system – or how well a potential problem like fires or damaging insects can be controlled. In such management systems the normal course is to reduce variability, maintaining constant high yields of the species from which the desired products come. Success may be concluded when such levels of yield are high and appear steady. But the monitoring may neglect variables which can build up and undermine the management system, for example by diminished resistance to drought, inbreeding in fish hatcheries, or the invasion of diseases and pests from areas of nearby habitat which were outside the monitoring system. Because these measurements of indicators of impending disaster are not available, the disaster can catch the managers unawares. And it is important that the statistics are complete: fisheries catch records, which are obviously essential as a basis for management, are hard to obtain in many developing countries because a lot of fish may be caught and consumed locally. In the Philippines it has been calculated that twice the marketable catch may be processed and consumed locally without being measured.

Complexity, diversity and uncertainty are all features of ecological systems and their management – and hence of sustainable development. Prediction has to be a matter of probabilities. Moreover, even when long time-series are available, it is often unclear whether an apparent trend is that, or part of a cycle of natural oscillation. If sustainable development is to be carried forward with confidence there must be a great improvement in relevant, statistically reliable, scientific measurements (Carpenter, 1994). Such measures need to describe the conditions of natural (and semi-natural) systems under various management practices, monitor trends in the condition of such systems, and their responses to natural and human-induced stresses and predict the outcome of proposed alternative management practices.

At the moment we are hampered by ignorance of ecosystem behaviour and evolution, and especially of response to stress. Natural variability in such systems is poorly understood, and may confound our interpretation of the changes we see. Sampling and analytical techniques are imprecise. Clearly an indicator is dangerous if it rests on poor measurement. In any assessment we need to be sure about the origins and quality of the data, their geographical coverage, their relevance to the problems under analysis, their application in that analysis, the importance of the analysis in determining the sustainability or unsustainability of development and the personal judgements involved in establishing the inter-relationships between different kinds of information, from different levels and scales.

There has been insufficient monitoring and research in many places, and over long enough time. Systems of resource use that have been in operation for several decades may appear sustainable – but that may be too short a timescale for certainty. And socio-cultural and other factors have sometimes slanted the interpretation of information to make it conform with political desire. This whole area is likely to be a priority for new studies and new methodology.

However, we cannot wait for such new insights. The development process has to go on, and one key to it is to stretch nature's limits. We may wish to do this by science, but we shall also have to accept trial-and-error learning. How to use nature – and especially the wilder components of nature – sustainably is the theme of Chapter 8.

C H A P T E R 8

USING NATURE SUSTAINABLY

The pressures of need

There is increasing pressure on the land in many countries, and it will get worse. The growth in world population, and the need to improve living standards for well over 1 billion people, imply that world food production should double over the next fifty years. If we were simply to substitute new land for that being lost through degradation, desertification, salinization and urban encroachment, we would have to convert around 300 million hectares not now being used for food production. To feed the 3 to 5 billion more people to be added to the world in the next fifty years, yet more would be needed (Tolba et al, 1992).

Yet the area of arable land worldwide increased by only 4.8 per cent between 1970 and 1990. In developed countries (where the food surpluses are) the increase was only 0.3 per cent, while in the developing countries, full of hungry mouths, it reached 9 per cent. But per head there was a *decrease* in available arable land, from 0.38 ha in 1970 to 0.28 ha in 1990 – and if present population trends continue and there is neither loss nor gain in the world's total of farmland, there will only be an average of 0.14 ha per head by the year 2100.

Despite its success in keeping food production ahead of human population growth in all continents except Africa, many trends in world agriculture are alarming. We waste far too much primary production. Too much land has been lost. Food surpluses are concentrated in areas with high standards of living, while acute shortages add to poverty and misery in the most underdeveloped regions. The demand for export earnings has boosted cash-cropping in many areas where food production for local use should have priority – and the crops grown have often aggravated the problems because neither they nor the cultivation methods used suit the regions. Too much grain has been fed to livestock rather than people. Soils that are the product of millennia of weathering and maturation have been eroded, waterlogged, or contaminated by excessive salt and alkali in a few years or decades. In some countries, including the western United States and Saudi Arabia, groundwater thousands of years old is being mined to irrigate crops for a few decades – water that will not be replenished once used.

According to a United Nations survey (Tolba et al, 1992), up to half the fertilizer applied to the land in some areas is lost from the soil system and does not benefit the plants. It contaminates groundwaters, rivers and coastal seas and causes acute environmental problems in many regions. Residues from intensive livestock husbandry aggravate the problem. Up to 90 per cent of pesticides do not reach their targets, but they do enter ecosystems and food chains and have profound ecological effects. There is also a natural selection of resistant strains of pest organism, and their number has increased from well under 50 in 1955 to over 500 in 1988 (Figure 15). Pests and pesticide manufacturers are engaged in a race, as the former adapt to pesticides, and the latter try to keep ahead by producing new products.

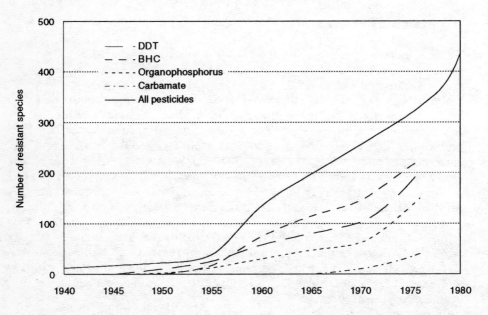

Source: Trappe, 1985 and Georghiu, 1989, cited in Tolba, 1992; Patton et al, 1980

Figure 15 The growth of resistance to pesticides

The evidence that much land is being mis-used is a challenge and at least a sign that there is capacity that could be re-gained if efficiency improves. On the other hand, there are concerns that farming is not truly sustainable in some of the most intensively used areas, because it depends on the injection of water, energy, machines and chemicals, at an increasing cost as production is boosted to ever higher and more artificial levels. What is to be done?

There are two, complementary, ways of responding. The first is to make better use of the land already being farmed, and the other to improve our use of those natural or semi-natural ecosystems that we crop but do not manage intensively – the oceans and coastal seas, the lakes and rivers, and the wild forests and rangelands.

The first policy is almost unavoidable, because much 'unused' land has poor soils or low rainfall, and hence little agricultural potential. Asia, for example, home to three-quarters of the world's population, and with a massive growth in numbers in prospect, has little additional land to convert to agriculture. China, which until recently succeeded in feeding 22 per cent of the world's people on less than 8 per cent of the world's farm land is now rapidly becoming a major importer of grain. In Africa and South America, most of the apparently available land is within fragile and environmentally sensitive systems, such as tropical rain-forests, acid savannas and semi-arid zones. And the opportunity is there because much land already under cultivation could be used better, avoiding waste like that which squanders a substantial proportion of crops after harvesting, and taking advantage of the infrastructure of settlements, roads, irrigation channels and other systems that are already in place. We can also hope for gains within the present agricultural sector because we use biological productivity very inefficiently. Additional improvement may come through the application of biotechnology.

The second policy is important because much land marginal for agriculture is valuable for its wildlife, genetic diversity, and the life-support services it provides. It supports vegetation that helps to regulate water flow, prevent erosion, protect coasts and so on. Moreover, such ecosystems, managed properly and cropped sustainably, contribute directly to people's food and economic welfare. The important lesson we have learned is that such land is most valuable in its semi-wild state. Extending agriculture onto it erodes biological diversity and can all too readily replace a valuable wildlife habitat with a fourth-rate pasture, launched from the very start on the downhill path of land degradation. Maintaining such 'wild' systems as assets complementary to the intensively managed land is part of the mosaic of sustainable development. It helps if we ensure that the value of the services they provide are properly entered in the economic ledger.

There is a continuous gradation between 'wild' and 'developed' lands. The latter are, after all, wild lands transformed through human use. As Rowan Martin of Zimbabwe pointed out at the 1994 IUCN General Assembly in Buenos Aires (Martin, 1994), any use of a wild species will cause a change in an ecosystem. Land now used unsustainably by farming and forestry may need to be moved down the spectrum of intensity, and so restored. Other wild lands need to move up the spectrum so that human communities, especially those on the ground, gain an interest in, and benefit from, their conservation or – where the soils, water supplies and other features are favourable – use them for more intensive food production.

Making the use of managed land more sustainable

Agriculture has been remarkably successful. It has greatly enhanced land productivity. In medieval Europe, in around AD 1200, farmers gathered around 0.5 tonnes per hectare of wheat (Cooke, 1970). With the new seed drills and four-course rotation of the 18th century, the output rose to around 1.75 tonnes/hectare. With fertilizers and selective weed killers and new short-straw varieties, the production lifted to around 3 tonnes/ha in the 1950s. In 1990 it had reached between 6.5 and 7.5 tonnes/ha in Germany, France, the UK and the Netherlands (Prescott, 1994). There is little doubt that further gains in production are possible in many areas of favourable climate and soil which are currently yielding far below this level.

Farmlands and managed forests are part of nature – nature 'developed' and modified by human action, to enhance useful productivity. Such lands are functioning ecosystems, with the essential components – primary producers, herbivores, carnivores and decomposers – in place, even if greatly skewed in proportion by human intervention. They are habitats for a wide range of species, despite tillage, elimination of trees and hedgerows, monoculture, fertilizers, and pesticides. Today, there is real interest in developed countries in lower-input farming – which may provide higher yields per unit of effort and use chemicals and energy more efficiently. Integrated crop management and reduced-input farming offer the prospect of agriculture that is not only more sustainable in production terms but more diverse biologically and more attractive scenically, thus contributing both to development and to conservation.

As Chapter 3 noted, *Caring for the Earth* listed 14 actions to make farm- and range-lands more productive, on a sustainable basis (IUCN/ UNEP/WWF, 1991) and *Agenda 21* devoted one of its longest chapters (Robinson, 1993) to the promotion of sustainable agriculture and rural development. Taken together, they provide a very long checklist. It includes making plans for sustainable agriculture an integral part of national strategies for sustainability (to get the farms in the right place, growing the right things, supported by the right policies and appropriate land tenure systems); enhancing food security; involving communities in decisions that will favour sustainable rural land use; providing better information, education, training and support; protecting the best farmland for agriculture; promoting a wide range of 'good husbandry' measures to manage water and land better; and encouraging integrated pest control and more efficient use of fertilizers. The action list urges that farming be backed up by measures to conserve genetic materials and wild relatives of crop species.

These actions are all sensible, and many are being followed. In the developed world one consequence may well be the creation of a new kind of land-use mosaic, with areas managed for food or timber, or even energy production, alongside others where the primary aim is to regulate water flow, curb erosion, or sustain biological diversity and amenity. It is likely to involve integrated crop management (ICM): 'a cropping strategy in which the farmer seeks to conserve and enhance the environment while producing safe, wholesome, food in an economic manner' (LEAF, 1994). ICM is based on understanding processes including nutrient cycles and the ecology of pests, weeds and diseases, and building management systems that favour the crop while injecting minimum amounts of chemicals. It demands cropping systems that maintain soil structure and fertility, and agricultural and ecological biodiversity. Crop rotations are used to avoid the build-up of pests and diseases. Resistant crop strains are chosen. Cultivation minimizes soil disturbance and erosion. Fertilizers are applied at rates that match crop growth and avoid 'leakage' of excess nutrients to river systems. Crop protection is selective, specific and carefully timed. And a long-term farm strategy for both cultivated and uncultivated land protects and enriches the whole habitat.

Whether or not this is the precise recipe, sustainable agriculture will certainly demand some changes in practice in many areas. In many developed countries this is very likely also to mean correcting the economic machinery and especially the subsidies that lead to over-production and excessive application of fertilizers and pesticides. It is likely to challenge the ossification of farming methods in the European Union, where quotas and other controls make it difficult for farmers to go in for long rotations and blend livestock husbandry and arable in a way that is best for the land. It may mean trying to make farming more, not less, labour intensive. And the switch from price support to conservation support will certainly mean reducing, if not ending, levels of subsidy which not only lead to unsustainable over-cropping at home but undermine the capacity of the developing countries to market their farm produce competitively on the world market.

In many developing countries, key areas of action are the better management of water (whether rainfall, run-off or irrigation), erosion control and more use of traditional cropping practices. It is important that these countries do not follow uncritically the recent farming methods of the North, with their high cost and dependence on artificial fertilizers and pesticides (one criticism of the 'green revolution' has been that it demanded a much more cash- and chemical-intensive cultivation system). Such countries should also not follow the North into subsidy or mis-use of resources (the use of ancient groundwater, delivered through vast centre-pivot irrigation systems to make Saudi Arabia an exporter of wheat, or of pumped water from the River Niger to irrigate rice paddy in Mali are two examples of unwise and unsustainable action). There will certainly be gains if integrated pest control can be established: in Indonesia, for example, pest management involving 4.5 applications of chemical pesticide in the year cost farmers three times as much, and the government over ten times as much as integrated management with only one pesticide application in alternate rice seasons, yet the yields were actually a little higher under the integrated system.

As Chapter 2 commented, the call in *Caring for the Earth* is for rather a rag-bag of actions, not all of equal priority in all areas. The most important are clearly those tied to soil, water and nutrient conservation – and to sound practices in irrigation, less wasteful use of fertilizers, and new techniques of integrated pest management (which are often ancient and local techniques rediscovered). New crop types and strains more appropriate to an area are a third key element. Integrated systems like agroforestry – another old system rediscovered – are also proving their worth. But the key is to begin on the ground, in the community, with a review of local needs, opportunities, current practices, aspirations, traditional wisdom and all the other ingredients. For governments the lessons include leaving local communities to decide their own land-use strategies, and empowering them to do as they want (for example by stronger land tenure), and the avoidance of misguided subsidy and cash-cropping policies that lead inexorably to unsustainability and future cost.

What about trees as a crop? Forestry as a land-use practice is still, in one sense, millennia behind agriculture in that it blends harvesting of wild vegetation – cutting of old-growth or naturally regenerated forests – with intensive cultivation in the shape of plantations. *Caring for the Earth*, the series of *Principles for a Global Consensus on the Management, Conservation and Sustainable Development of all types of Forest* (UN, 1992) adopted at Earth Summit in Rio de Janeiro, and *Agenda 21* address the whole spectrum. They call for nations to establish national forestry action programmes for the conservation and sustainable use of every nation's estate of natural and modified forest; to establish a comprehensive system of protected, natural forests; to establish and maintain an adequate permanent estate of modified forest; to increase the area of planted forest; to strengthen community management of forests; to strengthen forest-related institutions and improve technical and professional skills; to create a market for forest products from sustainably managed sources; and to adopt various economic measures to encourage sustainable forestry. The demand, in fact, is for just that kind of mosaic of conserved diverse systems, more intensively used semi-natural ones, and highly productive planted crops which is also being demanded in the agricultural landscape.

Such an approach offers real possibilities for combining conservation and sustainable resource use more effectively. It will have three components. First, there are good economic and ecological reasons for conserving large tracts of diverse natural forest (including old-growth woodlands in temperate zones), as reservoirs of biological diversity and sources of many products, including some used in a non-consumptive manner, for example through ecotourism.

Second, the very large areas of secondary forest and woodland in both tropical and temperate zones should be subject to multi-purpose management to yield timber, conserve soil and water, and shelter a substantial range of associated species. It is likely that much of the national need for timber in tropical countries can best be met by the sustainable use of such forest (Ayensu, 1993).

Third, countries need to develop a more effective plantation policy in which new woodlands are designed from the outset not only to supply a high yield of timber but to provide other services and to contribute to amenity and the conservation of biological diversity. The *Statement of Principles* endorses such action, emphasizing that 'planted forests are environmentally sound sources of renewable energy and industrial raw materials.' Their area is being increased in many countries. Overall, however, reafforestation is only covering some 1.1 million hectares per annum – about one tenth the area cleared. In tropical countries there were some 25 million hectares of man-made forest in 1990. China, Zambia and Cyprus are among the countries with substantial reafforestation programmes – although in the former much of the plantation is of introduced trees like eucalypts rather than native species.

There is a new interest in plantation forests today, as one means of dealing with the carbon dioxide added to the atmosphere through the burning of fossil fuels. Some United States enterprises have proclaimed that they will neutralize the impact of a new power station by planting an off-setting amount of forest in a developing country. Such action is unlikely to have more than a marginal impact on the problem – in order to balance the total human addition of carbon emission to the atmosphere we would have to reforest an area as big as Europe, from the Atlantic to the Urals (Nilsson, 1992). Moreover, developing countries are unlikely to welcome their land being afforested so as to allow developed countries to maintain their present wasteful use of fossil-fuel energy. On the other hand, growing coppiced trees to produce wood that replaces coal and other fossil fuels could be attractive, if the price is right. Argentina, Brazil and the Philippines have established 'energy plantations' to fuel power stations (Tolba et al, 1992).

It is, of course, a good idea to establish a permanent estate of natural, modified and plantation forest in every nation and manage it to meet the needs of society. The *Statement of Principles* adopted in Rio emphasizes that countries have the right to use forests for their social and economic development, but such use should be based on national policies consistent with sustainable development, and following environmentally sound guidelines. However, the strategy must give proper consideration to the vexed question of who should own the 'permanent estate' – the state, the local community or private individuals? Who should manage it? For whom? To meet the needs of which society – local or central, forest-dwelling or townee?

There are likely to be different interests in the three kinds of forest system just mentioned. The most natural forests are likely to be the home of indigenous and local peoples with their traditional systems of forest management and use. Here the *Statement of Principles on Forests* is clear. It emphasizes that:

> forest policies should support the identity, culture and rights of indigenous people and forest dwellers. Their knowledge of conservation and sustainable development should be respected and used in developing forestry programmes. They should be offered forms of economic activity and land tenure that encourage sustainable forest use and provide them with an adequate livelihood and level of well-being.

The implication is that such forests should continue to be used to supply many kinds of product, especially non-timber products, while at the same time meeting the call in *Caring for the Earth* to conserve forest genetic diversity.

Conversely, its demand that nations 'create a market for forest products from sustainably managed sources and use wood more efficiently' should apply especially to timber from secondary and plantation woodlands. But setting prices to reflect timber's full value and discouraging exploitation of stands of marginal commercial value comes up against basic questions of market intervention: who should do it, on what scale, and how will international trading systems work to improve sustainability? It is right that the capacity of lower-income countries to manage forests sustainably be increased, and that international cooperation in forest conservation and sustainable development be improved, but this calls for development assistance especially for planning and training, and the scale of such assistance has been reduced lately.

The fact is that many countries still do not have the capacity to manage their forests properly, few have worked out the priority for particular areas of the national forest estate, and we are a long way from having the guidelines for optimal, sustainable use of diverse old-growth forests, for the right mix of beneficiaries. These are matters dealt with in some detail later in this chapter.

Using the production of 'wild' lands better

The IUCN mission statement demands that any use of wild living resources (including forest species) is 'equitable and ecologically sustainable'. The Union has devoted an enormous amount of effort to developing general guidelines for such use (IUCN, 1993b). These state that:

> A use of a wild species is likely to be sustainable if:
>
> a) it does not reduce the future use potential of the target population or impair its long-term viability;
> b) it is compatible with the maintenance of the long-term viability of supporting and dependent ecosystems;
> c) it does not reduce the future use potential, or impair the long-term viability, of other species.

Five requirements, or basic operational conditions, must be met if these guidelines are to be fulfilled. They relate to information, management systems, legal frameworks, social or economic incentives to people, and acceptance of the precautionary principle and other safeguards. They are designed to apply to any wild or semi-wild plant or animal species used for human benefit, and to non-consumptive as well as consumptive uses. But clearly such rules can only be stated at the most general level. Plants and animals differ greatly in their life strategies and population dynamics: there is vast inter-specific variation in these respects, and aquatic and land habitats and ecosystems are also very different. For this reason, practical guidelines need to be worked out in the context of different ecological situations. They have also to fit the social context in which the resources are being used. In the following sections, their application to forests and to other environments on land and the balance between consumptive and non-consumptive uses such as ecotourism are considered in turn. Finally, the application of the same principles to the seas and oceans is analyzed.

Rowan Martin has suggested (Martin, 1994) that the two key principles of sustainable use are that it relies on an offtake – a harvest – which is proportional to the size of the population, and that economic returns are reinvested in the species and so benefit its status. However, several current regulatory approaches contradict these principles. For example, because a population is small, it does not mean that it cannot sustain a low level of use. Nor is it necessarily true that a declining population should not be harvested: it depends on why it is declining, and whether sustainable use would indeed help reverse the decline by making the species more valuable.

> When wildlife was protected in the commercial farming areas of Zimbabwe up until the 1960s it declined: when protection was removed and farmers were given rights to use it, animal populations increased. The CAMPFIRE (Community Management Programme For Indigenous REsources) programme in Zimbabwe was initiated in 1988 at a time when wildlife populations were declining universally throughout the communal lands. Evidence from air surveys in 1992 and 1993 indicate that populations of several wild species are now increasing, and it is highly likely that if the species which can be counted on aerial surveys (e.g. elephant and buffalo) are increasing, then the rest of the large mammal community is also increasing.
>
> (Martin, 1994)

Sustainable use of forests, especially in the tropics

Forests are the natural vegetation of much of the Earth's land areas. They are important as reservoirs of biological diversity, regulators of water flow and local climate, abstractors of carbon, and sources of many useful products – as well as for the intangible wealth represented by great natural beauty. As Chapter 1 documents, recent centuries have seen a reduction in the extent of the world's forests, with a consequent loss of biological diversity and decline in the pool of carbon held in the standing timber and organic forest soils.

As noted above, a mosaic of conserved old-growth forests, sustainably used secondary ones, and intensively used plantations is likely to prove optimal in most countries. It is highly desirable that countries establish a comprehensive system of protected forests, giving priority to the types that are most important for their biological diversity. As the *Statement of Principles* (UN, 1992) emphasizes, 'national plans should protect unique examples of forests, including old forests and forests with cultural, spiritual, historical, religious or other values.' Action for such conservation has moved forward in a number of countries, although ancient and diverse forest is still being lost in temperate countries (such as the United States, Chile and Tasmania) as well as in the tropics. But such protected woodlands are likely always to be the minority. Economic and social pressures will demand that most are used. How, and at what cost?

The issue, well stated by European forestry ministers in Helsinki in June 1993 (European Forestry Ministers, 1993), is how to achieve:

the stewardship and use of forests and forest lands in a way, and at a rate, that maintains their biological productivity, regeneration capacity, vitality and. . .potential to fulfil, now and in the future, relevant ecological, economic and social functions at local, national and global levels and. . .does not cause damage to other ecosystems.

This goal is clear. As in other spheres of resource management, the test is at the practical level. As Walt Reid of the World Resources Institute has put it (Reid, 1993), 'nowhere is the need for a transition to sustainable development more crucial than in the world's forests – and nowhere will the triggering of such a transition be more difficult or more challenging.'

The situation is complicated by what DS Cassells, addressing IUCN in Buenos Aires (Cassells, 1994), called 'myths, misinterpretations, misconceptions and miscalculations' in this field, namely:

Myth 1. Sustained yield equals sustainable management.
Myth 2. Good forestry practice is automatically good for the environment.
Myth 3. Temperate forests have a long history of sustainable management.
Myth 4. Sustainable management of tropical forests is an unachievable goal.
Myth 5. Sustainable forest management is not economically viable.
Myth 6. Developing countries can achieve sustainable management without international assistance.

These are bold statements and deserve a little elaboration. According to Cassells, the problem with the first is that the model of sustained yield forestry, developed especially in Germany, came from forests that had been altered greatly through many centuries of use, so that old-growth trees and associated diverse ecosystems had been virtually eliminated. The sustained-yield model sought to balance use with the growth of the forest: when trees reached a desired degree of maturity they were cut, regeneration was allowed to follow, and the cycle guided to the stage where harvesting was again possible. With a reasonable balance of blocks at different stages in the cycle the annual yield from the forest as a whole could be more or less constant. Such management is 'sustainable' in timber terms (and is continuing in a number of areas in Europe, such as the Swiss Jura and the German Black Forest) and also maintains the role of the forest in regulating water flow, stabilizing soils, and providing a sink for atmospheric carbon dioxide, but clearly reduces species and ecological diversity. If we insist that 'sustainability' demands the maintenance of full biological diversity these systems do not qualify (but neither would any other system of agriculture or forestry).

The European management system did not work when exported to the tropics or to North America and Australia, where there were diverse old-growth woodlands. And recent discussions have led to the recognition that forests produce far more products than timber alone. Sustainability today is taken (Botkin and Talbot, 1992) to be 'maintaining the integrity of the natural forest in terms of its structure (i.e. its species composition and biological diversity) and ecological processes, along with the environmental services it provides.' Any strategy for sustainable management must include provisions for maintaining biological diversity, and this is likely to demand mosaics of management pattern, including protected areas and areas managed to yield multiple products. This is a long way from the narrower sustained-yield approach. The issue is how much change is acceptable, under what circumstances, and what the dimensions of the parts of the mosaic should be.

The second myth hinges on what constitutes 'good forestry practice'. The term used to be applied to the silvicultural system which in turn guaranteed high and steady production of timber on the German model. 'Good forestry practice' can however be redefined as the system of management which delivers the multi-product, multi-benefit output now sought. New management techniques are clearly crucial, and Cassells (1994) quotes a series of immediate priorities developed for Asia:

- confining yield and annual logging areas to prescribed limits;
- ensuring that all felling is orderly and complete, and confined to the designated logging areas;
- retaining an adequate residual stand;
- protecting the residual stand against further logging or encroachment;
- carrying out post-harvest silvicultural work;
- defining an appropriate felling cycle, and ensuring that re-logging is not permitted between cycles;
- maintaining permanent roads and controlling erosion following logging;
- protecting unworked forest areas;
- developing and enforcing an appropriate working plan.

Clearly, these guidelines apply largely to the areas from which timber is extracted, and since Duncan Poore (1989) has pointed out that only a negligible area of tropical forest is currently being managed deliberately for sustainable timber production, they are something of a 'wish list'. But they could readily be compatible with wider goals if the working plan caters for all the elements in a multiple use and multi-product pattern.

Can this be done? Poore has stated that it is not possible to demonstrate conclusively that any natural tropical forest has been successfully managed for even the sustainable production of timber. He adds that there is a simple reason:

> the question cannot be answered with full rigour until a managed forest is in at least its third rotation, still retains the full forest structure, and possesses adequate regeneration and an intact soil and ground fauna. No tropical forest has been managed consistently for a sufficiently long period to fulfil all these conditions.

But, of course, many tropical forests have been *used* consistently for centuries, and modified woodlands like the 'forest gardens' of the Dyak people in Sarawak (Brookfield, 1993) or in Amazonia (Denevan, 1992) suggest that it is possible to harvest tropical forests sustainably, but not for timber as the sole product (this has never been the goal of traditional forest users). As Walt Reid (1993) has put it 'what the world needs now is sustainable-enough forestry, and this means choosing what's to be sustained – and for whom – and moving in that direction sooner rather than later.' Here Cassells' Myth 3 can itself be challenged: it may well be that ecological and species diversity are reduced in the German and Swiss forests, but those modified systems can none the less be sustainable in the sense of continuing to provide a spectrum of products indefinitely, and they do support considerable diversity as well as maintaining natural beauty and providing important recreational benefits. The *only* ecosystems which will maintain the full range of natural biodiversity indefinitely are those not subject to any human interference (if any such exist) – and even these systems will not be immune from natural changes, some of which may reduce diversity.

The same kind of argument arises when economic viability is examined. At present, as noted in Chapters 1 and 2, much forest destruction provides economic benefit to groups and treasuries that do not depend directly on the land for their livelihood. Destructive logging, followed by abandonment, is acceptable to such groups because they do not bear the social costs that follow, or the costs of rehabilitation. But reformed practices, including logging, can deliver benefits without a substantial increment of cost. In northern Queensland in the early 1980s new logging practices with reduced impact cost only 3 per cent more than the traditional methods (Gilmour, personal communication, quoted in Holdgate, 1993). World Bank studies in Malaysia have indicated that natural forest management with reduced-impact logging can produce higher economic returns than both current practices and many alternative land uses. If multi-product values and social benefits are taken into account the economic balance can tilt quite dramatically.

One way forward is illustrated by the communal forests of Nepal. A case study by Yam B Malla (1994) noted that while rural communities have been involved in the use and protection of forest resources for generations, the government has only recognized and backed the process of community forestry quite recently. The change of policy results from a realization that action in 1957 to place all forests under central government control was a mistake; that forests and trees are an integral part of local farming systems (yielding fuelwood, fodder, leaf litter, grass and timber on which farming communities depend); and that the problems of forest degradation are too large for the Forest Department to tackle alone. It has also been recognized that deforestation in Nepal is neither universal nor recent. Some areas still have plentiful forests and ample supplies of forest products. Others have suffered severe impact and scarcity. Solutions have to be tailored to local circumstances.

As a result, since 1978 the country has been following a new policy, which will hand over some 60 per cent of the country's forests to local communities, and involve them in their management. It is untrue that deforestation in Nepal has been caused by ignorance and incapacity. Local people know a lot about how to propagate many valuable fodder species. Many rural communities have developed their own rules and regulations, including sanctions, to govern the protection and use of communal forests. Many have been contributing cash or grains so as to employ local watchers to protect the forests. Local initiatives for forest management are in fact widespread in Nepal, and under the impulse of the new programme rural people have begun, or accelerated, the planting and protection of trees on their private farmland. These developments have taken place within a context of socio-economic change, including the involvement of rural people in off-farm cash-earning activities, growing cash crops for the market, purchasing inorganic fertilizers, abandoning cultivation of crops with low cash value and high labour inputs (such as millet), using some marginal land to grow fruit and timber trees as cash crops, changing livestock husbandry from free-range to stall feeding, and reducing the overall number (or changing the type) of farm animals. Many of these changes have brought environmental benefits.

The community forestry programme begins with the establishment of Forest User Groups (FUGs). These are active, community-based organizations. They mostly have committees reflecting the ethnic and caste composition of the community, and the majority include women. Support is given to the groups by the Forestry Department, which has altered its structure at district level, so that its staff serve more as extension agents, providing training and information. The FUGs are encouraged to develop forest management plans based on consultation within the community and the definition of local needs. As they get into action, many FUGs have accumulated funds through forest management activities, and they have used these not only for planting trees but to hire forest watchers, build schools and roads, and develop drinking water and irrigation facilities, thus improving quality of life and aiding farm production outside the forests. Most of the forests handed over have been effectively protected and regenerated, and improved in condition, while in many wild animals such as deer and leopards have increased also. Clearly biological diversity is being enhanced.

The process is developing slowly and has a long way to go. It has weaknesses. For example, the operational plans tend to focus on the supply of firewood, fodder, grass, leaf litter and timber rather than seek to develop other products like medicinal plants. There is also the problem that the

development of a cash market for forest products is raising questions of
equity. The community programme is largely directed to meeting rural
subsistence needs. But the market for wood and other forest products,
while providing an incentive to grow more trees, is slanted towards private
landowners. Powerful local elites may emerge and dominate community use
of communal lands, for cash rather than local support, and the economic
pressures could lead to unsustainable use and degradation of the resource.
The situation therefore requires close monitoring. But the programme does
provide a demonstration of the benefit of empowering local communities to
develop and use their resources.

A great deal of emphasis has been placed in recent times on the value of
non-timber forest products, especially in the tropics. Some details have
already been given in earlier chapters. It is, however, one thing to recognize these potential benefits and another to make them the foundations for
sustainable development which helps to lift communities out of poverty.
How far is it likely that people can increase their income from the sustainable use of non-timber tropical forest products, and make this the basis of
sustainable development that contributes both to local standard of living
and national economic welfare? The issue has been analysed by Richard
Godoy, Nicholas Brokaw and David Wilkie (1994).

People in poor rural economies often depend heavily on the forest for
food (mammals, birds, reptiles, fish and insects as well as fruits and nuts)
and also use wild plants for condiments, medicines, ornaments, fuel, fodder
and building material. The share of household income from such products
is high, and the process is sustainable if population pressure is low, technology simple and customary sanctions against over-use are effective. In richer
rural economies people tend to rely less on wild and more on sporadically
cultivated plants, and hunt fewer kinds of animals because domesticated
livestock replace wild species as a source of protein: the share of household
income from the forest therefore falls. But in the richer rural economies
ambiguities over ownership of land and trees tend to loom larger also.
Governments and local people often have competing claims. There is an
incentive to forage for the most gain obtainable in the short term – a sure
recipe for unsustainability. Moreover, as people become paid more they
value their time more highly and tend to forage for the most valuable forest
products.

Godoy and his colleagues worked among the Sumu of Nicaragua. These
people live in villages in moist tropical rain-forest. The study looked at
household monetary and non-monetary income (the Sumu people, who are
10,000 strong, vary considerably in monetary wealth) and the amounts of
the various products they took from the forest. The areas over which villages foraged, and the prices or values of each product were recorded. The
people collected wild fruits, firewood, vines, medicinal plants, barks, bam-
boos, vegetable oils and many animals and fish. However the study did not
find the expected relationship between income and the variety of non-timber forest products extracted. It was clear that non-timber forest products
amounted to over half the household income among the poor villages, but

less in areas where mines provided employment. The share of income from agriculture rose from 23 per cent in the poorer villages to 55 per cent in the richer ones (Godoy et al, 1994). It appeared that at the lowest income levels foraging was inhibited because the people could not afford to buy guns, good hunting dogs, rubber boots and good medicines for themselves or their dogs. As wealth rose, so these investments became possible and foraging increased. But when income per person rose above $250 the forest became less significant, because the people farmed more, got more education, and were better able to get jobs outside the rural economy. The conclusion was that the biggest threat of over-exploitation occurs when incomes rise enough from a small base to allow purchase of aids to substantial foraging, falling as wealth reduces interest in the forest products.

The value extracted per hectare from the forest also varies. The poorest villages only extracted about 1 dollar per hectare: richer villages obtained about US$35 per hectare and the richest, $93/ha. The latter return was however thought to be unsustainable. This contrasts with worldwide data suggesting a spread of from $0.75 to $420 per ha, depending on forest type and other conditions. Norman Myers' original calculation based on Southeast Asia (Myers, 1988) was of an average of $200/ha annually: a maximum figure from the upper Amazon, rich in natural rubber, was $700 a year from fruits and latex, while the Cooperativa Extractavista in Xapuri involves 325 people who channel the production of 500 families on 250 ha and derive a return of $410,000 per annum, or $1640 per ha (Holdgate, 1993). In Ecuador, the marketing of tagua nut from the Communa Rio Santiago area has yielded $100,000 between 1990 and 1993, 70 per cent of which has remained with the thousand or so people involved (Calero and Frank, 1994). Clearly income can be expected to vary greatly with conditions and only a locally based and critical survey can decide optimum sustainable patterns of resource use.

Ralph W Roberts and JH Cayford (1994) have examined how the generic IUCN Guidelines might be applied to forests. They emphasize that any resource management strategy involves a statement, first, of *objectives* – the broad goals of the process. The next step is to define *principles*, as general rules to be followed. Then come *guidelines*, as more specific statements that steer action, and these are followed by *criteria* – more specific still – and *indicators* as 'measurable variables' which in the present context will illuminate whether the goals of sustainability are being attained.

These elements may need to be elaborated at various levels, as Jeffrey Sayer (1994) has pointed out. There must be clarity over the spatial scale on which sustainability is sought. If the objective is to sustain all ecosystem components and functions, over the entire landscape, then very little intervention in tropical forests will be possible. If 'product optimization' is acceptable, at least in certain areas, with the best sites for timber being managed to yield it, and other values and products given preference elsewhere, then a mosaic of primary uses emerges and much more management flexibility will result.

Product optimization is normal policy in determining land allocation for agriculture, industry, plantation forestry and urban use. It seems both rational and inevitable that it will be pursued in areas of wild forest. But let us be clear. That approach rules out the notion, current in some conservation circles, that all ecosystem functions and components can be kept as they were before human intervention, across the whole landscape. That ideal, anyway, is likely to be an illusion. Even in Amazonia there were large human populations before European contact – possibly 8 million of them, almost as many as today (Denevan, 1992). They certainly modified the forests, just as forest dwellers in Kalimantan and Sarawak or the Bronze Age dwellers in Britain did by selection of the most valuable tree species.

Jeffrey Sayer (1994) has made a series of other cautionary comments about the sustainable use of tropical forests. His first point is that it is irrational to call for all ecosystem functions to be maintained in pristine form in such forests when this criterion is not applied to other kinds of human land management. It is also very hard, if not impossible, to apply the rule that the taking of target species should not prejudice the survival or productive potential of any associated species in tropical forests, where many invertebrate species are known to depend on particular tree species, and many of the species concerned may still not be known to science.

A second problem arises because there is a good deal of inequity in current conservation claims:

> In the present debate environmental lobby groups in rich Northern countries are placing infinitely high value on obscure organisms, whilst the poor people living in and around tropical forests attribute very little value to these organisms. There is also a perception in certain quarters that the rich in the North attribute rather little value to the right of the poor in the South to improve their immediate well-being (Sayer, 1994).

Sayer argues that the debate on sustainability can never reach a conclusion unless it is accepted that nothing can have infinite value, and that a great variation exists over space and time in the willingness of societies to pay for functions, products or components of forest systems. The implication is that the definition of use for tropical moist forests must recognize and provide mechanisms for societies to attribute different values to different components of forests (or landscapes), and to adjust these over time. Conservation and management strategies must be adaptable.

Jeffrey Sayer concludes that it is not useful to discuss sustainability as something that you either have or do not have. It is likely to be more productive to focus attention on finding equitable and participatory mechanisms for achieving the best possible use of a forest (or other ecosystem) to obtain the optimal range of products (including the conservation of ecosystem functions and diversity as a product, and including non-consumptive uses).

If the IUCN guidelines are to be applied to tropical forests the management regime must therefore recognize that in most cases the forest is already being used for something, that these uses will not stop, and that the goal of management is to improve the pattern of use. It should combine regulation and incentives, and must be relevant to poor people with short time horizons, while providing for equity between sectors of society and between generations. Conservationists need to recognize that for poor people ecosystem functions are very important, but canopy insects generally are not! The policy must recognize the legitimacy of aiming for product optimization, and should include participatory mechanisms to decide the baseline of ecological and social values which should be maintained in a particular area (Sayer, 1994).

This all accords with the process for defining management criteria reviewed by Roberts and Cayford (1994). They point out that it is logical that national or regional forest policy will have different guidelines, criteria and indicators from a management plan for a single area, or a component within a diverse forest. Both the International Tropical Timber Organization and the Working Group on Environmental Criteria of the conference held in Helsinki in 1993 under the auspices of the Convention on Security Cooperation in Europe (CSCE) have attempted to define criteria. They can be combined, also taking account of other proposals, in the list set out in the box below.

Criteria for sustainable forest policy

1 Maintaining ecological security
   (a) Maintaining soil characteristics and ecological processes.
   (b) Maintaining water flow and water quality.
   (c) Maintaining the functional integrity and biological productivity of the forest ecosystem.
   (d) Protecting the ecosystem against air pollution that exceeds critical loads.
   (e) Maintaining biological diversity.
   (f) Maintaining critical habitats for fish and wildlife.

2 Maintaining the continuity of timber production
   (a) Safeguarding the forest against fire, pollution and other impacts.
   (b) Controlling timber harvests within sustainable limits.
   (c) Ensuring that management is adjusted in the light of experience.

3 Ensuring an acceptable level of environmental impact

4 Maintaining socio-economic benefits
   (a) To local communities, especially indigenous forest dwellers.
   (b) To the nation as a whole.

5 Maintaining the contribution of the forest to global ecological cycles

---

At national level, attention is likely to pass from the more site-specific and ecological criteria to wider issues of social policy. They will include the institutions and infrastructure to provide for sustainable forest use and the means to ensure long-term supply of social and economic benefits (both to the communities on the ground and the nation as a whole). But, as Duncan Poore (1994) has pointed out, 'because of the complexity of the issues at stake, it is unlikely that it will be possible to identify any universally applicable quantitative criteria for the sustainable management of boreal and temperate forests as a whole.' The same holds true in the tropics, and the statement is likely to be valid also for wetlands, drylands and other ecosystems.

Balancing consumptive and non-consumptive uses of species and ecosystems

Many conservationists seek a way out of the dilemma by suggesting that non-consumptive uses, and especially tourism, can provide an income to dwellers in the richest and most beautiful areas of tropical or temperate forest, thereby eliminating the need to cut trees or tolerate other destructive acts.

Such nature-based recreation, or 'ecotourism' has been a modern growth industry. Worldwide, tourism is the largest civil industry, with annual expenditures of US $3500 billion. It employs 127 million workers and handled 450 million international travellers in 1991 (a number expected to grow to 650 million by the year 2000). Nature-based tourism is the fastest-growing segment, generating about 7 per cent of the total revenues (Ceballos L, 1994).

Ecotourism may be defined as 'environmentally responsible travel and visitation to relatively undisturbed natural areas in order to enjoy, study and appreciate nature (and associated cultural features)'. It takes many forms. To be sustainable it must have a low environmental impact (in parts of the Himalaya of Nepal, especially around the Mount Everest Base Camp, breach of this criterion has made remedial measures necessary), and it should bring benefits to local people. To guide it, there has to be knowledge of the country being visited and of its traditional uses and ecological tolerances. It may need regulation to prevent environmental damage. It is most important that it does not simply focus its impact on protected areas – indeed the concentration of impacts on National Parks can be extremely destructive. The industry clearly needs management, and the local people must be involved in the planning and management process as well as participate as guides and in the provision of living facilities. Ecotourism strategies need to be a part of the sustainable use strategies for rural areas, and education and training are an important component of the action.

In the South Pacific, ecotourism has also been seen as posing potential threats (Valentine, 1994). Target species may be upset by too much pressure (as from whale-watching in parts of Hawaii and in the Great Barrier Reef Marine Park in Australia). Non-target species can be disturbed (shark-netting to protect swimmers has had impacts on dugongs, turtles and dolphins). Tourists like to eat local delicacies – a cause of the near disappearance of the tasty Coconut Crab, *Birgus latro*, and damage through over-fishing in parts of the Pacific. And there are many indirect impacts, including those from pollution, construction, transport and the inadvertent introduction of alien species.

Strategies for sustainable ecotourism require:

- *information* about ecosystems, target species, proposed uses and proposed tourism activities;
- *a management system* that can respond rapidly to threats, involving the local people but also safeguarding them from unscrupulous and wealthy entrepreneurs;
- *a supporting legal framework* and its proper enforcement;
- *social and economic incentives* to local people to conserve the resources on which tourism depends, especially by giving them a proper share in the revenues provided;
- *a precautionary approach.*

Ecotourism is a classic example of non-consumptive use, and the problems encountered locally are a sufficient demonstration that people can still upset ecological balances and damage nature even if their motives are wholly benign. But non-consumptive uses go wider than ecotourism. Some 90 per cent of Canadians have one kind or another of involvement with wildlife, if watching TV and reading are taken into account alongside more direct contacts in the field (Table 8) (Foley and Brackett, 1994).

Table 8 Percentage of Canadians participating in wildlife related activities in 1991

Activity	At home	On trips	Unspecified
Watching TV, etc	-	-	78%
Watching live	57%	16%	-
Reading	-	-	54%
Visiting zoos or museums	-	-	40%
Feeding special foods	32%	5%	-
Studying	24%	6%	-
Photography	20%	7%	-
Purchasing art, etc	-	-	20%
Contributing to NGOs	-	-	9%
Recreational hunting	-	-	7%
Enhancing habitat	-	-	6%

Source: Foley and Brackett, 1994

Other uses of wild animals are radically different. Indigenous and local people have a traditional dependence on wild species, well illustrated in experiences from regions as far apart as northern Canada and Alaska and southern Africa. Hunting and trapping is a traditional lifestyle in northern Canada and traditional methods that tended to prevent over-harvesting are now partly replaced by quota systems worked out in dialogue with local people. For example, in the Inuvialuit region of Canada, dialogue in a local cooperative set a quota of seven grizzly bears for Tuktoyaktuk district after consideration of numbers between six and ten (Foley and Brackett, 1994). In northern Pakistan, villages have applied agreed conservation measures for Himalayan Ibex and juniper forests, and the ibex have now increased to the point where some income from a tiny amount of trophy hunting (4 animals in the 1993–94 winter) can begin (Rao, 1994). In the Andes of Chile, the vicuna, *Vicugna vicugna* reduced to a remnant population through decades of poorly controlled hunting, is now safeguarded in a large protected area and there are new plans for its sustainable management, especially for its fine wool (Torres, 1994). The local Aymara community are closely involved in this plan, which affects their own communal lands.

Rowan Martin (1994), basing his arguments on experience in Zimbabwe, argues that there are fallacies in many established beliefs among conservationists. One is that any species population which has undergone a serious decline should be 'rested' – a principle enshrined in the United States Endangered Species Act and reflected in the CITES Convention. The fact is that the cause of the decline needs to be understood, and it may well prove that complete protection is the worst action to take, because it deprives the species of legal value yet may not stop illegal destruction. In Zimbabwe:

> we. . .have a policy whereby any species whose numbers have *not* increased as a result of legal protection are now being 'deregulated' and, under cautious monitoring, various uses are being permitted. This seems to be producing positive results (e.g. with cheetah and roan antelope) and it gives the lie to the Precautionary Principle in the given circumstances (Martin, 1994).

Martin argues strongly for adaptive management based on monitoring, and on adjustment in exploitation rates should it become clear that hypotheses about the response of exploited populations or their habitats prove wrong, or the objectives of the scheme need to be modified. He also urges abandonment of the term 'sustainable use' – at least in the form where it is applied largely in terms of commodity production from single species. In Zimbabwe the wildlife industry is based on multispecies systems, and the issue at stake is whether *development* – the inevitable changes in use by human communities – proves sustainable. In any event, a multi-species (and habitat) approach is essential, and the socio-cultural dimension must be given more weight. Ecological principles alone are an inadequate guide.

Brian Child, also of Zimbabwe, has also analysed the CAMPFIRE programme (Child, 1994). He emphasizes that it is a reflection of the national policy that wildlife conservation outside protected areas should be based on sustainable utilization. It is 'one of the most successful and exciting conservation programmes on land managed by poor communities'. It works by giving local communities the power to manage and use their wildlife and benefit from the proceeds. The aim has been:

> to make its wildlife as valuable as possible by actively promoting utilization and higher prices. The result has been a significant shift from livestock monocultures to natural ecosystems having a wide range of indigenous

species. Elephants, antelope, zebra and giraffe live on ranches and are sold to safari hunters and tourists: this is more profitable than cattle.

Child concludes from experience that the key to success is to:

■ make wildlife so valuable that farmers conserve it;
■ recognize that resources compete for space and that in certain situations wildlife is the most productive and sustainable form of land use;
■ recognize that economic signals will decide the survival of wildlife outside protected areas, and therefore make sure that these signals reflect the true value of wildlife;
■ promote the value of wildlife in a situation where landholders and communities are resource proprietors;
■ recognize that people who live with wildlife ultimately decide its fate;
■ recognize that they will only manage it sustainably when there is an economic motivation to do so, and when they have secure rights to manage and reap the full rewards of their management inputs, and to prevent others from doing so.

Improving the use of the oceans, seas, and coastal and inland waters

Fisheries supply about 16 per cent of the world's consumption of animal protein – about the same share as beef or pork. Some 86 per cent of this fish comes from the sea, and the overwhelming bulk (90 per cent) of that from the coastal zone. The remaining 14 per cent of catch comes from inland waters. Fish farming in fresh waters produces about 7 million tonnes, while mariculture yields 5 million tonnes: Asia is the leading region for both. The proportion of fishery products from aquaculture is rising and may reach 25 million tonnes in the year 2010 (Tolba et al, 1992).

It is widely stated that the world fishery harvest from wild stocks is, at around 100 million tonnes a year, near the theoretical maximum. Indeed the present yield may not be maintained without better management. At present there is gross over-fishing in many areas. It has led to the severe reduction in the once super-abundant cod stocks off the Canadian coast, and the temporary closure of that fishery. In the past it led to catastrophic collapses in Icelandic and North Sea herring stocks. The problem has arisen especially because the seas have been treated as an 'open access' resource – a free-for-all – leading to a competitive rush to catch as much as possible. It is, as noted in Chapter 4, one of the worse manifestations of 'the tragedy of the commons'. The acceptance of exclusive economic zones in the coastal waters out to 200 miles from the shore should have made tighter regulation by coastal states feasible, but traditional rights of access and over-investment in fleets have proved strong obstacles to rationality. In Europe, the opening of the coastal waters of the various member states of the European Union has not been accompanied by sufficiently strict quotas, and has brought violent competition between national fishermen and those coming from other member countries. These problems erupted in 1995 in a widely publicized dispute between Canada and the European Union. Unless it is recognized that sustainability is determined by the productive capacity of the environment rather than past human practice, there is little prospect that the situation will be righted and yields increased. At present, wasteful over-subsidization of the fishing industry in many countries is leading to diminishing returns and only deferring political crisis when the inevitable crash occurs, and losses are greater and longer-enduring than they would have been had rational policies prevailed at the outset.

In many regions of the world, indeed, the situation is aggravated by the way in which coastal fisheries, which are often traditional, small-scale and partly outside the commercial sector, are being undermined by offshore commercial fishing, often the product of investment using official development aid money. A BBC Radio programme in January 1995 described how European Union fleets are depleting fish stocks in the waters off Senegal, to the detriment of local communities. The money from licence fees accrues to the national exchequer, not to those socially and economically disadvantaged by the sale of their traditional rights. As Table 9 shows, the world has two marine fishing industries yielding almost equal catches for human consumption – and the small-scale local component uses far less capital and energy, employs far more people, and destroys far less of non-target species as so-called by-catches. On any objective analysis except that of industrial yield and central government economics, the small-scale, locally based, more adaptable and more sustainable fishery would be favoured. The fact that it is not is another expression of the perverse consequences of investment and economic decision processes which do not take social or environmental costs and benefits into account.

Table 9 Comparison of the world's two marine fishing industries

	Large scale commercial	Small scale artisanal
People employed	0.5m approx	12m approx
Capital cost per job	$30,000–$300,000	$250–$500
Employment per US$m invested	5–30	500–4,000
Annual fuel oil consumption	14m–19m tonnes	1.4m–1.9m tonnes
Catch of fish for human consumption	29m tonnes approx	24m tonnes approx
Catch of fish for industrial processing	22m tonnes approx	Almost none
Fish caught per tonne fuel used	2–5 tonnes	10–20 tonnes
Fish destroyed annually as by-catch in shrimp fisheries	6–16m tonnes	0

Source: IUCN/UNEP/WWF (1991)

Caring for the Earth (IUCN/UNEP/WWF, 1991) urges 12 actions to promote the sustainable use of the seas and oceans, and these conform closely with those in Chapter 17 of *Agenda 21* (Robinson, 1993):

- Develop a national policy for the integrated management and sustainable development of coastal and oceanic marine waters (to plan and allocate uses, evaluate the impacts and benefits from each kind of use, deal with shoreline erosion and protection, reduce pollution, harmonize national and international laws, and provide for shared and sustainable use of marine resources outside national jurisdiction).
- Establish a mechanism to coordinate the planning and allocation of uses in the coastal zone (especially where populations are dense, conflicts of use exist or are likely, and mis-use or pollution is depleting productivity. Such plans should embrace inland drainage basins together with adjacent coastal ecosystems, include comprehensive waste management and pollution control, regulate agriculture and land use to control siltation and nutrient input, and include local and regional management plans).
- Allocate marine resource user rights more equitably among small-scale, large-scale and sport fisheries, and give more weight to the interests of local communities and organizations (because of the importance, but political marginalization, of local small-scale enterprises just noted).
- Use an ecosystem approach for the management of marine resources (a self-evident need).
- Conduct information campaigns to raise the profile of coastal and marine issues; and include a strong marine component in environmental education in all countries (making people understand the importance of the oceans and seas, the vulnerability of coastal systems, the risks to health from coastal pollution, and the need for established ownership, legal rights and strict controls to protect marine resources).
- Promote marine protected areas (marine conservation lags far behind action on land, but needs a systematic approach to safeguard a representative range of marine ecosystems, especially sites of high biological diversity).
- Conserve key and threatened marine species and gene pools (including whales, seals and turtles, and ban fishing methods like drift nets which kill many non-target species).
- Place high priority on preventing marine pollution from land-based sources (because most marine pollution comes from the land, in sewage discharges, run-off from farmland, industrial effluents, and plastics. So far there are only five international conventions covering discharges from land, and their scope is limited).
- Adopt procedures for effective prevention of pollution from ships and offshore installations, and for rapid response to emergencies such as oil spills. (Discharges of oil by tankers should be stopped, and ships' waste should be discharged in shore facilities; plastic materials should not be dumped, but should in any event have degradable sections to reduce the risk of their trapping animals.)

■ Ratify or accede to the United Nations Convention on the Law of the Sea (UNCLOS) and other legal instruments and develop an effective regime for sustainable use of open-ocean resources (obviously sensible, given the ineffectiveness of international action today).

■ Expand and strengthen international cooperation both regionally and among funding agencies and intergovernmental organizations (to help in research, planning and resource management).

■ Promote inter-disciplinary research and exchange of information on marine ecosystems (to help sustainable use and sound management).

But how can the productivity of marine ecosystems be evaluated? The sustainable yield of marine fisheries has been estimated at from 100 to 120 million tonnes, and 95 per cent of this is produced within 49 large marine ecosystems located in highly productive waters adjacent to the continents (Sherman et al, 1993; Sherman, 1994). Many of these areas are affected by over-exploitation, pollution and habitat degradation. A number have shown wide fluctuations in fish abundance and fishery yield, attributed to such factors as alterations in the currents and in the upwelling of nutrients; large-scale changes in water movements and temperatures; rising nitrate levels due to run-off from farmland; predation by the crown-of-thorns starfish; and excessive fishing. Management must be based on a deeper understanding not only of their ecological characteristics but of the socio-economic factors underlying their use. CS Holling was quoted in Buenos Aires as having suggested three needs in this context: first, the maintenance and restoration of critical ecosystem functions; second, the synthesis and communication of knowledge and understanding for economics; and third, the development and communication of the understanding that provides a foundation of trust for citizens.

Justin Cooke (1994) emphasized in Buenos Aires that most fishery resources have been 'mined' by over-exploitation to well below the optimal population size and biomass. As a result, yields are below the optimal sustainable level, and after a steady rise between 1950 and 1989, they are now falling. The old adage that 'there are more fish in the sea than ever came out of it' is no longer true, and world food production is being undermined by mis-use. According to FAO all 17 of the world's main fishing areas have either reached or exceeded their natural limits. Nine are in serious decline (James, 1994). This is despite the fact that most coastal states have declared Exclusive Economic Zones (EEZ) out to 200 miles from the shoreline. One problem is that fishing does not become unprofitable until stocks have been reduced to well below the level providing the maximum sustainable yield. To achieve sustainability there has to be a substantial cut-back in fishery effort now: if it is maintained, or if falling yields lead to ever more effort in an attempt to maintain production and economic return, the result will be collapse. Another problem is that 90 per cent of world landings come from fish stocks which range outside the EEZs of a single state. That is one reason why, in 1993–1994 the United Nations convened international negotiations on the 'management of migratory and straddling fish stocks'.

What does over-fishing involve? Justin Cooke (1994) summed it up in the following words:

> As a fish stock is depleted, catch rates decrease; the unit cost of the catch increases; the fish stock and catches become less stable and more prone to sudden changes in abundance, because there are fewer year classes to buffer fluctuations in recruitment, survival and growth. Even when a species has been reduced below the level at which it can continue to support a profitable directed fishery, it may continue to be caught in fisheries targeted at other species or in unselective fisheries, such that it continues to decline towards extinction. . .the drift towards extinction will continue inexorably so long as fishing effort remains high.

As target stocks decrease, and fishing intensity increases, with larger and more powerful vessels chasing fewer and fewer fish, the proportion of undersized fish and non-target species in the catch increases. Much of this is discarded. In some intensively fished areas, discards now exceed the landed catch. Many non-target species of fish and wildlife are showing evidence of decline and may be unable to survive in the sea in the long run if fishing at today's intensity continues. Many types of fishing gear cause severe disturbance to the benthos (the life on the sea bed), 'resulting in changes to the sea-bottom ecology which can reduce the breeding success of the target fish species, thus further exacerbating the downward spiral'.

Clearly such practices cannot be tolerated in a world with a desperate need to feed billions more people and a commitment at the highest level to sustainable development. A new style of management is needed. Its central objective must be to keep fishing under control so as to limit its impact both on target species and the ecosystems of which they are part. It will inevitably involve forgoing some of the potential short-term catch in favour of longer-term sustainability, at a higher catch level.

The IUCN guidelines on the sustainable use of living natural resources can be applied to fisheries. They require that there is:

- *protection*: there should be no reduction of future use potential of the target population;
- *low risk*: risk of seriously depleting the target population should be negligible;
- *restoration*: target populations that have been over-used in the past should be allowed to recover.

A precautionary management procedure must give a high probability that these criteria will be met. There needs to be a set of fixed rules relating action to the information available about the state of the resource. The procedure must include: collection and analysis of information both from the fishery itself and independent sources; the assessment of the status of the stock; decision rules for setting total allowable catches (TACs) for the season; monitoring of compliance and the enforcement of the management measures (Cooke, 1994).

It is essential that the procedure defines how the essential guiding information will be collected and evaluated. Assessments of fish stocks are prone to uncertainty. It is meaningless to say that the management procedure will involve harvesting half the estimated maximum sustainable yield (MSY) unless it is explained how the MSY is to be calculated from the available data. Indeed, as Justin Cooke points out, since MSY 'is not a determinable quantity either in theory or in practice, it cannot legitimately form the basis of a management procedure except in a purely notional sense'. Clear rules have to be laid down for determining the allowable catches from stocks, while maintaining a very high probability that such catches will not deplete the stocks.

A precautionary approach to management differs radically from traditional ones. In the past the normal practice has been to allow fisheries to expand unhindered until signs of overfishing (such as declining catch rates or falling fish sizes) become apparent, and then to start processes of enhanced scientific monitoring, and negotiation for catch limits. The precautionary approach, on the other hand, begins with a high scientific effort, and with international or national agreement on controls, and only allows catches to rise when the assessments inspire high confidence that this can be done without risk. There must always be enough data to implement the management process: where data are sparse, fishery levels must be severely restricted. It is therefore strongly in the interests of the industry itself that ample data of good quality are collected.

The most difficult area is the assessment of the wider ecological impacts of fishing, and the determination of how much precaution is needed to prevent undesirable ecological effects. Clearly, any harvest of a major species from an ecosystem has some effect – it is bound to alter the processes and make-up of the system as a whole. Fishing is bound to depress the abundance of some species while permitting increases in others. For example (and as noted in Chapter 1), it is commonly argued that the drastic reduction in the populations of all the larger whales in Antarctic waters, with a consequent reduction in the amount of krill (*Euphausia superba*) eaten by these species, may have lain behind the recent large increases in abundance of some seal and penguin species. As whale populations recover, it may be expected that there will be declines in some of these other species which were able, because of their shorter generation time and faster reproductive rate, to take temporary advantage of the resources made available by the destruction of the whales (Holdgate, 1967).

Whaling illustrates another dilemma. For it has provided not only one of the worst examples of destructive and unsustainable mis-management of a natural resource, but has also illustrated that exploitation of nature can be economically productive but socially and ethically unacceptable.

The first calls for a halt to commercial whaling were based on scientific common sense, and the kind of argument now pointing to the need to stop fishing for some stocks – like Newfoundland cod – altogether, while drastically reducing fishing effort for many more. For the increasing numbers of increasingly efficient whaling fleets this century first reduced the blue whale, the largest animal ever to have lived on Earth, to a tiny remnant, and then progressively devastated the stocks of the smaller fin and sei whales, its relatives. In the 1950s it was pointed out by three eminent statis-ticians that the best way to ensure the largest obtainable whale catches for the rest of the century would be to halt all whaling for a decade and then resume with a much-reduced catching effort (Chapman, 1964). Because of the failure of the International Whaling Commission (IWC) and the weak-ness of the Convention under which it works, this first opportunity was passed by and the devastation continued. By the time of the Stockholm Conference of 1972, blue, sei and fin whales had joined the right whales and humpback that had been devastated by earlier industry on the endan-gered list. Conservation arguments linked with earlier economic and new humanitarian ones to demand a ban on all commercial whaling. That ban has now been operating for nine years.

Today, in 1995, some species of whale show signs of slow recovery – at least in some populations like the South Atlantic humpback and southern right whales, and perhaps the fin and sei whales of the southern circumpo-lar ocean. But the blue whale hovers on the brink of extinction, with a tiny and widely scattered population of under a thousand. The most abundant large whale is the minke, *Balaenoptera acutorostrata*, which was never the tar-get of commercial whaling in the Southern Ocean and may have a popula-tion of around three-quarters of a million there (IUCN, 1991c).

One reason why the IWC failed was that the whole scientific basis for regulating whaling was inadequate. In the period of the commercial mora-torium, scientists and statisticians have been working on a revised manage-ment procedure (RMP) which will avoid these past errors and will express the precautionary principle. It would only be used as part of a revised man-agement system which included better monitoring and tighter supervision. There is no doubt that such an improved system could now be introduced – very cautiously, with only the minke whale as the target of new commercial action, and with a catch limit set at around 2500 a year out of the 750,000 or so living in the southern ocean. But should even this be done? Many leading conservation bodies argue that the Antarctic marine ecosystem is so disturbed by centuries of destructive sealing and whaling that it should be left to recover its balances – and this may take a century.

Others argue that while we could safely resume very limited whaling, we should not do so because of the wider values involved. Anyone who has seen whales at close quarters will have been struck by their majesty, and by their mystery – a vast mammal, clearly with a social structure and communi-cation ability as good as in any land animal, but whose way of life is largely shut away from human observation because we inhabit different media. Films, photographs, the sound recordings of whales 'songs', the first-hand experience of thousands of divers, and 'whale-watching' by thousands more, have brought these wonderful animals into view and stimulated revulsion at the prospect that they may once again be hunted by fast ships, gunned down with exploding harpoons, and cut up for so much oil and meat. The revulsion is strengthened by the relative inhumanity of current capture methods: while an explosive harpoon can kill instantly, about 10 per cent of whales harpooned take over 10 minutes to die. And, on the other hand, non-consumptive uses in the shape of whale-watching by tourists are bringing large revenues to coastal communities in areas where whales gather inshore at certain seasons, as in the Gulf of California or the Peninsula Valdez of Argentina.

A decision on whether to use a particular natural resource, in the seas or on land, in a particular way has to be taken after an analysis of all the benefits the various alternatives bring. And the welfare of the species concerned must be taken into account in that evaluation. This is an important ethical point, enshrined in the World Charter for Nature endorsed by the United Nations General Assembly in 1982 which states that all species warrant respect regardless of their usefulness to humanity. So while it is right that we assess objectively the ways in which living renewable resources might be used, especially to relieve world poverty and as a basis for meeting human needs, we must also recognize that those needs go beyond the material and that it will certainly not be a part of our future strategy to exploit commercially and consumptively every form of life that we could use. It was largely for this reason that in 1994 the IUCN General Assembly adopted recommendations that not only called for the continuation of a ban on all commercial whaling, but for the establishment of a sanctuary south of latitude 40 degrees South (IUCN, 1994b), and the IWC, meeting later that year, adopted both proposals, with some changes in the boundary of the sanctuary.

There are guidelines for bringing a fishery back to sustainability. They were set out by Justin Cooke in Buenos Aires (1994):

■ do not establish a new fishery, or expand an existing one, until a scientifically sound management plan has been drawn up and shown, by simulation or otherwise, to be capable of ensuring sustainability;

■ develop and apply such management plans also to existing fisheries by the year 2000, and where such plans are not in place by the deadline, reduce allowed catches by 10 per cent per annum until the management plan is adopted;

■ ensure that the intensity of fishing does not distort the character of the wider ecosystem – making sure that catches to not reduce the average biomass of either target or non-target species by more than 20 per cent unless it can be shown that a larger reduction will do no harm;

■ where data are inadequate, ensure that catches do not exceed 1 per cent of the estimated biomass of target and non-target species;

■ never establish a fishery in the absence of a reliable minimum estimate of the target species biomass;

■ do not deploy a fishing method which is new or new to an area until it has been thoroughly tested experimentally, and the results evaluated independently to confirm that they will not cause substantial ecological disturbance;

■ exclude any fishing method that involves substantial habitat disturbance from representative areas covering at least half the fishing ground.

These offer a framework for enhancing the use of the oceans and seas, but the detailed prescription must obviously be worked out stock by stock and area by area, and with value judgements like those applied for whales alongside the more strictly utilitarian criteria.

Conclusions: a spectrum of actions

The IUCN guidelines on the sustainable use of wild species are an important development, but we are far from the end of this debate. As Eduardo Fuentes of the World Bank (1994) has commented, there is a danger of circular argument: 'sustainable is what can be shown not to be non-sustainable'. It is almost impossible to prove that a use will be sustainable, but it can be shown that certain actions, at certain intensity levels will be unsustainable.

Any non-trivial human use is bound to cause changes in a target population, ecosystem or landscape. How can the acceptable be separated from the unacceptable, and regulated? Sustainable use of a priority target species or for particular products will very probably reduce overall diversity (as in forests) – can we define boundary conditions for acceptability? Some species may have particular economic value, whether for consumptive or non-consumptive uses – but depend on others not directly valued: how should the balance be reflected in management strategies? In developing countries, how can we ensure that poor people in rural areas benefit from sustainable use – for example from ecotourism revenues – if the tourist operators and concessionaires are based in the cities or even in the developed world? Who pays for the opportunity costs of sustainable use – for the quick revenues forgone in the longer term interest?

While very general criteria may be applicable everywhere, separate guidelines will be needed for marine and terrestrial systems, and more detailed prescriptions will be required for particular situations. Adaptive management must be emphasized. There must be flexibility, creativity and imagination. And we must always remember that sustainable use, sustainable development and adaptive management are all processes that are driven by human behaviour, within the sphere of social, economic and political life.

C H A P T E R   9

EMPOWERING COMMUNITIES

The context of action

Beliefs, values, information, education, knowledge of nature and understanding of how to use natural resources sustainably. All essential ingredients of action. But not action itself. That is largely taken within
communities. If sustainable living is to be achieved, communities must be
structured and empowered to put the decisions of the people that compose
them into effect.

A community, in some ways, is the social equivalent of an ecosystem. It is
an interacting group of people, together with their immediate physical
environment. As *Caring for the Earth* (IUCN/UNEP/WWF, 1991) puts it:

> A sustainable community cares for its own environment and does not
> damage those of others. It uses resources frugally and sustainably, recy-
> cles materials, minimizes wastes and disposes of them safely. It conserves
> life-support systems and the diversity of local ecosystems. It meets its own
> needs as far as it can, but recognizes the need to work in partnership with
> other communities.

Caring for the Earth emphasizes that three kinds of action are needed:

- actions that give individuals and communities greater control over their
  own lives;
- actions that enable communities to meet their needs in sustainable ways;
- actions that enable communities to conserve their environments.

At a greater level of detail, it demands six specific steps:

- provide communities and individuals with secure access to resources and an equitable share in managing them;
- improve exchange of information, skills and technologies;
- enhance participation in conservation and development;
- develop more effective local governments;
- care for the local environment in every community;
- provide financial and technical support to community environmental action.

There are now numerous accounts of how community action has worked out – or failed – in different situations around the world. Useful volumes emerged from a Workshop on Primary Environmental Care held in Siena, Italy, in 1990 (Borrini Feyerabend, 1991) and the Partnerships for Change Conference held in Manchester, England in 1993 (which is summarized in some detail in Chapter 10) (DOE, 1994). A comparison of action in ten countries has been prepared by Charles Pye-Smith, Grazia Borrini Feyerabend and Richard Sandbrook (1994). The conclusions fit together remarkably well. The conclusions?

First, communities and individuals must have secure access to the land and other natural resources on which they depend, and a role in their management. Without these things, they will not be motivated to cherish their resources and use them sustainably. In many countries land tenure needs to be reformed. Many countries have vested ownership in the state, and central governments are all too prone to disregard local wishes, or event to dispossess local people, when they perceive some short-term advantage to the central exchequer. Yet even hunters and nomadic herders need guaranteed access to hunting grounds and pastures. Farmers, including shifting cultivators, need clear title to their land, for this gives them the incentive to conserve soil and enhance productivity. In towns, people need a legal right to their sites or houses and this will give them the incentive to maintain and improve them. Where resources are shared, there needs to be an agreed and equitable system of allocation and management. All this demands decentralization of control and the strengthening of local democratic institutions. A third need is to build partnerships that really support local groups and actions. A fourth is to make markets work for people (Pye-Smith et al, 1994).

Such actions are a part of the process of applying the world ethic for sustainable living. They are essential if the quality of human life is to be improved. For that improvement depends on giving people a decent standard of life on a sustainable basis. They also need levels of health and nutrition that will permit a long and healthy life, education that allows each person to realize his or her intellectual potential and become equipped to contribute to society, and opportunities for rewarding employment. All these things, while properly a part of national strategies, can only be implemented at local community level.

Primary environmental care

Primary environmental care (or PEC for short) is the process by which local communities – with varying degrees of external support – organize themselves and strengthen, enrich and apply their means and capacities (know-how, techniques and practices) for the care of their environment while simultaneously satisfying their needs.

PEC seeks to integrate three objectives (Borrini Feyerabend, 1991):

- protecting the local environment;
- meeting people's needs;
- empowering the local community.

In a sense, primary environmental care is no more than a form of community-based sustainable development. But it is explicit in calling for a merging of environmental and social interests (recognizing that actions that favour one at the expense of the other will not work in the long run) and in calling for full local empowerment, especially through local bodies that take responsibility for resource management.

In her paper for the IUCN Symposium in Buenos Aires, Grazia Borrini Feyerabend (1994) emphasized that:

> PEC is not born out of some fertile minds in search of creative occupation, nor to capture funds that were idly floating in the corridors of development agencies. It is born out of lessons learned in the field, out of the frustration many of us felt in considering failure upon failure, the enthusiasm of reviewing cases of success – which, yes, do exist – and the patience needed to disentangle some plausible reasons why they succeeded.

Three particular lessons stand out from recent reviews and analyses. First, good management of *local* environments is essential if *national* environments and economies are in turn to be managed satisfactorily. Too often, development plans and environmental initiatives (including national strategies) focus on the large-scale at the expense of the local. Yet the 'local' is the dimension of real meaning. It is the place where activities must be carried out, where complexities, conflicts and knots are apparent and not disguised by an abstract planning language, and where environmental care or disruption and neglect have direct, immediate and severe consequences for people's health, well-being and income. Thinking globally and acting locally may be the wrong way about. Local thought and action may be the essential precondition for global success.

There is something of a dichotomy between people's recognition of the need to live more sustainably and their personal actions in response. Much the same gap exists at community level. Vast efforts are devoted to debating great global environmental problems while far less is done to help communities do what can be done today, with simple means and immediate benefits. This happens, as Grazia Borrini emphasized:

> despite the fact that there is little certainty about many outcomes of efforts to address global problems, while for most local environmental problems

the outcome is right in front of our eyes in the form of human death, disease and drudgery, irreversible ecological degradation, loss of biological diversity and waste of great economic resources. Can any country be prosperous when a myriad of local environmental problems remain unchecked and a myriad of communities live a life of misery and disease?

Indeed, this diversion of attention from the local, practical, and soluble to the global, general, and long-term is one of the major impediments discussed in Chapter 4. Addressing it is probably the central key to the solution of the unsustainability conundrum.

The second lesson is that for the management of local environments to be effective, environmental protection must be clearly linked with the satisfaction of the particular needs of local people. There are innumerable local environments in this diverse world, and for each of them 'environmental protection' means something different. It may mean restoring degraded areas, conserving habitats, stopping harmful practices, making sure that productive activities are sustainable, that pollution and waste do not stress ecosystems beyond their limits of resilience, and so on. The point is that all these activities imply some sacrifice on the part of the people living in close relationship with the environment itself. They may require an investment of labour or money, a reduction in the use of a particular resource, foregoing of immediate rewards, or accepting burdens, damages and opportunity costs.

'Can we expect people to be willing to make these sacrifices?' asked Grazia Borrini:

> The experience is that, yes, some people are willing to do so, but only when they make sense, when in return they get something they need and value. That something may be income, food, health, jobs, credit potential, cultural value, pride, recreation or whatever else they wish. Typically, it is something expected to stay, not to flee at the first gust of wind or change of administration. This is the real challenge of sustainable development: finding those ingenious solutions – unique for every environment and society – that meet the needs of the people while meeting the needs of the local environment.

The third lesson is that a human culture cannot be defined from the outside. Substantial initiatives and social changes are sustainable only when the concerned communities, groups and individuals are fully involved in creating them, deciding about them, and carrying them out. This means that the action for sustainability has to begin with the people, not be imposed by some top-down process from a higher level in government, perhaps with a notional 'consultative process' that seeks, and may appear to obtain, assent to plans that have in fact already been worked out in such detail that their originators have a major commitment to them.

Obvious? Yes, but it clashes against walls of power, professional presumption and inertia. There are many instances where large investments, especially of aid money, went astray because the presumed beneficiaries were not consulted about or involved in the initiatives. Their knowledge of their environment, and skill in managing it were disregarded. They had no stake in the scheme. Their labour and resources were not called upon. Indeed some such schemes have disrupted the communities that they were supposed to benefit. On the other hand, as some of the case studies in Chapter 5 and later in the present chapter demonstrate, when people are enabled to take part, and are given responsibility, results can often be obtained with little expenditure. Initiatives succeed when local knowledge and skills are put to full use and activities are designed in response to the complexities of society, and are closely monitored and adjusted along the way.

Drawing together the intelligence, experience, self-perceived interests and willingness of people to work together for a common objective is what primary environmental care is all about. But it is not an automatic or easy process. Conflicts will sprout, lack of knowledge and resources will be major stumbling blocks, and existing cultural limitations – such as degrading treatment of women, violence as a means of achieving power, conflicts with neighbours, or traditional practices that are environmentally damaging – will continue to impede progress. And neither should we romanticize the outside expert, sometimes depicted as the knight in shining armour, either. Many people argue, from experience, that the strongest obstacles to PEC come from outside rather than inside a community, and that many experts have led those they sought to assist astray (Chambers, 1993).

Grazia Borrini Feyerabend has summed up the conditions required in order to achieve primary environmental care as follows:

Some are clearly *political* such as:

■ the government allows people to organize and have a say in decisions over environmental management;
■ people feel secure in terms of access to resources and their ability to benefit tomorrow from the investments they make today. In other words, they have political stability;
■ society promotes an equitable distribution of resources and services, and in particular treats genders, ethnic minorities and indigenous communities fairly;
■ information circulates freely, and there is transparency in ruling and decision making by government agencies and representatives.

Other conditions are *technical*, such as:

■ professional disciplines and sectoral agencies recognize that communities have their own knowledge and skills, and are not arrogantly dismissive of them;
■ information, advice and the diffusion of new technologies are based on a dialogue with local people, building upon and integrating what they have (for example through participatory research, assessment and planning);
■ decentralized services, whether provided by government agencies or non-governmental organizations, are designed to respond to community needs rather than impose solutions and direct and control local activities;

Yet other conditions are *economic*, such as:

- there is a legislative framework that correctly assigns the costs and benefits of environmental protection and regulates the exploitative tendency of markets;
- communities have access to financial resources such as loan and credit facilities, and they can use as collateral the environmental resources they have effectively safeguarded;
- communities have access to regulated markets – that is, markets that use incentives and disincentives to value and promote environmental resources and the health and culture of people;
- communities have access to reliable information provided by such markets, which are expected to remain reasonably stable.

Finally, there is a need for sufficient *time* for people to understand, plan and develop specific agreements and 'contracts' with a variety of partners (this means no more quick projects concocted in far-away offices).

Successful communities

There are many examples of unsuccessful community action around the world. But there are also successes. It is important to analyse both. In this section 13 case studies are reviewed. They concern: date palms in Niger, fuelwood conservation in Mauritania, villages in the north-west frontier province of Pakistan and in the Usambara mountains of Tanzania, Italian National Parks, island communities in the Caribbean, the Australian Great Barrier Reef Marine Park, coastal conservation in Indonesia, wildlife use in rural Zimbabwe, community participation in sustainable development in Guinea Bissau, wetlands management in Uganda, agriculture in Hungary, and land care in Australia. They could be multiplied several times over from various other studies (Reid et al, 1988; Pye-Smith et al, 1994).

In the *Gaya region of Niger* (Daouda and Tiega, 1994), the palm groves have long been of great importance to the local, and indeed to the national, economy. They lie at the centre of agricultural and pastoral activities in the region, providing a wide range of products used as food for people and livestock, the construction of furniture and fishing gear, medicines, and through bee-keeping. They contain over 2 million feet of timber with a potential value of 24 billion CFA francs.

Historically, the palm groves were owned by local communities who had traditional ways of controlling their use and ensuring their protection. However, in the colonial era and at independence all natural resources came under the exclusive control of the state. The use of land and natural resources was not strictly controlled, and this, together with the loss of ownership by the local communities reduced the incentive for effective management and ultimately led to over-exploitation and degradation of the palms.

Today a new scheme is being tested in 52 villages. Responsibility for managing the palm groves is being devolved to them, along with the powers to regulate resource use. While still in its early stages, the project has already provided a number of lessons of wider application in the Sahel region. They include the need for an effective legal framework, the need to re-develop appropriate organizational systems in the communities, and the need to work with those groups that have been marginalized in recent years, and especially women and pastoralists. Another lesson is that funding agencies must be willing to take a long view: all these new systems will take some years to become fully effective. Nine particular needs, likely to be of wider application in the Sahel region, are for:

■ existence of an organizational structure which can represent and negotiate on behalf of the community;
■ recognition by the state and its agencies of the legitimacy of the local groups;
■ progressive transfer of decision-taking powers to the local level;
■ transfer of resource management responsibility to community level;
■ familiarity with the local structures and responsibilities among all concerned;
■ development of a mechanism for conflict resolution, especially where a resource can provide alternative products for different interest groups;
■ establishment of a climate of confidence in the communities;
■ development of a regulatory regime which can ensure conformity with the decisions of the community;
■ establishment of a system of information (including information transfer between communities) and training.

In *Mauritania*, people (and especially those who live in towns) often suffer from a shortage of charcoal and fuelwood. In the country as a whole, according to a 1990 estimate, almost 70 per cent of domestic needs are met by these fuels. The only city in the country, the capital, Nouakchott, accounted in that year for over 47 per cent of total energy consumption. These pressures were fast eroding the remaining forests. The aim of a recent effort (Thiaw, 1994) was to reduce consumption of fuelwood, and thus reduce pressures on woodlands, by distributing improved stoves. The underlying thinking was that despite the acute energy crisis it was unrealistic to expect people to switch rapidly from a fuel used for generations. Hence the first step had to be to reduce wood consumption through enhanced efficiency; only later, and progressively, could substitute fuels like butane or kerosene be introduced.

The project started with market surveys to find out how people cooked, with what utensils and equipment, how often, and using how much fuel. Prototype new stoves were then distributed to a group of households, who had been told that they should aim to reduce their charcoal usage by 30–50 per cent. The attraction of the new system was economic: the new stove saved costs as well as reducing cooking time and being more versatile. Craftsmen benefited because the market for new pots expanded (something that some unscrupulous people exploited). The campaign was linked to voluntary reafforestation schemes. Two particular lessons emerged: that people will support a conservation programme only if it does not restrict their daily needs unduly, and if they really feel the approaching threat and know that they will bear the consequences of non-conservationist lifestyles. These messages are probably equally valid in developed as well as developing countries.

Mauritania – predominantly a pastoral country – has also had some success in improving livestock management (Pye-Smith et al, 1994). The key has been making pastoral associations (PAs) responsible for regulating grazing, managing wells, and stopping destructive bush fires. The result has been increased production of hay and more healthy and productive animals. The PAs have diversified into vegetable and nursery gardening. Some reafforestation has begun, to combat erosion and provide fodder and fuelwood. This diversification of effort, building outwards from action to make the principal land use system more sustainable, is a good indicator of a successful scheme.

In the *north-west frontier province of Pakistan*, where despite the presence of some of the world's highest mountains and the largest glacier systems outside the polar zones, the valleys are arid and water management is of crucial importance, there are several development programmes with a strong element of primary environmental care. They all involve the creation of community-based organizations, and these have focused especially on the sustainable development of agriculture and the planting of trees (for wood, fruit and fodder) on communal land (Khattak, 1994). Several projects have also extended into the sustainable management of grazing land. The primary aim is the organization of village communities to help themselves through collective action. All sectors of the community are involved. Women's organizations have been created, regular meetings are held and savings are being accumulated for reinvestment and extension of the projects. Originally the communities were organized around physical infrastructure, such as the construction of water channels and the supply of gypsum for soil improvement, but agriculture, livestock and social forestry are now major preoccupations. The main challenge is to sustain the activity of the village organizations in the absence of help from either governmental or non-governmental organizations. The principal strategy is to create a strong capital base and village organization in each community, with trained volunteers who can continue to provide leadership after support from the enabling agencies has come to an end. Networks, linking village organizers, will, it is hoped, bring economies of scale.

There is much in common between this scheme, which has been led by the Aga Khan Rural Support programme for over ten years, and an IUCN-Tanzanian government partnership in the *eastern Usambara mountains of Tanzania*. Here the original stimulus was the need to protect diverse montane forests with many endemic species from the encroachment of village cultivators. It soon became clear that conservation had to proceed hand in hand with the strengthening of the village communities. Village organizers were appointed in each of 13 communities, in consultation with the people, and they were trained in skills including contour surveying and the development of nursery gardens for plants used for erosion control and as potential cash crops. Fishponds and fuelwood plantations were created. The whole process enhanced quality of life in the villages, diversified their economies and increased their revenues as well as taking the pressure off the forest reserves, which were demarcated as a part of the scheme by cutting a 10-metre swathe around them and planting it with a double row of teak cuttings.

In *developed countries*, much new effort is being devoted to planning sustainability in urban and industrialized communities. In the United Kingdom, where a national plan for sustainability has been adopted (UK, 1994b), over 20 local, neighbourhood and business *Agenda 21s* are now being developed. Experience has already demonstrated that people on the ground are very familiar with irritating problems like excessive road traffic cutting through residential areas, or street fouling by dogs, or encroachment of building on green space, but are less able to see how the overall pattern of city and local life can be made sustainable. Too many local plans have been prepared by specialists in city administration and then put out to a consultative process designed to adapt such plans at the margins rather than shape them wholly in sympathy with popular views. In the city of Reading, for example, the new process began with widespread public consultation on needs and objectives, in parallel with expert analysis, both contributing to the building of a plan. This approach closely resembles that followed 20 years ago in the alpine resort of Obergurgl (Holling, 1978) where citizens of the village, local government officials and independent scientists debated the issues and objectives and built a simulation model of what various alternative choices might lead to.

In Europe, people and nature co-exist closely and many of the National Parks are protected landscapes in which people live, farm, or use forest products. A new action plan for protected areas, entitled 'Parks for Life' emphasizes that all such areas must be integrated into the fabric of national and local life (IUCN, 1994c). Parks cannot be 'set aside from the mainstream of human concerns, as islands apart from surrounding areas and neighbouring communities.' They:

> protect vital watersheds; they safeguard areas of outstanding beauty and cultural significance; they provide homes for human communities with traditional cultures and protect landscapes reflecting a history of human interaction with the environment, and they are vital places for tourism, recreation and education.

Local people need to be involved as supporters, caretakers and managers. All the stakeholders in an area need to be involved in designing a management regime that is good for the area and good for the community.

A similar effort to link community and national institutions together in the management of local natural resources, within the framework of national resource management and social development policies, is being undertaken in many *Caribbean islands* (Renard, 1994). Here one key has been the definition of the rights and responsibilities of the various stakeholders and in particular their degree of involvement, degree of economic and social reliance on the resource base, historical and cultural relation with it, present and potential impact, treatment in terms of access to resources and the distribution of benefits. The relationship between interests and activities at local level and national conservation and development policies is also crucial.

It has been found that the essential requirements for a sound approach include participatory planning and decision-taking (using popular knowledge, integrating traditional management, ensuring that the agenda is shared and there is good communication, developing means of conflict resolution, and ensuring participation in both institutions and decision processes). The proper development of community institutions, NGOs and government agencies, a clear definition of their roles, and the vesting of authority in them (with legal reforms where necessary) is also essential. Various technologies and structures have been developed, to redress economic and social imbalance, enhance benefits and ensure environmental sustainability.

A rather similar approach has been adopted in the *Australian Great Barrier Reef Marine Park* (Kenchington, 1994). The marine park authority sought from an early stage to secure broadly based community support, and to do this it set out to involve people and give them an economic incentive to cooperate. A three-phase programme began by establishing public awareness of why the authority had been established, and what it did. Phase 2 sought to involve the public generally, and users in particular, in an effective public participation programme for the establishment and zoning of the marine park. In Phase 3 the public, and particularly users, were involved both actively and passively in the management of the park. Active involvement meant getting users to behave in accordance with park rules, and by peer-group pressure to get other users to do the same. Passive involvement was achieved by building awareness of, and support for, the management process in the park.

The mechanisms were a series of education and public awareness projects – posters, brochures, an aquarium and so forth. The message here was that the reef belonged to the community, it was wonderful and must be protected – and that the park authority as the vehicle for that protection needed the full cooperation of the public. The fishing community was a separate target group, and the message for them was that the survival of their industry, and the continuance of their livelihood, depended on their working together with the authority to protect and manage the resource base. It was also made clear to them that the authority needed their knowledge and perspective, since many of them spend 200 days or more a year on the reef and know it more intimately than many visiting scientists, who rarely spend more than 50 days a year there.

The principal lesson learned was that regulations and directions alone could not achieve the conservation objective, and that management was about achieving good results through enlisting the support of 'real people' – the individuals who live around, use, visit, or care about the Great Barrier Reef.

Marine conservation in Indonesia illustrates the problem of levels of delegation (Schoen, 1994). Indonesia is the world's largest archipelagic state, with some 81,000 km of coastline. Pressures on the coastal seas from unsustainable activities including over-fishing, dynamite fishing, coral mining and pollution have been expanding rapidly. In response, the government has established a series of marine protected areas covering 2.5 million hectares: the ambitious target is to expand this to 10 million ha in 5 years, and reach 30 million by the year 2000.

The first stage of action has been to gazette the proposed areas. This involves interactions between various non-governmental actors and agencies at national, regional and local levels. At local level there are consultations and discussions with local communities. Ministerial decrees establishing the area follow. The second phase is the development of a conservation management plan for each area, analysing threats and opportunities, stating conservation objectives, and indicating the instruments (such as subsidies, zonation systems and income-generating activities) to be used to achieve the stated goals. Participatory actions, including discussions, communication and education are a vital part of this stage. Phase 3 is one of implementation of the management plan, and phase 4 of monitoring and adjustment so that the action remains on course to achieve the objectives.

Experience suggests that the implementation stage is the difficult one. It is easy to make laws and prepare management plans, but these are not the answer on their own. Communication with the community is crucial, and different phases in the process need different communication approaches. Although progress has been made in Indonesia, it seems likely that a more community-based approach, in which the people in the area have more authority in framing the management plan and implementing it would be more effective that the rather top-down framework applied so far, with heavy emphasis on the role of government and its agencies.

In *Zimbabwe*, CAMPFIRE (Communal Areas Management Programme For Indigenous REsources) provides something of a contrast. For, as Chapter 8 explained, it is based on the principle that rural communities who suffer the costs of living with wildlife should receive the benefits from its use. It is 'concerned with the conservation and management of wildlife grazing, forestry and water. It offers communities a legitimate means to obtain direct, financial benefits from the exploitation of natural resources.' The local people are themselves the custodians of the natural resources and take the decisions about their sustainable management and use. The programme has involved a fundamental transformation of social relations, and abandonment of the traditional wisdom that it is the top decision-makers who know what is acceptable to, and workable for, grassroots communities. The programme (Martin, 1994) has introduced a system of group ownership with defined rights of access to natural resources, for the communities resident in the areas involved. It has provided appropriate institutions under which resources can be legitimately managed and exploited by the resident communities for their own direct benefits, and also provided technical and financial assistance to the communities which join the programme, so that they can realize these objectives.

CAMPFIRE began by emphasizing the use of wildlife, and especially by raising revenues from safari operators and their clients (Maveneke, 1994b). Animals killed provided meat, sold or distributed in the villages, and yielded other products which were marketed or used in craft industries. Most revenues came from licensed hunting of large animals. But as the programme evolved, communities came to demand a broader approach, with use of forestry products, fisheries, and revenue from photographic safaris. CAMPFIRE has been correctly described as 'not just a wildlife programme. . .[but] a people and institution development programme'. There are increasing demands to switch the management of tourism and safaris from outside operators to new groups based within the communities. This, of course, demands skill transfer through training.

The programme is based on multiple accountability. Legal authority to manage wildlife resources was granted in 1989 to the first two rural district councils involved: the number rose to 12 in 1991 and 23 in 1993. The Zimbabwe Trust is involved in developing community-level institutions. It has to work with the councils and with the Ministry of Local Government, Rural and Urban Development which is responsible for rural district councils. The Centre for Applied Social Sciences which is responsible for socio-economic baseline surveys works hand in hand with the World Wide Fund for Nature, the Zimbabwe Trust and the Department of National Parks and Wildlife Management.

CAMPFIRE works through democratically elected local committees. They are the forums in which people state their needs, discuss and agree plans for resource harvesting, and manage the revenues that result from marketing wildlife products. The Programme emphasizes that benefits, be they cash or projects, are returned to the local communities in the form that the communities demand them. This motivates the communities to regard the natural resources as their own, and so develop a positive attitude towards them.

The benefits have been considerable. In 1992 Muzarabani District communities earned Z$50,000 and used the money for drought relief. In the same year Mahenye Ward in Chipinge District distributed Z$180,000 as household dividends to 481 families and also set aside Z$52,000 for a community grinding mill. Similar levels and patterns of resource use have occurred in other districts. Investments have been in school classrooms, mills, water supplies and clinics. Training is a major investment in all districts.

There have, inevitably, been conflicts as well as cooperation, compromise and consensus-building. For example, some district councils give priority to investment in water-supply projects, while others seek to provide cash hand-outs to the people. Centrist versus community-based approaches introduce tensions in some areas, and it has been noted that the more income a CAMPFIRE project generates, the more there is a tendency for the councils to centralize funds! And while district councils have been adamant in demanding devolution of power from central government, they have been less keen to devolve their own powers to local levels. These tensions are an important feature of the programme and are yielding lessons, one of which is that local empowerment is indeed the best insurance against erosion of people's rights.

The lessons learned from CAMPFIRE are, first, that for meaningful conservation to take place, there must be positive economic benefits that outweigh the cost of living with wildlife. Second, there must be a clear identification of beneficiaries, and they must have an unfettered choice about how to use the benefits. Third, the programme must grow dynamically, and include social, political and economic elements. Fourth, local people must be able to empower themselves to face the challenges of rural development, and finally they must be allowed time to learn and adjust.

This issue of relative responsibilities between the state, its agencies, and local communities and NGOs is central to some of the debate in *Guinea Bissau*, both over the conservation of the last areas of dense forest and the management of the national park on the Orango Islands (Henriques, 1994). The two projects both address the basic question: 'how can we combine public participation with environmental conservation?' In the forest area, the priority is to secure the sustainable development of the people, and conserving the forest resources is an essential mechanism. In the Orango Islands conservation of the natural resources is central, with public participation the means to the end. In the first area, the approach is building on the recognition among the public that the accelerating degradation of their environment threatens their own future. Their awareness is being heightened by the work of non-governmental organizations. The local people have decided that saving the remaining forests is a priority, and they are looking for the best ways of doing so. In Orango, in contrast, the process has begun with an integrated study of the coastal zone, and the options for the conservation and use of its resources. But conservation for whom? Clearly the local people must be involved in the decision process, as a next step.

The state's role is to provide laws and judge between alternative possible actions. But in Guinea Bissau the position is complicated by the fact that some of the agents of the institutions responsible for protecting the environment have been principal causes of its destruction. They have granted concessions for deforestation, for charcoal burning, and for unsustainable fishery. Many of these concessions have been of greater benefit to foreign interests than to local communities. The country has behaved as if, being economically poor, it must of necessity also be poor in ideas, and has turned for solutions to Northern agencies whose development aid has complicated the problems. Clearly sustainability demands transfer of power to those living in and on the resources in question, but this will demand significant changes in attitude, administration, law and practice.

In *Uganda*, the government has conducted, with technical support from IUCN, a survey of the nation's rich wetland resources (Mafabi, 1994). These cover about 6 per cent of the country and have traditionally played an important part in its development. Traditional uses have been for fishing, harvesting of plant materials, grazing, and the growing of crops in 'wetland gardens'. Such practices have been sustainable, and also conserved the biological diversity of the resource. But modern pressures for arable land bring the threat of drainage for agriculture. There are also problems of pollution and the unsustainable harvest of wetland products. Moreover, the trends are bringing a shift in the sharing of benefits: the economic gains from wetland drainage often accrue to a relatively small number of people while removing the option of use of the areas by rural communities in times of need.

It was recognition of these problems that led the government of Uganda in 1986 to ban all wetland drainage until an adequate policy has been developed and implemented. The survey is aimed at defining the values and functions of the wetlands, and identifying how they can best be managed and used for long-term benefit, and how local communities can be given the skills and power to use them sustainably. It has involved a wide consultative process, with district development committees, local communities and individuals. The goal is national consensus.

The aim is to empower the people through formulation of a national wetlands policy, defining the best ways of managing wetlands and providing guidelines on their sustainable use. Local communities should be able to decide how their wetland areas should be developed, and have responsibility for management. Practical projects will demonstrate how wetlands can be used sustainably and raise public awareness of their value, so encouraging people to use them wisely.

The main lessons learned are very like those from the other study areas, namely that local communities should be consulted in all decisions about wetland management, since they know their own needs best; that local communities should be trained and given guidelines for sustainable wetland management; and that participatory programmes which provide hands-on experience of the values, functions, and means of wisely using natural resources are vital.

Uganda was also the scene of a study of primary health care in Palliso District, an area devastated by war and cattle-raiding (Pye-Smith et al, 1994). The district development plan was built around a student association, and funded by the people who wanted to join. It mushroomed, despite poverty and the tiny contributions participants could afford to make. Vaccination greatly reduced child mortality, and adult health improved. The next step was to build outwards into the community, addressing education, family planning, and environmental care. Improved farms, tree nurseries, and revenue-producing projects followed.

Central and Eastern Europe are in a stage of rapid change, and this is affecting agriculture profoundly. There is thus a historic opportunity to ensure that ecological protection and habitat restoration are integrated into the new policies, and that local communities (where livelihoods come especially from farming) and nature conservation agencies work together to achieve common interests.

Hungary has a relatively large farming population (11.5 per cent compared to an average of 6.9 per cent in the European Union), and agriculture contributes some 16 per cent of GDP as against 3.3 per cent in the EU. Present pressures arise because market forces rather than production targets govern activity, the market for products in the former Soviet Union has collapsed, and land is passing back into private hands. Agriculture is being intensified, and threatens to extend onto areas most valuable for nature conservation, many of which have sandy or alkaline soils or are marshy, and which until recently divided the farms that were scattered on the better land. Yet these sensitive areas are unlikely to be attractive to agriculture in the long term. Moreover, longer-term trends in Europe are more likely to favour taking marginal land out of cultivation than extending farmland. In Hungary, therefore, efforts are being made to maintain traditional farming practices and also to maintain the natural habitats on the poorer areas. The thrust of this initiative is at local level (Keleman, 1994). A pilot project has been set up in one area, under a steering committee chaired by the local Mayor and involving representatives of the Ministry for Environment and Regional Policy, the Ministry for Agriculture, local authorities, NGOs and the tourist sector. IUCN is providing independent expert support.

A survey of farmers shows that they are interested in a system which offers them information and advice, and a reliable market for their products. Younger farmers are interested in participating in a system of sustainable tourism that depends on a variety of rural services. They are also interested in courses on sustainable agriculture which will allow them to exchange ideas, learn about new, environmentally sound farming practices and products, learn how to market their products, and understand new legislation. The hope is that the pilot project will lead on to a wider campaign, with public and local community support, to help save Hungary's natural and cultural heritage and protect the well-being of its local communities.

In contrast, *Australia* is a country where rapid and drastic change is some decades old. The arrival of Europeans in 1770 led to major modifications of the landscape and wildlife: in less than 200 years about 100 species of plant and at least 27 species of birds and mammals have become extinct, and a further 209 species of plant and 59 species of vertebrates are recorded as endangered. Habitat destruction is the main cause, especially through the extensive clearing of the vegetation for agriculture, which has transformed or modified about 1,300,000 square kilometres, or 27 per cent of Australia's land surface. Changes in fire patterns, overgrazing by exotic animals like rabbits and domestic sheep and cattle, and the adoption of inappropriate cultivation regimes transferred from Europe have aggravated the situation. The result is a legacy of fragmented landscapes – urban development and vast areas of farmland interspersed with thin corridors of remnant forest and woodland along roads, railways or creeks, and as small patches on hilltops or the corners of paddocks.

This situation clearly needs correction, and a number of actions are now being taken in response (Mobbs, 1994). Emphasis is being placed on conservation outside protected areas, recognizing that many important habitats and species are not adequately protected in the national system of parks and reserves. A parallel move towards ecologically sustainable land-use is in progress, with the goals of protecting the land against erosion and salinity, providing shade and shelter for livestock, maintaining the quality of water in streams and rivers, and adding aesthetic appeal to the landscape.

The community has to be involved, and this is one aim of the National Landcare Programme established by the Commonwealth Government in 1989 (Campbell, 1994; Mobbs, 1994). It has four elements: a land and water programme, a natural resources management strategy, a Save-the-Bush programme and a tree-planting scheme ('One Billion Trees'). There are important common principles. They include recognition that nature conservation outside reserves requires all ages and sectors of the community to play a key role in protecting and managing local ecosystems, and that central governments cannot achieve goals of biodiversity conservation by themselves, but must work with the community. It is clear that there must be a sense of community ownership of the problems and solutions, especially among landholders; that ecologically sustainable development and conservation of biological diversity must be linked wherever possible; and that local knowledge, especially that of indigenous peoples, must be recognized.

Funds are available to help community groups to carry out projects within the four programme areas. In 1993/1994 there were around 1500 applications under the Save the Bush and One Billion Trees sectors alone, of which only 400 were funded. The actual grants are small ($5000 is average) and groups are expected to raise at least twice as much money themselves as they receive from the central organization.

There is no doubt that Landcare has been successful in developing a conservation ethic among a large cross-section of the Australian community. The alliance between the National Farmers Federation and the Australian Conservation Foundation has been important, as these two groups have often differed about land management. In 1994 there were about 1600 Landcare Groups in Australia, with some 39,000 members – a fourfold growth since 1989, despite recession. The key lessons learned have been:

- develop community commitment by involving people and allowing them to do something positive for the environment at local level;
- make the role of the government that of providing funds, back-up support, expertise and information, but not direction;
- ensure availability of an essential minimum of funds, but make these 'pump-priming', encouraging groups to raise most of the resources they need;
- supply back-up expertise and information – this can be more valuable than funds;
- provide information that is useful at local level, where knowledge of plants, animals and habitats may be inadequate (but encourage people to collect local information for themselves);
- build partnerships between governmental and non-governmental organizations;
- target the audience for the initiative;
- expand strategically.

Primary environmental care, community action and national strategies

The world is a diverse place, and numerous different methods and mechanisms are applied in primary environmental care (PEC) activities. Universal methods and mechanisms are difficult to develop, and may not be desirable anyway, given the variety of social and environmental circumstances. But it is clear that a key is what has been termed 'induced positive local participation' – which involves public meetings bringing together traditional leaders and trusted local advisers. The meetings explain environmental issues, find out the interests in the community, and help to change attitudes and develop a consensus. Other conclusions from discussion at the IUCN General Assembly in Buenos Aires (Anon, 1994a) were:

- surveys offer a good way of getting into a community;
- PEC should build on existing capacity, work with different interest groups, and create dialogue;
- local people should be helped to solve their own problems, and to resolve conflicts;
- the legal and policy framework provided by governments needs to be addressed and influenced;
- PEC projects should not depend on donors, and where possible should be carried forward by grants to local communities: this is a better way to build trust;
- replication and sustainability are crucial and hard to achieve, and the best approach is to involve local leaders in the project management group, allow the community to draw up the agenda, use local people as project staff, and devote a good deal of effort to education and training;
- it is essential to respect local culture and hence the best project leaders and trainers are local people, trusted by and sensitive to the community;
- an effective legal and policy framework is required;
- the community must own, or have substantial rights over, the resources on which it depends.

There is, however, an obvious gap between defining an approach like this and solving the conundrum of sustainable development. Some sustainable models do appear to exist at local level, although a number could easily be undone through external pressures, immigration or population growth. But there is no complete model for a sustainable industrial community. The present systems of the developed world, incrementally adjusted and even with wealth transfers like those in Germany, have not demonstrated an answer. What has been developed is a system of partnerships that at least make progress more likely, and some of these are reviewed in Chapter 10.

The process of preparing national conservation strategies, national sustainable development strategies, national environmental action plans and other strategic documents can undoubtedly contribute in a positive way to the development of national and local sustainability. Moreover, as public awareness increases and a stronger constituency for sustainability is built, so demands for increased financial investment in sustainable development will gather force and affect national budgets (Anon, 1994b). By investing in and strengthening local capacity, communities will become more self-reliant and adaptable. Many have this capacity, but it is often ignored, or its weakness is used as an excuse for external intervention, which can be less effective (Chitrekar, 1994). By creating participatory approaches local communities can become involved in managing local resources, but to get the best out of them there has to be change in the way national institutions operate (Shah and Bass, 1994). We must always recognize that there is no uniform model that works everywhere, and the key is to build on existing national and local plans, which must be guided by needs and priorities rather than be donor-driven (Aryamanya-Mugisha, 1994). By emphasizing that environmental plans must not just be 'add-ons' to other national policies, but start from a comprehensive review of economic, social and environmental goals, we can actually strengthen the latter.

But to succeed, strategy must be related to the local environment and to actual social circumstances. Obvious? Of course – but too often thinking has been transferred uncritically from developed to developing countries, and from elite 'expert' institutions to local villages whose traditional knowledge has been swept aside as outdated and irrelevant. Strategies must be built on local knowledge so that they meet the needs of the people concerned. Where external technical contributions are needed – and they often will be – they must fit within the local frame. Strategies must also be adaptable – for the development process is one of rapid change. They must be action-oriented and capable of ready implementation (again, the more they are rooted in local communities who help frame them and are committed to them, the more certain implementation becomes).

In Africa an estimated 70 per cent of the strategies prepared so far have not been implemented. This is partly because they were prepared as analyses rather than action programmes, and partly because their preparation was not linked to economic planning or other development processes. Duplication is another problem: national environmental action plans have been promoted in some countries with scant regard for the other strategies they already possess. Scarce human resources have been wasted in consequence, and the whole strategic process can easily be discredited as a waste of time, or resented as an imposition from outside. Unless a strategy is really owned by the community supposedly guided by it, it is very likely to be counter-productive.

Continuity is another need. By definition, an environmental strategy should be long-term. It deals with fundamental assets, and with processes that operate on a scale of decades if not centuries. Hence the strategies should be proofed against political oscillation, and continue despite changes in government. This is most likely to happen if they are the outcome of community-wide discussion, and reflect general consensus. They should also be cross-sectoral, and hence integrate environmental, economic and social policies. They should be produced by a flexible, consultative process, not designed to give effect to pre-determined government policies. While they may need support by legislation, they should go with the grain of social commitment and should employ economic incentives as well as regulation.

Analysis suggests that the conservation strategies and environmental action plans of the past fifteen years have had partial success only. On the credit side, they have helped to elevate environmental issues on the agenda of governments and communities. They have helped to inject environmental thinking into education, planning and technical development programmes. They have influenced both governmental and non-governmental organizations. On the other hand, many have been left on one side as the mainstream of economic and development planning flows by. If we are to give effect to *Agenda 21* and *Caring for the Earth*, this must change.

The key issue is how to turn the strategic planning process on its head, and make it truly participatory. This is the best way of ensuring that a strategy matches local circumstances, needs and capacities – and will be willingly implemented. The pace of implementation must match local capacity. If strategies are to lead to action rather than simply add to the load on bookshelves and the wastage of paper, they must meet certain criteria:

- They should start with a sensitization process which raises public awareness and generates a broad base of support. This is essential if they are to be accepted at political level and obtain the resources they need. When it comes to implementation, a clear public mandate is also essential, so that there is a groundswell of opinion behind the strategy.
- Local knowledge, values, traditions and ideas must be captured. Unless we work with the grain of culture we are unlikely to succeed.
- The process must be transparent. Information should be widely disseminated. All sectors of the community – members of the public, local interest groups, business industry and commerce, organized labour, the professions, local government and central government – must be able to participate. The result must be owned by the community at large – by both 'winners' and 'losers'.
- There must be dialogue between all the groups concerned, leading to a broad if not universal consensus. This demands the building of understanding, and may require special skills of conflict resolution. Strategies are as much a part of the political and social agenda as of the technical and environmental one. Scientific analysis alone cannot define the whole range of economic, social, and environmental options for meeting both present and future needs. The technique of adaptive assessment pioneered by CS Holling and his colleagues at the International Institute of Applied Systems Analysis (Holling, 1978) provides one model that could be followed.
- The strategy documents must be written in clear language and be widely available. It helps for them to be discussed in local communities, as the National Conservation Strategy for Botswana was, before any formal adoption by government.
- The benefits the strategy will bring must be obvious. It must be clear that the community as a whole will gain, and that while some people may lose relative benefit, they will be outnumbered by the 'winners'. The strategy must be explicit about how costs are likely to fall on different sectors of the community, with impacts on livelihoods and equity.

■ The costs of implementation must be clear – and the means of achieving it. Incentives are likely to be more effective than regulations when it comes to action. And attaching a proper value to environmental resources is crucial in helping governments and individuals make the right decisions.

■ Strategies should enlist the support of private landowners (for much of the action, in many countries, will be on private land), and should win so much public support that people effectively police the environmental impacts of actions by the state and others, bringing cases against those who do not follow environmental guidelines.

■ The process should be under the control of the country and communities concerned, and be carried forward at a pace they accept. Donor pressure should not impose an unwelcome strategy or press it forward so fast that it leaves the people behind.

■ All strategies should be seen as part of a continuous process of development, and they should include monitoring and review procedures. Moreover the review process should itself be broadly based in the community, and participatory.

Linkages are extremely important. In Europe, Africa and Asia environmental strategies have often been too narrowly sectoral and hence the mainstream of development has passed them by. Competition and rivalry between sectoral institutions has to be faced and dealt with at the outset. In Pakistan and Ethiopia this was done by placing the central body responsible for national planning in the lead, and giving all the principal ministries concerned a place in the steering committee. In Zambia and Tanzania parastatal agencies have been established to implement strategies. They are outside the line ministries and hence able to 'encourage' all departments to incorporate environmental needs and factors in their work. On the other hand, for this to succeed the agencies must be strong enough to avoid being marginalized by a combination of powerful 'mainstream' ministries.

Local capacity must be built, and in ways appropriate to local conditions. It is better to strengthen existing institutions than to create new ones. Capacity-building should start at the beginning of a strategy process and be an integral and continuing element of it. The work on the strategy should proceed at the pace local capacity can support, rather than rely excessively on external technical assistance. And capacity building in the non-governmental organizations, the legal community and the private sector should not be neglected. Governments alone cannot prepare or implement the kind of strategy that is now needed. Hence the process should include some kind of 'round table' or interactive group, and a network of people – 'stakeholders' – within and outside government who can advise on and contribute to the strategy process.

Strategic planning, like all decision processes, demands finance. Experience shows that it is unwise to rely on the recurrent government budget, which is undergoing structural adjustment in much of the developing world. Strategies need their own sources of funds. While donors can often provide short-term support for the formulation and initial implementation stages, it is better to develop strategies without undue reliance on them.

There are many ways in which the procedure can be adapted in detail. National strategies can be developed first, and then decentralized to regional levels, as was done in Pakistan, or they can be built up from regional initiatives as in Ethiopia. The choice depends on how the administration in the country concerned is structured, and how local communities, business, the non-governmental sector and the other actors are to be involved.

Participation is essential but is not easy. It requires a flexible approach, and the strategy process must not be de-railed by initial challenges or downright hostility. It requires finance. People may need to be empowered to participate by the adoption of some specific public policy, or by funding. It has to be done sensitively: for example in some cultures women and men will need to participate separately (at least in public gatherings).

The term 'participation' is replete with ambiguity. The dictionary defines it as 'taking part in some activity: having a share in something'. But it can be truly collaborative, in which all participants work together on an equal footing, or reactive, in which a dominant person or group sets the terms of the process. In community decisions about the environment, and specifically in the context of strategies, participation is likely to be most successful in the end if it is much more than a matter of reactive consultation. Some sharing of control and responsibility is needed. The ideal is to move as far through the sequence in Figure 16 as possible, in the direction of 'High participation' (Shah and Bass, 1994).

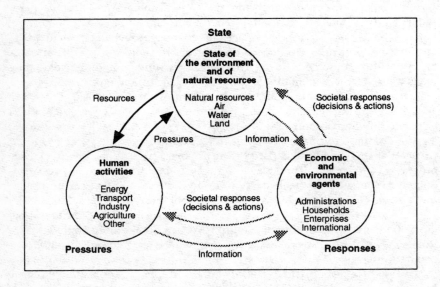

Source: after O'Connor, 1994

Figure 16 The pressure–state–response system

Social diversity, like biological diversity, is an asset. It is good that the strategy process involves the development of diverse perspectives both on the process and its goals. In India, for example, participation led to a greater attention to livelihoods, productivity and equity issues, and in turn made the resulting strategies more attractive to the people and more likely to succeed. Meeting local priorities first should be one outcome of a participatory approach. While this may deflect some effort from broader strategic environmental issues to start with, it will help bring local commitment and momentum to the strategy process overall.

The outcome of this analysis can be summarized in a series of positive rules for the process of strategic planning for sustainability, and the decisions that follow from it:

- Make sure that the process is a cyclical one, with successive stages of planning, action, feedback and evaluation, review and adjustment.
- Make sure that it is rooted in the communities concerned, and gains legitimacy from their support. In this way, develop a broad mandate for implementation, and as far as possible make strategies self-implementing through public commitment and political pressure.
- Ensure that capacity is developed from the start of the process, so that the strategy is the creature of the institutions in the country and community concerned.
- Go at a pace that the communities and institutions can bear. Never leave the people behind.
- Make sure that you know how to re-invigorate strategies that run out of steam.
- Make the strategies a part of mainstream economic and social development. They are about how to use the most precious assets of the community for the sustainable benefit of present and future generations.
- Seek funding that makes the development and implementation of the strategy as autonomous as possible.
- Recognize that a successful strategy will make the government or community concerned more self-reliant, more able to learn from experience, and above all, able to enjoy a steady improvement in its quality of life for an indefinite period.

Indicators of sustainability

Community participation is a mechanism for building a sustainable society. It has to be accepted that such societies are rare – especially in the developed world. The communities of the North are not the model, for they are too much geared to the linear throughput of materials, wastefulness in energy use, and the excessive consumption of materials and generation of pollution. There is a long way to go in designing sustainable societies, and the national and local strategies needed to implement *Caring for the Earth* and *Agenda 21* should start by establishing the criteria for them. All strategies should then include a monitoring process, in which indicators of sustainability are defined and progress towards them measured.

In recent years there has been a great deal of discussion of indicators of sustainability. Some people have portrayed them as a kind of mathematical index that allows uncertainty to be by-passed, and the success of the development process to be evaluated objectively. There are manifest dangers in such an approach. For a composite numerical indicator may appear to confer precision, yet be the aggregate of many judgements each of which has subjective elements. And the choice of the components within the indicator clearly determines how well it relates to the real world. Finally, is it meaningful to expect a single list of parameters to fit situations everywhere, and so provide a general yardstick? Almost certainly not.

The difficulties are well illustrated by the approach used in two United States cities – Jacksonville in Florida and Pasadena in California – which have adopted 74 and 112 indicators respectively (Corson, 1994). The Jacksonville list reflects trends in the economy, public safety, health, education, the natural environment, travel mobility, government and politics, the social environment and culture and recreation. Other indicators have been adopted at state level in Oregon and Minnesota, and yet others have been used in national programmes in various nations. One series, developed from a Latin American perspective (Winograd, 1994), includes erosion and the loss of soil fertility, desertification, deforestation and land-use change, use and exploitation of woodlands, rural land tenure and migration, the degradation of freshwater catchments, the loss of genetic and ecosystem resources, the deterioration of marine and coastal resources, the contamination of air and water and the quality of life in human settlements. A special set, termed 'Green Gauge', has been developed in the UK and covers biodiversity, habitat changes, and pollution. A recent overview and analysis was published by the World Resources Institute in May 1995 (Hammond et al, 1995).

Clearly, the lists commonly group two kinds of measure: those related to the health of the environment and those related to human welfare (Table 10). The World Resources Institute team believe that there are in fact four key aggregate indicators – pollution, resource depletion, ecosystem risk and environmental impact on human welfare (Hammond et al, 1995). The problem is that the use of several hundred physical indicators – such as appear in many national inventories of environmental statistics today – is unlikely to lead to a rational policy (O'Connor, 1994). For statistics like emission of sulphur dioxide or carbon dioxide, river quality, household waste generation or the area of nature reserves in a country need to be interpreted if they are to be useful. There has to be some conceptual model as a framework for designing sensible indicators – and it must span the political, social, cultural, economic and environmental spheres. Where measurements are made, the methods and units must be compatible or comparisons become impossible and confidence in the picture that results deservedly evaporates.

Many evaluations of the state of the environment use what is termed a 'pressure–state–response' system (O'Connor, 1994). In each area, indicators can be chosen and measured (more or less). Thus indicators of environmental pressure could include such things as emissions of carbon dioxide, sulphur dioxide or nitrogen oxides; generation of toxic, nuclear, municipal or other kinds of waste; rates of urban encroachment on farmlands; or human population growth. The state of the environment is clearly to be measured in terms of factors that can cause change – like concentrations of carbon dioxide in the atmosphere, or of chlorofluorocarbons in the stratosphere, or of ozone in the total air column, or ultraviolet B radiation penetration. Similarly the state of freshwaters and soils can be evaluated in terms of contaminant levels.

Table 10 Possible indicators of environmentally sustainable development

Issue	A Pressure	B State	C Response
I. Economic			
Production	inputs as % GNP	Value added per caput (NNP)	Efficiency of produced assets
Expenditure	Inflation	Gross national expenditure (GNP)	Saving (adjusted)/GNP
Income	Population (growth rate)	Distributional inequality	Spend on safety nets
Labour	Wages etc (share in GNP)	Human capital (educational attainment)	Spend on training and job creation schemes
II. Social			
Urbanization	Migration to towns	Urban population	Spend on towns
Housing	Population increase	% homeless; sq m dwelling per head	Spend on housing, shelter for homeless
Water Quality	Demand for clean water and sewerage	Drinking water quality	Spend on water and sewerage, and clean-up of water and air
Air Quality	Energy demand	Particulates, SO_2 etc	
Health	Disease (incidence)	Life expectancy	Spend on health
Nutrition	Underweight children	Dietary energy supply	Subsidy for school meals
Transport	Growth in road vehicles	Modal split, road/rail, passengers and freight	Spend on public transport provision; % petrol unleaded
Women's status, caring capacity	Maternal mortality rate	Total fertility rate; Females in school	Growth in female employment and education
III. Ecological			
Global commons			
Climate change	Greenhouse gas emissions	Greenhouse gas concentrations	Energy use efficiency
Stratospheric ozone	CFC consumption	CFC concentrations	Application of Montreal protocol
Oceans	Discharges	Pollution levels	Spend on controls
Marine resources	Fishing intensity	Marine stocks	Fishery controls

Natural assets

Biodiversity	Agrochemical use; Land use changes	Toxic residues in wild life; % of species threatened	Integrated pest management; spend on conservation
Water	Discharges of pollutants	Concentrations of metals in rivers	Spend on pollution control
Eutrophication	Phosphate, nitrate discharges	Oxygen, nitrate, phosphate in rivers	% sewage treated; nitrate control zones
Acidification	SO_2, NO_x emissions	Acidity of rain, mist and snow	Spend on pollution control
Toxic contaminants	Discharges to rivers	Concentrations	% petrol unleaded
Waste	Production of hazardous wastes	Volume disposed annually	Spend on disposal and recycling

Marketable Assets

Gas, oil and coal	Extraction rates	Proven reserves	Energy use efficiency
Metals, minerals	Extraction rates	Proven reserves	% recycled
Forest resources	Conversion and use rates	Areas and production	% used sustainably
Land and soil	Erosion and land degradation rates	Productivity, area of degraded land	Spend on erosion control, resotation

General indicators		Opinion polls on environment	Spend on controls; new laws

Source: Modified from O'Connor, 1994

But the state of the environment can also be expressed in terms of ecological characteristics, such as levels of biomass, biological diversity, agricultural productivity, soil erosion rates, areas of forests or wetlands, and – in the urban areas – extent of human settlements. Finally, responses are evidently to be measured in terms of social action, such as expenditures on pollution control, expansion of protected areas, enactment of laws and regulations, or installation of new social services to enhance urban environmental quality. Given the new recognition that a state of dynamic change is normal in ecosystems, and that some stresses may be essential to resilience, the prediction of the limits of tolerance is clearly very difficult. Yet how can an indicator be evaluated unless we can judge its significance as an ecological factor? The fact is that we do not have any agreed, reliable series of indicators yet. What we have are some provisional systems, like the list set out in Figure 16 and Table 10.

The 'clusters' in Table 10 imply that the economic, social and ecological issues can be grouped, and in the latter that 'global commons', 'national trusts', 'marketable assets' and 'carrying capacity' can be used as sub-headings. The four key indicators in the WRI report likewise group many components. But this approach has many difficulties. For example, climate change and stratospheric ozone depletion are themselves the result of measurable processes, but have an impact on biological diversity and ecosystem function and productivity (for which, probably erroneously, biological diversity is taken as surrogate). There is an element of double counting if a factor and effect are separately assessed.

There are other problems. The indicators most useful in one community are not necessarily appropriate to another. There is considerable concern in some developing countries that a set of universal indicators will be applied to measure national success in achieving sustainable development – and to criticize those who appear to be lagging. There is also concern that progress against certain indicators could be used to evaluate whether aid had been well used, and international obligations complied with. None of these applications is sensible in today's state of knowledge.

It is, indeed, far from clear that the indicators chosen from within the fabric of today's non-sustainable societies are the right ones. The indicators should come from the target society towards which communities are working. If so, they are likely to emphasize social goals (health, literacy, housing, urban service provision, employment opportunity, land and home ownership rights, rights of expression and levels of local community empowerment) and 'ecoefficiency' standards (per caput use of energy and materials, levels of recycling, levels of pollution, energy density in industry and so forth). A third cluster will certainly measure the health of the ecological systems on which society depends (productivity, diversity, contaminant levels, reproductive success of indicator species and so forth). There is a need for a critical analysis of just what pointers would be most useful, under various social circumstances. Probably the best course is for each community or nation to choose its indicators once it has adopted its strategy for sustainability – but there is a role for a body like the UN Environment Programme to suggest frameworks and approaches.

The wider context of decision

Empowering communities is important, but there is no guarantee that they will choose the path of sustainability. Anil Chitrekar of Nepal (1994) pointed out in the Buenos Aires workshop that 'the prevailing mind-set with many decision makers is that environmental management is important but should in no way hamper development' (by which they commonly mean technology, industrialization and urbanization). The biggest challenge in dealing with the issue of sustainability remains this human mind-set that considers the manufactured more valuable than the natural (whatever it costs to maintain). People find it hard to step back far enough and envision the new sustainable society they need, and the new environmental paradigm (Milbraith, 1989) they should follow.

Even if this hurdle is overcome, problems can arise if the desirable alternative is too expensive simply because the currently exploited resource is free. Fuelwood, for example, is free (where it can be gathered), whereas a methane gas plant requires investment. Why should a village make the change until forced to do so? Governments (as already noted) reinforce this distortion by treating natural resources as free goods, and by an ever-ready tendency to expropriate them as sources of revenue for the administration.

Decisions are taken on a basis of perceived benefit. Most people (most of the time) choose the option that seems likely to bring the best return for them personally, or for their immediate group. The selfish and competitive element behind many such choices is at the root of many of today's problems, ranging from the legacy of past industrial pollution and the destruction of the great whales to the inequities in the world trading and economic system. Getting the valuations right is one step. While a chopped tree has a cash value and a standing tree is worthless, people will mis-use forests.

Equity is universally conceded to be important, but is not universally respected in practice. Those who benefit from inequity tend to cling to their gains, while those who suffer are powerless to reverse the decisions. For example, people in Nepal have been removed from their homes in order to protect large areas of National Park, while commercial operators are permitted to open lodges and hotels there (Chitrekar, 1994). A similar situation has arisen in parts of East Africa, like the Ngorongoro Conservation Area in Tanzania, where Maasai people may not reside in certain areas or grow crops, yet where until recently only a fraction of the tourist revenues found their way back to the local communities. In Kenya the Maasai Mara National Park belongs to Narok District Council, yet over 90 per cent of the revenue it generates moves out of the district. Decisions for equity are hard to implement. And these kinds of distortion make it harder for communities to find the path to sustainability.

At global level, so long as emissions of air pollution per head in the rich North are ten to twenty times those in the South, there will be little sympathy for claims that the industrialization process in the poorer countries should be loaded with abatement costs. As Tewolde Berhan gebre Egziabher and his colleagues Gedion Asfaw and Worku Ayele have pointed out (Tewolde et al, 1994):

> the poorest countries of the South use only biomass for energy. The carbon dioxide they produce becomes new biomass, fuel for the next season. They do not thus cause any appreciable carbon dioxide accumulation in the atmosphere. It is the industrialized countries that do so. Any resulting change in climate, however, will affect all countries.

Global sustainability is obviously essential, but even if it is accepted as a common goal there will be a vast range of pathways towards it, because communities start from such different places and have differing priorities, differing cultural values and differing environmental constraints. It is obvious that both North and South need to change their lifestyles. The North needs to reduce consumption, pollution and waste, while the South takes measures to halt population growth, and strengthen economies and infrastructure. Both must cooperate to support sustainability and this will mean a change in their economic, trading and financial relationships. It will mean that many Northern societies stand more or less still at their present standards of living, while the disadvantaged catch up. But it will also mean that both converge on a new point where quality of life is provided through a far more efficient use of natural resources, and far greater concern for individual human fulfilment.

The thesis that if the idea of sustainability is voiced clearly enough, countries will automatically re-orientate themselves is clearly false. Cure does not follow automatically from diagnosis, any more than people practise what they preach. The opinion polls show that at an individual level people may be aware of the need to change their lifestyles for the good of other people and the common environment, but they do not do so. The same goes for nations, whatever their leaders said in Rio de Janeiro. Those leaders need to remember that there are great benefits to be gained from the regional and planetary security that sustainability will bring. And having seen it, they need to be willing to advance their own long-term interests by aiding others to achieve sustainability. That means joining in planetary alliances for peace-building through sound care of the environment. The following chapters address some of the ingredients.

BUILDING NEW ALLIANCES

Sustainable living is a matter of individual lifestyles: how people use, damage, care for and hand on their environment. But however well informed and motivated individuals are, they will not be able to live sustainably unless they are enabled to do so by others. Social traditions, financial constraints, laws, and the dictates of local and central governments can all impede, or facilitate, sustainability. And communities and governments are themselves constrained by the inertia of the past – the laws enacted by previous generations and the investments made a decade or more ago.

Sustainability demands change in the whole fabric of living. We all form part of a large, complex, diverse system whose functional rules are still only imperfectly understood. To treat that system as a single unit is clearly to over-generalize. To assume that it is all a matter of getting at individuals, firms, municipalities, religious groups or government ministers is equally incorrect. All have to be influenced, and all have to work together. Partnerships are frameworks for that association.

A *partnership* in this chapter is defined as a linkage between individuals or groups with a defined common objective – the pursuit of sustainable living. Previous chapters have described numerous examples. But what are the ground rules? What are the impediments to partnerships and how can these be overcome? These questions were explored by the 'Partnerships for Change' Conference held in Manchester, England, in September 1993 (DOE, 1994), and were also considered by the IUCN General Assembly in Buenos Aires. They are the focus of the present chapter, which summarizes the conclusions of a number of its workshops.

The structure of society

Most attempts to classify the structure of a society – national, state or provincial – stress the role of the formal governmental sector: the departments of state responsible for sectors of activity, and the official agencies responsible for implementing areas of policy. And at the level of detail the situation is often very complex.

Yet such schemes miss the fact that in any society there is a large and complex network of non-governmental organizations (NGOs), often loosely co-ordinated or not co-ordinated at all. Environment and conservation bodies may be members of IUCN and linked through a national committee, but this largely serves for information exchange in a restricted series of areas of interest related to international conservation, and there is little by way of real coordination. A quite different assemblage of NGO representatives may be constituted for other purposes – such as the steering committee that relates to the UN Commission on Sustainable Development (CFOCF, 1995). In the same way the industrial world may have groupings that bring together firms in a particular sector – the oil, chemicals, fertilizers, pesticides or motor-vehicle sectors for example – but national federations and chambers of commerce again provide common meeting grounds for information transfer and mutual expressions of concern rather than tight coordination. Information flow is clearly an essential linking mechanism.

Another linking system is in the fabric of governance itself – laws, administration, and financial policies. These are determined by legislatures and governments, and they provide the framework within which individuals, groups, local communities and industrial enterprises operate. Recent years have seen an apparent triumph of the system of government which is based on free-market economics over that based on planning. The reasons are complex, but in part arise from the lack of flexibility in planned systems, and their removal from individuals of the capacity for personal initiative. In developing and developed countries alike, empowering individuals to pursue their goals is of crucial importance, and allowing people to build for the future is central. Land tenure, home ownership, and an ability to save and invest for later years and generations are all stimuli that can lead directly to investments in environmental improvement.

But there are dangers in unbridled individualism. The human animal is all too easily stimulated into aggressive competition, whether at individual or group level. We live, as Lester Milbraith (1989) put it, in a dominator society. The long-running political debate between 'capitalism' and 'socialism' may have been resolved in favour of the former, but behind these labels lies a deeper dichotomy. 'Capitalism', as a word, derives from the Latin *caput*, head. It is the cult of the individual, and when it becomes the cult of the selfish individual uncurbed, becomes dangerous. 'Socialism' for its part comes from another Latin word, *socius*, friend or companion: at its best therefore it is the cult of the alliance. Sustainability at least demands that unbridled 'caputalism' is avoided, and that individuals use their personal freedoms to advance 'societalism', sustainable communities. It has implications for the structure of the frame of governance within which people and groups operate.

Sustainable living means curbing excessive consumption. It means curbing competition where this positively damages elements in the community, or other societies in other countries, or the prospects of future generations. It therefore means interfering in the market, altering the framework of governance. It means stating clearly that some forms of behaviour tolerated – indeed promoted – today, for example through the advertising process that drives rampant consumerism and tolerates waste, environmental degradation and the needless extinction of species, are *wrong* in a moral sense. It means using custom, the definition of the socially acceptable, the economic process, or even the law, to stop behaviour which is intolerable because it undermines sustainability. Sustainability, as IUCN has recognized in its new mission statement, must be built on *equity*. But equity is incompatible with repression, and striking the balance between freedom and constraint is the most difficult challenge.

There are grave doubts about the ways many societies will develop. As Maximo Kalaw of the Philippines (1994) put it in Buenos Aires:

> predictions for the next two decades forecast no growth in employment in Europe. They foresee long-term poverty for the majority of the human family. The globalization of markets, capital and technology will continue to result in disintegration of society where the majority of citizens cannot be market players. They acknowledge that the State is powerless to regulate and govern international finance flows, traffic in drugs and armaments, ethnic and religious conflict and trans-boundary destruction of planetary life-support systems. Such a situation provides the proverbial condition of 'crisis and opportunity' for civil society, and non-governmental organizations in particular.

Such a situation, of course, brings with it the opportunity – indeed the imperative – for fundamental change. If traditional systems of government are failing, partly because they have not cared either for their people or for those parts of the Earth that lie within their boundaries, then change will be inevitable – either through social and governmental breakdown such as is tragically evident in many countries today or through a smoother process of reconstruction, or both.

The challenge of the evident unsustainability in today's world therefore opens the way for a new kind of society, committed to new kinds of goal and following new pathways towards them. It is likely to demand decentralization from central to local levels, and the protection of groups against dominance and exploitation, by the agencies of government as much as by private sector entrepreneurs and employers. It is likely to be built from the citizen upwards, starting with personal values and ethics, aided by education and open, honest, public information. It will strengthen the role of the local community. We need to truly empower people. We need to re-enfranchise those who have long been exiled by the ideologies of the state from the domain of political and economic decision. We need to re-examine values that come from our deepest spiritual and cultural traditions. We need to build societal constraints on a broad consensus.

The non-governmental community can and should be major architects of that change. They can provide a third linking mechanism, drawing citizens together into groups that debate their goals and priorities. Being free from the inevitable commitments and inertia of governmental machinery, NGOs are able to be more innovative, more radical, and swifter in their reactions. They can harness active sectors in the community in a parallel organizational structure, which can sometimes by-pass the official machinery. But there are limits to NGO capacity. They are best as stimulants within the body politic. They should not demand too much, or they will face the accusation that they are grasping at power without responsibility – for they are accountable only to their members, where elected governments are accountable to everyone. The NGO community needs to review its own contribution to achieving sustainability within states and localities, and to organize itself accordingly.

The world of business, industry and commerce is another linking mechanism. It employs a large slice of the community and generates most of its wealth. It has its own international links, and operates on a larger scale than many governments – the ten largest international corporations are bigger, in financial terms, than some seventy of the world's states. But the business sector also needs to organize itself to contribute to sustainability. At present, many firms appear at best ambivalent, torn between pursuing their narrow financial goals and their contribution to the wider community. Despite the work of the Business Council for Sustainable Development and the International Chamber of Commerce, the business community has not taken up a position of leadership commensurate with its power in the world, or presented its own agenda for sustainable living in a sufficiently persuasive way.

Chapter 11 discusses some of the key actions in all these groups as we move to the future. But what is apparent is that none can act alone. Partnerships are essential.

Partnerships for change

Since the UN Conference on Environment and Development there has been renewed interest in how to focus the national and international quest for sustainability. Some countries have followed the lead of Canada and established round tables at both national and provincial level. These are meeting places for government, industry, the scientific and economic communities and environmental groups. Some countries have established a more complex system: the United Kingdom, for example, has a high-level Panel on Sustainable Development, giving authoritative advice, together with a round table which is intended to bring together representatives of the main sectors and groups and a Citizen's Environmental Initiative which is intended to 'carry the message to individuals and local communities' (UK, 1994b).

There is little point in seeking to review all the different structures worldwide. The important thing is that they are all designed to promote partnership within the community, and they need to be adapted in each country to its needs and priorities. And as Chapter 9 emphasized, the key is getting the action down to the local level and there establishing whatever mechanism fits the community best.

The same holds internationally. The United Nations system has pride of place as the intergovernmental forum for coordinating action, and in the environmental field, under the General Assembly and the Economic and Social Council, the Commission on Sustainable Development, the UN Environment Programme, and a number of specialized agencies all have a major role. But what is becoming clear is that the UN system alone cannot provide global sustainability: there has to be partnership with the non-governmental sector, including the world of business, industry and commerce and the environmental movement (UN, 1994a; UN, 1995f).

The Manchester conference was convened by the United Kingdom government, in response to a pledge made at Rio. It brought together over 300 people from all sectors and over 85 countries (DOE, 1994). The participants came from central and local government, business, industry and commerce, the trade union movement, environment and development NGOs, religious groups and the media. It included activists and academics (not always readily separated), planners and legislators, scientists and economists, managers and operators, young and old. And its conclusion?

> The overwhelming message of the Conference was that partnerships are applicable in all kinds of situations, in all places, and it is hard to think of instances where they are not appropriate. . .As one participant put it: 'sustainable development is a big problem, demanding big solutions'. 'Big solutions'. . .that show breadth of imagination, length of time horizon, and depth of commitment are surely only attainable when many different kinds of people are involved. It is often the alliances between the most unlikely partners that are most effective. And it is difficult to think of any kind of development that is likely to be sustainable unless all interests in a community – poor as well as rich; young as well as old; women as well as men; labour as well as employers; industry as well as environmentalists – are brought together and contribute, first to policy, and then to implementation.

The introduction to the published report identified a number of positive *factors in success*:

1 *Focus* – a clear set of parameters for the partners to address. All participants must start by making an effort *to understand the nature of the problems*.
2 While information and education are important, they must be *linked to what people have to say about their needs*.
3 Solutions must be *developed in context*: experience shows that ideas and methods imposed from outside will not win confidence or be taken forward.
4 While partnerships must be *innovative and flexible*, their success depends on good *planning* to sort out complex problems, good *management* to get the best out of people, *building capacity* at both personal and institutional levels, the sharing of *financial resources*, and *good communication*, because everyone must understand the positions of everyone else, and credit must be given to all contributors.

5   All partners must have a sense of *ownership* of the partnership, and this means opening it up to *wide participation* and showing that there are real benefits from cooperation.

6   There must be *transparency* and *accountability*, with the roles of each partner clear at every stage and with each being responsible to all the others for their contribution. A *formal agreement* may be necessary to that end.

Equally, there are common obstacles to success. The one most frequently encountered is *inequality* between the actual or potential partners. The present vast disparities in economic strength and access to resources make it hard for partners from the South to join those from the North with a feeling that they have equal weight in the arguments. Some sectors of society may even be excluded because their views are dismissed as of little importance:

> Such prejudices are not just exercised against those who lack economic power. They may be rooted in race, creed or just differing views of how the world works. Environmentalists, for example, can be just as unwilling to listen to the views of industry as the other way round. 'Experts' can be scornful of traditional learning that stems from centuries of experience (DOE), 1994).

It is clear that the role of governments needs a great deal of thought:

> At present there are too many areas of government policy, in far too many countries, that are actually in conflict with the processes needed to achieve sustainable development, and act to limit the effectiveness of any partnership. . .Governments have an inescapable role in sustainable development, but it is as much enabling as directional. They can and must create the conditions in which partnerships for sustainability can flourish (DOE, 1994).

The Conference suggested that this demanded action at several levels:

■   through *national and international frameworks* to bring bodies and agencies together;

■   through *government leadership in developing national sustainability strategies and action plans*;

■   through their willingness *to create the economic and administrative conditions for success* – which may include decentralising decision-making and action and giving more scope to local initiatives;

■   through ensuring that the national frameworks *integrate* the sectors and levels of government and harness them to the process of sustainability.

Finally, the Conference concluded that:

> Whatever the process, means must be found to *evaluate* success. This may be helped by establishing clear *goals, targets and indicators of sustainability* so that progress towards them can be monitored. There must be *open reporting* of the results of such monitoring – which must feed into the continuing process of discussion and adjustment. Partnerships – at whatever level – must have a *long-term view* as well as short-term objectives. Sustainable development is an unending process (DOE, 1994).

Many of these general points emerged time and again in the 36 workshop sessions. These addressed 12 basic themes, and some special United Kingdom perspectives. All the general workshop topics started with the question 'how can partnerships work...?'. They all began by raising certain basic issues, turned to consider what kinds of partnership were appropriate, looked at obstacles, considered cases of success and failure, and the reasons, and drew out the factors in success. Their conclusions are helpful to the wider debate, and are summarized in the following ten sections.

Achieving sustainable resource management

Many countries face the central issues of how to set priorities for the sustainable use of natural resources (including biological diversity), how to ensure rights of access and ownership and how to control communal natural resources and ensure that people share equitably in the benefits they provide. They have to confront problems of poverty, rural subsistence and the pressure of growing populations. They need to take account of special groups, such as nomadic communities and indigenous people, and recognize that women are often the custodians of the natural resources on which the community depends.

Decisions on such wide-ranging matters must be based on transparency, equity and trust. Because all sectors of the community are involved, broad-based partnerships are appropriate. Obstacles often arise because of unequal rights and uneven access and ownership. Relatively poor and uneducated communities cannot compete against powerful and affluent interests, whether in government or industry. Multinational corporations can have a dominant and distorting influence. The technology to use natural resources sustainably is often lacking, and where it exists it is not being shared. These problems have a major international dimension.

To move forward, clear objectives must be set. There must be proper participation of non-governmental as well as governmental sectors. Grassroots knowledge, including that of women and indigenous groups, is crucial. Guidelines on how to formulate sustainable lifestyles are needed, and must fit within the context of the communities concerned. Education and training should help local people towards more effective control of their resources.

We need a new approach to the representation of those who produce environmental products locally. There should be new machinery to transfer knowledge and technology to them. The economic system needs improvement, to deliver a more equitable distribution of profit and responsibility. Industries need to maintain high standards of health, safety and environmental care. Trade unions must mobilize and press for such high standards. The government must provide an institutional framework that ensures effective land-use planning and development control, safeguards biological diversity and protects vulnerable social groups. Sustainable development must start at home, in every country and district, and not just be seen as a global desideratum (or as something that collective humanity is failing to achieve). Most importantly, civil society should be mobilizing itself to look at problems and solutions within it, instead of shifting responsibilities to others who have, or assume, power.

We need new alliances between those who are locally wise and those who have the knowledge and skill of modern science. Such a fusion is the best way of developing sustainable resource-use methods that will work on the ground and within local communities. But we also need better knowledge to feed into the dialogue – especially now that ecological integrity, in many areas, is threatened by global climate change and unprecedented human population pressures. We must, therefore, develop our skills of theoretical ecology and environmental modelling. These will be needed to help define maximum acceptable yields from harvests of wild populations; to understand the responses of ecosystems to stress; to define the nature of ecological resilience; and to enlighten our thinking about 'carrying capacity', ecological integrity, and the true significance of biological diversity. We also need to develop the skills of the agronomist and the crop breeder.

At local level, we need combined local and international skills to define and value natural resources and work out the best ways of managing and using them. We need surveys to ascertain the wider potential of biological diversity. We need new techniques for predicting how systems will respond to human use. We need to make environmental impact assessment a more precise science. We need ability to balance local, national and global interests and to explain to people active at all three levels why a particular pattern is likely to be best.

At national and global level we need skills to define the importance of natural resources more clearly, and value them where they are susceptible to economic valuation. We need the ability to explain to governments the restraints nature will place on their political strategies. We need to understand the likely implications of pollution and climate change, so that adaptive strategies can be worked out. We need international scientific cooperation – like that in the Inter-Governmental Panel on Climate Change – to pool insights and present the best achievable consensus on global problems at global level.

Science and economics must be developed together. Political and commercial decisions throughout the world are more influenced by economic thinking than by any other single body of formal logic. The development of 'sustainable economics' is a key to the future. It is no good arguing that 'ecology into economics won't go' – if economic thinking continues to be environmentally unsound, and ecologists refuse to contribute their insight to the necessary reforms, the only result can be disaster. The question is how to redesign economics so that it remains a good tool for handling those aspects of social policy and decision that can be expressed in financial terms, while at the same time respecting the underlying values of care for the Earth, social justice and global responsibility. This is a case for partnership between economists and scientists.

The wider partnerships for environmental resource management need, therefore, a broad base. They should encourage communities on the ground to state the worth to them of elements in their environment, and then seek scientific definition of how those values can be maintained. They should apply new economic techniques, including those for proper pricing of environmental services, proper use of inter-temporal comparisons and discounting, proper use of economic instruments like prices, taxes and charges, and better means of measuring national economic activity. Economic analyses which are not explicit about their treatment of environmental parameters and the ways in which these have been arrived at should be rejected. All governments, leaders in local communities, and those taking decisions about the environment need to appreciate that environmental assets and services have economic value, which must be included in decisions if distortions and wrong judgements are not to result.

Strengthening the links between environment and health

Poverty, a lack of social justice in the allocation of resources, the investment of resources in care after the event rather than prevention, the adoption of wrong priorities and inefficient working practices (including among aid agencies), sectoralism, lack of information-sharing, and the political and economic dependence of poor countries and communities on insensitive lending institutions are all obstacles to social progress. In the sphere of community health, one serious problem is the difficulty in involving ecologists, urban planners, pollution controllers and the medical profession as real partners in preventive medicine, even though their cooperation could save much social cost and prevent much misery.

Successful partnerships have shared objectives. People need to be motivated and attitudes need to be changed, and for this the communication process is crucial. There are innumerable potential partners, but local communities are critical: there must be authority and responsibility at local level. The health-care sector needs to be decentralized to the grassroots, and organizational capacity strengthened at local level. In Colombia, for example, health has been the responsibility of central government, but this is changing as primary care is being devolved to municipalities. In India, the most successful partnerships have been at grassroots level, involving government departments, NGOs and the people at whom the help is targeted. In Sri Lanka, such local partnership organizations were strengthened by being granted the same legal rights as national organizations. Development of the economy, providing jobs and markets, is a positive factor also in supporting health. Social justice, conflict resolution, good collective agreements between employers and workforce, and open access to information are also important enabling conditions.

People often do not understand the real nature of environmental and health hazards, and the gap between perception and reality can waste resources, especially if scares are not founded on real risk. Health should be seen as a collective phenomenon as well as an individual problem. Once it is accepted that health is shared by the community, the importance of a healthy environment for all becomes obvious. Education, training, recognition that all members of the community should contribute, sensitivity to local cultures, traditions and needs, provision of adequate funding, and a means for the community to evaluate success and ensure that the partners are accountable are also important. Examples of the way ahead are provided by the World Health Organization's 'Healthy Cities' programme, and all communities need to build health issues into their local plans and frameworks for sustainable development.

Building sustainable urban and rural communities

Cities are created by and for people. The world's urban population is growing rapidly and it is essential that technology and resources are applied to make cities sustainable and improve the lives of their inhabitants. Three central elements need consideration – the people (including community groups) who make up a city; the social and economic activities they pursue; and the physical environment including land, air, water and the plants and animals with whom people share their living environment. Partnerships in the city need to deliver clean and sufficient water, clean air, food, health, a quiet environment, housing, education and training, employment, efficient transportation, energy efficiency, clean industry, good waste management, conservation (and restoration where necessary), leisure and entertainment. The linkages between these services (and those supplying them) and between the city and its hinterland are of crucial importance. Unplanned urban growth (and the attitude 'pollute now, control later') must be avoided. Urban immigration can undermine the best of plans for sustainability and must be tackled; where there are large immigrant groups they must be involved in the partnerships. Land supply for housing, and ownership of dwellings, should not be constrained by restrictive laws.

Partnerships need to be related to the distinctive features and needs of the city. They should embrace central government, local authorities, the business community and private sector, non-governmental organizations and community groups, and local people (both men and women). They should pay particular attention to groups representing interests that are commonly marginalized (such as women's groups, indigenous groups, labour unions and grassroots bodies). The city partnerships should reach out and link with those in adjoining areas. Key factors in success include recognition of the interdependence of the city and its hinterland; encouragement to the local authority to plan ahead and provide more infrastructure at costs the local people can bear; maintenance of close consultation between the municipal authorities, NGOs and the individual members of the community; good management of the partnership process, with continuing monitoring and evaluation; good education and information; an ability for all partners to discuss, plan and negotiate on equal terms; devolution to local authorities of freedom and power to decide their future; proper recognition and involvement of grassroots initiatives; good mutual assistance between the partners; encouragement and funding of the process by governments; and flexibility.

The view of the city must be holistic. There must be a clear vision that empowers the community and promotes sustainability. All citizens must have a stake in their city. At the same time, it must be recognized that all cities are different, and the perspectives and interests of each community and country need to be reflected in the overall plan. Specific tools for action include creating local community forums for education, leisure, housing, industry and employment, conservation and amenity. Case studies of success (and failure) should be exchanged between the cities of the world: there could be a role here for the UN Centre for Human Settlements (Habitat).

The same holds for rural areas. But here the nature of the resources available, and alternatives for their use, are crucial factors. In such communities, other questions arise over 'partnerships' – are these at individual, family, community, regional or national level? Every person is useful and can do something, regardless of his or her level of experience – but what? In some rural areas of the developing world, the issue of poverty looms large. Many communities are in crisis so far as finance and education go. Most rural settlements do not have community organizations, and these need to be stimulated. Levels of organization vary widely, and some do not take people's interests and values into account. At the outset, we need to identify the resources needed to create a partnership, recognizing that people are the most important resource. Such partnerships need to yield cash, knowledge and capacity-building.

If partnerships are to work, in this as in so many other fields they must begin at local level and with existing organizations. They must address the basic problems of poverty, illiteracy, unemployment, deprivation, poor health, and unsound use of natural resources. They must recognize the dependence of many rural communities on outside markets and should develop capacity for self-reliance in the community and for improved production and enhanced finance. As the scale expands to regional, national and international levels, issues of linkage, information flow, resource allocation and technology transfer gain importance. But at all levels key objectives include improving quality and effectiveness of community action, identifying opportunities for new partnerships, encouraging efficiency, flexibility and innovation; fostering self-reliance; recognizing the importance of each partner and the value of its contribution and achieving the objectives without exposing the rural community to needless financial and social burdens.

To succeed, partnerships must add value and benefit all participants. The first essential is that they be based on respect for the rural community. They must help transfer knowledge to the community. They must have economic relevance. They must provide for communication, education and awareness – including education of women. As the workshop record commented, 'if you educate a man, you educate an individual, but if you educate a woman you educate the whole community'. They must provide information about market opportunities to community members.

Strategic thinking is essential. Partnerships also need an animator – a driving force – from within the community, who understands group dynamics and vested interests. Skills of conflict resolution are important. The diverse groups in the community need to be brought together. Networking is essential. There must be understanding of social and environmental responsibility. Partnerships should not be exploitative, but should create climates in which other partnerships can grow. They must build capacity and create infrastructure. Above all, they must recognize that rural communities are the people, and all must be involved in the decision process. 'Sustainability has to be created by people working in partnerships ...that can inspire confidence, local initiative, self-reliance and self-respect.'

Creating sustainable development policies for business

People accept that business, industry and commerce are agents of change in the world. They provide employment and wealth. They develop technology. They have a major impact on the environment, both because they consume non-renewable and renewable resources and generate pollution and other impacts.

Numerous recent conferences and books have analysed the role of business in building sustainability, and the imperative for its involvement with other sectors of the community. There have been two World Industry Conferences on Environmental Management (WICEM), at Versailles, France, and Rotterdam, the Netherlands, respectively (Sallada and Doyle, 1986; Willums, 1991). The Business Council for Sustainable Development was established by Maurice Strong, Secretary General of UNCED, as a part of the preparations for Earth Summit in Rio de Janeiro, under the chairmanship of the Swiss industrialist Stephan Schmidheiny, and produced an important book, *Changing Course: A Global Business Perspective on the Environment* (Schmidheiny, 1992).

Changing Course begins with the environmental crisis and the need for sustainable development. It recognizes that this will:

obviously require more than pollution prevention and tinkering with environmental regulations. Given that ordinary people – consumers, business people, farmers – are the real day-to-day environmental decision makers, it requires political and economic systems based on the effective participation of all members of society in decision making.

It accepts the need for 'clean, equitable economic growth' which it rightly regards as the largest single challenge in the whole sphere of sustainable development. The new vision is that the avoidance of pollution and waste is not only a proper display of corporate citizenship, but a way for industry to become more efficient and competitive. The name of the game is 'eco-efficiency'.

Companies are adopting and committing themselves publicly to strategies for sustainable development. They are broadening the partnerships which have always been an internal feature of industry to bring in neighbours, public interest groups (including environmental non-governmental organizations), customers, suppliers, governments and the general public. They are becoming much more open about their activities – and their impacts on the environment (deterred only by the fear that such openness may lead to legal action by some of those to whom industry is trying to be accountable). And this means changes in economic valuation, more efficient energy use, changes in trade and capital finance systems, alterations in corporate structure (with environmental concerns elevated higher up the hierarchy and commonly into the Chief Executive Office), innovation, cooperation in technology, and new partnerships with the developing world.

The need for such advances is widely accepted. Questions arise over the kind of partnership industry, business and commerce should seek to build, and how. The main doubts arise from fear that business will retain hidden agendas and be unable to over-ride its financial interests in the cause of sustainable development; that competitiveness and adversarial attitudes will dominate; that there will be too much rhetoric; that standards will not be made uniform or applied with equal commitment everywhere, and that some would-be partners, especially environmental NGOs, are not ready for true partnership. Conversely, the environmental movement still looks on industry with distrust.

Key factors in success therefore begin with openness and the building of trust. It requires dialogue to establish common ground, a clear focus and purpose, good leadership from the top, common terminology, equality between partners and a genuine willingness to share:

> Equality in the partnership should not just be measured in money and monetary resources. There is also sharing of technology and know-how. The sustainable enterprise will be that business organization which ensures its long-term viability and profitability by meeting the needs and demands of all stakeholders in the business. This involves establishing and maintaining the confidence of those stakeholders in the management's ability positively to address the potential environmental impacts, human and ecological, of the local business operation (DOE, 1994).

Industry will have to concern itself increasingly with the social value of its products (and techniques such as life-cycle analysis may be useful here). It will have to take note of the social context in which it operates, and in developing countries this means sensitivity to the goals of local partnerships in addressing poverty, technology-sharing, and other issues. And industry may need legislation to define the context of its operations, so that it can apply competitive processes on a 'level playing field' that also guarantees proper attention to environmental benefits.

At the same time, industry needs to state to its other partners – both governments and consumer groups – what is needed if it is to contribute effectively to sustainable economic growth. It should be far more emphatic about the ways in which externally-imposed regulation and standards, self-regulation, economic incentives and taxation impede or facilitate sustainability. It should be blunt about where policies and actions of government undermine progress. As our principal wealth creator, the world of business, commerce and industry should speak far more clearly.

Reconciling the aims of sustainable development and employment

When recession bites, the first thing workers in developed countries fear for is their jobs. The first thing the masses of unemployed and poorly paid people in developing countries care for is jobs. As a speaker from such a region commented in Manchester, people say: 'I would rather be able to feed my family now and die in ten years' time than see my children starve'.

How can we address the problems of unsustainable, over-consuming, wasteful communities in the North without creating unacceptable unemployment? How can we give meaningful jobs to the poor and unemployed in the South without creating there the problems that plague the rich countries? Clearly, environmental policies that put people out of work, or deny people work they could have, will be socially unacceptable even if they meet the criteria of environmental sustainability in other respects.

Dialogue between businesses, government and trade unions must form part of the package of readjustment for sustainable living. Unions themselves should be at the forefront of negotiations that will move people from the old kind of damaging industrialization to a new and sustainable mode. They should be pressing for polluting plant to be cleaned up, since it if is shut down jobs will be lost. They should be pressing for environmentally friendly production that also creates jobs. Society should also realize that there are alternative ways of creating jobs to industrialization – such as investment in health, education, and social services – provided that the wealth-creating section of the economy is strong enough to support them. This is one way in which people no longer employed in mechanized and computerized manufacturing industries may find new opportunities.

The partnerships we need must be based at local level and be multilateral – employers, the workforce, local government and environmental and health groups, with central government ministries of environment and industry participating and supporting. Traditional tripartite partnerships need expanding to bring in the environmental dimension. In the developing world in particular, partnerships with international financial institutions are also important.

The chief obstacles are poverty, fear that environmental concerns will lead to job losses, negative feelings towards unions, a misguided emphasis among the latter on jobs rather than environmental care and quality of life, a reluctance on the part of governments to adjust their basic policies in the light of consultations, and inefficiency in organizations (including environmental ones). They are best overcome if the different industrial sectors are tackled separately, and if local plans are tailored to local needs. Such plans should include some kind of framework to guide industrial and employ-ment development, with clear standards. They should also cater for educat-ing the workforce about the environment, the need for sustainability, and the way in which they can help (and press) the employing organization to adopt high environmental standards, which will in turn help to guarantee continuing employment. The basis of taxation also needs attention: it makes much better sense to tax resource use and pollution than jobs.

Free political expression is vital. The more there is mass engagement and commitment of the workforce, the higher performance standards are likely to be – they need therefore to feel 'ownership' of the firm's environ-mental policies. Employers need to change their culture accordingly, and there needs to be free sharing of information between the four partners – labour, employer, government and environmental movement.

We do face a dilemma. Undoubtedly mechanization and the widespread use of information technology have eliminated much drudgery and made modern workplaces far cleaner and healthier than the ones they replaced. But the reduction in unskilled jobs has forced a number of people out of employment and widened the gap between incomes at the extremes of soci-ety. The trend will continue: imagine the impact, only a few years away, of word processors that will transcribe voice to text reliably, and render the audio-typist redundant. The pace of change has removed the career secu-rity on which many people built their lives. In the United Kingdom, for example, seven out of ten new jobs are for fixed contracts, or temporary and self-employment. Less than fifty per cent of the population of working age now have full-time jobs. Much the same holds throughout the OECD countries. Yet sustainability has to be seen in human terms, and employ-ment is a social necessity. The way financial and labour markets interlock, and are both affected by technology, needs close attention, and new part-nerships to examine the likely futures are essential.

Partnerships for technology transfer

Technology is not just equipment. It is a complex system of relationships (including power relationships) which may increase or reduce dependency between North and South or affluent and poor sectors within a community. We need to tell people about practical examples of new technology that really work for sustainability. The needs and capacities of users must be starting points in the development process, and we must stop the marketing of inappropriate technology which simply profits the vendors. We should start by considering what technology will help daily life and development in poor rural and urban areas. We need to see technology within the setting of lived experience.

There is much talk at present about transfer of technology from North to South. This process needs great care. If the North's environmental agenda drives the introduction of advanced technology to protect the environment in the south as industrialization proceeds, the costs need to be shared.

Transfer should not increase the economic dependence of South on North, poor on rich. Where environmental improvement causes technologies to be phased out in the North, they should not then be 'dumped' in the South. But developing country governments for their part must realize that prevention is cheaper in the long term than clean-up and that it is in their interests to impose and enforce stringent environmental standards.

Partnerships may be made difficult by tradition, by incompatible and hidden agendas, by ignorance of cultural values so that proposals do not fit context, by conflicting interests, by undue pressures for change from donors when recipients are not ready (or find the changes inappropriate), and above all by self-interest among the dominant partners. The way ahead is first to identify problems and conflicts of interest and then face them directly. Dialogue should demonstrate that there will be real mutual benefit. The transfer or sharing of technology should be seen as a means to an end, not an end in itself, and hence the technology and system adopted must always fit the wider social plan for sustainability. Local people should control the technology and its transfer.

We should always speak about 'sharing', not 'transfer' (UN, 1994a; UN, 1995f). Transfer is, or can all too easily become, an uncritical process by which techniques developed in one country are implanted in another. All too often, the result is disaster. European agricultural techniques have devastated large areas of Australia. German and British forestry techniques have undermined the sustainable, multi-purpose use of tropical forests. If technology is to be shared, it has to work, sustainably, in the place it is going to. Providers and users must work as partners before, during and after the process of transfer. It has to be chosen to meet the needs of those who will use it. It should be user- rather than supplier-driven. It must be evaluated against clear criteria of sustainability in the new setting.

Only good technology is worth sharing. Too much has been written about the 'dumping' of outmoded methods and products in the poor countries by companies or governments that have outgrown them at home. Dirty factories using processes outlawed in the rich countries should not be accepted in the developing world, even if they bring employment and an apparent gain in wealth, because the externalization of costs will undermine those gains.

Such externalization of costs in the shape of environmental damage should be unacceptable everywhere. The principle of 'prior informed consent' which was imposed on the export of wastes should apply to technology. A company should not be permitted to construct a factory or introduce a process in a country without notifying the government and local community concerned of the nature of the process or product and its environmental impacts. If that process or product infringes environmental standards in the country of origin, or anywhere else known to the industry, that fact should be disclosed and explicit consent should be obtained before construction begins. Efforts should be made to develop internationally agreed standards, and place internationally agreed seals of approval on processes and products.

Partnerships may require a willingness on the part of governments and development aid agencies to change their procedures and outlook, for governments to work in cooperation with business to secure investment in cleaner technologies, for business to enter into long-term technology cooperation arrangements (with associated training and education), for multilateral finance institutions such as the World Bank and Regional Development Banks to play a role in supporting such new partnerships between governments and business, and for governments and development agencies to move towards the support of demand-driven technology cooperation.

Adapting financial institutions to meet the needs of sustainable development

Banking and financial services are there to make money rather than improve the environment. Competition between them can further bar their involvement in long-term environmental care. The partnerships in this area have to be built around the areas where cooperation is practical, while permitting competition to continue. The central area of common interest is in the mutual desire of financiers and the champions of sustainable development for long-term, sustainable returns. A first step is likely to be the establishment of a wider local or national strategy for sustainability within which all financial institutions and processes must operate. This gives the working context, and will include: clear goals for sustainable development, priorities for investment to secure it, specification of the social and environmental benefits the investment process should provide and rules of operation that bear on financial institutions at home and abroad, create a 'level playing field' for the competitive process and define the information they should provide and the transparency which should be a feature of their operations.

In many countries, priority is likely to be given to investment that addresses and ends poverty, provides health care and a clean environment, and creates employment. Education and social welfare will be high up the list. The financial institutions will be expected to define and make public the environmental criteria they use to guide their operations, and to insist that their customers meet such guidelines. They should move towards longer-term investment, which will, in many cases, have to be underwritten by governments. Governments can help the flow of private funds especially if they consider beneficial lending rates for projects with a particular value in advancing sustainable development. Financial institutions should also join in dialogue with local governments, grassroots community groups and environmental non-governmental organizations as a means of defining environmental goals, and they should inform the public about their activities. Internally, they may find these partnerships useful in educating their staff about wider environmental and social objectives. They should accept the need to support small customers, including local grassroots groups and community enterprises.

We are a long way from clear understanding of how financial institutions can best contribute to partnerships for sustainability. The Business Council for Sustainable Development accepted that capital markets will be important to the future but commented (Schmidheiny, 1992) that 'little is known about the constraints, the possibilities, and the inter-relationships between capital markets, the environment and the needs of future generations...' It went on to emphasize that sustainable development will certainly require increased investment in both industrial and developing countries; that this means capital investment that respects environmental sensitivities; and that much of the finance will have to come from capital markets – which 'may be one of the most important factors conditioning corporate behaviour, and are therefore a key issue in the future of the planet'.

People tend to speak as if the dominant source of investment for environmental goals was development aid, yet in practice, and even with the welcome establishment of the Global Environment Facility of the World Bank, the UN Development Programme and the UN Environment Programme, this is relatively small and accounts for financial transfers one or two orders of magnitude below those undertaken by the private sector. How can private capital markets be made effective agents of sustainability? *Changing Course* suggests that we should start by defining, presumably at global level, clear and closely refereed rules for capital markets, and these must obviously be broadened, in partnership with government and environmental experts, to incorporate goals of sustainability.

Partnerships between the world of finance, government regulators, investing industry and the environmental agencies need to focus on some practical goals. *Caring for the Earth* suggested that Northern financial institutions should refuse to finance unsound projects, and should develop proactive lending and investment policies which relieve poverty directly and promote sustainable development. It also urged them to help provide services for the management of debt, explore ways of assisting areas which are exposed to climate change and other environmental threats, develop methods to expose the ways current cost accounting tecnhniques make the irrational exploitation of the environment appear acceptable, and explore measures to restrict capital flight.

But such action would clearly need to be carried forward in partnership with the financial institutions and governments in the developing world, rather than be imposed unilaterally.

Mobilizing people through effective education and awareness

As Chapter 6 demonstrated, education is not only about classrooms and lecture theatres. Nor is it just directed at the mass of the people. Those in authority – for example in financial institutions – also need educating about environmental issues and the goals of sustainable living. Environmental education should reach all people and groups, and is essentially about giving people information which will allow them to respond in an effective way

to the challenge, and improve their own lifestyles. It is as important to educate employers and workers in the business sector as any other component
of society, and partnerships between industry, trade unions and non-governmental organizations have a role here.

Seven major obstacles to partnerships in this field have been identified
(DOE, 1994). They are: lack of trust in all levels of government; loss of
identity by some partners; loss of credibility with local communities; lack of
continuity; inequality between the parties; compartmentalization within the
community; and institutionalization, which can impair the flexibility of a
community group or organization. As to factors for success, these have been
identified as:

- Never over-estimate the value of formal education or under-estimate
  the value of traditional wisdom. There are often unrecognized experts
  in the community.
- Recognize that there is a difference between literacy and education, and
  that people in the community may be wise even if not literate.
- Avoid treating science and technology as mystic things: they are practical aids to social goals and need to be understood in that way.
- Avoid stereotypes: there is no 'correct' way of educating, and what is
  needed is what works in the community.
- Take time to listen to, and learn from, the community.
- Make services community-based and low-cost, reducing the dependence
  of the community on government or international agencies.
- Focus especially on the poorest 10 per cent of the community. If they
  are helped, the whole society will gain.
- Support informal education at community level, for it is crucial in
  achieving awareness and helping to change attitudes.
- Make sure that any partnership is based on sharing, not giving or taking.
- Do not be frightened of debate and conflict: they are needed in order to
  achieve change.
- Ask the right questions at the right time!

How far should partnerships in this field be linked internationally, thereby
drawing support from the widest possible network and benefiting from
experience elsewhere? There is clearly a role for such networks so long as
they do not impose solutions from outside. International NGOs, in particular, and also bodies like UNESCO, need to give attention to ways they can
help local and grassroots level NGOs in developing countries.

The people who join in partnerships for education and awareness need
themselves to be enthusiasts. They must realize that awareness is created by
action – and this is the sign that communication has succeeded. They need
humour, staying power, and passion to fight against exploitation and social
injustice.

Producing sustainability strategies and plans

Chapters 2 and 9 have analysed much experience in creating such documents, and clearly they must involve partnerships. These will change over

time, and obviously differ from country to country and between the national and regional levels. There must be a broad-based mechanism to pull together inputs from different sectors and coordinate, monitor and evaluate the strategy. The participants are likely to include government, non-governmental organizations and major groups (including religious bodies, trade unions, business, industry, communities, local government, and those representing women and indigenous peoples). A central core group of people drawn from the major groups concerned is likely to oversee the process. A constitutional and legal mechanism and one to promote public awareness are also required.

At local level, local government and locally based NGOs will clearly have a stronger role in the partnership than at national level while the role of central government and major national groups will be reduced (although not entirely absent). National NGOs should indeed support local ones and help them to develop capacity to join in preparing and implementing local sustainability strategies. International links between cities (for example extending the concept of 'twinning' to provide real help between cities in developed and developing countries) should be built.

There are many obstacles to overcome. They include: undemocratic legal and governance systems that exclude participation; lack of commitment at high level; the imposition of a vision from outside; unrealistic objectives; conflicting aims (which means the process of dialogue and partnership has simply not worked properly); corruption; political conflict, and even war within the country; financial policies that over-ride national and local interests or fail to provide the investment needed to make the strategy work; exploitation of one group by another (a further sign of failure); and the dominance of one partner by another (a balance is needed between the influence of conservationists and of developers); insensitive planning, which makes people lose faith in plans and strategies and – as always – pervasive poverty that makes any kind of long-term strategy seem of doubtful priority.

Some of these obstacles (like war and strife) are clearly likely to negate the whole process. Unless there is a broad agreement in the community that there should be a local sustainability strategy, and a willingness to base it on common ground, clearly the process is doomed from the outset. On the other hand, so long as there is an element of agreement, even if it is small, partnerships can be built and the area of consensus widened. Many of the obstacles can be overcome if the right partnerships are built in the right atmosphere.

The partnerships should involve all sectors and major groups, so that the product is owned by all sectors of society, who have a consensus as to its value (even if everyone does not agree with everything) . There should be an agreed agenda and targets. The process must begin by identifying the needs of the community, and then look at how it can best meet these. It must take account of local social, cultural, economic and political conditions and standards, and provide for environmental and social diversity. There must be leadership, open participation, accountability, transparent motives on the part of all partners (especially the business community), trust, clear definition of the roles of each partner, and good information flow to the community at large. Public education and awareness-building is crucial, for this will in turn stimulate participation. Groups often left out of the decision process – such as women and the poor – must be brought in. NGOs working at local level must not compete with one another, but ensure that their efforts are complementary. The strategy itself must be people-centred, visionary, flexible and with phased goals, building on existing institutions but creating new ones where required. It must gain acceptance in the political leadership. International knowledge and expertise must be used where relevant.

Partnerships in decision-making at all levels

People will join in partnerships if the process is right: if they feel it is worthwhile for them, and helps them to achieve something they could not get in other ways. The group that met in Manchester suggested that there were ten guiding criteria for success (DOE, 1994):

- there must be open, timely and adequate information;
- the actors must be deeply involved;
- the stakeholders and partners must be representative of the groups within the community and have legitimacy;
- the participants must be sure that they will not be put at risk through participation;
- there must be money to help those with limited resources to participate equally;
- there should be independent facilitation and agreements reached should be recorded;
- participation must be voluntary, and tasks assigned clearly;
- representation must be balanced;
- there must be transparency and accountability;
- partners must have the right to dissent and if necessary, to withdraw.

This adds up to a blueprint for free, equal and balanced partnership, and for assurance that collective decisions will be honoured.

A framework for society

Caring for the Earth emphasized the need for a national framework for integrating development and conservation. It went on (IUCN/UNEP/WWF, 1991):

> It is essential to build a public consensus around an ethic for living sustainably, and to enable individuals and communities to act...But it is equally important to ensure an effective national approach, and for this purpose governments must provide a national framework (and in federal countries, provincial or state frameworks as well) of institutions, economic policies, national laws and regulations, and an information base.

The specific actions called for were:

- adopt an integrated approach to environmental policy, with sustainability as the overall goal;
- develop strategies for sustainability and implement them directly and through regional and local planning;
- subject proposed development projects, programmes and policies to environmental impact assessment and to economic appraisal;
- establish a commitment to the principles of a sustainable society in constitutional or other fundamental statements of national policy;
- establish a comprehensive system of international law and provide for its implementation and enforcement;
- review the adequacy of legal and administrative controls and of implementation and enforcement mechanisms, recognizing the legitimacy of local approaches;
- ensure that national policies, development plans, budgets and decisions on investments take full account of their effects on the environment;
- use economic policies to achieve sustainability;
- provide economic incentives for conservation and sustainable use;
- strengthen the knowledge base and make information on environmental matters more accessible.

These actions clearly remain relevant, and many are being implemented in the various strategies and partnerships already reviewed. The overall framework at national level has to integrate these, and this is commonly done through three linking mechanisms: economic policy, law and administration. Good information keeps the public aware of these kinds of action, and maintains the sense of commitment and partnership which is an essential criterion for success.

Economic developments

It is a self-evident fact that political and commercial decisions throughout the world are more influenced by economic thinking than by any other single body of formal logic. Because governments measure success in terms of advance towards economic goals – especially higher personal or national wealth or higher sales of products – the development of 'sustainable economics' is a key to the future. If economics is so constructed as a discipline that its application leads to perverse and unsustainable conclusions, then it is socially necessary either to change economics or to ensure that it is one element only in the decision process.

There are divergent views over whether the new economics should have an ethical component. While classical economics has no overt ethical base, it is clearly founded on tacit or implicit values. The question is how to redesign economics so that it remains a good tool for handling those aspects of social policy and decision that can be expressed in financial terms, while at the same time respecting the underlying values of care for the Earth, social justice and global responsibility. This need has been addressed, particularly, by Hermann Daly and John Cobb in their book *For the Common Good* (Daly and Cobb, 1989).

Like science, economics gives us techniques. One major recent debate has been over how to improve those techniques and so ease the way to sustainability. It is agreed (to quote David Pearce and colleagues) (Pearce et al, 1989) that 'sustainable development involves a substantially increased emphasis on the value of natural, built and cultural environments.' And 'it is important to ensure that economic growth is measured "properly".' 'The broad concept of wealth bequest needs supplementing with a concern to avoid irreversible losses of environmental assets. But there are strong reasons to think of sustainable development involving a further constraint, namely that the stock of environmental assets as a whole should not decrease...'.

Valuing the environment is likely to be neither comprehensive nor precise, and some attributes like solar energy are so fundamental that they are literally beyond price. But at least by seeking to put a monetary value on environmental attributes, we emphasize the fact that they have worth. Moreover, some *can* be valued in money terms, and prove to represent 'natural capital' not inferior in the national balance sheet to the capital accumulated by human effort. By debating and assessing such values we are forced to explicit statements in place of emotional assertions. The techniques need further advance, but they are important.

There is one other aspect of valuation that is rarely discussed but important. It is the value set on security (or risk), and the compensation sought when people are harmed. It is well known that popular concern over risk is not strictly related to its probability: in terms of risk of death for an hour's exposure, cigarette smoking is at least twice as hazardous as air or car travel, which is twice as risky as coal mining, 50 times as hazardous as rail travel, and 100 times as risky as exposure to radiation from nuclear power stations (Whyte and Burton, 1980). Yet popular concerns over the risk of exposure to radiation remain very great. And courts of law have tended, especially in the United States, to award immense financial compensation to people who claim to have suffered injury from environmental damage, even when it results from actions that fully met the legal standards and scientific knowledge of the time when the risks were created. There is real danger that investment in new, sustainable technology will be deterred if open-ended risk liability remains, and societies may need to consider redefining legal rights and responsibilities in this respect.

The linkages needed between economic, social and political development in a changing world were reviewed by the High Level Advisory Board (HLAB) to the Secretary General of the United Nations in March 1994 (UN, 1994a; UN, 1995f). It concluded that the globalization of production and of international finance by transnational corporations and financial institutions have greatly changed the economic envelope within which countries and governments operate. The long period of low prices for many commodities has had a big impact on the economies of states, especially those dependent on a relatively small range of primary commodities. Developments in technology have reduced demands for unskilled labour while telecommunications has been a major factor in creating the new global finance and business systems. New supra-national groupings of states including the European Union (EU), the North American Free Trade Association (NAFTA), the Common Market of the Southern Cone (MER-COSUR), the Association of South East Asian Nations (ASEAN), and the Asia Pacific Economic Cooperation (APEC) have emerged and gained strength. All this means that countries cannot any longer think of themselves as economically detached, and we need new attention to economic instruments that may help carry sustainability forward within this context.

The HLAB considers that *all* apparent conflicts between development and the protection of the environment can be traced to six causes:

■ government failure – by creating incentives to use the environment wastefully and inefficiently;
■ market failure – because prices set by market mechanisms do not fully reflect the costs of production and consumption;
■ missing markets – because there are no property rights for environmental services, so that those who exploit environmental resources lack economic interest in sustainability;
■ poverty – that is, situations in which the poor do not have access to income-earning opportunities which will sustain their lives without depleting natural capital;
■ failure to recognize the need for enhanced political, economic and social diversity in the process of development;
■ scientific ignorance or error leading to unsustainable practices or the introduction of damaging products.

Many people believe that while law is important, market incentives which provide voluntary rather than coercive mechanisms are likely to prove more efficient. *Caring for the Earth* indeed urged that these be developed, and there has been much talk about how best to do this. UNEP's review, *The World Environment, 1972–1992* (Tolba et al, 1992) records that 153 economic instruments were in use in OECD countries by 1988, 81 of them being charges of some kind and 41, subsidies. The High Level Advisory Board urged consideration of:

■ indicators of sustainable development which are capable of monitoring the sustainability of supply or production as well as the sustainability of demand or consumption;
■ the application of the 'polluter pays' principle, ensuring that the cost of reducing pollution is borne by those who inflicted (or would otherwise inflict) damage, and by the purchasers of their products, but with compensation when this would harm the poor;
■ transferable development rights which oblige purchasers or developers of land to meet conservation objectives (a kind of analogue of the 'polluter pays' principle which might be called the 'developer pays' principle);

- introducing environmental safeguards into primary commodity agreements, under which consumers would pay producing countries (or land
  managers) for the costs incurred when they produce a particular commodity in a more sustainable way;
- tradable emission permits, within the total of what is environmentally
  tolerable, so that the market is used to find out the most efficient way of
  meeting standards.

A great deal more needs to be done to refine and apply such economic policies, and their development is surely a matter for an international partnership between governments, economists, industrialists and environmentalists. One issue they will need to address is that of double (or multiple)
standards for countries at different stages of development. As Laura Westra
(1994) has pointed out, *Agenda 21* does state that 'standards that are valid in
the most advanced countries may be inappropriate and of unwarranted
social cost for the developing countries'. But this is to imply acceptance of
standards set in terms of national economic capacity rather than the need to
safeguard the environment and guarantee sustainability. Westra argues that
if social costs of maintaining high standards are too much for the developing world, then it is the responsibility of the North to redress the balance.
The argument extends wider into issues of trade and environment which
became prominent in the GATT Uruguay round, and must receive international attention now within the World Trade Organization. Some of the
ingredients of the necessary approach are considered in Chapter 11.

Advances in law

There has been an enormous growth in the volume of environmental law in
recent years. In the OECD countries 64 national laws on environmental
issues were adopted between 1970 and 1979, and a further 23 between
1980 and 1984, as against only 24 in the whole period between 1950 and
1969. At international level the growth has been dramatic: the UNEP
Environmental Data Report catalogues only 6 such instruments on environmental themes before 1950 whereas there were 52 by 1970 and 140 by 1988
(UNEP, 1988–1992).

Environmental treaties and national laws alike have traditionally been
sectoral in nature:they have addressed themes like the protection of the
atmosphere and oceans; preserving species and habitats; preventing the
pollution of rivers and lakes; controlling hazardous wastes; safety in the
working environment; and the degradation of the environment through
military activities (Adede, 1994). International law is none the less changing
rapidly. Yet, according to Nicholas Robinson (1994):

> most environmental treaties, and many national laws, are very successful at
> designing systems for gathering data about environmental conditions and
> do establish and clearly state broad norms for the protection of nature and
> human health. Unfortunately, as yet they do little to actually protect the
> environment because these norms have not been transformed into action.

Law must progress. Nicholas Robinson emphasized how:

> Classic International Law was the law of nations. It is being supplanted, albeit gradually and not without opposition, by the law of environment. Peoples are linked more by their water supplies, watersheds, weather patterns, coastal regions and migratory species than they are by national borders or alliances among nation states. Even as cultural self-determination erodes large national states into confederations or even separate communities, at the same time these localities increasingly see themselves as part of a greater global village expressed in the words 'Only one Earth'.

Environmental law is evolving as part of the vision of interdependent social and natural systems. It is also applying the ethic of sustainability and the principle of equity. As Lothar Gundling (1994) pointed out in Buenos Aires, this already applies where international and shared watercourses are concerned: the resource has to be used in such a manner that every bordering state receives its fair share. Equitable principles also apply in the international law of the sea and are the decisive criteria when delimiting maritime zones. The International Court of Justice has ruled that 'the legal concept of equity is a general principle directly applicable as law'. But what is equity in this context? Sir Shridath Ramphal reminded the IUCN General Assembly of the statement by Aristotle: 'Equity among unequals does not require reciprocity: it requires proportionality.'

This is a hot issue when it comes to international action to protect the atmosphere, whether against the agents that deplete stratospheric ozone or those liable to cause climate change. There has to be international partnership, but Aristotelian equity surely demands that the greatest effort and cost falls on those states that are having the greatest impact. But should this be measured per head of population or per state – something of great importance where carbon emissions are concerned because several developing countries, including China, India and Brazil are large emitters as nations, whereas per head of population they have a much smaller impact than the developed states. Again, in the context of biological diversity, the countries that safeguard the bulk of the world's species are relatively poor developing nations while those with technologies geared to exploit their products lie in the affluent North. How should the burden of cost fall? In each case the agreement in international law is that it will be borne especially by the wealthy developed states.

The Rio Declaration emphasized equity in seven principles, dealing respectively with: the right to development, the eradication of poverty, special considerations relating to developing countries, common but differentiated responsibilities, the reduction and elimination of unsustainable patterns of production and consumption, the strengthening of capacity for sustainable development and the rights of all citizens to participate in decision making (Adede, 1994; UN, 1993). Inter-generational equity is also stressed in many discussions today, but goes deeper to the heart of sustainable living.

MOVING FORWARD

The elements of action

Although the age of the global environmental conference and the world strategy is far from over, it is clear that the key to success is the translation of a mass of ideas, and the lessons from a lot of experience, into action. Well, yes, all right, what can we *do*?

The preceding chapters have established that action has to be at all levels in the community. It cannot be left to the United Nations or to governments, though they have an essential role. It cannot be left to individuals, for they can do little unless provided with the information, opportunity and power. Action has to be built throughout society, so as to:

■ strengthen vision and insight, and reinforce acceptance of the environmental ethic;
■ build self-reliance at both the individual and community level;
■ involve people throughout the community, and link all the sectors of society;
■ end needless hostility between 'greens' and other groups within society, confining the debate to arguments rather than stereotypes;
■ empower people and communities to care for their environments, but at the same time bridle private initiative with equity;
■ accept industrial development and private sector investment as important agents of change, and cater for both within the overall process of sustainable development;

■ build more effective international cooperation, in the non-governmental as well as the intergovernmental community.

Sustainability will demand a new style of governance, and new politics. There are a number of more specific rules or precepts for that process:

■ there is no single, universal pattern: the approach must be designed to fit diverse social, cultural, economic and environmental circumstances;
■ top-down approaches are out: action from the upper echelons of social governance must enable and reinforce initiatives from below but cannot succeed without them. And arrogance, whether on the part of governments, industrialists, economists, scientists or other 'experts', must be avoided;
■ we have to start with people, and the key is to ensure that they believe in what is proposed and are themselves prepared to lead in the action;
■ information and communication are therefore at the heart of the action, but informing people is not enough:they have to be enabled to act;
■ humility is essential: we all have to be prepared to listen and to discuss, on the basis of respect for other cultures and traditions.

These in turn lead to the key questions that need direct answer, such as:

■ what should I do?
■ what should my village or my firm do?
■ what should my non-governmental organization do?
■ what should my city, canton, land or state do?
■ what should my country do?
■ what should the world institutions do?

Personal action for sustainability

Many people do understand their environment, and want to live sustainably. But they are at the mercy of many forces – cultural, social and economic – which block their actions. The answer to the first question may have to be constrained by hard realities. But each of us can make a contribution by:

■ being a witness for sustainable living and care of the Earth;
■ minimizing our personal impact on the Earth;
■ joining a green neighbourhood group;
■ joining groups that press for sustainability, and for the removal of barriers which stop us living sustainably;
■ urging sustainable policies and actions in our villages, companies, cities and countries.

What do these mean? Personal witness of commitment to the ethic for living sustainably means speaking, writing and acting in accordance with it. It means being vigilant about our own actions, judging them against a yardstick of environmental impact. It means demanding information – for example about the products we buy, and the policies of the groups and societies we belong to, so that we can judge whether they conform to the goals of sustainability and equity. It means speaking out when our group, neighbourhood or community is clearly on the wrong track. But it does not mean taking to a tent in the wilderness – an unsustainable lifestyle for most people – or becoming angrily confrontational. Nor does it mean rejecting the benefits of modern society. It means showing that there is a way of easing our personal footprints on the Earth, and sharing our experience.

Sometimes, this will mean reaching back to an older wisdom. Yasuo Goto, of Keidanren, Japan, spoke in Buenos Aires of the values of earlier insight, often driven out by the advent of the modern consumer society. He said (Goto, 1994):

> In Japan we have a word 'mottainai', which is not used often today. It means:
>
> a humble state of mind, inspired by awe;
>
> a feeling of gratitude;
>
> a sense of regret over wasted time or materials.
>
> The basic concept of that word is that we should love, value and make the best use of ourselves and everything on the earth. We Japanese used to use this 'mottainai' quite often and tried very hard not to have meaningless luxury and waste in our daily lives. We believe that we should recognize this word again.

Such an attitude is indeed an expression of the basic environmental ethic, and of the philosophy of *Caring for the Earth*. It is a reminder of the fact that living sustainably is about living ethically, and in a mood of reverence and respect for the natural world. We need to cultivate this sense in ourselves and try to re-awaken it in others. One small step on that way is to try to make the parts of the environment we control as beautiful and biologically diverse as we can.

Minimizing our personal impacts on the Earth can have many ingredients. In developed countries they may include:

■ Minimizing the pollution we release to air and water by burning clean fuels (like gas, rather than coal), using energy efficiently in the home and in transport, and purchasing non-polluting detergents and goods made in a non-polluting way.
■ Minimizing the waste of energy in our homes, by good insulation, low-energy light bulbs, energy-efficient equipment of all kinds, good heating and ventilating controls, and switching energy-using devices off when not required. The extreme of unsustainability is running the central heating and the air conditioning at the same time (if this seems absurd, try some hotels in the richest countries).

- Choosing products that are efficient in their use of energy and materials, are not swathed in useless packaging, have not been made by environmentally damaging processes or through slave labour, and can be mended when they go wrong and recycled when they wear out. We should demand that a rigorous 'sustainability standard' is developed and applied to products. The timber community is beginning to do this through the Forest Stewardship Council (Elliott, 1994), which will monitor the inspection and certification of forest products, demanding that its seal is only applied to those that come from forests that are managed in ways that are environmentally appropriate, socially beneficial and economically viable. We need to press for similar schemes, and only buy products that meet the standard.
- Disposing of all practicable wastes to recycling, while pressing for more outlets to be made available.
- Using water carefully.
- Buying fuel-efficient cars fitted with pollution control devices, ensuring that they are regularly maintained and driving them economically and quietly. And, using other means of transport including muscle-power when this is practicable....
- Avoiding making a lot of noise! In many towns it is the form of pollution with the most obvious impact on other people's quality of life.

There are innumerable other things we can attend to. Some are obvious – like making sure that our dogs (especially in town) never foul public places. We can try to make our gardens something that other people enjoy looking at as well as ourselves. We can grow flowers in window boxes in our houses. We can grow some wild plants, and species attractive to insects in our gardens. We can encourage birds (and try to stop our cats from eating them). We can pick up litter in our streets as well as on our own patch.

Some are less obvious. A healthy diet is an investment in minimizing our impact on the Earth. Avoiding needless medication, for many medicines have residues better kept out of the sewage systems and the rivers. Stopping smoking. Cultivating a critical attitude of mind, able to judge the likely truth and importance of media stories. The list is almost endless – and will look very different from culture to culture. Perhaps we should write our own checklist, and try to score our success rates (we will find that when it comes down to personal brass tacks our efforts leave a lot to be desired). But while a checklist is always helpful, the attitude of mind is more important. The price of sustainability is likely to be eternal effort.

But sustainable living should not just be the observance of a set of negatives. It should be an enriching experience, for it is driven by reverence for the Earth and for nature, in all its mystery and beauty, and by respect for others. It should be positive and creative. It should remove the fetters with which we have bound nature, and allow the wonder of the natural world to shine out, as it will, and enrich all our lives. It is the expression of the sense of stewardship, of responsibility as trustees for the planet and the human future, which is deep within many religions and at the heart of the environmental ethic.

The faith of life is a listening faith – open to the ideas of others, and sharing experience that may help each one of us to live better. Because it is centred on the individual, it accepts that every individual is of value and has an important contribution to make. Because it starts there, it is participatory and enabling, rather than dictatorial and repressive. It is a caring, sharing, approach, drawing on many cultures. It is an expression of what most religions teach about our responsibilities to one another and to the creation.

Collective actions for sustainable living: the local community

Sharing starts at home, and moves outwards. We are all members of various groups – the family; the work group; the school; the church, mosque, synagogue or temple; the club; the voluntary organization; the village. It is through group action – alliance and partnership in a unit of between 10 and 100 people – that many of us make our most effective contribution. It is, after all, commonly said that our personal decisions are largely influenced by no more than twenty other people whom we particularly trust.

Many of the key actions for sustainable living have to be group actions. They fall into several classes:

■ actions to share understanding – and so reinforce our personal contributions to sustainable living;
■ joint actions by the group to achieve more sustainable living within it and within the areas it controls;
■ 'upward and outward' actions to alter how the wider community behaves.

The first kind of action can be very informal. It is likely to involve discussion, and the exchange of written information. 'I went to a Conference last week and heard what they are doing in Seattle...or Curitiba...or Manila...or Manchester...We could...' 'Have you heard about Greenfreeze – the fridges that don't use the chemicals that destroy the ozone layer?' (Rose, 1994). 'They've got a new scheme for consulting people about the environment in Reading, which we could copy here. . ..' And so on.

The second kind of action is really joint planning for sustainability. The first step could well be the creation of a 'green neighbourhood group'. What is that? The model is that of the 'neighbourhood watch' scheme now found in many developed country residential areas, as a defence against crime. The idea is that a group of householders club together, each keeping an eye over what is happening in the street or district and reporting anything that looks suspicious. A 'green neighbourhood group' would similarly be a group of households that met together and discussed the environmental needs of the street or village, worked together to keep things as attractive as possible (as by clearing litter, maintaining green spaces, and helping one another, for example with composting of garden and kitchen wastes if there were no central facilities), and debated the line to take at the higher social level of the city or district. There is nothing very new in this idea – 'best kept village' awards are a feature of Britain and Switzerland and pride in the village is familiar throughout the world.

Such a group could share tasks and benefits – like a group of gardeners or allotment holders working together to grow the crops best suited to their individual plots and sharing the surpluses. It could discuss personal approaches to sustainable living and help all its members to lighten their footprints on the Earth. It could help its members to choose larger groups to join, actions to push, and policies to advocate in the wider community. Meetings of caring, like-minded, people seeking the way forward can strengthen everyone's commitment and effectiveness, just as meetings for prayer strengthen religious groups. The initiative could move on to full commitment by a village to primary environmental care and to the kinds of scheme that are working in the various places described in Chapter 9.

Each community needs to discuss how to set about such action. The agenda must be set from within, rather than imposed by outside 'experts'. The latter may be helpful as facilitators, so long as they recognize that their role is to subordinate themselves and help the real community to discuss its needs and frustrations, and propound its own solutions (Chambers, 1983; Chambers, 1993). Experts are there as living reference books – people who can be questioned, as a help to the group's own conclusions.

Each community needs to mobilize its strengths. This means drawing in all the kinds of expertise it holds – farmers, fisherfolk, craftsmen and women, painters, poets, scientists, priests, writers, builders, doctors, nurses, teachers, architects, engineers and all other trades (Robert, 1993). But it must not be an elitist process. Women as well as men, young and old as well as those in the earning bracket, unemployed as well as workers, workers as well as bosses, have to be involved. Indeed, those who are unemployed in a conventional sense, and the retired, may have an especial part to play because they have time to give – and may, in turn, find new energy and satisfaction in the process.

There are, as earlier chapters have suggested, certain basic rules for community action. They include:

- Creating a forum in which everyone can join equally in discussion of the goals of the community, and especially of their path to sustainable living (where social tradition demands that genders participate separately, the findings of the two forums need to be brought together in a manner acceptable to both). It is important that thoughtful young people are involved, for many young people are more visionary and original in their challenges than their elders.
- Discussing what sustainable living means for all members of the community, in their particular social setting, which aspects of present life are likely to be sustainable, which are not, and what options are open to the group as a whole.
- Reviewing the knowledge available to the community about the environment, the products and processes available and their impact, and the likely impacts of alternative actions. For example, how far do we have accurate information about consumer goods – and especially their economy in materials and energy, durability and capacity for ultimate recycling, and the social acceptability of the ways in which they are made? How can we get better information?

- Discussing the adequacy of education and supportive services like health care, which are also vital for sustainable living.
- Preparing information (such as newsletters) about the local environment and the choices open to the community. The media should be drawn into the consultative process, and their role considered. Curricula for education that teach people about the environment, our dependence on it, our responsibility to other people, and the bases for sustainable living might be demanded.
- Creating a mechanism by which the community can put its communal decisions into action (making sure that the rights of individuals are not unduly sacrificed in that process). Where key decisions rest with representative government, the local community might press for these to be referred back for endorsement at local level.

Some of this analysis can be done within the community, but some may need to involve specialists from outside. Such experts – provided that they accept their role as listeners and supporters rather than dictators – can help answer many difficult questions, such as:

- What should be the essential features of a village, or area, or group plan for sustainability? For example, what must be done to conserve soil, fuelwood, water, fishing grounds, pastures or forests? Can fertilizers be used more efficiently, and money saved through adopting integrated pest control? What are the priorities? How can the community feed itself – and cater for population growth? What about employment and hard currency earnings – can new products be generated for sale, thereby increasing the capacity of the community to pay for new heath care, training, better housing, water supplies or other essentials?
- How can community industries be stopped from polluting air or water? Can human sewage and surplus farm wastes be put through biogas plants rather than shed into streams? What about slaughterhouse effluents, silage liquors, tanneries, charcoal burning and so on?
- What are the limitations within which the community will have to work? For example, how far does it own or have entrenched rights in communal lands, including forests and water resources, or the power to manage wildlife and benefit from its sustainable use?

The analysis is likely to lead on to action that goes beyond the community:

- Where it is clear that the community is being frustrated by outside forces, how can these be checked or converted into allies? How, for example, can national or state policies for transport, agriculture, industry or urban growth be made sensitive to local desires?
- Where new empowerment is needed in order to allow primary environmental care to happen, how can this be achieved – who must be persuaded, and what must they do? How can the community ensure that it cannot be disenfranchised or dispossessed by central or provincial governments or by industries ? What legal and social protection is needed against exploitation by richer and more powerful people?

■ Where it is clear that some injection of financial, technical and human support will be essential if the community plans are to be put into action, where can this come from, and on what terms?

One area where new efforts may be needed is in the understanding of the environment. Often this demands a process of liberation rather than lecturing. As we have learned more of traditional wisdom, it has become increasingly clear that an enormous body of knowledge is held in rural societies that have lived for generations in a region, and used it in ways perfected over the centuries. People are not necessarily ignorant because they have not received advanced education: the poor can be wiser than the rich (Chambers, 1983). Problems arise when population pressure or the imposition of new demands from outside make that traditional approach inadequate, and the pace of imposed change is faster than the capacity of the community to devise new adaptations. Other problems arise when teaching from outside – whether by religious missionaries or missionary scientists – sets out to discredit the traditional insights because they are either not understood or are associated with ways of life considered 'primitive' and 'improper'. How can we state traditional wisdom and get it listened to alongside new insights?

We need new alliances between those who are locally wise and those who have the knowledge and skill of modern science. Such a fusion is the best way of developing sustainable resource use methods that will work on the ground and within local communities. We need a combination of local and international skills to define and value natural resources and work out the best ways of managing and using them. We need surveys to ascertain the wider potential of biological diversity. We need new techniques for predicting how systems will respond to human use. We need ability to balance local, national and global interests and to explain to people active at all three levels why a particular pattern is likely to be best.

Another essential basis for sound community action is a proper valuation of nature, and the incorporation of those values into the local decision process. And the values should be those of the local community, not just those of academic economists or resource managers in capital cities. But it will be necessary to state those values in money terms, as far as possible. Cost–benefit analyses are central to many decisions – not least about how far central or international authorities will invest to support a local initiative. It follows that the specialists who do such analyses need to encourage communities on the ground to state the worth to them of elements in their environment, and these should then be valued economically in as rigorous a manner as possible.

The sustainable company

Companies (indeed the whole world of business, industry and commerce) are extremely important social units, with an immense part to play in building sustainability. They are the main employers in urban areas. They are major investors in the developing world (private sector finance flows far exceed those of official governmental development aid agencies).

Agenda 21 calls on business and industry to take a wide range of actions (Robinson, 1993). These have also been spelled out in the report of the Business Council for Sustainable Development (BCSD), *Changing Course* (Schmidheiny, 1992). The fact is that unless businesses reshape their approach and change their pattern of operations, we shall not achieve the sustainable development the world needs. The BCSD emphasized that such a development will require 'far reaching shifts in corporate attitudes and new ways of doing busines'. They go on to outline six essential elements:

■ strong leadership from the top;
■ sustained commitment throughout the organization;
■ clear plans of action for each firm, with proper monitoring of progress towards the stated goals;
■ attention to the entire life cycles of products and the changing needs of customers;
■ 'ecoefficiency', defined as ever more efficiency while preventing pollution through good housekeeping, materials substitution, cleaner technologies and cleaner products, and more efficient use and recovery of resources;
■ technology cooperation between those enterprises that have the essential knowledge and those that require it, especially in the developing world.

Much the same approach is evident in the 16 principles of the Business Charter for Sustainable Development, produced by the International Chamber of Commerce (ICC) (Willums and Golucke, 1992), and the 7 principles of the Caux Round Table (1994).

The Caux principles centre on two ethical ideas, one summed up by the Japanese word 'kyosei' which means 'living and working together for the common good'. They embrace the responsibilities of businesses; their economic and social impact; the need to cultivate a spirit of trust; respect for international and domestic rules; support for multilateral trade; respect for the environment; and the avoidance of illicit operations. The 16 ICC principles are more down-to-earth, covering corporate priority; integrated management; process of improvement; employee education; prior assessment; products and services; customer advice; facilities and operations; research; precautionary approach; contractors and suppliers; emergency preparedness; transfer of technology; contributing to the common effort; openness to concerns and compliance and reporting.

What is significant is that both sets of principles – indeed all the emerging thinking in the corporate sector – place environmental concerns in a wider social and operational context. The ICC report which launched the Charter called it *The Greening of Enterprise '92*. But it makes clear that while many companies have made real strides, 'companies' credibility...remains to be judged upon the proper implementation of the Charter in the field'.

There is a paradox about the corporate sector. On the one hand, they are a dominant engine of change in the world, handling vast sums of money and dominating investment in the development process. They have also shown increasing signs of recognizing the need for environmental responsibility. But the sector as a whole has not sought to lead communities forward towards sustainable living. Many firms give the impression of following the trend rather than seeking to make it. Perhaps this is partly because they have been put on the defensive by the green environmental movement, and sensitized by the tendency, especially in the United States, to take firms to court over every misdeed, real or imagined. But if the world of business, commerce and industry is to help the world community towards sustainability, it will have to come out and take a more positive, leadership, line.

There is a clear need for all members of an enterprise to be committed to the goal of sustainability. Ecoefficiency involves the shop floor as well as the office of the chief executive and the boardroom. Anyone working in a business enterprise should make a positive effort to advance its sustainability. For this to happen, the lead from the top – the board and chief executive – is clearly important. They must make the individual efforts welcome, and see that they get further than a suggestions book. They must see that reactionary elements in middle management do not stifle ideas from more junior people. They must encourage representatives of the labour force – the trade unions – to join in the process. Training and information schemes are needed. People should be encouraged to develop their own ideas about how they can be more ecoefficient.

It will help if people who invest their money in a company ask about its environmental commitment and ecoefficiency. There are now a number of investment trusts which select enterprises on the dual ground of economic profitability and environmental policy. Such trusts ask questions about firms, and assess them before including them in their lists (Jupiter, 1994). Do they publish environmental policy statements, conduct environmental audits, have a formal environmental management system, publish annual environmental reports, assess the environmental merits of their trading partners, operate programmes for efficient use of energy and raw materials, maintain a register of significant environmental effects? Is there a main board director with responsibility for environmental matters?

The relationship between the enterprise and the community around it is vital. Companies must expect to publish their environmental action plans and the statistics of their emissions to the environment. They must join in dialogue with the community so that people living around them understand their activities, and can for their part state social goals the business enterprise should contribute to. The vision set out by the BCSD, and the practical detail of the ICC Charter, are most likely to be achieved if industrial enterprises make themselves part of the wider community and open to its influence through dialogue. The new World Business Council on Sustainable Development, formed through the merger of the BCSD and the World Industry Council for the Environment, could guide and lead this process.

We need to shed a number of unhelpful attitudes in the environmental community as well as in industry. Many 'green movements' have developed a culture of hostility towards industry (two successive General Assembly sessions in IUCN have rejected any idea of admitting industrial enterprises as associate members). This has some past justification. Yes, many firms were secretive, hostile to questioning, and dishonest in their statements. Yes, many firms did gloss over their pollution or take refuge in the threadbare argument that its was the unavoidable price the community paid for employment. Yes, when pressed, many firms did suddenly find that pollution prevention paid anyway (Royston, 1979; Willums and Golucke, 1992). But this is no basis for rejecting partnerships with those companies that do commit themselves to sustainability. Without healthy, clean, ecoefficient industry, providing employment and creating wealth, sustainable development will not be achieved.

This, in turn, may demand rejection of the extreme litigiousness of recent years, especially in the United States, where whenever anyone is disadvantaged by anything they seem to expect to be able to extract large sums of money in compensation (were Acts of God open to such claims, the Almighty would surely be bankrupt by now). Such an attitude is counterproductive in many ways. First, it denies the natural risk we must all take in a world liable to tempest and flood and where such impacts may get worse as the climate changes. Second, it fails to make allowance for the fallibility of honest humans, striving to do their best. Third, it makes companies less willing to be open about their activities in case they provide evidence for some pressure group to use against them. Fourth, it stifles dialogue about partnership for sustainability, because it pits individuals against their communities and their employers.

Absolutism is far too evident in many communities. It manifests itself in the so-called NIMBY (Not In My Back Yard) reaction when a company or government agency proposes to site a new factory or waste disposal site. Its extreme manifestation is BANANA (Build Absolutely Nothing Anywhere Near Anybody). Perhaps the silliest manifestation is seen in connection with very low level radioactive wastes. Virtually every major hospital generates these as a part of the treatment everyone expects. The level of radiation is tiny – very little more than in many soils and rocks. Yet when it is proposed to dump such wastes in a properly engineered facility within the community that gains the medical benefits there is an outcry on a scale more appropriate to a planned dump of surplus atom bombs. That same community is likely to be equally strident in opposing the building of equipment to burn its own wastes and sewage sludges, never mind dealing with wastes from other parts of the country, or from overseas, even though it makes sense to operate a relatively small number of highly efficient plants to treat the most difficult materials. Action for sustainability demands a rational attitude towards industrial actions on the part of the community, based in turn on openness, good information and consultation.

Employees and members of local community groups must therefore work to promote the culture of ecoefficiency in their own businesses. We should all press the firm we work for, or those in our neighbourhood to:

- participate fully in community discussions of development goals, contributing their special knowledge and helping to lead society towards sustainability;
- be open with local communities about the nature and impact of the processes and technology they use, publishing information about their environmental management, emissions, goals and policies;
- explain the nature and likely impacts of any planned new developments, and release an environmental impact statement. The principle of prior informed consent should be applied (but, at the same time, local communities should reject the foolishness of NIMBY and BANANA, and avoid a situation in which hostility to industry and the continued threat of litigation deters openness);
- apply high environmental standards wherever they operate, and adopt the BCSD's six points and the ICC Business Charter for Sustainable Development;
- adopt the three rules for the transfer of technology set out in Chapter 10, namely:
  1. that it has to work, sustainably, in the place it is going to and meet the needs of those who will use it; it must be evaluated against clear criteria of sustainability in the new setting;
  2. that only good technology is worth sharing – dirty processes, no longer tolerated in the developed countries, should not be exported to the developing world, providing cheap products at the expense of the environment;
  3. that externalization of costs in the shape of environmental damage should be unacceptable everywhere;
- ban transfers of technology that are not based on dialogue within the industrial or commercial sectors in the country of origin and country of receipt.

We should press these firms to join in or support, through the industrial organizations they belong to, the continuing development of international standards of sustainability under the International Standards Organization, the International Chamber of Commerce and the World Business Council for Sustainable Development. We should also press governments to adopt a mix of regulations and economic incentives to make industries safer, less polluting and more efficient in their use of materials and energy. They should set standards for the future, as goals to be achieved at specified dates. And they should lead in establishing new and innovative partnerships with business and financial institutions. This is one way to overcome the problem that much transfer of advanced technology is unattractive because of the costs and the long pay-back periods involved.

Action within the non-governmental organizations

Non-governmental organizations are, in the most basic sense, groups of concerned people who share a particular mission and have agreed to work together to pursue it. Usually, however, they have gone further than that and adopted some kind of collective identity – often a constitution, structure of governance and legal registration under the law of the country or countries they work in, so that they can raise and hold funds and gain the special benefits open to many charitable bodies.

There are literally thousands of NGOs, and the number continues to grow apace. They cover a vast range of topics, from politics through education, science, environmental protection, wildlife conservation, animal rights and the prevention of cruelty, development, humanitarian aid, and the arts. All should be concerned with sustainable living, for (apart from some religious sects with visions beyond this world, and anarchist groups dedicated to destruction) all their missions depend on its accomplishment. Hence the quest for sustainable living is not just the business of the conservation and sustainable development movement, even in its widest sense. It involves virtually the whole NGO community. All should examine their missions and approaches in the light of *Agenda 21* and *Caring for the Earth*, and see what adjustment is needed.

The non-governmental community can and should be a major architect of the change towards sustainability. But to succeed it needs to be clear about its role. The chief task is to empower people's organizations and help communities towards self-reliance and self-governance. The criterion for success is to achieve a situation in which the community can take care of its own interests. NGOs have to act as partners in that process, within the structure of society. This means partnership with one another, and also with government at all levels and with the world of business, industry and commerce. And NGOs should not worry if sustainable development leads to their own future marginalization, because their work has been done (Kalaw, 1994).

There is always tension between creativity and consensus. Creativity involves the development of new ideas and challenges, and the process of consensus-building inevitably tends to narrow this diversity about a common theme. There is room for both challenge and consensus in any society, because the world does not stand still, and new solutions to new and old problems should be sought. One of the major contributions the NGO community can make is to press their visions with courage and passion – so long as they are also guided by honesty, and do not present warped arguments because they feel that the end justifies the means.

But this does not mean rejecting the effort to rally about common ground. It does mean, however, that the consensus should not be forced, artificial or premature. Members of the non-governmental community have a particular role as champions of sustainability, advocates of environmental education, and leaders in the quest for care for the Earth, and some have a message which is, at present, disturbing to established consensus politics – to the dominant social paradigm of Lester Milbraith (1989). They are being brought into the new dialogue with governments and industry, and this is good for it will advance the process of social learning. But they must not let their voices be drowned in a sea of established political doctrine. In so far as *Caring for the Earth* is a new book of minor prophecy, its advocates may have to adopt the dangerous role of the prophet. Nothing else is likely to break through the barriers of inertia.

This approach will demand courage – which the NGO movement has displayed in abundance – and change. The NGO movement has so far been dominated by the thinking of the Northern, developed, world. Its very success in creating and driving the global conservation movement has brought problems (Smillie, 1994). First, it has grown at an immense rate. There were over 3000 NGOs with a mission somehow related to development in the OECD countries in 1992: each had to carve out a special niche, fly a special flag, and raise funds, often in competition with its natural allies. Second, and more seriously, many Northern NGOs which had seen their mission as solving the problems of the South tended to impose their philosophy and approach. Now, a similar wave of growth in the non-governmental sector is occurring in the developing world, and these new Southern NGOs reflect their own cultural heritage and have their own priorities, based on the needs of the communities to which they belong. It cannot be assumed that (say) an Argentine NGO will behave like a Swedish one, even though they are working on very similar issues. The Northern organizations must prepare to pass the torch South.

Governments have often found the NGO movement a nuisance, and they have often handled it badly. In the former centrally-planned states of Central and Eastern Europe, NGOs were seen as subversive because, by definition, the state was the expression of the will of the people and the custodian of their welfare, and all citizen's groups had to lie within the envelope of the state. Yet those same NGOs – not least those in the environmental sphere – were important spearheads in the liberation movement. All NGOs who work to accomplish their missions are inevitably forced into politics. They must not de-politicize their message, for this would guarantee its ineffectiveness. This means, of course, that they will run into barriers.

At the same time, the NGO movement must accept that government – central or local – has a duty to ensure that there is informed and sensitive debate within communities about their road to sustainability, and that communities must then be permitted to follow the path they choose so long as it lies within the defined envelope of sustainability, and does not deprive individuals of their rights. This can mean – yes – that when an NGO has made its case, and the community as a whole has rejected it, that rejection is accepted and the NGO does not seek to subvert the action that follows.

The non-governmental movement is at present gaining increasing acceptance with national governments in many parts of the world, and in international circles. But this, in turn, is forcing many organizations to re-think their separate and collective roles. Ian Smillie (1994) suggested to the IUCN session in Buenos Aires that they will need to place 'higher values on pluralism; on the need for honesty and transparency; on the need to find common ground where it exists, and to recognize where it does not'. In some cases governments or intergovernmental institutions will be agents of change, and in others the NGOs will transform themselves. Governments may need to create financial mechanisms that support NGOs – 'because they do good work, because they are expressions of public concern, not because they raise money through emotive and increasingly sophisticated market techniques.' One of the difficulties here is how far governments will be willing to fund NGOs if this simply means 'feeding the hands that bite them' (to quote one politician's inverted metaphor).

The justification must be that 'governments see NGOs as valued development agencies in their own right, not simply as delivery mechanisms, executing agencies and adjuncts to the work of official agencies'. And, especially in developing countries (and some others, like Japan, where non-governmental bodies have not fitted easily into the culture) there needs to be recognition that a committed NGO can be of positive value in advancing social debate and promoting wise social action even if they do from time to time question established thinking. There is a difference between a challenge and a threat.

What should the NGO community do in its quest for sustainability? What should we do as members of such bodies? At least the following:

■ Make sure that all NGOs are open, democratic and accountable. There are some small, closed, pressure groups that use the NGO label as a cloak for advocacy. The status of any NGO must be clear, and the NGO community as a whole should adopt a stricter scrutiny of its members.

■ Ensure that the groups we belong to review their mission and action agenda in the light of *Agenda 21* and *Caring for the Earth*, and are truly committed to sustainability. Each NGO should prepare its own *Agenda 21*, as a clear statement of the contribution it hopes to make. We should resign from any group that is not interested in creative dialogue with other sections of the community.

■ Make sure that each NGO builds effective working partnerships with other NGOs in the same village, city, state and country.

■ Make sure that our NGO does enter into dialogue with central and local government, for example participating in round table discussion groups and the like even when they appear to be inadequate. We should always work from within such structures, to strengthen them, rather than snipe at them from afar.

■ Speak clearly, passionately, and yet truthfully about the cause that drives the group, be it small or large scale. Avoid premature consensus, but be willing to support wider actions that reflect the mission and blend it with other initiatives, even if there has to be some blurring at the margin.

■ Recognize that NGOs are the creatures of their cultures, and do not seek to impose our cultural vision in other parts of the world. We should try open dialogue, guided by humility instead, and be prepared for a two-way learning process.

■ Accept the unpopularity of the prophet, without rushing towards martyrdom. And do not try to martyr other visionaries, even if we passionately disagree with them.

Action in the city, district, state or canton

The city or rural district, or in countries with a federal constitution the land, canton, state or province, is often the level at which citizen's groups,

NGOs and businesses can most effectively come together and work for sustainability. Many cities have got the message. There are numerous conferences on 'the sustainable city'. Some, like Curitiba (Taniguchi, 1994) or Seattle (Lawrence, 1994), have developed detailed action plans to that end. In the latter, the first key action was the rejection of the elected leadership, and insistence on a new framework with far more citizen participation!

The key in Seattle was the emergence of a series of groups at several levels, all interacting in a structured yet flexible way. Citizen groups organized themselves around particular concerns (waste disposal was the literally burning issue that catalyzed the whole process). A discussion forum on environmental priorities, a comprehensive plan built around the outcome of that consultation, and a citizen effort to prepare a report card against which the performance of private and public enterprises would be judged were the other components.

Five key areas of action have been proposed for third world cities (Hardoy et al, 1992):

- respond to citizen demands for safe and healthy living and working environments;
- ensure that laws and regulations protect citizens from exploitation by landlords and employers;
- penalize polluters, but also provide incentives for reducing pollution, minimizing resource consumption and recycling wastes;
- manage urban growth so that environmental capital is used as well as possible and social and economic goals are met;
- identify and support new economic activities which enhance both the city's economic base and its environment.

These are things that we as citizens – North or South – should press on our municipal and district authorities. But the essential, first step is that they set up the consultative framework so that the ideas of individuals, neighbourhood groups, firms and NGOs can be brought together. This means a forum. It also means that each ward or electoral unit in the city may need to have its discussion process, in which the elected representatives as well as city or district officials are fully involved. But above all it means that the output must be taken seriously when final decisions are taken.

Too often, city authorities mount massive consultation exercises on the basis of plans that have been prepared in detail before they are laid before the public or before consultative forums. The result is that the officials or elected representatives that prepare them 'own' and defend them by the time they are opened for discussion. They are tightly articulated so that altering one bit upsets the fabric of the whole. There are always reasons for resisting change at this stage. We need to press for a real citizen involvement 'upstream' of the written plan.

Another need is for direct feedback loops from government to people. In Switzerland, popular votes are commonly conducted when enough people demand that the general will of the community is tested in this way. In other countries (like the United Kingdom) the word 'referendum' is treated by Ministers and Members of Parliament as the ultimate in unspeakability. There is no logic in this argument, and in many ways it is absurd to postulate that a nationwide election every four or five years on the basis of thirty-page general manifestos is enough to give a mandate for government of a complex society. People should press for their city or district governance systems to be more directly accountable and the use of occasional votes on key issues – like a local plan – is one useful mechanism.

A third need is for everyone to be involved in the business of their city, district, land or canton. Too often local elections are greeted with apathy. Too many people take no interest in policy at this crucial level of government. Those concerned with sustainable living should reject such an attitude. Most elected members would welcome closer links with their constituencies. But it goes further than that, for it means incorporating proposals for sustainability in political manifestos, and debating them in an electoral context. It means getting all political parties to accept sustainable living as a goal, and making them set out alternative proposals for action so that the political debate focuses on the pathways the community should follow. The NGO movement should insist that participatory local democracy is a vital element in the sustainability process, and should make sure that their members take part in the electoral debate, as well as seek meetings with their elected councils to discuss the way ahead. They should only by-pass the councils and campaign against them when dialogue has defined the issues clearly and both sides understand what the row is about.

'Subsidiarity' is an ugly word, but it has an important meaning – that in government, issues should be decentralized to local level wherever possible. They should be pushed as far down the ladder of government as they can be. This makes good sense in the context of sustainable living. The implication is that the NGO community should also work as far as possible at local, district and city level and should stop the present heavy emphasis in many countries on national politics. They are important, but the real environment is commonly managed at a lower level of government.

Finally, we should press for real empowerment of the city, district, state, land or cantonal layers of government. This means power to manage and develop the environment. To raise money to that end. To hold discussions and referenda. To involve people. Central government must set a frame, and can usefully adopt national strategies. It has to have laws constraining local governmental mavericks. But it should not try to manage the cities for their people. If the empowerment is real, then people will see that it is worth their while being active in these crucial units of society. And democracy does mean allowing groups of people to get it wrong – within limits, and provided they do not damage other people and future generations.

Accordingly, the process of sustainable development demands that we all press for action to:

■ incorporate sustainability as a goal of all political parties, and debate alternative social policies for attaining it as a major element in the local electoral process;

- establish, in every sub-national level of government (urban or rural), a system of discussion between elected representatives and officials and citizen groups, NGOs, and local business, industry and commerce;
- make this process of consultation the starting point for planning, with feedback loops so that the resulting plans and proposals are endorsed by as wide a community process as possible;
- ensure that every local community has its own *Agenda 21*, built through this consultative process;
- support citizen groups as partners in the process of implementation – there is no reason why NGOs and 'green neighbourhood groups' should not actually undertake some of the actions on behalf of the community: it may well be cheaper than using the machinery of the state or city;
- build essential protection of the citizen into local and city plans (for example with local controls on pollution, traffic, noise, building, industrial processes and with insistence on adoption of environmental impact assessment and proper review of development proposals), but also provide incentives for sustainable living (for example using economic incentives);
- get our national governments to decentralize to local level responsibility for guiding action for sustainability on the ground.

Action by governments

We may be just emerging from the age of national sovereignty that has dominated the world for a century or more. In the 1970s everyone agreed that the way to deal with the problems of the world environment was to get the governments together – and the UN Conference on the Human Environment at Stockholm was the result. We have seen a massive proliferation of national environmental laws and international agreements since then. Yet – despite the reaffirmation of national concern at the highest level at Earth Summit in Rio in 1992 – these have not led on to the action needed.

There are two areas of deficiency. Internally, in the way nations are governed and internationally, in the way governments interact with one another and with supranational institutions like the United Nations agencies, multinational corporations and global non-governmental organizations.

Internally, sustainable development in many states is being frustrated by:

- defective or perverse political theory;
- imperfect distribution of power between government and other parts of the community, and between levels of government;
- sectoralism;
- bad internal communications in government;
- poor training of government officials, and poor explanation of their roles;
- inadequate laws and economic regulations;
- corruption.

Land ownership is a vexed question in many countries. Some still hold to the belief that the land – the environmental resource of greatest importance – should be vested in the state on behalf of the people. In theory this is to prevent exploitation of one group or individual by another: it is perceived as a way of avoiding the situation that does occur in a number of countries where a tiny proportion of the population controls a large proportion of the land. For example, in Paraguay in 1987 1 per cent of landowners had possession of 80 per cent of the land, and in Brazil 60 per cent of the arable land was held by 2 per cent of landowners. However this kind of situation was not peculiar to the developing world: in the United Kingdom the total farmland was owned by 2 per cent of the population, and the poorer half of the population owned less than 1 per cent of the land.

The issue is really less about ownership than about power and responsibility. Many individual land owners use their land well and seek to pass it on to future generations 'in good heart'. The reduction in the proportion of the population owning land has been a natural part of the development process in many countries, as people have moved to the cities and to other trades and professions. State ownership in many countries, on the other hand, has signally failed to care for the land or to give people living in rural areas security of tenure: even urban dwellers often lack title to their homes. The result is little incentive to conserve or improve. Again, this is a Northern as much as a Southern problem, as the failure of collective farms in the former USSR testifies. Where control and responsibility has been given back to individuals and to local communities, sustainability has risen – and this applies also to rights to wildlife resources, as the Zimbabwe CAMP-FIRE project, repeatedly described in this book, has shown.

Another flawed doctrine is that there must be plans and strategies for everything. Such an idea is seductive, for it implies that there will be very thorough and informed analysis of options, and that government as a whole will be committed to what is proposed. In practice, the top-down, rigid nature of much central planning has brought disaster to many regions, notably in central and eastern Europe, but also in parts of Africa. The need is to reverse these kinds of thinking and start with attention to needs and perceptions on the ground. What do the communities seek? What can they tell about the capacity of their lands and the best ways of using their natural resources? How can the expertise, finances and supporting strengths of central government and its agencies, of business and of non-governmental organizations, best support such endeavours?

Confidence is best achieved by good governance. Forbidding capital transfers defeats itself if it makes the country unattractive to inward investment, for example because firms fear that they will never be able to move the profits they earn out again. The philosophy of the new European Energy Charter Treaty addresses this point, its articles on investment promotion and protection emphasizing that 'once an investment is made, the foreign investor must be accorded fair and equitable treatment and be entitled to use, enjoy and dispose of his investments free of unreasonable or discriminatory measures' (DTI, 1994). Governments need to create the confidence which will in turn attract investment in a country by its own wealthy, rather than transfer all they can to safe-deposits in Northern banks. In the same way, they need to motivate people to work in and for the society, to acquire skills, and to trust that should they have the energy, ability and good fortune they can really contribute to building their local community and nation.

Sectoralism has been condemned in a succession of reports, over the past several decades. Yet it is inherent in many societies. It is easier to carve up the fabric of government and the operations of society into units that deal with particular aspects – agriculture, forestry, fisheries, nature conservation, outdoor recreation, transport, housing, planning, finance, defence, economic affairs and so on. Many government officials spend their whole working lives within such a sector, or still narrower segments within it. The result makes for well-structured governance, because people understand what they are doing and can develop and apply skills and insights. But it fails the test of sustainability because environmental resources cannot safely be parcelled up in this way. If practical administrative necessity demands a degree of sectoralization, then cross-links and inter-sectoral discussions become of paramount importance.

There is an interesting inconsistency and intellectual tension here. Cross-sectoral approaches are commonly urged by environmentalists, because the environment underlies all that we do, and bridges the stratifications imposed by human societies. National conservation strategies, national sustainability strategies and national environmental action plans are commended as solutions. But what are these but codified central plans? How can they escape the drawbacks and failures of centralized planning? Is the fact that so many exist on paper, but have proved hard to apply on the ground, a further testimony to the ineffectiveness of central planning? Maybe. The answer is that cross-sectoral strategies are not in themselves a means of governance. They are not, nor should they be, central plans. Their purpose is to enable decentralized as well as centralized action, and to draw the local and sectoral into a common focus and look at how it all adds up. We have still not worked out how to do this. Sustainable governance remains largely a theory – and is a challenge for the next few decades.

Internal communications are a key to avoiding the undermining of sustainable development by sectoralism. They should prevent one sector or agency being unaware of the work of others or failing to see how the actions it takes can affect them. But what kind of communications? A strategy is best seen as one communications form – a way of exchanging information – rather than a machinery for rigid direction. Meetings, committees, seminars and all those devices beloved of bureaucrats come into the same category. Again, societies generally waste a lot of time in these things. A lot has to be done to make them more effective than they now are.

Poor training is another factor. Very few people are actually trained for public governance – unless training on the job (a crude form of trial-and-error learning) counts. Hardly any government officials are being trained in modern thinking about sustainability, and its environmental and social implications. Changing this is also the best way to develop cross-sectoral thinking, and if environmental education is done well in school and university; if environmental economics is taught to all economists and practical environmental scientists; and if ideas of sustainability and what limits it are part of the general educational background, then people are likely to enter even a sectoralized government with cross-sectoral ideas. They may then be better able to use cross-sectoral communications channels.

Very often deficiencies in governance are blamed on bad laws, or worse enforcement. The criticisms are often valid. Environmental protection laws can be evaded. Development control barely exists in many countries. Wildlife protection and national parks often exist largely on paper. But all the laws in the world are unlikely to succeed unless they go with the grain of society. As earlier chapters have shown, where people feel an ownership of their environment and its resources, they are likely to be moved to cherish it, and will be the best agents of law enforcement. So, once again, education and communication are keys to success, and laws follow after and express what has already largely become a matter of social consensus. They are there primarily to constrain the minorities who would otherwise abuse power.

And corruption. In some countries, it does undermine governance and sustainability. It is the most blatant abuse of power, converting resources and influence entrusted by the community for personal gain. But once more, the climate in which it flourishes is one of weak social structure, no consensus on goals, no shared strong moral codes of visions, no social demand for compliance with community actions, no self-enforcement of the law, and no communications systems which expose the corrupt and force the institutions of the law to act.

We should press for governments to correct these obstacles to sustainable development. But in a real sense, such corrections are just a first step. The goals and programmes of many national governments are not compatible with sustainability. They tend to press for economic growth at virtually all costs, regardless of what they have signed up to in *Agenda 21*. They spend immense sums on military equipment, very little of which is actually needed for defence against potential aggressors. Several developed countries engage in competitive marketing of arms to recipients that do not need them and cannot afford them, thereby retarding development, aggravating social ills and adding to the debt burden. Few national *Agenda 21*s or strategies for sustainability look hard at these issues.

Of course nations need means to defend themselves. But there is a balance. All nations should review the best means of striking that balance. They should in that context review the value of the United Nations as a peace-building as well as a peace-keeping organization.

Sustainability is every bit as much a political issue at national as at local level. It follows that there should be discussion of national goals for sustainability, and of policies to attain them in party political manifestos and electoral debate. In recent years, at least in Europe, the 'Green Parties' have been swallowed up by older political bodies that now claim to have absorbed the best of their ideas and incorporated them within wider and more balanced agendas. Maybe. But few 'mainstream' political parties admit that sustainability is about more than fine tuning and slow readjustment of the current social paradigm (Milbraith, 1989). Society in developed countries has been led to expect endless economic growth and a steady stream of consumer goods from the Great Cornucopia. We need a more challenging and informed political debate, for like the legendary giant's horn that the god Thor drank from, the end of that cornucopia rests in the environment, and draining it too vigorously can only lead to disaster.

Among the actions we should seek from national governments are the following:

- They should place the commitment to sustainable development at the top of the political agenda.
- They should express this commitment in practical action to care for the 'natural capital' of the environment.
- All political parties should set out their plans for sustainability in their election manifestos, and ensure that the choices and costs are laid squarely before their electorates.
- Governments should prepare national strategies for sustainability through a broad consultative process. These should look honestly at the need for continuing economic growth, the way it is defined and measured, and the extent to which the country should invest in military hardware and personnel. The arms trade should be scrutinized from an ethical as well as an economic standpoint.
- Fundamental issues like land ownership, support for population limitation through health care and birth control facilities, universal education and training, the construction of truly participatory democracy, and international equity should also be discussed openly, and addressed in national policies and actions.
- Governments should accept that sustainability will only be achieved if all citizens, citizen groups, NGOs, business enterprises, and local authorities are enabled to play their full part. They should promote dialogue within the community, at all social levels and across all sectors, about the need for sustainable living and the way it can be carried forward.
- The principle of subsidiarity should be adopted, and local communities empowered. National policies and strategies should be built from below up, and founded in realism, rather than top down, and based on political theory.
- Governments should build social and personal commitment. This is the best defence against corruption and inefficiency, the best means of law enforcement, and the best foundation for sustainable development. An informed, committed, citizenship is best secured through universal environmental education, good training, and good communications. The national media need to set themselves high standards – to tell the truth, the whole truth and nothing but the truth.

■ While supporting individual and group choice, governments should adopt guiding laws that prevent excessive power being mis-used for personal short-term gain. Economic and social incentives that plough wealth back into investment that in turn promotes sustainability should be promoted. Inward international investment should be attracted, and measures put in place to ensure that it is profitable, within the necessary safeguards to prevent abuse of power.

■ Governments should make sure that their national machinery (and especially financial policies) truly assist sustainable development. While sectoral departments are likely to remain essential, there must also be good across-the-board coordinating mechanisms.

■ All governments should affirm their commitment to international alliances that will move the global community towards sustainable development. All should adopt and enforce the essential international conventions and agreements to safeguard the world environment. They should reject narrow nationalism, and the nonsense that any nation in today's world can achieve sustainability on its own.

International action for world sustainability

Caring for the Earth emphasized the environmental, social and economic interdependence of nations. It quoted the South Commission (1990):

> If the multiple bonds that characterize interdependence are convincingly present in any field, it is that encompassing development and the environment. Human civilization is moving towards a global state. That is apparent in all dimensions: social, economic, cultural and political as well as environmental. But the transition is not occurring smoothly and harmoniously: it is turbulent and beset with conflict.

For the past twenty years it has been assumed that international action could be equated with intergovernmental action. In 1995 the intergovernmental dimension indeed still stands strong. Many economic decisions are taken by groups of governments – in the Group of 7 leading industrialized nations, in OECD, in regional economic groupings like the European Union, ASEAN, NAFTA, MERCOSUR and so on. Such groupings are multiplying as states realize that they offer prospects of mutual support and enhanced economic growth. But governments do not act alone. The private sector of business, industry and commerce also works internationally, with many multinational corporations active in fifty or more countries, and not a few having financial turnovers substantially greater than the poorest 50 of the world's nations. Science has always been international, but modern telecommunications and information transfer makes this cooperation swifter and wider. The media foster world consciousness, and the whole global community knows almost instantly of a triumph or disaster.

Despite this global interlinkage, global harmony seems as elusive as ever, while consensus within nations is declining and internal dissent threatens to rip states apart. As Sir Shridath Ramphal said in Buenos Aires (1994), our record is tangled and disquieting. The rich – individual and national – have grown richer, and the poor, poorer. As the cold-war era closed, the peace that followed was rent apart by terrible new tribal divisions and ethnic and religious tensions. The events in Somalia, the former Yugoslavia and Rwanda are shameful failures. For all too many people, peace and security have been illusions. Four factors seem likely to re-shape the international and national future: continuing population growth, the unequal prospects of people, a shifting economic centre of gravity and the weakening of nation states.

The centre of human gravity is shifting south. In 1945, 33 per cent of the world population lived in developed countries: in 1992 it was 24 per cent. In 2025 Africa will have more people than the countries that today consti-tute the developed world. The centre of world economics is also shifting out of the OECD countries, which together only account for about half of world GDP. China is now the world's second largest economy, with India sixth and Brazil and Mexico in the top ten. As non-European countries rise to the top of the economic league the G7 countries will be seen as less and less representative. These factors may be more influential than traditional poli-tics in strengthening the calls for global governance.

Human prospects are even more starkly different than two decades ago. Gulfs in wealth – made evident by the information revolution and the mass media – are fuelling envy and frustration. The poor cannot be expected to put up with economic injustice for ever. Communist regimes originated with fundamental ideas of equality and justice, and inequity and injustice remain potent breeding grounds for revolution even though it is now accepted that market economies will shape the future. Criminal violence and strife between religious and ethnic groups are symptoms of today's social disease.

Nation states are being eroded. Global financial systems and finance flows make national frontiers less relevant. Environmental concerns also span such arbitrary lines on the map. Where ethnic relationships and reli-gious beliefs do not match frontiers, the security of states is undermined. These vulnerabilities make new international alliances essential for the secu-rity and sustainability of human life.

The 1939–1945 war ended in a near-universal determination that global society (especially under the new shadow of the atomic bomb) must never again tear itself apart in this way. The new global security system was built on an alliance of nation states in the United Nations System and the linked financial institutions created following the conference at Bretton Woods in 1944 and so bearing its name. A 'frenzy of institutionalization overtook the world in the 1940s and continued into the 1970s' (Holdgate, 1994b). Several pre-existing bodies like the International (now World) Meteorological Organization and the International Labour Organization (created in 1873 and 1919 respectively) were swept into the UN system as specialized agen-cies, to be joined by the Food and Agriculture Organization, the General Agreement on Tariffs and Trade, the International Fund for Agriculture

Development, the International Maritime Organization, the UN Educational, Scientific and Cultural Organization, the UN Industrial Development Organization, the World Health Organization, the World Intellectual Property Organization and the World Tourism Organization. The special Bretton Woods financial agencies, the International Monetary Fund, the International Bank for Reconstruction and Development, the International Development Association and the International Finance Corporation were all created between 1944 and 1960.

These bodies are 'specialized agencies' with their own international governing councils, and a substantial measure of independence (although they report to the UN General Assembly through the Economic and Social Council, ECOSOC). But there is an extraordinary tangle of other bodies, one, the International Atomic Energy Agency constitutionally independent although under the aegis of the UN, two described as 'organs of the UN' (UNICEF, the UN Children's Fund, and the UN Conference on Trade and Development, UNCTAD), one joint organ of the UN and FAO (the World Food Programme), two UN Programmes (the UN Environment Programme, UNEP, and the UN Development Programme, UNDP), three Commissions (on Population, Human Settlements and Transnational Corporations), one Committee (on the Development of New and Renewable Sources of Energy), one subsidiary organ of the General Assembly under the administrative authority of UNDP (the UN Population Fund), and several Special Offices like those of the Disaster Relief Coordinator and the High Commissioner for Refugees. And then there are Regional Commissions for Europe, Africa, Latin America and Asia and the Far East – and some special regional offices like that for the Sudano-Sahelian region.

As in government, this sectoralism makes coordination difficult. Coordination for environmental action – parcelled out among many agencies and special groups – was the cry at the UN Conference on the Human Environment at Stockholm in 1972, and led to the creation of the UN Environment Programme with its 'small, co-ordinating secretariat', and its governing council, designed to articulate the world's priorities for environmental action and to stimulate a response through the concerted action of the UN agencies. Success was only partial, and best where UNEP itself took direct action, as it did to establish an 'earthwatch' monitoring system, create an information base on chemicals liable to cause environmental problems, and to develop new international conventions and laws (where there were spectacular successes in dealing with the problems of regional seas, but also in action to safeguard the ozone layer and deal with hazardous wastes). In Rio, coordination was again uppermost on many people's rhetorical agendas, and this time UNEP the coordinator became the coordinated, with a new body, the Commission on Sustainable Development taking this role, and with a stronger internal mandate for the UN Administrative Committee on Coordination.

Two major realizations dawned slowly, especially at and after the Rio Earth Summit. The first was that the UN system really had major weaknesses to overcome. The second was that the intergovernmental action would never, alone, create the right kind of alliance.

Seven weaknesses are evident in the UN system (Holdgate, 1994b):

- It has never been *integrated*. The central machinery has never been able to control the agencies. The Bretton Woods financial institutions really function as a separate system.

- It has never been truly *pro-active*, with a clear strategy for its work on environmental issues, and well-defined priorities (*Agenda 21* is, in this context, far too broad a shopping list).

- It has failed *to address the big socio-economic issues* like the widening poverty gap between nations, the defects in the world economic and trading system, and the need to curb wasteful over-consumption and pollution in the developed world.

- It suffers from *insularity*. Intergovernmental bodies are dominated by governmental delegations, and they have not been good at building links with the non-governmental and business worlds.

- Its *legitimacy* depends on that of the nation states that constitute it, and as their authority is eroded, so the UN is weakened.

- It is easily *distracted by political crisis*, as witness the immense growth in its recent peace-keeping role, to the detriment of longer term peace-building through sustainable development.

- It has led in the adoption of much environmental law, but *has not been able to make this law enforceable*.

One consequence is a serious lack of confidence in the UN, on the part of rich as well as poor nations. It can be argued that the Bretton Woods institutions have similarly failed to deliver (Rich, 1994). They have been too prone to work through big loans to governments, which are at best unwieldy and at worst recipes for disaster because sustainable development is advanced far more efficiently through smaller-scale and local action. Major projects have disrupted communities and displaced large numbers of local people, largely because the cost-benefit analyses undertaken have followed traditional central government economic valuation systems and undervalued traditional uses and natural capital. The World Bank, despite major efforts to strengthen its staff competence in the environmental area, does not enjoy a high reputation for its environmental projects. Although the alleviation of poverty is a major goal, many World Bank projects are alleged to have aggravated it (Rich, 1994). In 1995 there are many signs that the Bank has 'got the message', and is working in much closer partnership with other parts of the UN system and with the expert NGO community, but there is much reconstruction still to do.

Many people looked to the Global Environment Facility – the only significant source of 'new money' following the Rio Earth Summit – as a way of accelerating sustainable development and dealing with the major world problems. Some of these hopes were misplaced. The GEF is, by world stan-

dards, a small fund (only US$2 billion). It is directed to specific global prob-
lems (it is not a general fund for sustainable development). It does not
address the subjects listed in *Agenda 21* except for issues of climate change
and the conservation of biological diversity. While the GEF has an important role within its defined mandate, and should change the balance of its
support towards smaller-scale projects by local-level groups, quite new ways
will have to be found to advance sustainable development priorities in the
developing world (Khosla, 1994).

A new and more equitable basis for international trade is widely
regarded as an important element in the development of global sustainability. There is concern that GATT, the General Agreement on Tariffs and
Trade, could actually work the other way, and in the zeal to remove barriers, might obstruct the efforts of governments to insist that marketed products were produced in ways that meet high standards of sustainable
management. Article 11 of the General Agreement prohibits restrictions on
exports and imports, subject to exceptions to protect human life or health,
and to conserve exhaustible natural resources (Akao, 1994). The implication is that exceptions to protect the health of ecosystems or species other
than the human are not admissible (though it is of course possible to argue
that human life depends on the maintenance of a healthy ecosystem and
the avoidance of pollution). Hence the desire for a new 'green round' of
GATT following the completion of the long drawn out agony of negotiation
over the so-called 'Uruguay Round'. GATT is now being converted into a
new World Trade Organization with a standing Working Group on Trade
and Environment issues. It remains to be seen how well it will work.

A global alliance has to go wider than the United Nations system – or,
indeed, intergovernmental systems. This is conceded in *Agenda 21* and has
been the subject of increasing discussion since Earth Summit. The High
Level Advisory Board to the Secretary General of the United Nations concluded that partnerships between the United Nations system and non-governmental bodies are necessary because the latter have special knowledge,
active memberships and a capacity to build awareness and promote action,
and this in turn allows them to facilitate the work of the UN system internationally and of governments nationally. It went on (UN, 1994a):

Partnerships should bring all sectors together in a common understanding of what is needed, and then advance implementation....The partnerships between the United Nations system and non-governmental entities
should operate as a two-way relationship....The United Nations and its
Agencies should:

(a) strengthen their linkages with appropriate intergovernmental
    bodies and non-governmental entities in order to draw upon their
    expertise;

(b) seek to enhance national action by developing and promulgating
    models for partnership, based on case studies of success;

(c) improve the effectiveness of consultative processes with non-gov-
    ernmental entities, especially through the establishment of *consul-
    tative forums*;

(d) develop and promulgate models for partnership based on success, emphasizing the need for flexibility, practicality, adaptability, cost-effectiveness and accountability;

(e) facilitate the process of sustainable development by coordinating the development of indicators and strategies for sustainability;

(f) promote and support training programmes led by partner institutions;

(g) encourage the promotion of awareness, down to grassroots level, and especially through UNDP, support capacity building;

(h) encourage the establishment of electronic information networks as effective ways of publicizing the work being done, and as a means for promoting cooperative action.

The NGO community should enhance its own capacity to contribute to partnerships with United Nations bodies, including by organizing themselves into representative coalitions and by inviting United Nations participation in their activities.

The non-governmental movement is involved in a wide range of activities following the Rio Conference (Kalaw, 1994). At global level the Earth Council is organizing itself to monitor how states are complying with *Agenda 21*; Earth Action Network is seeking to build a constituency for global issues with monthly alerts on peace, human rights, development and environment while the International NGO Forum, which facilitated the drawing up of NGO 'treaties' in Rio is looking at how to create alternatives based on community and civil society experiences. Major groups of NGOs are coming together to prepare joint position papers, as inputs to the UN Commission on Sustainable Development and other bodies. The UN institutions are now reviewing the formal basis of their relationship with the NGO community. There is a vast mass of national NGO activity. What Maximo Kalaw has called 'a wave of NGO action' is developing.

Quite evidently, if the Commission on Sustainable Development is to succeed in promoting the sharing of technology, or if the World Trade Organization is to balance trade and environment issues sensibly, the world of business, industry and commerce must be involved. For it is a dominant force in today's world. To quote Yasuo Goto of Keidanren, Japan (1994):

improvement in the global environment calls for all the players to join in a common front line. Whether a player belongs to a national government, a local government, an NGO or a company, he or she must respect other participants as equal partners...Partnership...is defined as a dynamic state of human relationship in which both partners do their best to reach for their common goal and thereby learn from each other...Partnership in the true sense does not mean indulgence or dependence on each other.

There are other ingredients in the mix. International conventions and agreements are important. They can define the framework for cooperation between governments, and they can be used also as mechanisms in which the non-governmental sector can come in and contribute. Dr Andronico Adede (1994) has suggested that we need a new breed of international convention – and that we must revitalize those that are moribund, and stop competing and conflicting initiatives between others. To secure a good convention:

■ there must be consensus that a legal instrument is needed;
■ the process of negotiation must be accepted as sound, conferring legitimacy on the product;
■ there must be wide participation, especially of developing countries;
■ a funding mechanism should be established, to assist compliance.

Where the conditions – and consensus – are not met, it is wiser to proceed via a soft law such as an agreed set of guidelines.

This could be the position with the proposed Covenant on Environment and Development, being developed by IUCN (Hassan, 1994). The covenant is envisaged as 'a global instrument embodying general environmental legal principles'. It is to draw on soft-law statements like the Declaration of the UN Conference on the Human Environment, held at Stockholm in 1972, the World Charter for Nature, adopted by the UN General Assembly in 1982, and the UN Conference on Environment and Development, held at Rio de Janeiro in June 1992, but is to go further because it would be 'hard' law, a series of binding commitments, which combined new general principles with the accepted dicta of a number of extant international legal instruments. It would in this sense complement 'the kind of visionary declarations and aspirations that might find expression in the Earth Charter'.

The Charter, Covenant and other such documents are mission statements for the world community. As such:

they need to articulate:

■ the concept of common concern of humanity;
■ the concept of inter-generational equity;
■ the precautionary principle by virtue of which lack of full scientific certainty is not to be used as a pretext for postponing action to protect or avoid harm to the environment;
■ recognition of the right to development, and
■ the need to balance the obligations relating to consumption patterns and those relating to demographic policies (Adede, 1994).

But all the treaties and covenants in the world are useless unless they are implemented, and the record of treaty implementation, especially by developing countries, is not encouraging. One reason is that the importance of the environment is not properly recognized by public or government. Another is the lack of expertise and resources. Amado Tolentino of the Philippines (1994) suggested that the answer lies in the preparation of 'implementation packages' which set out the objectives of an international agreement or treaty and the legislative and administrative requirements for its implementation nationally and at local level and back them up with clear blueprints for implementation. Local experts can then pick up the details set out in the package and apply them within their own communities and districts. Someone – and this may not be done best by conferences of the parties, which tend to see things from national perspectives and achieve highest common factors rather than new advances – needs now to settle to prepare such a package.

The challenge to the leaders of the nations, working in partnership with the leaders of world commerce, world science and world conservation, is to choreograph the ballet we are all dancing on the world stage. Just as at national level, the need is for support, facilitation and freedom rather than direction and dominance: for drawing together the lessons learned by those working to care for areas of the Earth and use its resources sustainably; for keeping up with change and removing barriers to adaptation.

At one level, the international community has a mechanistic, an institutional task – to create groupings which advance world sustainability as a common mission, by sharing experience, removing barriers and inequities, and genuinely supporting those who need help. This means:

- reforming the UN system, making the Commission on Sustainable Development and other cross-sectoral groups work effectively and perhaps following the Commission on Global Governance's proposal (1995) to establish a Social and Economic Security Council and reconstitute the Trusteeship Council as a Security Council for the Global Commons and the Global Environment;
- emphasizing the UN's role in peace-building rather than peace-keeping, averting strife rather than stepping in after it has riven communities apart;
- providing more finance for investment in sustainable development in the poorer countries, recognizing that this is an investment in a sustainable future for the whole world community;
- removing barriers like the burden of debt;
- ending the perverse and wasteful haemorrhages of the arms trade, replacing it by guarantees of international security in which the poorer nations can trust;
- using global networks in science and information to provide the knowledge nations, communities and individuals need in order to attain their goals.

But the greatest need is for international vision and inspiration. It has to build from the inspired and committed individual through the active community to the national framework and the world alliance. 'The power of man is as his hopes', wrote John Masefield. The hope of a new dawn and brighter day lies deep even in the most despondent. For many generations, people of many cultures have been led by visionaries rather than by functionaries: by prophets, poets and kings. If we are to come through the shadows and recapture the sense of vision, care for the Earth needs to be inspired not only by practical realization that the world of nature is the foundation of our lives, but also by the deeper truth that the world of nature is wonderful, beautiful, an object of reverence and a manifestation of what people of many faiths have seen as the divine.

BIBLIOGRAPHY

Abaza, H (1992) The present state of environmental and resource accounting, and its practical application in developing countries. *Environment and Economics Series, Paper 1.* New York: UN Development Programme

Adams, W M (1990) *Green Development. Environment and Sustainability in the Third World.* London & New York: Routledge

Adede, A (1994) A close-up look at the Draft International Covenant on Environment and Development. Paper delivered to Workshop 1 on Ethics and Covenant, 19th Session of the IUCN General Assembly, Buenos Aires, Argentina, January 1994

Akao, N (1994) Prospects for a GATT Green Round. Paper presented to Workshop 10 on IUCN on the World Stage, 19th Session of the IUCN General Assembly, Buenos Aires, Argentina, January 1994

Alcock, D J (1994) Education and extension: management's best strategy for the Great Barrier Reef Marine Park. Paper presented to Workshop 7 at the 19th Session of the IUCN General Assembly, Buenos Aires, Argentina, January 1994. Edited text in Palmer (1995)

Ambio (1993) The Royal Colloquium: tropical and subtropical coastal management: a question of carbon flow in a closed society. *Ambio* XXII, No 7, November 1993

Anon (Editorial) (1989) The Gospel of Chief Seattle is a Hoax. *Environmental Ethics,* Vol 11, No. 3 195–196

Anon (1994a) Summary of Workshop 8: Environmental Care for Communities, 19th Session of the IUCN General Assembly, Buenos Aires, Argentina, January 1994

Anon (1994b) Summary of Workshop 9, Public Participation in National Policy Making: The role of Strategies for Sustainability, 19th Session of the IUCN General Assembly, Buenos Aires, Argentina, January 1994

Arensberg, W (1994) The Role of Strategies in Capacity Building. Address to Workshop 9, at the 19th General Assembly of IUCN, Buenos Aires, Argentina

Aryamanya-Mugisha, H (1994) Lessons learned with national strategies. Paper presented to Workshop 9, Public Participation in National Policy Making: The role of Strategies for Sustainability, 19th Session of the IUCN General Assembly, Buenos Aires, Argentina, January 1994

Ashby, E and Anderson, M (1981) *The Politics of Clean Air*. Oxford: Clarendon Press

ASTAF (Council for Tropical and Subtropical Agricultural Research) (1991) *Astaf Circular*, 28, 17. Cited in WRI/IUCN/UNEP (1992)

Ayensu, E (1993) Conservation of tropical forests and other terrestrial ecosystems. In *Environmental Change in Rain Forests and Drylands*. Tokyo: UN University

Barclay, W S (1926) *The Land of Magellan*. London: Methuen

Barney, G O (Director) (1980) *The Global 2000 Report to the President. Entering the Twenty First Century*. Washington DC: US Government Printing Office

Beckerman, W (1995) *Small is Stupid. Blowing the Whistle on the Greens*. London: Duckworth

Benton, M J (1985) Mass extinction among non-marine tetrapods. *Nature*, 316, 811–814

Berry, B L (1990) Urbanization. Chapter 7 in Turner, B L, Clark, W C, Kates, R W, Richards, J F, Mathews, J T and Meyer, W B *The Earth as Transformed by Human Action*. Cambridge: University Press with Clark University

Berry, R J (1994) The underlying ethics of 'The International Covenant on Environment and Development'. Paper delivered to Workshop 1 on Ethics and Covenant, 19th Session of the General Assembly of IUCN – The World Conservation Union, Buenos Aires, Argentina, January 1994

Beversluis, J (Ed) (1993) *A Source Book for the Community of Religions*. Chicago: Council for a Parliament of the World's Religions

Blanchard, K A (1994) Seabird conservation on the north shore of the Gulf of St. Lawrence: the effects of education and attitude on behaviour towards a marine resource. Paper presented to Workshop 7 at the 19th Session of the IUCN General Assembly, Buenos Aires, Argentina, January 1994. Edited text in Palmer (1995)

Boer, B (1994) Report on Oceania. Paper presented to Workshop 9, 19th Session of the IUCN General Assembly, Buenos Aires, Argentina

Bolin, B, Houghton, J and Meira Filho, L G (1994) *Radiative Forcing of Climate Change. The 1994 Report of the Scientific Assessment Working Group of the IPCC*. Geneva: World Meteorological Organization, and Nairobi: United Nations Environment Programme

Borrini Feyerabend, G (1991) *Lessons Learned in Community-Based Environmental Management. Proceedings of the 1990 Primary Environmental Care Workshop*. Rome: ICHM

Borrini Feyerabend, G (1994) Introductory overview on primary environmental care. Paper presented to Workshop 8 on Environmental Care for Communities, at the 19th Session of the IUCN General Assembly, Buenos Aires, Argentina, January 1994

Bos, Peter (1994) Strategic planning of environmental education in the Netherlands. Paper presented to Workshop 7 at the 19th Session of the IUCN General Assembly, Buenos Aires, Argentina, January 1994. Edited text in Palmer (1995)

Botkin, D B and Talbot, L M (1992) Biological Diversity and Forests. In Sharma, N P (Ed), *Managing the World's Forests: Looking for Balance between Conservation and Development*. Dubuque, Iowa, Kendal/Hunt

Bramwell, A (1989) *Ecology in the 20th Century*. New Haven: Yale University Press.

Brookfield (1993) Farming the Forests of South-East Asia. In *Ecological Changes in Forests and Drylands. Report of the Second UNU Global Environmental Forum*. Tokyo: United Nations University

Brown, J H (1988) Species Diversity. Chapter 3 in Myers, A A and Giller, P S (Eds), *Analytical Biogeography*. London: Chapman and Hall

Brown, L R and others (1984–1994) *State of the World: A Worldwatch Institute Report on Progress towards a Sustainable Society*. Annual volumes. New York & London: W W Norton

Brown, N J and Quiblier, P (Eds) (1994) *Ethics and Agenda 21*. New York: United Nations Publications

Cairncross, F (1995) *Green, Inc. A Guide to Business and the Environment*. London: Earthscan

Caldwell, L K (1984) *International Environmental Policy. Emergence and Dimensions*. Durham, North Carolina: Duke University Press

Calero, R and Frank, R (1994) The Tagua Nut Initiative. In DOE, *Partnerships in Practice*. London: Department of the Environment

Calvo, S (1994) The coordination of environmental education in Spain. Paper presented to Workshop 7 at the 19th Session of the IUCN General Assembly, Buenos Aires, Argentina, January 1994. Edited text in Palmer (1995)

Camacho, L (1994) Metro Manila Women's Garbage Recycling Programme, the Philippines. Case Study 7. In DOE *Partnerships in Practice*. London: Department of the Environment

Campbell, A (1994) The Landcare Programme, Australia. Case Study 8. In DOE, *Partnerships in Practice*. London: Department of the Environment

Capra, F (1986) Paradigms. *ReVISION*, Vol 9, No l, p14 (cited in Milbraith, 1989)

Carew Reid, J, Prescott Allen, R, Bass, S, and Dalal-Clayton, B (1994) *Strategies for National Sustainable Development. A Handbook for their Planning and Implementation*. London: Earthscan with IUCN and IIED

Carpenter, R (1994) An Overview of Biological and Physical Indicators. Paper delivered to Workshop 3, on Developing and Measuring Sustainability, 19th Session of the IUCN General Assembly, Buenos Aires, Argentina, January 1994

Carson, R (1963) *Silent Spring*. London: Hamish Hamilton

Cassells, D S (1994) Sustainable Forest Management. Some Myths, Misinterpretations, Misconceptions and Miscalculations. Paper presented to Workshop 3, on Sustainable Use of Renewable Natural Resources, 19th Session of the IUCN General Assembly, Buenos Aires, Argentina, January 1994

Caux Round Table (1994) *Principles for Business*. Minneapolis: Minnesota Center for Corporate Responsibility

Ceballos Lascurain, H (1994) Overview on Tourism around the world: IUCN's Ecotourism Programme. Paper presented to Workshop 3, on Sustainable Use of Renewable Natural Resources, 19th Session of the IUCN General Assembly, Buenos Aires, Argentina, January 1994

CFOCF (1995) NGO Steering Committee Members for the CSD. Centre for Our Common Future Special Report. *The Network, the Independent Sector's Newsletter*, 45, April/May 1995

Chalbi, Hassania (1994) The role of women as an indicator of sustainability. Paper delivered to Workshop 2 on Defining and Measuring Sustainability, 19th Session of the General Assembly of IUCN – The World Conservation Union, Buenos Aires, Argentina, January 1994

Chaloner, W G and Hallam, A (Eds) (1989) *Evolution and Extinction. Proceedings of a Joint Symposium of the Royal Society and the Linnean Society held on 9 and 10, November 1989*. Cambridge: University Press

Chambers, R J H (1983) *Rural Development: Putting the Last First*. London: Longman

Chambers, R J H (1993) *Challenging the Professions: Frontiers for Rural Development*. London: Intermediate Technology Publications

Chapman, D G (1964) Final Report of the Special Committee of Three Scientists. *Report of the International Commission on Whaling*, 14, 39–92

Charig, A J (1989) The cretaceous-Tertiary boundary and the last of the dinosaurs. *Philosophical Transaction of the Royal Society of London*, B, 325, 387–400

Child, B (1994) Using Zimbabwe's CAMPFIRE Programme to assess the value of IUCN's proposed Guidelines for the Ecological Sustainability of Nonconsumptive and Consumptive Uses of Wild Species. Paper delivered to Workshop 3, at the 19th Session of the IUCN General Assembly, Buenos Aires, Argentina

Chileshe, J (1994) National Conservation Strategy, the National Environmental Action Plan, and the Environmental Education Strategy for Zambia. Paper presented to Workshop 7 at the 19th Session of the IUCN General Assembly, Buenos Aires, Argentina, January 1994. Edited text in Palmer (1995)

Chitrekar, A (1994) Public Participation in National Policy Making: The Role of Strategies for Sustainability. Discussion paper presented to Workshop 9 at the 19th Session of the IUCN General Assembly, Buenos Aires, Argentina

Commission on Global Governance (1995) *Our Global Neighbourhood*. Geneva: Commission on Global Governance

Cooke, G W (1970) The carrying capacity of the land in the year 2000. In L R Taylor (Ed) *The Optimum Population for Britain. Institute of Biology Symposium 19*. London: Institute of Biology

Cooke, J (1994) Application of the IUCN Sustainable Use Guidelines to Pelagic Fisheries. Paper presented to Workshop 3, on Sustainable Use of Renewable Natural Resources, 19th Session of the IUCN General Assembly, Buenos Aires, Argentina, January 1994

Corson, W (1994) Linking Sustainability Indicators to Performance Goals at National and Subnational Levels. Paper delivered to Workshop 2 at the 19th Session of the IUCN General Assembly, Buenos Aires, Argentina

Cotter, B and Boer, B (1994) Local Conservation Strategies in Australia. Paper presented to Workshop 9, 19th Session of the IUCN General Assembly, Buenos Aires, Argentina

Craik, W (1994) 'Carrying Capacity' and the Great Barrier Reef Marine Park Authority. Paper delivered to Workshop 6, on Carrying Capacity, 19th Session of the IUCN General Assembly, Buenos Aires, Argentina, January 1994

Crosby, A W (1986) *Ecological Imperialism: The Biological Expansion of Europe, 900–1900*. Cambridge: University Press

Daly, H E and Cobb, J B (1989) *For the Common Good. Redirecting the Economy towards Community, the Environment and a Sustainable Future*. Boston, Mass: Beacon Press

Daouda, I and Tiega, A (1994) Land tenure and land management of the Ron palm in Niger. Paper presented to Workshop 8 on Environmental Care for Communities, at the 19th Session of the IUCN General Assembly, Buenos Aires, Argentina, January 1994

Davidson, J, Handley, J, Wilmers, P, and Hunt, P (1994) Groundwork. UK Case Study 2. In DOE, *Partnerships in Practice*. London: Department of the Environment

Denevan, W M (1992) The Pristine Myth. The landscape of the Americas in 1492. *Annals of the Association of American Geographers*, 82(3), 369–385

Deneve, R (1994) Drought is not the Major Sahel Problem. Paper delivered to Workshop 6, on Carrying Capacity, 19th Session of the IUCN General Assembly, Buenos Aires, Argentina, January 1994

Detwyler, T R (Ed) (1971) *Man's Impact on Environment*. New York, McGraw-Hill

Diamond, J. (1989) The present, past and future of human-caused extinctions. *Philosophical Transactions of the Royal Society of London*, B 325, 469–476

Dingwall, P (1994) Tourism Carrying Capacity in the Antarctic Region. Paper delivered to Workshop 6, on Carrying Capacity, 19th Session of the IUCN General Assembly, Buenos Aires, Argentina, January 1994

DOE (1994) *Partnerships in Practice. Report of the Partnerships for Change Conference*. London: Department of the Environment

Dower, N and Tarasofsky, R G (1994) Ethics and Covenant. Rapporteur's summary, Workshop 1 on Ethics and Covenant, 19th Session of the General Assembly of IUCN – The World Conservation Union, Buenos Aires, Argentina, January 1994

DTI (1994) *The Energy Charter Treaty. Key Points for British Business*. London: Department of Trade and Industry

Earth Council (1994) *The Earth Council: Its Mission and Programmes*. San Jose, Costa Rica: Earth Council

Earthscan (1984) *Cropland or Wasteland: The Problems and Promises of Irrigation*. London: Earthscan

Elliott, C (1994) The Forest Stewardship Council and Timber Certification. In *Countdown to 1995: A Future for Forests. Proceedings of WWF's Timber Seminar held on 17 March 1994*. Godalming, UK: WWF-UK

Encalada, M (1994) The need for long-term education approaches to raise steady awareness in developing countries. Paper presented to Workshop 7 at the 19th Session of the IUCN General Assembly, Buenos Aires, Argentina, January 1994 and published in Palmer (1995)

Engel, R (1994) Our Mandate for Advancing a World Ethic for Living Sustainably. Paper delivered to Workshop 1, at the 19th Session of the IUCN General Assembly, Buenos Aires, Argentina

Erwin, T L (1982) Tropical Forests: their richness in Coleoptera and other arthropod species. *The Coleopterists Bulletin* 36, 74–75

European Forestry Ministers (1993) Conclusions of the Inter Ministerial Conference held in Helsinki, June 1993

Foley, J, and Brackett, D (1994) The Sustainable use of Wildlife: A Socioeconomic Approach. Paper presented to Workshop 3, on Sustainable Use of Renewable Natural Resources, 19th Session of the IUCN General Assembly, Buenos Aires, Argentina, January 1994

Fowler, C and Mooney, P (1990) *Shattering:Food Politics and the Loss of Genetic Diversity*. Tucson, Arizona: University of Arizona Press. Cited in WRI/IUCN/UNEP (1992)

Frakes, L A, Francis, J F E and Syktus, J I (1992) *Climate Modes of the Phanerozoic*. Cambridge: University Press

Fuentes, E (1994) Relevance of IUCN's Guidelines to the Global Environment Facility. Paper presented to Workshop 3 on Sustainable Use of Renewable Natural Resources, 19th Session of the IUCN General Assembly, Buenos Aires, Argentina, January 1994

Georghiu, G P (1989) *Pest Resistance to Pesticides*. New York: Plenum Press

GESAMP (1990) *The State of the Marine Environment*. UNEP Regional Seas Reports and Studies, no 115. Nairobi: United Nations Environment Programme

Glasby, G P (1995) Concept of sustainable development: a meaningful goal? *The Science of the Total Environment* 159, 67–80

Glowka, L, Burhenne-Guilmin, F, and Synge, H (1994) *A Guide to the Convention on Biological Diversity*. Gland, Switzerland: IUCN – The World Conservation Union

Godoy, R, Brokaw, N, and Wilkie, D (1994) The effect of income on the extraction of non-timber tropical forest products by indigenous people. Model, hypotheses and preliminary findings from the Sumu Indians of Nicaragua. Paper presented to Workshop 3, on Sustainable Use of Renewable Natural Resources, 19th Session of the IUCN General Assembly, Buenos Aires, Argentina, January 1994

Gosling, D (1990) Religion and the Environment. In Angell, D J R, Comer, J D and Wilkinson, M (Eds) *Sustaining Earth*. Basingstoke and London: Macmillan Academic and Professional

Gosling, D (1992) *A New Earth: Covenanting for Justice, Peace and the Integrity of Creation*. London: CCBI

Goto, Y (1994) Address to Workshop 10 on IUCN on the World Stage, 19th Session of the IUCN General Assembly, Buenos Aires, Argentina, January 1994

Grassle, J F (1989) Species diversity in deep-sea communities. *Trends in Ecology and Evolution* 4, 12–15

Greene, G (1994) Caring for the Earth. Report on Reports. *Environment* 36, No 7, 25–28

Gundling, L (1994) Equity in international environmental law. Paper delivered to Workshop 1 on Ethics and Covenant, 19th Session of the General Assembly of IUCN – The World Conservation Union, Buenos Aires, Argentina, January 1994

Hamilton, L S and King, P N (1983) *Tropical Forest Watersheds: Hydrologic and Soils response to major Uses or Conversions.* Boulder, Colorado: Westview Replica Editions, Westview Press

Hameed, S and Dignon, J (1992) Global emissions of nitrogen and sulphur oxides in Fossil Fuel Combustion, 1970–1986. *Journal of Air Waste Management Association*, 42, 159–163

Hammond, A, Adriaanse, A, Rodenburg, E, Bryant, D and Woodward, R (1995) *Environmental Indicators: A Systematic Approach to Measuring and Reporting on Environmental Policy Performance in the Context of Sustainable Development.* Washington DC: World Resources Institute

Hardin, G (1968) The Tragedy of the Commons. *Science* 162, December 1968, 1243–1248

Hardoy, J E, Mitlin, D S and Satterthwaite, D (1992) *Environmental Problems in Third World Cities.* London: Earthscan

Hassan, P (1994) The IUCN Draft Covenant on Environment and Development. Paper delivered to Workshop 1, at the 19th Session of the IUCN General Assembly, Buenos Aires, Argentina

Henriques, A (1994) Les populations et leur developpement durable. Organisation des communautes en Guinea Bissau. Paper presented to Workshop 8 on Environmental Care for Communities, at the 19th Session of the IUCN General Assembly, Buenos Aires, Argentina, January 1994

Hill, Julie (1994) Experiences from Europe. Paper presented to Workshop 9 of the 19th Session of the IUCN General Assembly, Buenos Aires, Argentina

Hogan, C (1994) Environmental citizenship: a Canadian case study. Paper presented to Workshop 7 at the 19th Session of the IUCN General Assembly, Buenos Aires, Argentina, January 1994. Edited text in Palmer (1995)

Holdgate, M W (1967) The Antarctic Ecosystem. *Philosophical Transactions of the Royal Society of London,* Vol 252, No 777, 363–383

Holdgate, M W (1979) *A Perspective of Environmental Pollution.* Cambridge: University Press

Holdgate, M W (1993) Sustainability in the Forest. *Commonwealth Forestry Review,* Vol 72 (4), No 231, December 1993, 217–225

Holdgate, M W (1994a) The Sustainable Use of Global Oceanic Resources. Paper delivered to the First International Symposium on Sustainable Fish Farming, Oslo, 28–31 August 1994

Holdgate, M W (1994b) The United Nations system after Rio. Paper presented to Workshop 10 on IUCN on the World Stage, 19th Session of the IUCN General Assembly, Buenos Aires, Argentina

Holdgate, M W (1994c) Hopes for the Future. Chapter 12 in Polunin, N and Nazim, M (Eds) *Population and Global Security.* Geneva: Foundation for Environmental Conservation

Holdgate, M W (1995a) Economic Valuation and Ecological Values. In Willis, K and Corkindale, J (Eds) *Environmental Valuation: New Perspectives*. CAB International

Holdgate, M W (1995b) How can Development be Sustainable? Prince Philip Lecture, Royal Society of Arts. *Journal, Royal Society of Arts* (in press)

Holdgate, M W (1995c) The Ecological Significance of Biological Diversity. The Carl Gustaf Bernhard Lecture, Royal Swedish Academy of Sciences. *Ambio* (in press)

Holdgate, M W, Kassas, M and White, G F (Eds) (1982) *The World Environment, 1972–1982*. Dublin: Tycooly International

Holling, C S (Ed) (1978) *Adaptive Environmental Assessment and Management*. Chichester etc: John Wiley & Sons

Holling, C S (1993) Investing in research for sustainability. *Ecological Applications* 3 (4), 552–555

Houghton, J and Bolin, B (1992) *The 1992 Supplement: Scientific Assessment of Climate Change*. Geneva: World Meteorological Organization and Nairobi: UN Environment Programme

Houghton, J, Jenkins G J and Ephraums J J (Eds) (1990) Intergovernmental Panel on Climate Change *Climate Change. The IPCC Scientific Assessment*. Cambridge: University Press

Hutchison, R (1991) *Fighting for Survival: Insecurity, People and the Environment in the Horn of Africa*. Gland, Switzerland: IUCN – The World Conservation Union

ICIHI (1988) *Winning the Human Race?* Report of the Independent Commission on International Humanitarian Issues. London: Zed Books

IFRC (1993) *World Disasters Report, 1993*. International Federation of Red Cross and Red Crescent Societies. Dordrecht, The Netherlands: Nijhoff

Imbach, A (1994) State of Strategies for Sustainable Development in Latin America. Address to Workshop 9, 19th Session of the IUCN General Assembly, Buenos Aires, Argentina

IPCC (1990) Scientific Assessment of Climate Change. The Policymaker's summary of the Report of the Working Group I of the Intergovernmental Panel on Climate Change. Geneva: WMO/UNEP

IUCN (1991a) *The IUCN Sahel Studies, 1991*. Gland, Switzerland: IUCN – The World Conservation Union

IUCN (1991b) *A Strategy for Antarctic Conservation*. Gland, Switzerland: IUCN – The World Conservation Union

IUCN (1991c) *Dolphins, Porpoises and Whales of the World. The IUCN Red Data Book*. Gland, Switzerland, and Cambridge, UK: International Union for Conservation of Nature and Natural Resources

IUCN (1992) IVth World Congress on National Parks and Protected Areas, Caracas, Venezuela. Regional Reviews: 1 Marine and Coastal. Gland, Switzerland: IUCN – The World Conservation Union

IUCN (1993a) *Status of Multilateral Treaties in the Field of Environment and Conservation*. Gland, Switzerland:IUCN – The World Conservation Union

IUCN (1993b) Draft Guidelines for the Ecological Sustainability of Non-Consumptive and Consumptive Uses of Wild Species. Gland, Switzerland: IUCN – The World Conservation Union

IUCN (1994a) *Proceedings. 19th Session of the General Assembly of IUCN – The World Conservation Union, Buenos Aires, Argentina, 17–26 January 1994*. Gland, Switzerland: IUCN – The World Conservation Union

IUCN (1994b) *Resolutions and Recommendations of the 19th Session of the General Assembly of IUCN – The World Conservation Union*. Gland, Switzerland: IUCN – The World Conservation Union

IUCN (1994c) *Parks for Life. Action for Protected Areas in Europe*. Gland, Switzerland: IUCN – The World Conservation Union

IUCN (1994d) *Report of the Global Biodiversity Forum. IUCN Headquarters, Gland, Switzerland, 7–9 October 1993*. Gland, Switzerland: IUCN – The World Conservation Union

IUCN (1994e) *1993 United Nations List of National Parks and Protected Areas*. Gland, Switzerland and Cambridge, UK: IUCN

IUCN/BGCS (1989) *The Botanic Gardens Conservation Strategy*. Gland, Switzerland, and Richmond, UK: IUCN, BGCS and WWF

IUCN/UNEP/WWF (1980) *The World Conservation Strategy: Living Resource Conservation for Sustainable Development*. Gland, Switzerland: International Union for Conservation of Nature and Natural Resources

IUCN/UNEP/WWF (1991) *Caring for the Earth: A Strategy for Sustainable Living*. Gland, Switzerland: International Union for Conservation of Nature and Natural Resources

IUDZG/IUCN (1993) *The World Zoo Conservation Strategy*. Chicago: Zoological Society

Jacobs, P and Munro, D (Eds) (1987) *Conservation with Equity. Strategies for Sustainable Development*. Gland, Switzerland: IUCN – The World Conservation Union

James, D (1994) Marine Living Resources: Present Utilization and Future Prospects. Paper delivered to the First International Symposium on Sustainable Fish Farming, Oslo, 28–31 August 1994

Johnson, S P (1994) *World Population – Turning the Tide*. London, Dordrecht, Boston: Graham and Trotman/Martinus Nijhoff

Johnson, T (1994) Countries of Ultimate Responsibility. Presentation by the World Conservation Monitoring Centre to Workshop 5, The Biodiversity Strategy and Convention, 19th Session of the IUCN General Assembly, Buenos Aires, Argentina, January 1994

Jupiter (1994) Jupiter Asset Management Ltd Questionnaire on Environmental Performance. London

Kabilsingh, C (1994) Elements of a sustainable world ethic: Buddhist perspective. Paper delivered to Workshop 1 on Ethics and Covenant, 19th Session of the General Assembly of IUCN – The World Conservation Union, Buenos Aires, Argentina, January 1994

Kalaw, M (1994) Crisis and Opportunity in the wave of NGO Action. Paper delivered to Workshop 10 on International Actions for Sustainable Development, 19th Session of the IUCN General Assembly, Buenos Aires, Argentina, January 1994

Keating, M (1993) *The Earth Summit's Agenda for Change. A Plain Language Version of Agenda 21 and the other Rio Agreements*. Geneva: Centre for Our Common Future

Keleman, J (1994) Agriculture and Nature Conservation in Hungary. Paper presented to Workshop 8 on Environmental Care for Communities, at the 19th Session of the IUCN General Assembly, Buenos Aires, Argentina, January 1994

Kelleher, G (1992) *Conservation of Global Marine Biodiversity: The Role of Marine Protected Areas*. Report to the World Bank. Canberra: Great Barrier Reef Marine Conservation Area Authority

Kemf, E (Ed) (1993) *The Law of the Mother. Protecting Indigenous Peoples in Protected Areas*. San Francisco: Sierra Club

Kenchington, R (1994) Great Barrier Reef Marine Park education approach. Paper presented to Workshop 7 on Changing Personal Attitudes and Practices, at the 19th Session of the IUCN General Assembly, Buenos Aires, Argentina, January 1994

Khattak, G M (1994) Applying primary environmental care in North-West Frontier Province, Pakistan. Paper presented to Workshop 8 on Environmental Care for Communities, at the 19th Session of the IUCN General Assembly, Buenos Aires, Argentina, January 1994

Khosla, A (1994) Should the Global Environment Facility be the central pole for financing environmental development in developing countries? Paper presented to Workshop 10 on IUCN on the World Stage, 19th Session of the IUCN General Assembly, Buenos Aires, Argentina, January 1994

Krishna, S (1994) Addressing urban environmental issues through environmental education. Paper presented to Workshop 7 at the 19th Session of the IUCN General Assembly, Buenos Aires, Argentina, January 1994. Edited text in Palmer (1995)

Large, E C (1940) *The Advance of the Fungi*. London: Jonathan Cape

Lawrence, G (1994) Sustainable Seattle, USA. Case Study 1. In DOE, *Partnerships in Practice*. London: Department of the Environment

LEAF (1994) *A Practical Guide to Integrated Crop Management*. London: Linking Environment And Farming

Leakey, R B (1981) *The Making of Mankind* London: Michael Joseph

Lynch, J D (1988) Refugia. Chapter 10 in Myers, A A and Giller, P S (Eds), *Analytical Biogeography*. London: Chapman and Hall

McBurney, S (1990) *Ecology into Economics won't Go. Or Life is not a Concept*. Bideford, Devon: Green Books

McCormick, J (1989) *The Global Environmental Movement*. London: Belhaven Press

McNeely, J A (1988) *Economics and Biological Diversity*. Gland, Switzerland: International Union for Conservation of Nature and Natural Resources

McNeely, J A (Ed) (1993) *Parks for Life:Report of the IVth World Congress on National Parks and Protected Areas*. Gland, Switzerland: IUCN – The World Conservation Union

McNeely, J A, Miller, K R, Reid, W V, Mittermeier, R A and Werner, T B (1990) *Conserving the World's Biological Diversity: Keeping Options Alive*. Gland, Switzerland: IUCN for the World Resources Institute, Conservation International, World Wildlife Fund and the World Bank

Mafabi, P (1994) Giving communities their say in wetland management. Lessons from Uganda's National Wetland Policy. Paper presented to Workshop 8 on Environmental Care for Communities, at the 19th Session of the IUCN General Assembly, Buenos Aires, Argentina, January 1994

Major, J (1988) Endemism: A Botanical Perspective. Chapter 5 in Myers, A A and Giller, P S (Eds), *Analytical Biogeography*. London: Chapman and Hall

Malla, Y B (1994) Sustainable use of Communal Forests in Nepal. Paper presented to Workshop 3, on Sustainable Use of Renewable Natural Resources, 19th Session of the IUCN General Assembly, Buenos Aires, Argentina, January 1994

Marland, G, Boden, T A, Griffin, R C, Huang, S F, Kanciruk, P and Nelson, T R (1989) Estimates of carbon dioxide emissions from fossil fuel burning and cement manufacturing, based on United Nations energy statistics and the US Bureau of Mines cement manufacturing data. Oak Ridge, Tennessee: Oak Ridge National Laboratory publication ORNI/CDIAC-25, NDP-030

Marshall, L G (1988) Extinction. In Myers, A A and Giller, P S, *Analytical Biogeography*. London: Chapman and Hall.

Martin, P S and Wright, H E (Eds) (1967) *Pleistocene Extinctions: the Search for a Cause* Yale University Press

Martin, P S (1971) Prehistoric Overkill. Page 621 in Detwyler, T R (Ed) *Man's Impact on Environment*. New York: McGraw Hill

Martin, R B (1994) Alternative Approaches to Sustainable Use. What does and doesn't work. Paper presented to a Conference on Conservation through Sustainable Use of Wild Life, University of Queensland, Brisbane, Australia, 8–11 February 1994 and summarized to Workshop 3 on Sustainable Use of Renewable Natural Resources, 19th Session of the IUCN General Assembly, Buenos Aires, Argentina, January 1994

Matthews, E (1983) Global vegetation and land use: new high-resolution databases for climatic studies. *Journal of Climate and Meteorology*, 22, 474–487

Maveneke, T N (1994a) The Campfire Programme in Zimbabwe. Paper presented to Workshop 7 at the 19th Session of the IUCN General Assembly, Buenos Aires, Argentina, January 1994. Edited text in Palmer (1995)

Maveneke, T (1994b) Matching benefits with inputs: the CAMPFIRE Programme in Zimbabwe. Paper presented to Workshop 8 on Environmental Care for Communities, at the 19th Session of the IUCN General Assembly, Buenos Aires, Argentina, January 1994

May, R M (1988) How many species are there on Earth? *Science*, 241, 1441–1449

May, R M, Lawton, J H and Stork, N E (1995) Assessing Extinction Rates. In Lawton, J H and May, R M (Eds) *Extinction Rates*. Oxford: University Press

Meadows, D H, Meadows, D L, Randers, J and Behrens, W W (1972) *The Limits to Growth*. New York: Universe

Milbraith, Lester W (1989) *Envisioning A Sustainable Society*. New York: State University of New York Press

Mitlin, D and Satterthwaite, D E (1994) *Cities and Sustainable Development. A Guide to the main issues in implementing Agenda 21 in Cities*. Report prepared for the Department of the Environment, UK. London: International Institute for Environment and Development

Mobbs, C (1994) Community involvement in conservation of biological diversity in Australia. Paper presented to Workshop 7 at the 19th Session of the IUCN General Assembly, Buenos Aires, Argentina, January 1994. Edited text in Palmer (1995)

Montenegro, R (1994) The educational programme of the Foundation for the Defence of Nature (FUNAM). Paper presented to Workshop 7 at the 19th Session of the IUCN General Assembly, Buenos Aires, Argentina, January 1994

Moriarty, F (Ed) (1975) *Organochlorine Pesticides: Persistent Organic Pollutants*. London: Academic Press

Morowitz, H J (1968) *Energy Flow in Biology*. New York and London: Academic Press

Morris, D W (1995) Earth's Peeling Veneer of Life. *Nature*, 373, 25

Mowat, F (1954) *People of the Deer*. London: Michael Joseph

Moya, H J (1994) Environmental education strategies: Venezuelan experiences. Paper presented to Workshop 7 at the 19th Session of the IUCN General Assembly, Buenos Aires, Argentina, January 1994

Myers, N (1988) Tropical Forests: Much more than stocks of wood. *Journal of Tropical Ecology*, 4, 1–13

Myers, N and Simon, J (1994) *Scarcity or Abundance. A Debate on the Environment*. New York and London: W W Norton

Naess, A (1973) The Shallow and Deep, Long Range Ecology Movements: A Summary. *Inquiry* 16, 95–100

Naess, A (1986) The Deep Ecological Movement: Some Philosophical Aspects. *Philosophical Inquiry* 2, 10–31

Ness, G D (1994) The long view: Population-Environment Dynamics in Historical Perspective. In Ness, G D, Drake, W D and Brechin, S R (Eds) *Population Environment Dynamics: Ideas and Observations*. Ann Arbor, Michigan: University of Michigan Press.

Nijhoff, P (1994) Account of linkages between resource uses in the Netherlands and other countries. Contribution to Workshop during the 19th Session of the IUCN General Assembly, Buenos Aires

Niklas, K J, Tiffney, B H and Knoll, A H (1983) Patterns in vascular land plant diversification. *Nature*, 306, 614–616

Nilsson, A (1992) *Greenhouse Earth*. Chichester: John Wiley & Sons

Nobel, P S (1973) Free energy, the currency of life. In Calder, N (Ed) *Nature in the Round*. London: Weidenfeld and Nicholson

Norse, E (1993) *Marine Conservation Strategy*. Washington DC: Center for Marine Conservation

North, R D (1995) *Life on a Modern Planet. A Manifesto for Progress*. Manchester and New York: Manchester University Press

O'Connor, J (1994) World Bank Initiatives. Paper delivered to Workshop 3, on Developing and Measuring Sustainability, 19th Session of the IUCN General Assembly, Buenos Aires, Argentina, January 1994

Odum, H T (1967) Energetics of World Food Production. *The World Food Problem*, 3, 55–95

OECD (1985, 1991) *The State of the Environment*. Paris: Organization for Economic Cooperation and Development

Olson, J S, Watts, J A and Allison, L J (1983) *Carbon in Live Vegetation of Major World Ecosystems*. Oak Ridge National Laboratory, Tennessee, Environmental Sciences Division, Publication No 1997

Padua, Suzana M (1994) Environmental education for Natural Areas in underdeveloped countries:a case study in the Brazilian Atlantic forest. Paper presented to Workshop 7 at the 19th Session of the IUCN General Assembly, Buenos Aires, Argentina, January 1994. Edited text in Palmer (1995)

Palmer, Joy A (1994a) Changing Personal Attitudes and Practices. Rapporteur's summary of Workshop 7, at the 19th Session of the IUCN General Assembly, Buenos Aires, Argentina, January 1994

Palmer, Joy A (1994b) Postscript: Emergent Issues and Conclusions. Edited as concluding paper in Palmer, Joy A (1995)

Palmer, Joy A (Ed) (1995) *Towards Better Planning of Education to Care for the Earth*. Volume based on papers delivered at Workshop on Changing Personal Attitudes and Practices, held during the 19th Session of the IUCN General Assembly, Buenos Aires, Argentina, January 1994. Gland, Switzerland: IUCN – The World Conservation Union

Pande, B D (1994) Experiences in the implementation of the NCS environmental education and awareness programmes: Nepal. Paper presented to Workshop 7 at the 19th Session of the IUCN General Assembly, Buenos Aires, Argentina, January 1994. Edited text in Palmer (1995)

Parry, M (1990) *Climate Change and World Agriculture*. London: Earthscan

Patton, S, Craig, I and Conway, G R (1980) Insecticide and Acaricide Resistance. In Conway, G R (Ed) *Pesticide Resistance and World Food Production*. ICCET Series E, 2: London: Imperial College Centre for Environmental Technology

Pearce, D, Markandya, A and Barbier, E B (1989) *Blueprint for a Green Economy*. London: Earthscan

Pearce, D W (Ed) (1991) *Blueprint 2: Greening the World Economy*. London: Earthscan

Pearce, D W (Ed) (1993) *Blueprint 3: Measuring Sustainable Development*. London: Earthscan

Pickett, S T A, Parker, V T, and Fiedler, P L (1992) The New Paradigm in Ecology: Implications for Conservation Biology above the Species Level. In Fiedler, P L and Jain, S K (Eds) *Conservation Biology: the Theory and Practice of Nature Conservation, Preservation and Management*. London: Chapman and Hall

Polunin, N, and Nazim, M (Eds) (1994) *Population and Global Security*. Geneva: Foundation for Environmental Conservation

Poore, M E D (1989) Conclusions. In Poore, M E D, Burgess, P, Palmer, J, Rietbergen, S, and Synott, T, *No Timber without Trees: Sustainability in the Tropical Forest*. London: Earthscan

Pope John Paul II (1994) *Crossing the Threshold of Hope*. New York: Alfred A Knopf

Prescott, J (1994) *Sustaining UK Food Production and Our Countryside. Centenary College Lecture, Wye College*. Wye College: Occasional Paper No 94/2

Prescott-Allen, C, and Prescott-Allen, R (1986) *The First Resource: Wild Species in the North American Economy*. New Haven and London: Yale University Press

Pye-Smith, C, Borrini Feyerabend, G and Sandbrook, R (1994) *The Wealth of Communities*. London: Earthscan

Rackham, O (1986) *The History of the Countryside*. London and Melbourne: Dent

Ramphal, S (1992) *Our Country the Planet*. Washington DC: Island Press

Ramphal, S (1994) Opening address to Workshop 10 on IUCN on the World Stage, 19th Session of the IUCN General Assembly, Buenos Aires, Argentina, January 1994

Rao, A L (1994) Village Management of renewable natural resources in Pakistan. Paper presented to Workshop 3, on Sustainable Use of Renewable Natural Resources, 19th Session of the IUCN General Assembly, Buenos Aires, Argentina, January 1994

Reid, W V (1992) How many species will there be? In Whitmore, T C and Sayer, J A (Eds) *Tropical Deforestation and Species Extinction*. London: Chapman and Hall

Reid, W V (1993) Foreword. In Johnson, N and Cabarle, B, *Surviving the Cut: Natural Forest Management in the Humid Tropics*. Washington DC: World Resources Institute

Reid, W V, Barnes, J N and Blackwelder, B (1988) *Bankrolling Successes. A Portfolio of Sustainable Development Projects*. Washington DC: Environmental Policy Institute and National Wildlife Federation

Renard, Y (1994) Participation, Community Empowerment and co-management. Lessons from the insular Caribbean. Paper presented to Workshop 8 on Environmental Care for Communities, at the 19th Session of the IUCN General Assembly, Buenos Aires, Argentina, January 1994

Rich, B (1994) The World Bank after 50 Years. No more money without total institutional reform. Paper presented to Workshop 10 on IUCN on the World Stage, 19th Session of the IUCN General Assembly, Buenos Aires, Argentina, January 1994

Robert, K-H (1993) *The Natural Step. From consensus to a cyclic society*. Information Pack. Bristol, UK: Natural Step, UK

Roberts, R W and Cayford, J H (1994) The IUCN Guidelines for the ecological sustainability of non-consumptive and consumptive uses of wild species and their relevance for validating the sustainability of timber harvesting from the world's production forests. Paper presented to Workshop 3, on Sustainable Use of Renewable Natural Resources, 19th Session of the IUCN General Assembly, Buenos Aires, Argentina, January 1994

Robinson, J G (1993) The Limits to Caring: Sustainable Living and the Loss of Biodiversity. *Conservation Biology* 7, No 1, March 1993

Robinson, N (Ed) (1993) *Agenda 21: Earth's Action Plan*. IUCN Environmental Policy and Law Paper No 27. New York, London, Rome: Oceana Publications

Robinson, N (1994) Ethical Premises in International Law. Paper delivered to Workshop 1 on Ethics and Covenant, 19th Session of the IUCN General Assembly, Buenos Aires, Argentina, January 1994

Rose, C (1994) Greenfreeze: the world's first completely ozone-safe fridge, Germany. Case Study 6 in DOE, *Partnerships in Practice*. London: Department of the Environment

Royston, M G (1979) *Pollution Prevention Pays*. (Quotes alleged letter from Chief Seathl to President of the United States. See also Anon, 1989). Oxford: Pergamon Press

Sallada, L H and Doyle, B G (Eds) (1986) *The Spirit of Versailles: The Business of Environmental Management*. Report of the First World Industry Conference on Environmental Management. Paris: ICC Publishing SA

Sayer, J A (1994) A plethora of Guidelines for Sustainable Use of Forests – which ones do we follow? Paper presented to Workshop 3, on Sustainable Use of Renewable Natural Resources, 19th Session of the IUCN General Assembly, Buenos Aires, Argentina, January 1994

Schmidheiny, S (1992) *Changing Course: A Global Business Perspective on Development and the Environment*. Cambridge, Mass: MIT Press

Schoen, R-J (1994) Education and communication support to the establishment of protected area systems. Paper presented to Workshop 7 on Changing Personal Attitudes and Practices, at the 19th Session of the IUCN General Assembly, Buenos Aires, Argentina, January 1994

Shah, P and Bass, S (1994) Participatory methods at national, regional and local levels. Paper presented to Workshop 9, Public Participation in National Policy Making: The role of Strategies for Sustainability, 19th Session of the IUCN General Assembly, Buenos Aires, Argentina, January 1994

Sheail, J (1985) *Pesticides and Nature Conservation: The British Experience, 1950–1985*. Oxford: Clarendon Press

Sherman, K (1994) Carrying Capacity of Large Marine Ecosystems. Paper delivered to Workshop 6, on Carrying Capacity, 19th Session of the IUCN General Assembly, Buenos Aires, Argentina, January 1994

Sherman, K, Alexander, L M, and Gold, B D (Eds) (1993) *Large Marine Ecosystems. Stress, Mitigation and Sustainability*. Washington DC: AAAS Press

Shrader-Frechette, K (1994) Environmental ethics, uncertainty and limited data. In N J Brown and P Quiblier (Eds) *Ethics and Agenda 21*. New York: United Nations Publications

Simon, J (1994) Pre-debate statement in Simon, J, and Myers, N *Scarcity or Abundance. A Debate on the Environment*. New York and London: W W Norton

Smillie, I (1994) NGOs, Governments and all that. Paper presented to Workshop 10 on IUCN on the World Stage, 19th Session of the IUCN General Assembly, Buenos Aires, Argentina, January 1994

Smith, J E (Ed) (1970) *Torrey Canyon Pollution and Marine Life*. Cambridge: University Press

Smith, W A (1994) Behaviour, Social Marketing and the Environment. Paper presented to Workshop 7 at the 19th Session of the IUCN General Assembly, Buenos Aires, Argentina, January 1994. Edited text in Palmer (1995)

Smyth, J C (1994) Developing national strategies in environmental education – A Scottish case study. Paper presented to Workshop 7 at the 19th Session of the IUCN General Assembly, Buenos Aires, Argentina, January 1994. Edited text in Palmer (1995)

South Commission (1990) *The Challenge to the South*. Oxford: University Press

Southwood, T R E (1976) Bionomic Strategies and Population Parameters. In May, R. M. (Ed) *Theoretical Ecology: Principles and Applications*. Oxford: Blackwell

Sprengers, S, Douma, W, and Vellinga, P (1994) The Local and Global Carrying Capacity: A Dual Strategy for Setting the Limits of Climate Change. Paper delivered to Workshop 6, on Carrying Capacity, 19th Session of the IUCN General Assembly, Buenos Aires, Argentina, January 1994

Tabaziba, C (1994) A world ethical statement. Paper delivered to Workshop 1 on Ethics and Covenant, 19th Session of the General Assembly of IUCN – The World Conservation Union, Buenos Aires, Argentina, January 1994

Taniguchi, C (1994) Curitiba City, Brazil. Case Study 2. In *Partnerships in Practice*. London: Department of the Environment

Tewolde Berhan gebre Egziabher, Gedion Asfaw and Worku Ayele (1994) Strategies for Sustainable Development through the next Decade: Applying Past Experience. Paper presented to Workshop 9, Public Participation in National Policy Making: The role of Strategies for Sustainability, 19th Session of the IUCN General Assembly, Buenos Aires, Argentina, January 1994

TIE (1971) *Man in the Living Environment: Report of the Workshop on Global Environmental Problems*. London: The Institute of Ecology

Thiaw, I (1994) The subtle charms of the desert. Paper presented to Workshop 7 at the 19th Session of the IUCN General Assembly, Buenos Aires, Argentina, January 1994. Edited text in Palmer (1995)

Tickell, C (Convenor) (1995) *British Government Panel on Sustainable Development. First Report*. London: Department of the Environment

Tolba, M K, El Kholy, O, El Hinnawi, E, Holdgate, M W, McMichael, D F and Munn, R E (Eds) (1992) *The World Environment, 1972–1992*. London: Chapman and Hall on behalf of the UN Environment Programme

Tolentino, A S (1994) The draft Covenant on Environment and Development from the perspective of a developing country. Paper presented to Workshop 1 on Ethics and Covenant, 19th Session of the IUCN General Assembly, Buenos Aires, Argentina, January 1994 ·

Torres, H (1994) Planning the sustainable use of the vicuna in the Parincota management area to benefit the Aymara community in the Andes of Chile. Paper presented to Workshop 3, on Sustainable Use of Renewable Natural Resources, 19th Session of the IUCN General Assembly, Buenos Aires, Argentina, January 1994

Toth, F (1994) Scales of Carrying Capacity. Paper delivered to Workshop 6, on Carrying Capacity, 19th Session of the IUCN General Assembly, Buenos Aires, Argentina, January 1994

Trappe, A Z (1985) The impact of agrochemicals on human health and environment. *Industry and Environment*, 8, 10

Trends 90 (1990) Oak Ridge, Tennessee: Oak Ridge National Laboratory Carbon Dioxide Information Analysis Centre

Trudel, M and N'diaye, R (1994) Environmental Education and changes of behaviour. Facing up to Constraints. Experiences in the Sahel. Paper presented to Workshop 7 at the 19th Session of the IUCN General Assembly, Buenos Aires, Argentina, January 1994. Edited text in Palmer (1995)

Trudel, M (1994) Case Study: Western Africa/Sahel. Paper presented to Workshop 7 at the 19th Session of the IUCN General Assembly, Buenos Aires, Argentina, January 1994. Edited text in Palmer (1995)

Trzyna, T and Osborn, J K (Eds) (1995) *A Sustainable World. Defining and Measuring Sustainable Development*. Papers delivered to Workshop 2 at the 19th Session of the IUCN General Assembly, Buenos Aires, Argentina. Sacramento and Claremont: California Institute of Public Affairs for IUCN – The World Conservation Union

Tunstall, D B and van der Wansem, M (Eds) (1992) *Country Environmental Studies. An Annotated Bibliography of Environmental and Natural Resource Profiles and Assessments*. Washington DC: World Resources Institute, IIED and IUCN

Turner, B L, Clark, W C, Kates, R W, Richards, J F, Mathews, J T and Mayer, W B (Eds) (1990) *The Earth as Transformed by Human Action*. Cambridge: Cambridge University Press

UK (1994a) *Climate Change: The UK Programme*. London: HMSO, Cm 2427

UK (1994b) *Sustainable Development. The UK Strategy*. London: HMSO, Cm 2426

UN (1992) *Statement of Principles on Forests*. Appendix VI in Robinson, N (Ed) (1993) *Agenda 21: Earth's Action Plan*. New York, London, Rome: Oceana Publications

UN (1993c) *Report of the United Nations Conference on Environment and Development, Rio de Janeiro, 3–14 June 1992. Volume I: Resolutions adopted by the Conference*. New York: United Nations publication E.93.I.8

UN (1994a) *Report of the High Level Advisory Board on Sustainable Development on its Second Session, New York, 17–22 March 1994*. Economic and Social Council paper E/CN.17/1994/13. New York, United Nations

UN (1994b) *Report by Secretary General to First Substantive Session of the Preparatory Committee for the World Summit for Social Development*. New York: United Nations General Assembly Paper A/CONF. 166/PC/6

UN (1995a) *Integrated Approach to the Planning and Management of Land Resources. Report of the Secretary General*. UN Economic and Social Council paper E/CN.17/1992/2. New York: United Nations

UN (1995b) *Report of the Ad Hoc Intersessional Working Group on Sectoral Issues of the Commission on Sustainable Development*. Economic and Social Council Paper E/CN.17/1995/10. New York: United Nations

UN (1995c) *National Information. Report of the Secretary General*. Economic and Social Council Paper E/CN.17/1995/24. New York: United Nations

UN (1995d) *Review of Sectoral Clusters, Second Phase: Land, desertification, forests and bio-diversity. Conservation of Biological Diversity. Report of the Secretary General*. Economic and Social Council Paper E/CN.17/1995/7. New York: United Nations

UN (1995e) *World Summit for Social Development: Draft Declaration and Draft Programme of Action*. New York: United Nations General Assembly paper A/CONF.166/PC/L.22. (Final version available June 1995)

UN (1995f) *Report of the High Level Advisory Board on Sustainable Development on its Third Session, New York, 17–21 October 1994*. Economic and Social Council paper E/CN.17/1995/25, New York: United Nations

UNDP (1991) *Human Development Report, 1991*. New York and Oxford: Oxford University Press for the UN Development Programme

UNEP (1987) *Montreal Protocol on Substances that Deplete the Ozone Layer*. Nairobi: UN Environment Programme

UNEP (1988–92) *Environmental Data Reports*. Oxford: Basil Blackwell

UNEP (1991a) *Status of Desertification and Implementation of the United Nations Plan of Action to Combat Desertification*. Nairobi: UN Environment Programme

Valentine, P (1994) How sustainable is eco-tourism in the light of the Requirements? Experiences in the South Pacific. Paper presented to Workshop 3, on Sustainable Use of Renewable Natural Resources, 19th Session of the IUCN General Assembly, Buenos Aires, Argentina, January 1994

Vavrousek, J (1994) Searching for human values compatible with sustainable ways of living. Paper delivered to Workshop 1 on Ethics and Covenant, 19th Session of the General Assembly of IUCN – The World Conservation Union, Buenos Aires, Argentina, January 1994

Vitousek, P M, Ehrlich, P R, Ehrlich, A H and Matson, P A (1986) Human appropriation of the products of photosynthesis. *Bioscience* 36, No 6, 368–373

Wace, N M and Holdgate, M W (1976) *Man and Nature in the Tristan da Cunha Islands*. IUCN Monograph No 6. Morges, Switzerland: International Union for Conservation of Nature and Natural Resources

Wagner, W H (1980) Origin and Philosophy of the ground plan – divergence method of cladistics. *Systematic Botany*, 5, 173–193

Ward, B and Dubos, R (1972) *Only One Earth. The Care and Maintenance of a Small Planet*. London: Andre Deutsch

WCED (1987) *Our Common Future*. Report of the World Commission on Environment and Development. Oxford and New York: Oxford University Press

Westra, L (1994) Ecosystem Integrity and Agenda 21. Science, Sustainability and Public Policy. Paper delivered to Workshop 1, 19th Session of the IUCN General Assembly, Buenos Aires, Argentina, January 1994

Whitmore, T C and Sayer, J A (1992) *Tropical Deforestation and Species Extinction*. London: Chapman and Hall

Whitmore, T M, Turner, B L, Johnson, D L, Kates, R W and Gottschang, T R (1990) Long-term Population Change. In Turner, B L et al (Eds) (1990) *The Earth as Transformed by Human Action*. Cambridge: University Press with Clark University

WHO (1976) *Environmental Health Criteria 1: Mercury*. Geneva: World Health Organization

Whyte, A and Burton, I (Eds) (1980) *Environmental Risk Assessment. SCOPE 15*. Chichester: John Wiley & Sons

Williamson, H (1942) *Story of a Norfolk Farm*. Quotes passage drafted by T E Lawrence for *Seven Pillars of Wisdom*, said to have been omitted in final edition. London: Faber and Faber

Williamson, M (1988) Relationship of Species Number to Area, Distance and other Variables. Chapter 4 in Myers, A A and Giller, P S (Eds), *Analytical Biogeography*. London: Chapman and Hall

Willums, J-O, (Ed) (1991) *WICEM II Conference Report and Background Papers*. Paris: ICC Publications

Willums, J-O, and Golucke, U (1992) *From Ideas to Action. Business and Sustainable Development. The ICC Report on the Greening of Enterprise 9*. Oslo, Norway: ICC and Ad Notam Gyldendal

Winograd, M (1994) Indicators of Sustainability for Latin America and the Caribbean. Paper delivered to Workshop 3, on Developing and Measuring Sustainability, 19th Session of the IUCN General Assembly, Buenos Aires, Argentina, January 1994

Wirth, C L (1962) National Parks. In Adams, A B (Ed) *First World Conference on National Parks.* Washington DC: National Parks Service, Department of the Interior

World Bank (1991) *Environmental Assessment Sourcebook.* (2 vols). Washington DC: The World Bank Environment Department

World Bank (1991a) *World Development Report 1991: The Challenge of Development.* New York: OUP

World Conservation Monitoring Centre (1992) *Global Diversity: Status of the Earth's Living Resources.* London: Chapman and Hall

World Population Report (1992) Chapter III: Demographic Impact of AIDS in 15 African Countries. New York: United Nations

WRI (1986) *World Resources Report, 1986.* New York: Basic Books

WRI (1987) *World Resources Report, 1987* New York: Basic Books

WRI (1990) *World Resources Report, 1990–1991* New York and Oxford: Oxford University Press

WRI (1992) *World Resources Report, 1992–93* New York and Oxford: Oxford University Press

WRI/IUCN/UNEP (1992) *Global Biodiversity Strategy. Guidelines for Action to Save, Study and Use Earth's Biotic Wealth Sustainably and Equitably.* Washington DC: World Resources Institute, World Conservation Union and United Nations Environment Programme

Wright, K (1994) Sustainable citizenship: Scottish Environmental Forum. UK Case Study 3. In DOE, *Partnerships in Practice.* London: Department of the Environment

Zaba, B and Scoones, I (1994) Is Carrying Capacity a Useful Concept to Apply to Human Populations? Paper delivered to Workshop 6, on Carrying Capacity, 19th Session of the IUCN General Assembly, Buenos Aires, Argentina, January 1994

Zimmermann, E C (1948) *Insects of Hawaii.* Vol 1, Introduction. Honolulu: University of Hawaii Press

I N D E X